GANDHI

In His Time and Ours

THE INDIAN CENTURY

Series Editors

Ramachandra Guha and Sunil Khilnani

GANDHI

In His Time and Ours

DAVID HARDIMAN

ASHOKA UNIVERSITY

in association with

permanent black

Published by

PERMANENT BLACK
'Himalayana', Mall Road, Ranikhet Cantt,
Ranikhet 263645
perblack@gmail.com

in association with

ashoka
UNIVERSITY

Distributed by

ORIENT BLACKSWAN PRIVATE LTD
Bangalore Bhopal Bhubaneshwar Chandigarh
Chennai Ernakulam Guwahati Hyderabad Jaipur
Kolkata Lucknow Mumbai New Delhi Patna
www.orientblackswan.com

First published in hardback 2003
First paperback printing 2005
Sixth Impression 2018

ISBN 81-7824-114-5

Printed and bound by Sapra Brothers, New Delhi 110092

In memory of

John Hardiman

(1916–2000)

and

Harshad Trivedy

(1931–2001)

Foreword

This book inaugurates a new series called 'The Indian Century'. Each book in the series will deal with a compelling subject in modern Indian history. The titles planned include works on Ambedkar and Ambedkarism, feminism, the city, the discourses of democracy, the novel and society, and the cultural history of music. As General Editors we shall take special care to match authors with subjects while leaving authors free to decide how their subjects should be treated. We ask only that the books not be narrowly focused. While each book might draw on an individual's experience of a particular state or region, each will be pan-Indian in scope. And while it might pay close attention to a particular slice of time, each book will deal with the period before as well as after Independence. For, one date, 15 August 1947, has too long divided History from the Social Sciences, to the impoverishment of both. By contrast, books in this series will breach the boundary by considering events and processes in both colonial and postcolonial India.

'The Indian Century' begins with David Hardiman's *Gandhi: In His Time and Ours*. This is a landmark study by a fine and experienced scholar. Hardiman is the foremost modern historian of Gandhi's cultural region, Gujarat. He is an acknowledged pioneer in the study of popular protest. And he has had a lifelong interest in Gandhi.

Most recent books on Gandhi fit tidily into one or the other of the 'Life' and 'Thought' categories. On the one hand, there are biographies which provide a chronological account of the life; on the other, works of political thought which study Gandhi's ideas on religion, non-violence, the state, or economics. Here, however, is a book that systematically and skilfully links life and thought. A distinctive feature is its discussion of Gandhism after Gandhi—that is, of movements in India and Europe inspired by Gandhi's ideas.

Hardiman's book is empathetic but by no means uncritical. It is widely researched and extremely well written. It is wise, insightful, and, above all, historically subtle. It will be read with great interest within the academy and beyond, and for many years to come. We are delighted and honoured that this book should start our series, 'The Indian Century'.

RAMACHANDRA GUHA AND SUNIL KHILNANI

Contents

Illustrations

(between pp. 84 and 85)

Preface

In this book I examine Gandhi's legacy as the creator and advocate of a radical style of politics that fought the many insidious divides found in his own and other societies. Political cultures—both democratic and authoritarian—have had a tendency to give rise to a populist demonising of people who are considered to be 'different' in one way or another. This may be directed against an external enemy, or it may be engaged within a society against minorities or those who lack social and political power. Often, though not necessarily, it is associated with a chauvinistic nationalism. Many examples may be cited, of which the case of Nazi Germany is only the most striking. In India, in Gandhi's own time, Hindu extremists spouted a hate-filled bombast against Muslims and Christians, who were depicted as 'traitors' and 'anti-nationalist'. Separatist Muslims countered them, demanding their own nation state—Pakistan. This led to inter-community strife and a series of tragic massacres.

This divisive politics had, and continues to have, several features. It involves defining an antagonist—an 'other'—who is seen to stand apart from the community to which the 'self' is perceived to belong. The difference might be perceived as religious, ethnic, racial or caste-based. It might target a minority or an assertive lower social class or community that 'needs to be taught its place'. All members of the 'other' community are seen to be culpable, and all may become objects of what is held to be a legitimate attack, regardless of any particular individual attitude or loyalty. Such enmity might also be directed against an occupying or colonial power that is defined on racial, religious and other such grounds, leading to terrorist attacks that are fuelled as much by a spirit of hatred and revenge as by any tactical need in what might well be an otherwise legitimate struggle. Debate and discussion with the 'other' is avoided lest it compromise the resolve to eliminate. The aim is always to bring about a polarisation of sentiment, leaving no middle ground between 'self' and 'other'.

Gandhi, I argue in this book, resisted such a politics with his whole being. He refused to accept the validity of such divides, arguing that humans everywhere share much in common, and that there are always grounds for a fruitful dialogue that can lead to a resolution of conflicts and a breaking down of difference. He resisted nationalists who preached hatred against the coloniser and who tried to assert a warped sense of masculinity through assassinations and terror-bombings. Instead, he validated what he depicted as 'feminine' principles of non-violent opposition and civility. He insisted that Britishers were welcome to stay in India if they relinquished their domineering and exploitative sovereignty and applied their many talents to improving Indian society in harmony with Indian sentiments. He forged a method of resistance that sought to build bridges with an opponent, while at the same time refusing to accept injustice. He directed a powerful spotlight on the injustices that ran through his own society, such as the practice of untouchability and the exploitation of low-caste and 'tribal' groups by the high castes, and he fought these abuses with great energy and commitment. He abhorred conflict based on the hatred of one religious group for another, seeing it as a negation of all that he defined as 'religion'. He was disgusted by Christian missionaries who railed against Hindu 'superstition' and 'idolatry', as well as by Hindus and Muslims who attacked one another for various alleged violations of their religious sentiments.

In resisting such polarities, Gandhi put his life on the line, and in the end was assassinated by a votary of the politics that he abhorred. In the process, he forged a method of moral activism that was to provide a beacon for many women and men in subsequent years. Such people, in speaking what they believed to be the truth to those in power and in fighting injustice through non-violent civil resistance, have also laid their lives on the line, and they have suffered and sometimes died for their principles. The final three chapters of this book examine Gandhi's legacy in this respect, both in India and on a global stage.

The book began as a result of a suggestion from Ramachandra Guha that I write a book on 'Gandhism in the Twentieth Century'. I took up the idea because I felt that Gandhi's beliefs, practice and legacy were due for reassessment in the light of many disturbing developments that had occurred during the 1990s both in India and the world, and no more so than in Gandhi's home region of Gujarat, where Hindu chauvinists carried out murderous attacks on Muslims in 1992. The events of 2002 in Gujarat—when the same elements launched a carefully planned pogrom against Muslims, and then months later swept the polls in the state elections through playing on fears of 'Muslim terrorism'—have strongly reinforced my feelings in this respect.

For reading and commenting on the manuscript, I would like to thank David Arnold, Ramachandra Guha, Gyanendra Pandey, Parita Mukta, Mahesh Rangarajan, Ajay Skaria; for the editing, Rukun Advani; and for invaluable help with my research in India, Kanu Bhavsar.

While I was writing this book, and within the space of less than two years, my father, John Hardiman, and my father-in-law, Harshad Trivedy, died. Both, in their own and very different ways, put into practice their admirable visions of public and private civility. I dedicate this book to the memory of them both.

Note: The references to *Collected Works of Mahatma Gandhi* (*CWMG*) are from *Mahatma Gandhi: Electronic Book* (CD Rom version of *CWMG*), Publications Division, New Delhi 1999. The version of the *CWMG* used for this CD Rom differs from some of the earlier versions of *CWMG*, in both volume and page numbers. Although I used both the printed volume and the electronic version while writing this book, for the sake of consistency I have ensured that all references conform to the volume and page numbers of the latter.

1

Introduction
The Gandhian Dialogic

Mohandas Karamchand Gandhi has today become an iconic figure, a symbol of many things for many people. He is seen variously as the great opponent of European colonialism, as a champion of civil rights for racial, religious and other minorities, as an important critic of the industrial system of production, as a great pacifist, or as a person who stood for the need to resist injustice non-violently in a way that provides a vivid demonstration of the superior morality of the protester. Some believe that his greatest quality lay in his ability to reach out to the poor and oppressed. As the Indian political leader Rammanohar Lohia once stated: 'tens of millions throughout the world saw in him their spokesman, the solace and the remedy for their sufferings and distress.'[1]

In its last issue of the twentieth century, *Time* magazine selected Gandhi as joint runner-up (with Franklin Roosevelt) to Albert Einstein as 'person of the twentieth century'. He was singled out as the century's foremost representative of 'the crusade for civil rights and individual liberties'.[2] A commentator in this issue stated that 'Gandhi is that rare great man held in universal esteem, a figure lifted from history to moral icon.'[3] Nevertheless, however great the esteem, Gandhi has always been

[1]Rammanohar Lohia, *Marx, Gandhi and Socialism*, Rammanohar Lohia Samata Vidyalaya Nyasa, Hyderabad 1963, p. 121.

[2]*Time: The Weekly Newsmagazine*, 31 December 1999, p. 6. Other qualities for which he is remembered are listed on p. 86.

[3]Johanna McGeary, 'Mohandas Gandhi', *Time*, 31 December 1999, p. 95.

a controversial figure. Not least, this was because he took a strong stand on many important issues, in the process coming into sharp conflict with a range of opponents. Born on 2 October 1869 in the seaport of Porbandar within Kathiawad (or Saurashtra) in western India, he trained as a lawyer in England and then took up work in South Africa in 1893. From the start, he refused to accept the inferior status imposed on Indians by a racist ruling class and resolutely fought the various restrictions that had been imposed on his fellows there. In the process, he developed the new technique of civil resistance now universally known as *satyagraha*, deploying it to powerful effect against the white rulers in South Africa and, later, opponents in India. He also developed his idiosyncratic social vision there—representing another sharp challenge to accepted ways of thought—and established small communes in which an alternative way of life could be practised on a daily basis. His political, social and spiritual development during those years led to his manifesto of 1909—*Hind Swaraj*, or 'Indian Self-Rule'—a work that was considered so scandalous by the British that it was banned in India and which is now considered by many to be his tour de force.

Gandhi returned to India in 1915, and, after a period of settling in, soon established himself as a champion of the peasantry, leading to confrontations with white indigo planters in Champaran in 1917 and the colonial tax bureaucracy in Kheda in 1918. He also led a successful strike in Ahmedabad—his base at that time—by textile workers against Indian mill bosses. In 1919 he staged his first all-India protest—the Rowlatt Satyagraha—and followed this up in 1920 by gaining control over the Indian National Congress and launching the Non-Co-operation Movement, in which Indians withdrew their support for British colonial institutions. This was followed in later years by two more powerful confrontations with the British—the Civil Disobedience Movement of 1930–4 and the Quit India Movement of 1942.

While struggling against colonial rule, Gandhi also sought to build alternative social, political and economic institutions in India through his 'constructive programme'. This brought him into conflict with many powerful vested interests within Indian society. The area he focused on in particular was the practice of untouchability. He saw this as a social disgrace and a blot on Hindu religion, and his stance inevitably led to a clash with many high-caste Hindus whose privileges rested on this practice. In time his work in this sphere led also to a bitter dispute with a new leader of the Untouchables, B.R. Ambedkar. As an Untouchable by birth, Ambedkar resented what he experienced of Gandhi's paternalistic manner, and during the 1930s he became increasingly critical of Gandhi's whole approach to the issue, feeling that it provided no adequate means for the successful assertion of his community.

Gandhi was also in dispute with Marxists and socialists within the nationalist movement. Many on the political left saw him as merely the leader of an emerging bourgeoisie who was playing a 'historical role' in mobilising the Indian masses, deploying a rhetoric and appeal which provided a link between a traditionalist peasantry and the Indian middle class. They argued that while Gandhi appeared to stand for the interests of the masses, he was in fact an agent of the bourgeoisie, always serving their interests when it came to the crunch.[4] He was, furthermore, criticised on the left for his focus on social and moral issues, such as untouchability and the 'evil' of liquor-drinking, which were seen to be 'distractions' from the central struggle against colonialism and class-based exploitation.

Gandhi found himself in sharp disagreement also with Islamic separatists who became of increasing political importance in India from the mid-1920s. Muslims made up about a quarter of the entire population of the subcontinent and were in a majority in the north-west and in east Bengal. The demand led, in 1940, to the demand for a separate nation-state for Muslims in the Muslim-majority areas, to be called Pakistan. Muhammad Ali Jinnah, an old political rival of Gandhi, became the leader of this movement. Jinnah took the issue to the streets in 1946, which led to terrible riots in Calcutta and then other parts of India. The Congress leaders began to view Muslim-majority areas as a possible liability for the fledgling nation-state, and decided reluctantly in 1947 to agree to the division of the subcontinent into two nations—India and Pakistan. Gandhi believed this to be a tragic mistake that negated the secular principles of the nationalist movement. His fears were realised when the process of partition, which began on 15 August 1947, led to a genocidal conflict between Hindus, Muslims and Sikhs

[4]See for example R. Palme Dutt, *India Today*, Victor Gollancz, London 1940, p. 517.

in the north-west of the subcontinent. Hundreds of thousands died and millions became refugees. Gandhi worked tirelessly to alleviate the suffering of that terrible time, fasting to maintain communal peace, and insisting that the Muslims who remained in India should be treated as full and respected citizens of the new nation-state. Many Hindus saw him as pandering to these supposed 'traitors from within', and in January 1948 a Hindu extremist assassinated him at a prayer meeting in Delhi.

From all this, it is clear that Gandhi had many opponents, detractors and enemies throughout his life. He was accused, variously, of being an irresponsible trouble-maker by his colonial masters, a destroyer of social harmony by Indian traditionalists, a backward-looking crank by modernisers and progressives, an authoritarian leader by those within the movement who resented his style of leadership, a Hindu chauvinist by many Muslims, and a defender of high-caste élitism by lower-caste activists.

Some historians have argued that Gandhi's significance was limited to a specific historical situation—that of the decline of European colonialism at a time when it was in any case a waning force in the world. It is argued that Gandhi could only have succeeded against the relatively benign and liberal British; more ruthless rulers would have crushed him and his movement without a qualm. Others argue that Gandhi's particular brand of nationalism was important in mobilising the masses, but that it had to give way in time to the more hard-headed nationalism of state power and rapid economic development. Partha Chatterjee has thus described the Gandhian period in Indian history as a 'moment of manoeuvre', arguing that it was superseded by a more mature national capitalist ideology in the Nehruvian 'moment of arrival'.[5] Gail Omvedt has claimed in like vein: 'The events of independence and partition brought a near-complete *marginalisation of Gandhi and Gandhism*.'[6]

[5]Partha Chatterjee, *Nationalist Thought and the Colonial World—A Derivative Discourse?*, Zed Books, London 1986, pp. 131–66.

[6]Gail Omvedt, *Dalits and the Democractic Revolution: Dr Ambedkar and the Dalit Movement in Colonial India*, Sage Publications, New Delhi 1994, p. 226, emphasis in the original.

The problem with arguments such as these is that they fail to help us understand the reasons why Gandhi's ideas continue to resonate in the world today. It is hardly adequate, for example, to see Gandhi merely as a backward-looking representative of a 'traditional' culture that was being destroyed inexorably by the forces of modernity. Although a few of his admirers may have been and continue to be driven by a nostalgia for a romanticised past, the majority have been and are moved by a strong desire to evolve a better world in the light of existing realities. We have to try to situate Gandhi's controversial legacy within the modern world in a more satisfactory manner.

In this book, I intend to examine Gandhi as a figure whose life and work represented a dialogue between the many complex strands of thought of his day, both Indian and extra-Indian, as well as his legacy in India and the world since his death. Gandhi, on the one hand, cast a critical eye over his own society, deploying against it some of the values of the European Enlightenment, such as the doctrines of human rights, egalitarianism and democracy. On the other hand, being a colonised subject who resented most keenly the inferior status imposed on him by an imperial system, his positions were inevitably highly critical of many strands of this thought, such as its belief in the superiority of Western culture, its materialism and what he regarded as its amoral pursuit of knowledge. He claimed that in many areas of life, Indian values were better by far.

In his debate with the British who ruled India in his day, Gandhi deployed several thinkers who came from the European intellectual tradition. Those whom he endorsed most strongly tended to be ones who were most critical of the ruling ideologies of their societies, and Gandhi drew on them to advance his own critique of the systems of thought associated with the hegemony of British imperialism. In this respect he was involved in a continuing dialogue with thinkers located outside India who were by no means marginal figures, but, in many cases, respected theorists whose critiques might be disputed, but could hardly be ignored.

In India, he sought to open up a series of dialogues with his many opponents and rivals. In trying to establish a common ground as a basis for an agreement, he was often willing to alter his own views if he found them to be inadequate to the situation. He was thus involved in a series of long-running debates with Indian thinkers, such as the leader of the Untouchables B.R. Ambedkar, the Congress socialist Jayprakash Narayan, the Bengali sage Rabindranath Tagore, the left-wing liberal Jawaharlal Nehru, and Marxists such as M.N. Roy. These debates were sustained over decades, and in many cases both sides moved considerably in their position as a result of the dialogue. M.N. Roy, for instance, who began as an outspoken critic of Gandhi from a Marxian perspective, gradually came to appreciate Gandhian methods, in particular the emphasis on the ethics of struggle.[7] Gandhi similarly moved in his final years towards a more socialistic understanding of the need for an element of class conflict in the struggle for greater social equity, and this was because he kept an open mind towards his socialist critics.

Gandhi's style of writing was, similarly, dialogic rather than monologic. Rather than providing clear-cut authorial statements of the sort defined by the 'Bakhtin circle' theorist V.N. Volosinov as 'linear' or 'rational dogmatic'—a style seen most strongly during the period of the European Enlightenment[8]—Gandhi presented both sides of the case, but in a manner which might lead both himself and his adversary towards a resolution, which he considers the 'truth'. This is seen very clearly in the work that is often taken as seminal, *Hind Swaraj*, which is set out in the form of a debate between an 'Editor' (Gandhi) and a 'Reader' (Gandhi's adversary). According to Gandhi, the book reflected an actual debate that he engaged in with fellow nationalists at that time.[9] He appears also to have been influenced in part by the example of Socrates, and cites a book called *The Death and Defence of Socrates* in his list of recommended further reading at the end of the work. Possibly more importantly, he appears also to have been guided by the debate between Krishna and Arjun as set out in the *Bhagavad Gita*. Here a mortal debates with a deity and, as might be expected, is made to accept an unpalatable higher Truth.

[7]Dennis Dalton, *Mahatma Gandhi: Nonviolent Power in Action*, Columbia University Press, New York 1993, pp. 82–90.

[8]V.N. Volosinov, *Marxism and the Philosophy of Language*, translated by Ladislav Matejka and I.R. Titunik, Seminar Press, New York 1973, p. 123.

[9]'Preface to *Indian Home Rule*', 20 March 1910, *CWMG*, Vol. 10, p. 457.

We find this quality also in Gandhi's autobiography, where the debate was more of an inner one, documenting his personal struggles to arrive at guiding principles in life through continuing experiments in living.[10] Elsewhere, his body of thought was set out to a large extent in newspaper editorials, letters to individuals, speeches to audiences, dashed-off memos and the like. His statements were highly contextualised, and framed in relation to an individual or a particular group always likely to fire back a quick reply. Because fresh situations often required new thinking, Gandhi was not afraid to change his mind.

Gandhi never sought to provide a grand political theory, e.g. an ideological system. He worked out his theory—his 'truth'—as praxis, and understood that it had to evolve constantly in relation to his and other people's experience. He understood that this quest could lead to inconsistencies, because life is like that. On this he said: 'I must admit my many inconsistencies. But since I am called "Mahatma", I might well endorse Emerson's saying that "foolish consistency is the hobgoblin of little minds." There is, I fancy, a method in my inconsistencies.'[11] The method was, essentially, the dialogic—one in which knowledge is seen to arise from discussion, rather than from a unified philosophical system which is provided in the form of a treatise from which the internal contradictions have, ideally, been removed. As V.N. Volosinov argued: 'Any true understanding is dialogic in nature.'[12] By this, Volosinov meant that understanding does not come through individual revelation, but is reached through dialogues. Through such dialogues, systems of knowledge are both challenged and enriched. Gandhian knowledge

[10]There are interesting parallels between Gandhi's autobiography and the reminiscences of the sixteenth-century Baniya of north India, Banarasidas, known as the *Ardha-Kathanak*. Like Banarasidas, Gandhi provides a seemingly frank and self-confessional chronicle of his search for a transcendent Truth. See R.C. Sharma (trans. and ed.), 'The Ardha-Kathanak', *Indica*, 7:1, March 1970. The socio-historical implications of such a style of writing and its class situation would bear investigation, of a sort alluded to by Volosinov in *Marxism and the Philosophy of Language*.

[11]'My Inconsistencies', *Young India*, 13 February 1930, *CWMG*, Vol. 48, p. 314.

[12]Quoted in Pam Morris (ed.), *The Bakhtin Reader: Selected Writings of Bakhtin, Medvedev and Volosinov*, Arnold, London 1994, p. 35.

was set forth as a debate between people with opposing points of view, but there was always a search for a common ground, allowing a compromise and a going forward.

Ronald Terchek has argued that in this respect Gandhi adopted the Enlightenment position of valorising rational debate over coercion to solve problems. However, whereas it was a confident belief of the Enlightenment *philosophes* that rationality was indivisible and general, Gandhi understood that different peoples have their own definitions of what is 'rational', and to insist on the universality of one form of 'rationality' over another, and to thereby justify the imposition of one's will on others, represents no more than coercion by another name. In the process, alternative rationalities are silenced.[13] Gandhi thus insisted that we should try always to be open to the voice of the adversary, that is, the ego's Other. In other words, Gandhi's was a dialogic, as opposed to coercive, form of rationality.

Something of the quality of Gandhi's beliefs in this respect come through from a statement he made at a conference in East Bengal in 1940, when he was faced with hostile slogan shouting by supporters of Subhash Chandra Bose.

> I just now heard some people shouting, 'Down with Gandhism.' Those who want to put down Gandhism have every right to say so. Those who have come to hear me will please keep quiet and not get excited by hostile slogans nor shout counter-slogans of '*Gandhijiki Jai*'. If you are non-violent, you should calmly tolerate such slogans. If there is any trace of untruth in Gandhism, it must perish. If it contains truth, lakhs and crores of voices clamouring for its destruction will not destroy it. Allow freedom to those who want to say anything against Gandhism. That will cause no harm. Do not bear any grudge or malice against them. You cannot realise ahimsa unless you can calmly tolerate your opponent.[14]

Although Gandhi believed that there was a universal Truth that he equated with God, he never believed that he or any other human could

[13]Ronald J. Terchek, *Gandhi: Struggling for Autonomy*, Rowman and Littlefield, Lanham, Maryland, p. 7.

[14]Speech at Khadi and Village Industries Exhibition, Malikanda, Dacca, Bengal, 20 February 1940, *CWMG*, Vol. 77, p. 350.

ever comprehend this absolute in an adequate way. Human 'truths' were for him contingent and contextual, being reached through experience, praxis, debate and dialogue. His 'truth' was thus evolving and changing constantly; being in fact a series of 'truths'—with the 't' in lower case—rather than '*the* Truth'. In this respect, his approach to knowledge was not in practice so different to that of the scientist. He abhorred certainties, preferring debates and honest disagreements to unthinking assent. As his follower, Ramachandra Rao, once said 'Gandhi was bored by those who always agreed with him. He always enjoyed discussion and argument when there was a basis of agreement which made the exchange of differing ideas meaningful.'[15] Gandhi did not view the scriptures of any religion as being in any way exempt from moral scrutiny. Rather, he viewed such texts as human creations that had to be approached dialogically. He therefore scrutinised each in the light of his own lived experience. If the text came into conflict with his beliefs, then he was not prepared to give it credence.[16]

In this, Gandhi was by no means certain of his own personal truths; he doubted himself constantly, being torn between his Reason and his Faith by a powerful anguish. In seeking to resolve these contradictions through a courageous praxis, Gandhi reached out to make his suffering a matter of deep public concern. Just as Marx doubted whether he would qualify as a 'Marxist', so Gandhi distanced himself constantly from 'Gandhism'. As he stated:

> I love to hear the words: 'Down with Gandhism'. An 'ism' deserves to be destroyed. It is a useless thing. The real thing is non-violence. It is immortal. It is enough for me if it remains alive. I am eager to see Gandhism wiped out at an earlier date. You should not give yourselves over to sectarianism. I do not belong to any sect. I have never dreamt of establishing any sect. If any sect is established in my name after my death my soul would cry out in anguish.[17]

[15]Hugh Grey, '"Gora", Gandhi's Atheist Follower', in Peter Robb and David Taylor (eds), *Rule, Protest, Identity: Aspects of Modern South Asia*, Curzon Press, London 1978, p. 149.

[16]Terchek, *Gandhi*, p. 63.

[17]Speech at Gandhi Seva Sangh Meeting, Malikanda, Bengal, 22 February 1940, *CWMG*, Vol. 77, p. 378.

In truth, I myself do not know what Gandhism means. I have not given anything new to the country. I have only given a new form to the traditional [wisdom] of India. It would therefore be wrong to call it Gandhism.[18]

I assure all my admirers and friends that they will please me better if they will forget the Mahatma and remember Gandhiji ... or think of me simply as Gandhi.[19]

Ashis Nandy has pointed out, in this respect, how Gandhi did not attempt to provide a strongly systematised theory or ideology or utopia. Rather, he provided a vision of a society that stood in constant opposition to the oppressions, hierarchies and technologies that prevailed in the world of his day. His approach represented a state of mind rather than a clear-cut theoretical system.[20]

Being human, and always in the thick of a constant clamour for his attention, with momentous consequences often hinging on his pronouncements and actions, Gandhi did not always practice his principles adequately. He could at times be querulous, intolerant and not at all open to dialogue. For example, when Ramachandra Rao wrote to Gandhi in 1941 stating that he had been campaigning against untouchability from an 'atheistical angle' and wanted to discuss the matter with him, Gandhi replied with an irritated and curt: 'atheism is a denial of the self. No one has succeeded in its propagation.' Rao, unlike many others, did not give up. Two years later, Gandhi gave him some time and quickly realised that this particular atheist was a like-minded seeker after truth, deserving his full support.[21]

Gandhi can however be seen as closing himself off to dialogue in more important respects. In his own family, he acted the high-handed patriarch, coercing his wife and sons into following the path he decreed as 'true'. He often ran his ashrams in an autocratic manner, disciplining

[18]Speech at Khadi and Village Industries Exhibition, Malikanda, Dacca, Bengal, 20 February 1940, *CWMG*, Vol. 77, p. 350.

[19]'Notes', *Young India*, 12 June 1924, *CWMG*, Vol. 28, p. 142.

[20]Ashis Nandy, 'From Outside the Imperium: Gandhi's Cultural Critique of the "West"', *Alternatives*, Vol. 7, Number 2, 1981, p. 173.

[21]Hugh Grey, '"Gora", Gandhi's Atheist Follower', pp. 147–8.

those who did not accept his dictates. While travelling the length and breadth of India he was constantly irritated by the huge crowds that pressed to see him, resenting what he saw as their harassment. He came to distrust the motives of many of his low-class followers, seeing in them a propensity towards violence that required strong control. He was accordingly reluctant to allow them their head in agitations. In addition, those who acted in his name often lacked his breadth of spirit and were frequently élitist in the way they related to subaltern groups. In all this, there was a constant tension, making any analysis of Gandhi's dialogue with truth difficult and problematic.

This book has two main dimensions. It involves, first, a scrutiny of Gandhi's own desired practice, that of striving to keep a wide range of dialogues open with people in many different areas of life, some of whom were his strong opponents. His not infrequent failure to live up to this ideal will be examined critically. Second, it involves an examination of dialogues between, on the one hand, a variety of political and social actors, and on the other Gandhi and his ideas and practices, both during his lifetime and after his death, in India and outside India. Thus, while providing a reading of Gandhi as a theoretical proponent of a dialogic approach, the book will at the same time seek to interrogate the ways in which he and his followers and admirers have sought to implement Gandhian ideals in practice. And last, but not least, it is a product of my own troubled dialogue with Gandhi, carried out over the past thirty years, beginning with a strong emotional commitment, developing into much profound disillusion, but with a subsequent emergence of a greater appreciation of what he stood for in the light of many horrific developments in India and the world in recent years.[22]

[22]My personal trajectory in this respect is hardly unique. As Ramachandra Guha has noted—speaking we must assume for his own generation and intellectual class—there is within many of us 'a Gandhian and a Marxist struggling for supremacy'. Having been engaged with India intellectually for much of own life, I can certainly recognise this tension in myself. Ramachandra Guha, *An Anthropologist Among the Marxists and Other Essays*, Permanent Black, New Delhi 2001, p. 1.

2

An Incorporative Nationalism

In the popular narrative of Gandhi's life—as told and retold in modern India—his nationalism is seen to have been forged through his personal experience of the dark underside of colonial rule. His autobiography provides a powerful chronicle of the series of humiliations and traumas that provided the milestones in this process. The first occurred in 1892, when he suffered the indignity of being ejected roughly from the office of the Political Agent in Rajkot when he made a request that was considered out of order. In a previous fleeting encounter in England the official had treated Gandhi in a civil manner, and Gandhi had expected the same in India. When Gandhi approached the eminent nationalist Pherozeshah Mehta with his tale of this humiliation, he was told that he would have to accept such treatment from British officials as a fact of life for Indian lawyers. He was advised to 'pocket the insult'. For Gandhi, this advice 'was as bitter as poison'. He had discovered that very different social rules prevailed in Britain and in India. He later stated: 'This shock changed the course of my life.'[1]

Less than a year later, Gandhi ran the full gamut of racist abuse in an epic journey from Durban to Pretoria.[2] He arrived in Durban from

[1]*An Autobiography*, *CWMG*, Vol. 44, pp. 163–4.

[2]The journey is central to the popular account of Gandhi's life; e.g.—to take some examples at random—in Richard Attenborough's film, *Gandhi*; in rather crude illustrations in Ramanlal Soni's illustrated book for children, *Shishu Gandhi Katha* (Gujarati), no publication details, pp. 9–10; also in a series of melodramatic tableaux which can be viewed in the exhibition in Birla House, Tees January Marg, New Delhi.

India to find himself transposed in South Africa into a mere 'coolie barrister'. He attempted to deny this status by travelling out of Durban first class on the railway, and when he refused to go to a third class seat was thrown out of the train onto the platform at Maritzburg. Once again, fellow Indians told him that such experiences were their daily lot. Then, on the stage to Johannesburg, he was made to sit on the outside of the coach with the driver, rather than inside with the white passengers. When even this seat was required, he was told to sit on a dirty sack on the footboard. His protests led to a beating. When he reached Johannesburg, he was refused a room in a hotel and had to find accommodation elsewhere. He remained defiant, insisting on continuing his journey first class. On this occasion the only other passenger in the compartment, an Englishman, told the guard that he was prepared to tolerate the company of an Indian with a valid ticket. And so he reached Pretoria, somewhat vindicated.[3]

Throughout this journey, Gandhi was consistently advised by other Indians to tolerate the humiliations and adopt a low profile. However, he refused to play by the largely unwritten rules of discrimination—he insisted on his right to equality as a citizen of the Empire. He consistently took a stance that forced matters to a head: provoking either a crude and violent counter-attack or an embarrassed and shame-faced retreat. In the end, as in a parable of his life, the colonial system was made to stage a strategic withdrawal and he gained his place of uneasy equality with the Englishman. In his actual life, the struggle with imperialism and racism was of course only just beginning.

Over the next decade and a half, Gandhi continued his fight for equal citizenship. He recruited an Indian ambulance corps to care for wounded British soldiers during the Boer War, leading the South African Indians to claim the epithet 'sons of Empire'—a status soon denied in the post-war settlement.[4] In 1906 he again raised an ambulance corps during the Bambata war (the so-called 'Zulu revolt'). He continued to be moved by a feeling of sincere loyalty to the Empire: 'I then believed that the British Empire existed for the welfare of the world.'[5] On reaching

[3] *An Autobiography*, *CWMG*, Vol. 44, pp. 171–8.
[4] Ibid., p. 251.
[5] Ibid., p. 323.

the front, he quickly discovered that the authorities had magnified a trivial incident of resistance to a colonial tax into a mighty 'rebellion' that justified a draconian response. When he and his fellow volunteers were assigned to care for wounded blacks he felt a sense of relief, as he believed them to be the wronged party. He found, to his outrage, that the whites were not prepared to give medical treatment to the blacks and even taunted them with lewd racist abuse while the Indian volunteers were treating them. He also discovered that the blacks whom they were treating had not been wounded in battle: some had been taken prisoners and flogged mercilessly, leaving festering sores. Others had not been involved in the protest but had been shot by the white soldiers 'by mistake'. He realised to his horror that the soldiers were going from village to village slaughtering innocent people. 'This', he discovered, 'was no war but a man-hunt ...'[6] This experience—more than any other—cleared his mind of delusions about British imperialism. Thereafter, he was only too aware that its liberal façade served merely to mask a brutal and systematic racism. The only honest choice open to him in the circumstances was to become an out-and-out opponent of British rule, in India and in the Empire at large.

Gandhi's progress towards a more militant nationalism during this decade was not of course unique, as the focus on his biography might imply. It was an experience shared by many of his generation and class. In the final decades of the nineteenth century, British liberals had begun to move towards a policy of devolving power within India to the Indian people, while at the same time British conservatives had fought a rearguard action in which they did their best to prevent any substantial weakening of colonial control. It was asserted in a racist manner that 'natives' lacked moral backbone, and that India could only deteriorate into chaos if they were given greater power. All this created an explosive mix of expectation and hurt pride. The first major nationalist upsurge occurred in Bengal in the period 1905–8 in what is known as the Swadeshi Movement.[7]

The manifesto that reflected Gandhi's new sentiments was the booklet

[6]Ibid., p. 325.

[7]The classic account of this movement is Sumit Sarkar, *The Swadeshī Movement in Bengal 1903–1908*, People's Publishing House, New Delhi 1973.

of 1909 entitled *Hind Swaraj*. This melded his revulsion towards imperialism with the economic nationalism of the Swadeshi Movement. In his own account, this was another position that he claimed to have come to in a surge of emotion. He describes here how he wept when he read R.C. Dutt's *Economic History of India*, with its narration of the terrible economic damage that had been inflicted on India by the British.[8] His own programme for economic nationalism was to be built on this foundation. *Hind Swaraj* provided a powerful statement of this new spirit of nationalist militancy. It went far beyond anything the authorities in India were prepared to tolerate, and they banned it as soon as it was published there.

During the following decade, Gandhi voiced his Indian nationalism in the strongest possible terms. In 1917 he asserted: 'Only if I die for India shall I know that I was fit to live.'[9] He did not accept the argument, put forward most notably by Rabindranath Tagore, that nationalism was corrupting *per se*. Tagore believed that the end result of such an assertion was a state with greatly enhanced power, and, possibly, greater tyranny. Tagore could see only greed and violence in nationalism, and when Gandhi launched his campaign of non-cooperation in 1920, he stated that the Mahatma was playing with fire.[10]

Gandhi countered this by arguing that he was trying to forge a nationalism of a very different sort to the violent and aggressive form found in the West. He most emphatically rejected a nationalism that sought freedom through violence. He argued that terrorist methods were a foreign import and alien to the nature of Indian religion, which was suffused with the principle of *ahimsa*.[11] Violence not only had a tendency to escalate, but it also precluded dialogue. The aim should be to seek to persuade the British of the wrongness of their ways and bring about a change of heart through *satyagraha*. 'The force of arms is powerless when matched against the force of love or the soul.'[12]

[8]Gandhi, *Hind Swaraj*, *CWMG*, Vol. 10, p. 303.

[9]Concluding Speech at the Conference, Broach, 21 October 1917, *CWMG*, Vol. 16, p. 106.

[10]On Tagore's arguments, see Dalton, *Mahatma Gandhi*, pp. 67–74.

[11]Speech at YMCA, Madras, 27 April 1915, *CWMG*, Vol. 14, p. 424.

[12]Gandhi, *Hind Swaraj*, *CWMG*, Vol. 10, p. 290.

Gandhi saw his goal as self-determination for the Indian people, who would then be free to work out their own destiny on their own terms. He rarely used the term 'nation', preferring concepts such as *swaraj*, *swadeshi*, and 'Indian civilisation'. As Bhikhu Parekh argues: 'Since the civilisation Gandhi wanted the Indian state to nurture was sympathetic, tolerant, spiritual and open, his vision of India had little in common with the collectivist, monolithic, aggressive and xenophobic nationalism of some of the Western and central European countries.'[13]

And, one might add, of many Hindu chauvinists in India.[14] In 1925 he stated very firmly that although his patriotism was focused on India, it was not narrow, for—

> it included not merely the welfare of India but the whole world ... In my opinion, it is impossible for one to be an internationalist without being a nationalist.
>
> Internationalism is possible only when nationalism becomes a fact, i.e., when peoples belonging to different countries have organised themselves and are able to act as one man. It is not nationalism that is evil, it is the narrowness, selfishness, exclusiveness which is the bane of modern nations which is evil. Each one wants to profit at the expense and rise on the ruin of the other. Indian nationalism has, I hope, struck a different path. It wants to organise itself or to find full self-expression for the benefit and service of humanity at large.[15]

Gandhi's nationalism was thus broad and catholic. He hardly regarded India as a nation in a narrow sense; rather it was a civilisation with its own particular qualities. He did not condemn Europe in any blanket fashion—in contrast to those demagogic nationalists who whip up support by playing on popular ethnic and racial antagonisms. Too often, the critique of the latter of Europe and 'eurocentricity' is deployed to condemn anything which they dislike in the modern world—e.g. human

[13]Bhikhu Parekh, *Gandhi's Political Philosophy: A Critical Examination*, Macmillan, Basingstoke 1989, p. 194.

[14]Notably V.D. Savarkar, whose *Hindutva: Who is a Hindu?*, Nagpur 1923, excluded from Indian nationality anyone who was not ethnically Indian or whose religion was non-Indian in origin.

[15]'Nationalism v. Internationalism', *Young India*, 18 June 1925, *CWMG*, Vol. 32, p. 12.

rights, women's assertion, democracy, socialism, secularism and religious toleration—while the modern technologies of organisation and disciplinary control which are of use to them—e.g. the authoritarian state, new forms of surveillance, policing, torture and armaments—are all absolved from being eurocentric or antinational. Gandhi had experienced many facets of Europe and had absorbed many doctrines propounded by European thinkers within his own philosophy of life. He also had many fast friends who were British, such as C.F. Andrews. Being very aware of this, he refused to stigmatise the British for *being* British, and insisted he would be happy to accept the British as fellow-citizens of India if they changed their ways profoundly.[16] He was not interested in chauvinistic nationalism—he aspired to a universalism that soared above narrow political goals.[17]

Gandhi saw India as occupying a unique position in a differentiated family of nations. Western nations were lands of *bhoga*, whereas India was the land of karma, so that 'India is fitted for the religious supremacy of the world'.[18] Both the words used by Gandhi are complex. In Gujarati, bhoga means both enjoyments and pleasures, as well as an offering to a deity—for the enjoyment of the deity—and, by extension, a sacrifice. There is thus a suggestion that, in the West, material pleasure had attained a spiritual dimension. Karma means action, deed, conduct, behaviour, fate, luck, religious rite, the effects of past lives on the present, evil, immorality and sin. Gandhi's invocation of the quality of karma by no means sought to flatter his Gujarati audience. Rather, it reminded them of their hard destiny which made them different from the populations of the West.

Gandhi believed that India was essentially a nation even before the coming of the British. When in *Hind Swaraj* the 'reader' puts forward the argument that British rule provided the basis for Indian nationalism—in particular by providing railway communication, which allowed disparate people to come together—the 'editor' (i.e. Gandhi) replies that India was already a nation before colonial rule. The fact

[16]Gandhi, *Hind Swaraj*, *CWMG*, Vol. 10, p. 282.

[17]Arnold, *Gandhi*, p. 105.

[18]Speech to First Gujarat Political Conference, 3 November 1917, *CWMG*, Vol. 16, p. 116.

that the four primary places of Shaivite pilgrimage had long been established in each extremity of the subcontinent showed this.[19] Gandhi sought to define Indian nationhood in terms of certain cultural markers of an assumed antiquity. This exercise entailed a series of inversions of colonial epistemologies of knowledge/power. For example, the colonial depiction of an Orient steeped in religion and superstition was inverted into a statement of the cultural superiority of an ancient civilisation that was based on a soaring spirituality.[20] The colonial depiction of the caste-ridden, stagnant Indian village was inverted into an argument for a harmonious and smoothly functioning social system in which humans were happy because they were comfortable with their destinies.[21] In all of this, Gandhi advanced highly essentialist arguments about the culture of each nation.

Gandhi believed that it was vital to nurture a dynamic political space that was separate from state power and which could act as a constant check on that power. Private property, held in a spirit of trusteeship, provided one such counter to state power: 'in my opinion the violence of private ownership is less injurious than the violence of the State.'[22] Another counter was provided by organisations devoted to public welfare. He thus advised members of bodies such as the Gandhi Seva Sangh, which was founded in 1923, not to expend their energies in what he called 'power politics', which included 'the politics of the Congress and elections and ... groupism.'[23] In 1948 he even advised the Congress Party to disband itself, as it had achieved its objective of winning independence for India, and he suggested putting in its place a Lok Sevak

[19]*Hind Swaraj*, *CWMG*, Vol. 10, p. 268.

[20]Chatterjee, *Nationalist Thought and the Colonial World*, p. 38.

[21]Nicholas B. Dirks, 'The Conversion of Caste: Location, Translation, and Appropriation', in *Conversion to Modernities: The Globalization of Christianity*, ed. Peter van der Veer, Routledge, New York 1996, p. 135.

[22]Interview to Nirmal Kumar Bose, 9–10 November 1934, *CWMG*, Vol. 65, p. 319. It is notable in this respect that John Locke, who first propounded the notion of civil society, saw rights of property as one of the chief cornerstones of such a society. See Dipesh Chakrabarty, *Provincializing Europe: Postcolonial Thought and Historical Difference*, Princeton University Press, Princeton 2000, p. 230.

[23]Speech at Gandhi Seva Sangh Meeting, Malikanda, Bengal, 21 February 1940, *CWMG*, Vol. 77, p. 371.

Sangh (Association for the Service of the People) which would be able to distance itself from the cut and thrust of party politics.[24] This did not mean that such social activists should not relate to politics, for he refused to see their welfare work as being in any way 'non-political'. It was only that their politics were to operate primarily outside and beyond the struggle for direct control over the levers of power. He even went so far as to say that without such non-governmental forces operating in a dynamic and independent way 'Gandhism is sure to perish'.[25] Gandhian ideals, in other words, could only flourish within a realm of politics that was separate from the state. All this marked off his position in a radical way from that of most political theorists and activists of his day.

Later in his life, Gandhi tempered his antagonism to state power with a realisation that the state provided perhaps the firmest guarantee available in the circumstances of the day to protect the rights of the most vulnerable in society. It could legislate to eradicate various social and economic injustices, such as untouchability, unemployment, and disparities in land ownership.[26] This was however only required as a temporary measure. He believed that as people became empowered and learnt to take full responsibility for their own affairs and developed a concern for their fellow citizens, society would develop and flourish outside the sphere of statist power politics. His ideal, in fact, was to strive towards a situation in which 'there will be no political institution and therefore no political power.' He described this as a condition of 'enlightened anarchy'.[27] He accepted that no such condition existed—or had ever existed—in the world. However, if it were to come into being anywhere, that place would be India. But a long and continuing struggle would be required.[28]

[24]Draft Constitution of the Congress, 29 January 1948, *CWMG*, Vol. 98, pp. 333–5.

[25]Speech at Gandhi Seva Sangh, Malikanda, Bengal, 21 February 1940, *CWMG*, Vol. 77, p. 371.

[26]Terchek, *Gandhi*, pp. 166–7.

[27]'Enlightened Anarchy—A Political Ideal', *Sarvodaya*, January 1939, *CWMG*, Vol. 74, p. 380.

[28]'Congress Ministries and *Ahimsa*', 15 September 1946, *CWMG*, Vol. 92, pp. 128–30.

Critics of Gandhi have argued that there was no reason to believe that India was suited to such a political order, as there was no tradition of stateless societies. On the contrary, Hindu political theory enjoins a strong and autocratic kingship tempered by dharma. This was necessary to counter the general human tendency towards wickedness.[29] Scholars such as Burton Stein and David Ludden have argued, however, that power in medieval India was by no means as monolithic as is assumed by such arguments, and in fact there was often very strong segmentation of power.[30] It can also be noted that there were many Indian traditions that Gandhi could invoke in his favour, though clearly he applied them in novel ways in the climate of his day.

Gandhi often quoted Thoreau's maxim: 'that government is best which governs least.'[31] Many have seen a congruence between Gandhi's ideas on the state and anarchist doctrine.[32] Like Gandhi, anarchists see the modern state, with its claim to a monopoly of the legal instruments of coercion, as an obstacle to the development of a genuinely democratic, co-operative and free social order. They too demand a decentralization of power, asking that local groups be given considerable degree of self-determination. Likewise, they place obedience to one's own conscience above that of obedience to the state, and moral authority over and above legal and political authority. However, while Western anarchists of Gandhi's day believed that a sharp revolution-

[29]For a review of such literature see Geoffrey Ostergaard and Melville Currell, *The Gentle Anarchists: A Study of the Leaders of the Sarvodaya Movement for Non-Violent Revolution in India*, Clarendon Press, Oxford 1971, pp. 29–30.

[30]Burton Stein, *Peasant State and Society in Medieval South India*, Oxford University Press, New Delhi 1980; David Ludden, *An Agrarian History of South Asia, The New Cambridge History of India*, Volume IV:4, Cambridge University Press, Cambridge 1999.

[31]Henry Thoreau, 'Civil Disobedience' in *Walden and Civil Disobedience*, Penguin, Harmondsworth, 1983, p. 385. For Gandhi's quoting of Thoreau see 'Enlightened Anarchy—A Political Ideal', *Sarvodaya*, January 1939, *CWMG*, Vol. 74, p. 380.

[32]For example, George Woodcock, *Gandhi*, Fontana, London 1972, pp. 78–89. See also Ostergaard and Currell, *The Gentle Anarchists*, pp. 32–4, 37–40 and 42; and Joan Bondurant, *Conquest of Violence: The Gandhian Philosophy of Conflict*, Princeton University Press, Princeton 1958, p. 178.

ary break was required before liberation could be achieved, Gandhi believed in gradual change through slow and patient constructive work. Also, Western anarchists were mostly atheists who saw religion as being deployed by states to bolster their power, and who regarded their beliefs as arising from a secular rational enquiry, whereas Gandhi appealed to faith, and asserted that there was no conflict between true freedom and the divine, God being Truth. An even more important difference was that anarchism was in many respects a culmination of a particular strand of liberalism that stressed the need to defend the liberty of the individual against that of the state. In such a formulation, state power is seen as fundamentally repressive and coercive. Against this, anarchists have sought, characteristically, to express their distance from power and their freedom from control by asserting their individuality, often through a bohemian lifestyle with a lack of sexual inhibition. Gandhi, by contrast, opposed the state not because he opposed control and discipline as such, but rather because he did not believe that the state should be the instrument of its expression. Instead, he demanded of himself and his followers a strongly puritanical self-restraint with a strong mental control over one's sexuality, which was far more rigorous than anything that the state might impose. In this respect, Gandhi's position was the antithesis of much Western anarchism.[33]

Gandhi believed that his ideals could be best realised through a system of decentralised self-government, which he preferred to describe as swaraj (self-rule) rather than 'democracy' which, in its Western constitutional form, was highly statist. He proposed a system of tiered councils with a large amount of autonomy at village, sub-district, district, provincial and national levels. Each council was to elect the members of the one above it. In this way, voters would know those whom they voted for personally. From around 1930 onwards, Gandhi modified his views somewhat as he came to realise that the poor and oppressed often required support from the state. In 1946–7 he saw also that communal violence could be contained by a strong state.[34]

[33]I am grateful to Ajay Skaria for some suggestive comments that I have drawn on freely here.

[34]Parekh, *Gandhi's Political Philosophy*, pp. 113–21.

Forging a Nationalist Hegemony

Gandhi believed very strongly that the nation had to incorporate within it all the different cultural and religious groups of the subcontinent. In *Hind Swaraj* his 'reader' raises the problem of the Hindu–Muslim divide; doesn't this make it impossible to speak of India as one nation? The 'editor' replies that nationalism cannot be defined by religion in India. In the past there was no profound enmity between Hindus and Muslims; the British created divisions. These divides can be overcome, for 'religions are different roads converging to the same point.'[35]

The 'reader' in this passage raises the question commonly asked by colonial officials in India at that time: how could the Indian people claim nationality when they were so divided by caste and religion? The Bengali nationalist Bipin Chandra Pal had sought an answer in his concept of 'composite patriotism', which he first put forward in 1906. He held that Hindus, Muslims, Christians, and other religious minorities (including the 'animistic' tribals) should preserve their distinctive religious cultures while fighting together for freedom. This provided an important secularist modification of the late-nineteenth-century Hindu nationalist idea of *adhikar-bheda*, which involved the belief that each level or group should have its distinct rituals and beliefs while accepting that it was a part of a wider Hindu whole. Pal had extended the principle to include non-Hindus within the fold. His proposition was criticised in 1907 by Tagore for its essentialism. Tagore wanted to move towards an ever evolving and ultimately hybrid national *mahajati*.[36] A decade later, in 1917, Annie Besant endorsed Pal's line by arguing that Indian youths should be brought up so as 'to make the Mussalman a good Mussalman, the Hindu boy a good Hindu ... Only they must be taught a broad and liberal tolerance as well as enlightened love for their own religion, so that each may remain Hindu or Mussalman, but both be Indian.'[37] After his return to India in 1915 Gandhi extended

[35]Gandhi, *Hind Swaraj*, *CWMG*, Vol. 10, p. 271.

[36]Tapan Basu, Pradip Datta, Sumit Sarkar, Tanika Sarkar, Sambuddha Sen, *Khaki Shorts and Saffron Flags: A Critique of the Hindu Right*, Orient Longman, New Delhi 1993, p. 7.

[37]Annie Besant, *The Birth of a New India: A Collection of Writings and Speeches in Indian Affairs*, Theosophical Publishing House, Madras 1917, p. 36.

the idea of a composite nationalism to include not only religious groups but castes and communities in general. In doing so he tapped into a wide range of movements for caste and community assertion, such as that of the Patidars of his own Gujarat.[38] One historian has argued that this allowed a massive expansion of the nationalist movement in India: 'Because Gandhi had a realistic picture of India as a loose constellation of classes, communities and religious groups, he was able to activate the peoples of the subcontinent in a way no one had done before, or has since.'[39] Gandhi sought to bind this loose coalition together through moral appeals, such as outrage against the Rowlatt Acts of 1919. At the same time, he championed sectional demands, such as that of the Khilafat Movement. This move was condemned by many Hindu nationalists, as well as secularists within the Congress. Despite this, he managed for two years to hold this uneasy coalition together.

It has been argued that there were certain parallels in this respect between Gandhi and Lenin, both of whom were trying at this time to form alliances of disparate groups so as to remove oppressive rulers.[40] Lenin, who theorised his strategy in *What is to be Done?*, envisaged forging a revolutionary alliance under the hegemony of the proletariat. This was seen as a tactical move; once power had been won, the other classes within the alliance would be gradually brought into line with the interests of the proletarian revolution.[41] Lenin believed very strongly in the universal value of such a revolution. Gandhi, in building the alliances that would remove the British, sought to bind together various ethnic, caste, class, religious and regional groups, all of which were enjoined to work out their destinies through the cleansing fire of nationalist activism. He however refused to accept the idea of the

[38]See Anil Bhatt, 'Caste and Political Mobilisation in a Gujarat District', in Rajni Kothari (ed.), *Caste in Indian Politics*, Orient Longman, New Delhi 1970.

[39]Ravinder Kumar, 'Class, Community or Nation? Gandhi's Quest for a Popular Consensus in India', in R. Kumar, *Essays in the Social History of Modern India*, Oxford University Press, New Delhi 1983, p. 51.

[40]This comparison was made as early as 1922 by the Gandhian intellectual Acharya Gidwani. See Indulal Yagnik, *Atmakatha*, Vol. 3, Vatrak Khedut Vidhalay, Mehmedabad 1956, p. 114.

[41]Ernesto Laclau and Chantal Mouffe, *Hegemony and Socialist Strategy: Towards a Radical Democratic Politics*, Verso, London 1994, p. 55.

hegemony of the working class or any other class within such an alliance—this was too narrow and sectional—with all the potential for violence and tyranny that it implied. For Gandhi, it was imperative that the integrity of each group's struggle be recognised through an acceptance of a fundamental right of each minority to follow its own way of life after independence had been won. He was trying to forge a polity bound together not by congruent 'interests', but by a sense of 'neighbourliness' in which each group would respect the beliefs, and even prejudices, of its fellows for the good of the wider whole.[42] It was on such terms that Gandhi's movement achieved a strategic hegemony at this juncture in Indian history. He was to do the same at other crucial moments, such as in 1930–1 and 1942.[43]

In all cases, there was a continuing problem of articulating the national-level organisation—with its secular-democratic principles and bureaucratic structure—with local solidarities and their very different systems of belief and culture. Shahid Amin's study of the local understanding of Gandhian politics in Gorakhpur district in 1920–2 shows how at times there was a profound chasm in this respect between the national leadership and local supporters of the movement.[44] There were inevitable tensions that could generate feelings of bad faith on both sides, particularly when Gandhi suddenly called off his protests for reasons that had nothing to do with such localised struggles. Gandhi for his part was often uncomfortable and sometimes horrified with the way in which his message was received by the masses. He was often critical of the way in which his lieutenants sought to extend the movement on the ground.[45] At times, however, the different levels were

[42]On this, I have benefited from the unpublished paper of Faisal Fatehali Devji, 'A Practice of Prejudice', 2001.

[43]There are other important differences between Lenin and Gandhi. For example, Lenin was working within a longstanding Russian radical tradition of violent revolt against a highly authoritarian state, whereas Gandhi can be placed more in the Indian nationalist tradition of putting pressure on the British through strategic protests aimed to bring about constitutional reforms. I am grateful to Mahesh Rangarajan for making this point.

[44]Shahid Amin, 'Gandhi as Mahatma', in Ranajit Guha (ed.), *Subaltern Studies III*, Oxford University Press, New Delhi 1984.

[45]I have described the way in which he distanced himself from one such

articulated with striking success, as in Bardoli in 1928. In this case Gandhi allowed his second-in-command in Gujarat, Vallabhbhai Patel, full rein to organise a campaign of non-violent civil disobedience within a confined area, in which a small army of Congress activists reinforced the peasant protesters. The government was forced to capitulate in a most humiliating way.[46]

Antonio Gramsci has argued that the elite and subaltern classes structure their discourses in relationship to each other through 'a series of negations'.[47] Although this can produce tension, it can also lead to a working through of difference and a contingent resolution that requires a shift in the mentalities of both parties. It is in other words a dialogic process. In this process a certain hegemonic consensus may be forged, in which certain attitudes and mentalities come to be accepted as a matter of everyday common sense.[48]

We can see this process being worked through in a number of spheres. For example, the secular nationalist belief in equality before the law, and Gandhi's insistence on the right of all to voice their demands through a dialogic form of civil resistance, became a matter of common sense for large numbers of poor Indians. Many areas of Indian identity came to be accepted as given, as with the Gandhian 'national dress' or the Indian flag that was fought for in a series of 'flag satyagrahas'.[49] Even

---

campaign, which involved a local nationalist activist trying to gain a base amongst some Adivasis by claiming that their gods had endorsed Gandhi. See *The Coming of the Devi: Adivasi Assertion in South Gujarat*, Oxford University Press, New Delhi 1987, pp. 168–71.

[46]Ghanshyam Shah, 'The Experience of Bardoli Satyagraha (1920–28)', *Contributions to Indian Sociology*, new series, 8, 1974; Shirin Mehta, *The Peasantry and Nationalism: A Study of the Bardoli Satyagraha*, Manohar, New Delhi 1984; David Hardiman, 'The Roots of Rural Agitation in India 1914–47: A Rejoinder to Charlesworth', *The Journal of Peasant Studies*, Vol. 8, n.3, 1981.

[47]Antonio Gramsci, *Selections from the Prison Notebooks*, Lawrence and Wishart, London 1971, p. 271.

[48]Ibid., pp. 323–31.

[49]Emma Tarlo, *Clothing Matters: Dress and Identity in India*, University of Chicago Press, Chicago 1996, pp. 62–93: Arundhati Virmani, 'National Symbols under Colonial Domination: The Nationalization of the Indian Flag, March-August 1923', *Past and Present*, 164, August 1999.

Gandhi's somewhat extraordinary belief in the intrinsic civilisational non-violence of the Indian people was accepted to a surprising degree by large numbers of Indians at the time. There were however obvious failures, the greatest of all being the emphatic rejection of both the principle of non-violence and that of a subcontinental national unity that cut across religious divides in the terrible events of the Partition of 1947 and in subsequent campaigns of communal aggression.

The Disciplined Nation

For Gandhi swaraj entailed above all what he called a 'disciplined rule from within'.[50] In this, he distinguished swaraj from mere 'freedom' or 'independence', which he claimed were English words lacking such connotations and which could be taken to mean a license to do whatever one wishes. His swaraj allowed no such irresponsible freedom, but demanded rather a rigorous moulding of the self and a heavy sense of responsibility. Above all it required *tap* or *tapas*—Hindi terms meaning an ascetic and rigorous self-discipline.[51] Tapas involved much hard work and sweat, which reflects the Sanskrit root of the term, that of *tap*, or 'heat'. The devotee was supposed to expose the body to 'five fires'—that of the four seasons and to the sun burning from above.[52] For the ascetic, tapas was the path to liberation and spiritual power.

Discipline has in fact a dual character—it is both empowering and repressive. This truth is stated most succinctly in the Gujarati proverb: 'discipline is power: power is discipline' (*tapne ante raj, ne rajne ante tap*).[53] In his analysis of power, Michel Foucault has emphasised the latter quality, equating body-discipline with docility. Gandhi by contrast

[50]Interview with Journalists, 6 March 1931, *CWMG*, Vol. 51, p. 220.

[51]In a letter of 1915, Gandhi translated *tapas* as 'discipline'. 'Letter to Maganlal Gandhi', after 14 March 1915, *CWMG*, Vol. 14, p. 385. For a definition of *tap/tapas*, see R.S. McGregor, *The Oxford Hindi-English Dictionary*, Oxford University Press, New Delhi 1993, p. 437. The word had a similar meaning in Gandhi's own Gujarati.

[52]Bondurant, *Conquest of Violence*, p. 114.

[53]See M.B. Belsare, *An Etymological Gujarati-English Dictionary*, H.K. Pathak, Bombay 1904, p. 578.

tended to deploy the term in the sense of *tap*, which is of a rigorous training designed to give oneself internal strength and to develop a powerful conscience.[54] He argued that a conscience that had been developed without such effort was worthless.[55] Non-violence could only be achieved through strong self-discipline.[56] As he stated in 1924: 'the richest grace of *ahimsa* will descend easily upon the owner of hard discipline'.[57] Without *tapasya*, India would never be free: 'We can be certain that once the spirit of discipline comes to pervade our lives, we shall be able to get anything we may want.'[58] He was clear in his mind that such *tap* was different from repressive forms of discipline. For example, when describing the party discipline imposed by the whips of the British Parliament, he described this as a 'so-called discipline'.[59] *Tap* was very different, for 'restraint self-imposed is no compulsion.'[60] However, as we shall see, he resorted to an unqualified language of coercive discipline at certain historical junctures.

For Gandhi, one of the strongest paths to the achievement of *tap* was celibacy, or *brahmacharya*. In *Hind Swaraj* he stated that 'Chastity is one of the greatest disciplines without which the mind cannot attain requisite firmness.'[61] In an important article in *Young India* of 1920, he demanded that celibacy be central to national reform.[62] Sexuality was for him a very public concern. In this, he tapped a chord among the literate public in India. When he published a booklet in 1927 called

[54]'Under Conscience's Cover', *Young India*, 21 August 1924, *CWMG*, Vol. 29, p. 25.

[55]Speech at Meeting in Lausanne, 8 December 1931, *CWMG*, Vol. 54, p. 270.

[56]'Power of *Ahimsa*', *Young India*, 7 May 1931, *CWMG*, Vol. 52, pp. 59–60.

[57]'No Limitations', *Harijan*, 8 December 1947, *CWMG*, Vol. 98, p. 14.

[58]'Speech on Indian Civilisation', Indore, 30 March 1918, *CWMG*, Vol. 16, p. 378.

[59]*Hind Swaraj*, *CWMG*, Vol. 10, p. 256.

[60]'Speech at Prayer Meeting, Sabarmati Ashram', *Young India*, 23 January 1930, *CWMG*, Vol. 48, p. 244.

[61]*Hind Swaraj*, *CWMG*, Vol. 10, p. 296.

[62]'In Confidence' *Young India*, 13 October 1920, *CWMG*, Vol. 21, pp. 356–60; 'How Celibacy can be Observed', *Navajivan*, 10 October 1921, *CWMG*, Vol. 25, pp. 78–80.

Self-Restraint vs. Self-Indulgence, the first edition sold out in one week, and it was reprinted many times. In his preface to the second edition of this work Gandhi wrote: 'Let young men and women for whose sake *Young India* is written from week to week know that it is their duty, if they would purify the atmosphere about them and shed their weakness, to be and remain chaste and know too that it is not so difficult as they may have been taught to imagine.'[63] He also claimed that: 'Though a body that has been developed without *brahmacharya* may well become strong, it can never become completely healthy from the medical point of view.'[64] He held that sexual indulgence undermined health. Constipation, for example, was caused by sexual arousal. He attributed his own illnesses, such as pleurisy, dysentery, and appendicitis to his 'imperfect celibacy'.[65] Gandhi advocated celibacy as the surest means through which the Indian people could sustain their health and decolonise their bodies.[66]

In this, Gandhi was inspired in part by European writers, such as the Frenchman Paul Bureau who published a book in 1920 titled *L'Indiscipline des moeurs* which made a strong appeal for French moral nationalism. Gandhi quoted Bureau's concluding statement—'The future is for those nations who are chaste.' He also cited William Loftus Hare, who in *Generation and Regeneration* had argued that sex had an enervating physiological effect. Gandhi also found a supporter in William R. Thurston, a major in the United States Army, who provided statistical evidence to back a claim that frequent sexual intercourse undermined the health of both men and women, leaving them unable to care properly for their families.[67]

Influenced by such polemics, Gandhi had a disturbing tendency to resort to a crude Malthusian and Social Darwinist language. He

[63]Quoted in Joseph S. Alter, *Gandhi's Body: Sex, Diet, and the Politics of Nationalism*, University of Pennsylvania Press, Philadelphia 2000, p. 8. Alter argues on the same page that: 'Even the journal title *Young India*—connotes an imagined celibate nation.'

[64]Ibid., pp. 15–16.

[65]Ibid., p. 18.

[66]Ibid., p. 27.

[67]Gandhi read the English translation of Bureau's book in 1925. Ibid., pp. 8–9 & 11–12.

stated, for example that excessive intercourse bred too many children: 'Do we think that the world is going to be saved by the countless swarms of such impotent children endlessly multiplying in India and elsewhere?' Early marriage and early sexuality led to the breeding of 'a race of cowardly, emasculated and spiritless creatures'. Self-restraint would allow the emergence of 'a nation of strong and handsome well-formed men and women'.[68]

As these quotations reveal, Gandhi was often exasperated by the failure of the masses to live up to his disciplinary ideals. When faced with the chaotic enthusiasm of the crowd during periods of mass agitation, Gandhi had no qualms about deploying the language of coercive discipline: 'The great task before the nation today is to discipline its demonstrations if they are to serve any useful purpose.' 'The nation must be disciplined to handle mass movements in a sober and methodical manner.' He demanded from the crowd 'implicit obedience.'[69] This was to be applied by trusted followers who shared his values.

In this emphasis on the need to maintain an austere discipline at all times during the course of a struggle, Gandhi distanced himself firmly from the more carnivalesque elements of popular culture. In this, he was clearly not in tune with Mikhail Bakhtin. In *Rabelais and his World*, Bakhtin celebrated popular carnival, which he saw as mocking and rejecting the medieval valorisation of asceticism and otherworldly spirituality. Through carnival, the 'immutable' and 'eternal' were brought down to earth.[70] The problem with this argument is that while the powerful may be lampooned or 'shamed' at such times of role reversal, vulnerable minorities are frequently targeted as well in an often vicious manner. Such festivities can cause great social damage while at the same time doing little to change oppressive relations of power in any meaningful way.[71] Gandhi had reason to insist on the overriding

[68]All these quotations from ibid., p. 11.

[69]All these quotes by Gandhi are from Ranajit Guha, 'Discipline and Mobilize', in Partha Chatterjee and Gyanendra Pandey (eds), *Subaltern Studies VII*, Oxford University Press, New Delhi 1992, p. 108.

[70]Mikhail Bakhtin, *Rabelais and his World*, translated by Hélène Iswolsky, Indiana University Press, Bloomington 1984.

[71]As Ranajit Guha has argued, festivals of reversal such as Holi have in India tended to strengthen structures of oppression rather than undermine them

importance of a dignified civility within any act of moral opposition.

Gandhi's concept of discipline was, therefore, full of tension. He worked it through in his own life in his own idiosyncratic manner. His followers had to do the same, with varying degrees of success. In some cases, the desire for discipline had questionable sexual overtones. There is for example the case of a Tamil Brahman follower of Gandhi who recounted the feelings he had shared with other satyagrahi when faced by state aggression during the Civil Disobedience movement in Bombay:

> Whenever a man was struck down, two others rushed up to be struck down in his place ... I remember a young man in front of me that a soldier was threatening with his raised rifle-butt, while shouting, 'Get back or I'll hit you!' 'Hit me then!' answered the young man. 'I shall imagine that you are my father and that you are doing it for my good.' Such a spirit of grace spread among the rioters that it was almost tangible. I felt it on the nape of my neck like a warm breath. When it was my turn to pass under the blows, I received them without feeling anything. I even think that I have never been so close to happiness.[72]

Taken to this level, from a process of protest to that of a search for ecstatic experience, such self-discipline becomes troubling and problematic, for it is being taken outside the realm of mass assertion to that of an individualistic sadomasochistic sexuality, in which—in this case—the young man desires violent discipline from patriarchal father-figures. It is hard to describe this as a commitment to the principles of Gandhian non-violence, as Lanza del Vasto, who recorded the statement, seeks to do.[73]

There has been a tendency for many self-perceived 'Gandhians' to apply a mechanical, narrow-minded and self-righteous discipline to

---

significantly. *Elementary Aspects of Peasant Insurgency in Colonial India*, Oxford University Press, New Delhi 1983, p. 34.

[72]As told by the Tamil Brahman in 1937 to Lanza del Vasto, in *Return to the Source*, translated from the French by Jean Sidgwick, Rider, London 1971, pp. 90–1.

[73]Some have however argued that there was a sadomasochistic streak in Gandhi, seen in his mortification of the body in fasts. For example, Burton Stein, *A History of India*, Blackwell, Oxford 1998, p. 301.

themselves and others in a way that is deeply unattractive. Whereas Gandhi tempered his discipline—of both kinds—with a strong sense of compassion and personal humility, as well as a self-deprecating sense of humour, many of these 'Gandhians' have willed themselves to carry out social, charitable and political work not because they feel for the suffering of the poor but because they see it as a path to personal moral salvation. Such people have helped create an image of a 'Gandhian personality' that is reviled rather than revered in popular imagination in India.

The former Prime Minister of India Morarji Desai, who always made great show of his 'Gandhian' principles in his day-to-day life, provides a good example. His autobiography is written in a style that imitates Gandhi's own autobiography, the difference being that he seems to be blind to the possibility that he could ever have made any mistakes. In one chapter of this work he describes in a self-satisfied manner how he expended great energy, while Home Minister of Bombay in the late 1940s, in disciplining the masses. Among other things he forced commuters to stand in orderly queues at bus stops, even posting police to create the correct atmosphere of 'discipline'; he censored films 'which could lead society astray and also prove harmful to the maintenance of social morality'; and, as a postscript, he orchestrated the brutal suppression of strong communist-led movements of workers and Adivasis throughout the state. When the police shot down some eight or nine protesters in Amalner he refused to sanction any enquiry, stating that: 'If the police, whose work on such occasions was difficult, were not given protection, then those who create disturbances would get encouraged and succeed in their mischievous aims.'[74] This trait of murderous intolerance towards dissidence was revealed again after he finally achieved his goal of becoming Prime Minister of India in 1977. In a conversation with the Naga rebel leader Z.A. Phizo in London in 1978, he was heard saying that 'I will exterminate the Nagas without compunction.'[75]

[74]Morarji Desai, *The Story of My Life*, Vol. 1, Macmillan, Madras 1974, pp. 220–5.

[75]Luingam Luithui and Nandita Haksar, *Nagaland File: A Question of Human Rights*, Lancer International, New Delhi 1984, p. 120. I am grateful to Mahesh Rangarajan for this reference.

Another Gandhian known for his inflexibility was Vinoba Bhave, whom Ramachandra Guha has characterised as 'a pious, puritan, and self-righteous man, devoid of humour and the capacity for self-criticism', who constantly sought to impress his superior virtuosity on those around him.[76] His taste for discipline extended beyond the realm of the personal to that of violent state repression. This was revealed most strikingly when he backed Indira Gandhi's declaration of Emergency in 1975, with its informing slogan: 'Discipline is the Need of the Hour'. With men such as Desai and Bhave, the notion of discipline was emptied of the qualities it had with Gandhi, being invested instead with a coercive and deathly monologic.

Invented Histories of the Nation

Nationalist ideologues have almost invariably sought to construct histories that have defined, valorised and naturalised the community that is said to form the nation, while excluding those who are seen to lie outside its bounds. In nineteenth-century India, this typically involved a celebration of the ancient Indian Hindu polity, as against that of the later Muslim and British invaders. In particular, the military valour and power of old Hindu rulers was invoked, the message being that salvation for India lay in a return to such values. This was a plea for an aggressive and militaristic nation-state which would wipe away the shame of centuries of subjugation of the Hindu by 'outsiders'.[77] The divisive communal implications of such a stance are obvious, and it was countered most typically by a secular-nationalist historiography which sought to align both Muslim and Hindu against the colonial 'Other' by stressing a shared syncretic past. The lesson of history in this case was seen to be that religious tolerance was a necessary basis for a successful polity. This strand of historical understanding laid less stress on a militaristic ethos, the emphasis being on the need for a strong but enlightened centralised state power.[78] Other groups sought to valorise different histories, such

[76]Ramachandra Guha, *An Anthropologist Among the Marxists*, p. 102.

[77]Ranajit Guha, *Dominance without Hegemony: History and Power in Colonial India*, Harvard University Press, Cambridge, Mass., 1997, p. 206.

[78]The seminal statement of this kind was by Jawaharlal Nehru, *The Discovery of India*, Signet Press, Calcutta 1946.

as the Dravidian nationalists of Tamil Nadu who depicted the Aryan invaders as the oppressors of the indigenous Dravidians, replacing an egalitarian social system with a rigid and oppressive caste hierarchy.[79]

These various nationalisms have all been rooted in a mode of reasoning which treats history as a narrative of a unilinear progress towards an ideal. In the case of nationalism, this becomes the nation-state, but in other formulations it may be different ideals, such as liberalism, socialism, communism. In all cases, the study of history is seen as a 'scientific' exercise undertaken both to reveal the path of this progress as well as to analyse setbacks and regressions in a manner that will help the observer to avoid making such mistakes in future. History is seen to be driven forward by conscious acts of human will rooted in such a historical consciousness.

Gandhi was profoundly sceptical of this way of thinking. He realised very acutely that his own willed action often produced the most unexpected consequences. He refused to accept the notion of unilinear historical time, understanding that the present was suffused with the past in a way that constantly undercut the working of the rational will to modernity.[80]

In this, Gandhi was almost certainly influenced by the writings of Tolstoy, whose translated works he had read avidly during his days in South Africa.[81] In the second part of the epilogue to *War and Peace*, Tolstoy set out a lengthy critique, stretching over twelve chapters, of the discipline of history. Tolstoy condemned the belief held by most 'general historians' that history was formed out of the rational exercise of power by great men: 'general historians almost invariably return to the idea that power is one which does produce events, and that it stands to events in the relation of cause to effect.'[82] 'Historians of civilisation', on the other hand, argue that history represented the working out of rational ideals. Yet, Tolstoy noted, the idea of the equality of man had

[79]M.S.S. Pandian, '"Denationalising" the Past: "Nation" in E.V. Ramasamy's Political Discourse', *Economic and Political Weekly*, 16 October 1993, pp. 2284–5.

[80]Sunil Khilnani, 'Gandhi and History', *Seminar*, 461, January 1998.

[81]Martin Green, *The Origins of Nonviolence: Tolstoy and Gandhi in their Historical Settings*, Harper Collins, New Delhi 1998, p. 3.

[82]Lev Nikolaevich Tolstoy, *War and Peace*, J.M. Dent and Sons, London no date, Vol. III, p. 430.

led to the terror of the French Revolution—the very negation of that idea.[83] It is thus absurd to hold that formative events of the past have been the product of the dreams of intellectuals.[84] Historical events are produced by a great many people acting in a whole range of ways, with highly unpredictable outcomes.[85] People often believe that they are free agents in all this, whereas they are in fact governed by forces beyond their control, which Tolstoy describes as 'the unknown substance of life'.[86] He ends his great novel by concluding that 'denial must be made of a freedom which is non-existent, and recognition be accorded to a dependence of which we are not personally conscious.'[87]

What was this 'unknown substance of life' on which we all depend? There is no clear answer in the novel, but the subsequent trajectory of Tolstoy's thought was to recognise this as the divine. Gandhi's study of Tolstoy appears to have helped him frame his own critique of the whole methodology of history-writing. When in jail between 1922 and 1924, he read Edward Gibbon's *History of the Decline and Fall of the Roman Empire*. Several of his English friends had strongly recommended that he read this massive work. He also read J.L.Motley's *Rise of the Dutch Republic*—a history of the Netherlands in the seventeenth century—and Lord Rosebery's *Life of Pitt*. He appreciated the breadth of knowledge and scholarship of Gibbon's work in particular. However, he felt that although Gibbon and Motley claimed to present the 'facts and nothing but the facts'—thus allowing the reader to supposedly exercise his or her judgement—'facts' were always open to dispute. Taking a passage from Rosebery, he remarked wryly that even Pitt's supposed 'last words' were denied by his butler. What remained, therefore, was a presentation of an argument by each author. Gandhi found that these histories were in reality no more than biographies of states, whether of the Roman or British empires, or the Dutch Republic.[88]

[83]Ibid., p. 431.
[84]Ibid., p. 440.
[85]Ibid., p. 451.
[86]Ibid., pp. 453–4 and 465.
[87]Ibid., p. 469.
[88]'My Jail Experiences—XI', *Young India*, 11 September 1924, *CWMG*, Vol. 29, p. 135.

For Gandhi, academic history was thus an exercise in bad faith—claiming objectivity in relation to the myths that it sought to construct. The great myths of the past, most notably the *Mahabharata*, were more honest in this, as they did not claim to be factual or scientific. Because facticity was such a dubious matter, Gandhi preferred to judge all narratives of the past not in terms of their historicity, but in terms of the spiritual truths to which they provided access. In this respect, he believed the statist histories of Gibbon and Motley to be very inferior to the *Mahabharata*, a work of profound and lasting truth. He concluded: 'Truth transcends history.'[89]

In Gandhi's view, human betterment thus lay in the realm of ethics (his 'truth') rather than in the working out of an illusory historical progress. Action dictated by an abstract historical need could never achieve the desired results, It was by defining an ethical life, and living according to that ideal in a very direct way, that one could do good in the world. Gandhi thus refused to try to justify his beliefs through an appeal to any historical meta-narrative. Although he frequently evoked a time of past harmony rooted in the self-sufficient village community, he never sought to historicise this structure of being but allowed it to remain amorphous. It represented for him a space that was non-conflictual, non-militaristic, and imbued with a spirit of neighbourliness. It was a clearly mythical construct, but so—he argued—were all of the others, and it had the advantage of allowing a space for dialogue, rather than foreclosing it, as the other more historicised mythical constructs tended to do.

Ashis Nandy has argued that Gandhi valorised myth over history, thus adopting a 'traditional' Indian stance towards the past. He distinguishes this from a 'Judeo-Christian cosmology' that sees history as developing dialectically and materially in a way which limits the possibilities for the future, as people cannot, in this view, transcend the dialectic of a given time and period. This is why it is considered important in the latter tradition to study the details of history, for each situation produces its own unique dialectic. Gandhi, Nandy asserts, refused to be limited by such determinism, preferring in its place the

[89]Ibid.

openness of myth. Myth, rather than history, established the parameters for his action.[90] Sunil Khilnani has claimed that in this respect Gandhi displayed a deep empathy with the subaltern world of groups that lacked 'history', and whose imaginings were of a mythic past that was punctuated by the appearance of saintly figures.[91] Ashis Nandy speaks similarly of 'the salience given by Indian culture to myth as structured fantasy which, in its dynamic of the here-and-the-now, represents what in an other culture would be called the dynamic of history ... In Gandhi, the specific orientation to myth became a more general orientation to public consciousness.'[92]

There are two problems with this sort of argument. First, Gandhi himself did not counterpoise myth against history in such a way. He saw no need to valorise myth over a historicised consciousness, as if the two form binary and contradictory opposites. He held that ethics transcended both. As he well realised, myth in itself is no better as a guide to ethical action than history. It can inspire such action, but it can also give rise to unethical behaviour. This becomes apparent if we examine the recent appeal by Hindu chauvinists to the myth of Ram Janmabhumi in Ayodhya as a justification for vicious attacks on Muslims.[93] Neither myth nor history is infallible in this respect; in the last instance one has to be guided by one's core beliefs. There is a certain circularity in this, for these core beliefs are themselves forged through a complex dialogic which engages a person's life experience with both myth and history. Gandhi had a strong sense of history that was expressed most strongly in his critique of colonialism, and he was guided by it in part in his political choices and strategies. His understanding of history was at times profoundly insightful, at times highly dubious, but never less than lively and engaged.

Furthermore, and this is a secondary problem, Gandhi's ethics were

[90]Ashis Nandy, *The Intimate Enemy: Loss and Recovery of Self Under Colonialism*, Oxford University Press, Delhi 1984, pp. 56–63.

[91]Khilnani, 'Gandhi and History', p. 114.

[92]Nandy, *The Intimate Enemy*, pp. 56–7.

[93]Neeladri Bhattacharya, 'Myth, History and the Politics of Ramjanmabhumi,' in Sarvepalli Gopal (ed.), *Anatomy of a Confrontation: The Babri Masjid-Ram Janmabhumi Issue*, Penguin Books India, New Delhi 1991.

by no means in accord with many popular structures of feeling, as expressed in myth. Thus, while poor peasants and pastoralists of Mewar and Saurashtra valorised the mythical *bhakti sant* Mirabai for her resistance to Rajput patriarchy, or for the persecution and hardship which she suffered in exile, Gandhi projected her as a sanitised ideal of Brahmanical widowhood.[94] And, when the peasants of Gorakhpur created their own myth of the mahatma from a highly selective appropriation of his 'saintly message', their veneration was to lead to a blood-drenched and disastrous clash with the police and a strong public condemnation by Gandhi.[95] Subaltern mythology frequently valorised the physical prowess of male heroes in epics of violent resistance, acts of conspicuous consumption or sexual aggression, revealing a 'wild' consciousness far removed from the Gandhian ethos.[96]

If we believe that history is a discipline rooted in the paradigms of unilinear evolutionary progress and state-centred narrative, then Gandhi's critique has great value. Dipesh Chakrabarty has described this as 'an imperious code that accompanied the civilizing process that the European Enlightenment inaugurated in the eighteenth century as a world-historical task.'[97] However, this paradigm is widely challenged today by historians whose narratives seek to show that there are many competing histories and possibilities, and that the subject of the discipline can also be the poor and powerless—the groups which have been described as the 'fragments' which lie outside the history of the nation state.[98] Some of these histories engage in a critical manner with

[94]Parita Mukta, *Upholding the Common Life: The Community of Mirabai*, Oxford University Press, New Delhi 1994.

[95]Shahid Amin, *Event, Metaphor, Memory: Chauri Chaura 1922–1992*, Oxford University Press, New Delhi 1995.

[96]For a study of narratives which celebrate such forms of subaltern 'wildness', see Ajay Skaria, *Hybrid Histories: Forests, Frontiers and Wildness in Western India*, Oxford University Press, New Delhi 1999.

[97]Chakrabarty, *Provincializing Europe*, p. 93.

[98]The concept of the 'fragment' does not imply that the history of the subaltern was fragmented in an actual sense, only that it appears as such when viewed from the perspective of a state-oriented history. See Gyanendra Pandey, 'In Defence of the Fragment: Writing about Hindu-Muslim Riots in India Today', *Economic and Political Weekly*, Vol. 26, Nos. 11 & 12, March 1991; Partha Chatterjee, *The Nation*

popular consciousness, folk narratives and myth as a means for entry into the mental world of the subaltern.[99] Such historians certainly do not consider myth as a 'primitive' form of history or the product of a 'savage' mind, as Ashis Nandy claims is the case in general within what he labels as 'Western social analysis'.[100] Neither do they seek to reify suffering through a historicist argument, as Nandy alleges is fundamental to the 'modern world view'.[101] Gandhi himself seems to have recognised the need for such a history when he stated that, 'whereas generally history is a chronicle of kings and their wars, the future history will be the history of man.'[102] For him, the ethics of such a history would be clearly superior, though never infallible.

---

and Its Fragments: Colonial and Postcolonial Histories, Princeton University Press, Princeton 1993.

[99]In recent years this has become a distinct genre of the discipline, far removed from the history based primarily on elite documentation. Ajay Skaria has defined it as a 'hybrid history'. See his *Hybrid Histories*.

[100]Nandy, *The Intimate Enemy*, p. 60.

[101]Ibid., p. 61.

[102]Speech at Hindustani Talimi Sangh, 24 April 1938, *CWMG*, Vol. 73, p. 126.

3

Dialogic Resistance

Mass civil resistance—a form of non-violent protest carried out by large numbers of people within complex state systems—emerged in Europe in the ferment of the post-French revolutionary period. It came from the sphere of civil society—the site of a free association of individuals in public bodies, associations and the like—which were valorised in the political thought of the Enlightenment as providing a means for checking and correcting the excesses of state power and governmental authority. Civil Disobedience entailed in part an assertion of new demands for equality and liberty within state systems that claimed to represent the will of the people but were also becoming increasingly centralised and bureaucratic. In some cases it entailed a demand for self-determination by nationalities within the old dynastic empires, such as that of the Hapsburgs. In Ireland, nationalist peasants protested against British colonial rule by refusing to pay their rents and taxes. In Britain, this politics was associated with new social tensions and demands arising out of the industrial revolution, which saw on the one hand the growth of reformist campaigns by the emerging middle class, on the other a demand for rights by the working class. This all gave rise to movements which involved mass mobilization, petitions, monster demonstrations, strikes, boycotts and the courting of arrest. These various tactics were developed and sharpened during the course of the nineteenth century, creating a new language of protest. Modern bureaucratic states resting on an industrial base are often considered to be particularly susceptible to this form of protest, as they operate through a complex process of co-operation that can be disrupted relatively easily. In the early twentieth century, we find certain groups like the suffragettes in Britain deploying such forms of resistance with great skill and to powerful effect.[1]

Civil resistance has been used to particular effect within polities that claim to conform to a rule of law while at the same time seeking to monopolise violence and criminalize any application of violence that is not wielded by the state. Modern states are geared towards dealing with violent forms of opposition, such as terrorism, and in fact they thrive on countering them, as it gives the excuse for legal increases in police power, surveillance operations, counter-terrorist measures, imprisonment without trial, summary forms of justice and the like. What they are less comfortable in dealing with is opposition that is non-violent in principle. They may try to delegitimise such protest by asserting that dissent should be expressed through the ballot box at election-time. But this argument is too obviously self-serving to carry conviction.

These forms of struggle developed in embryonic form in India long before Gandhi emerged as a leader. Notable were the indigo revolt in Bengal in 1859–62, the anti-landlord movement in Bengal of the 1870s, and the no-tax campaign in Maharashtra in 1872–3.[2] These were all mass movements in which peasant protest was supported by fractions of the élite, such as English-educated, middle class and generally high-caste Indians, certain paternalistic colonial officials, and socially concerned missionaries. The arguments advanced by these sympathetic élites were designed to appeal to the concerns and morals of the colonial rulers. There was a stress on the need to grant concessions so as to stave off a discontent which could assume dangerous proportions if left to fester. Appeals were made to liberal values concerning civil rights and equity, and to a neo-classical economic morality that was seen to be

[1]Michael Randle, *Civil Resistance*, Fontana Press, London 1994, pp. 11, 36–8 & 101–2.

[2]Blair B. Kling, *The Blue Mutiny: The Indigo Disturbances in Bengal 1859–1862*, University of Pennsylvania Press, Philadelphia 1966; Kalyan Kumar Sen Gupta, *Pabna Disturbances and the Politics of Rent 1873–1885*, People's Publishing House, New Delhi 1974; Ravinder Kumar, *Western India in the Nineteenth Century: A Study in the Social History of Maharashtra*, Routledge and Kegan Paul, London 1968, pp. 174–7.

violated by feudal practices. Leaders, like the Reverend James Long in Bengal in 1860, opened themselves up to imprisonment in defence of such principles, and in so doing embarrassed the government into backing down.[3]

Gandhi was inspired and influenced by these various protests in India and elsewhere. In 1907, for example, he praised the campaigns of passive resistance waged by the Hungarian nationalists against the Hapsburgs between 1849 and 1867, and by Sinn Fein against British rule in Ireland.[4] He came to understand very clearly the weak points of the modern polity, and deployed his particular form of protest to powerful effect. His stress on the imperative for non-violence in civil resistance represented a highly creative intervention within both political theory and practice. For him, non-violence was a 'truth' that could be worked through and understood only through a disciplined and arduous application in specific situations. In this way he took such resistance on to a new level, with a resonance that was global in extent. This has been acknowledged by Michael Randle in his book *Civil Resistance*, in which he argues that Gandhi is 'the figure whose actions and ideas have most crucially influenced the development of civil resistance in the twentieth century ...'[5] In this chapter we shall examine the various ways in which Gandhi forged this new praxis. It was based in part on the forms of civil resistance that had been developed in Europe, the United States and India; in part on his own strong moral principles, and in part through a dialogue with various modes of moral protest and mass resistance already practised in India.

Popular Forms of Mass Resistance in India

Popular resistance took many forms in India in the past, as Ranajit Guha has shown in his seminal study on the subject.[6] These acts of resistance may be situated at varying points on a scale that ranges from

[3]Kling, *The Blue Mutiny*, pp. 203–9.

[4]'Benefits of Passive Resistance,' *Indian Opinion*, 7 September 1907, *CWMG*, Vol. 7, pp. 183–5. Gandhi equated the Irish '*sinn fein*' ('ourselves alone') with the Indian term 'swadeshi', p. 184.

[5]Randle, *Civil Resistance*, p. 52.

[6]Ranajit Guha, *Elementary Aspects of Peasant Insurgency in Colonial India.*

the coercive to the dialogic. In situations in which the ruling classes were closed to any dialogue with the people and in which they enforced their will by brute force, action by insurgents was likely to involve counter-violence. This frequently involved a complex politics of ritual shaming, in which the object of popular hatred was seized and humiliated. For example, peasants of the Indian Himalaya would catch an unpopular official, shave his hair and moustache, blacken his face, and parade him around the village mounted backwards on a donkey.[7] It was rare for insurgents to kill even the most violent of oppressors.[8]

In situations in which channels were kept open for dialogue, protests might be almost entirely non-violent. In the Himalayan hill states there was a practice known as *dhandak* in which the aggrieved people marched to the capital city and demanded an audience with the monarch. There was a certain ritual to this—the ruler would appear before them and promise to look into the matter, after which they would disperse. The people believed that they were helping their ruler by drawing his attention to a rottenness within his state.[9]

Similar sorts of dialogic protest were institutionalised within the Rajput states of Rajasthan. For example, in June 1921 around 10,000 peasants of Udaipur state marched to the capital and camped before the palace of the maharana, Fateh Singh, demanding an audience. They threatened to stop all produce from being brought into the city if their grievances were not looked into. They had to wait several days before Fateh Singh agreed to receive a delegation. The maharana was under the impression that their grievances related to various oppressions carried out by local Rajput chiefs and state officials, though he also blamed political incitement coming from British India. He refused to accept that his subjects were in any way discontented with him. In this frame of mind, he discussed the grievances in detail and agreed to remedy several of them.[10]

[7]Ramachandra Guha, *The Unquiet Woods: Ecological Change and Peasant Resistance in the Himalaya*, Oxford University Press, New Delhi 1987, pp. 67–8.

[8]Guha, *Elementary Aspects of Peasant Insurgency*, p. 161.

[9]Ramachandra Guha, *The Unquiet Woods*, pp. 67–8.

[10]P.C. Jain, *Tribal Agrarian Movement*, Himanshu Publications, Udaipur 1989, pp. 87–8; Hari Sen, 'Popular Protest in Mewar in the Late-Nineteenth and Early-Twentieth Centuries', unpublished Ph.D. thesis, University of Delhi 1996, p. 317.

Another important form of dialogic resistance was that of mass migration, or *hijrat*. During the Mughal period, peasants often protested against excessive tax demands by migrating to the territory of another ruler.[11] This weapon was deployed not only by peasants. There was a famous case involving the Baniya community of Surat during the reign of the Mughal emperor Aurangzeb. In 1665–6 the emperor had appointed a reactionary theologian to act as *qazi*, or civil judge, of Surat city. The qazi began a campaign of converting merchants to Islam. Several Baniya merchants were forced under pressure to become Muslims. The turning point came when a Baniya clerk serving in the qazi's establishment committed suicide after being circumcised by force. Eight thousand Baniyas left the city in protest in September 1669, going to Bharuch. All trade and business in the city came to a halt. The qazi threatened that unless they returned he would destroy the Baniyas' temples and circumcise any who remained in Surat. The Baniyas replied defiantly, saying that they would go to the emperor for justice. A lengthy correspondence followed between the merchants, the qazi and Aurangzeb. In the end the emperor dismissed the qazi and wrote a letter to the Baniyas promising them security and greater religious freedom. They then returned to Surat.[12] Gandhi was well aware of this particular tradition of resistance, as it was still being used in Saurashtra when he was a youth. As he stated in 1909: 'I remember an instance when, in a small principality, the villagers were offended by some command issued by the prince. The former immediately began vacating the village. The prince became nervous, apologised to his subjects and withdrew his command.'[13]

There were also certain forms of protest that combined an appeal for dialogue with varying forms of self-inflicted suffering and violence. The aim was to emphasise the hurt which the aggrieved person or group claimed to have suffered, and in doing so lay the opponent open to social censure. It was commonly believed to be both dishonourable and

[11]Irfan Habib, *The Agrarian System of Mughal India 1556–1701*, Asia Publishing House, Bombay 1963, pp. 328–36.

[12]G.Z. Refai, 'Anglo-Mughal Relations in Western India and the Development of Bombay 1662–1690', unpublished Cambridge Ph.D. thesis, 1967, pp. 128–35.

[13]Gandhi, *Hind Swaraj*, *CWMG*, Vol. 10, p. 296.

inauspicious to ignore such an appeal, and in this way a ruler or a superordinate could be shamed into submission.

This form of protest was carried on from ancient times in India. For example, the *Manusmrti* mentions a protest called *carita*, which involved sitting at debtors' door so as to embarrass them into paying their debt. In some cases, the lender tied his wife, son or cattle at the door, or sat there without taking food.[14] A Marwar inscription of 1141–2 mentions the practice, using the term *kaya-vrata*.[15] In the eighteenth century such an act was known generally as *dharna* or *tukaza*, and it was deployed most frequently by creditors against debtors. The word *dharna* comes from the Sanskrit *dhri*, meaning to hold, and it meant a holding out.[16] In many cases, special protesters were employed to perform the task. They would go and sit before the alleged wrongdoer's house in a clamorous manner, advertising the grievance to the world. Timing was important; if a moment of celebration was chosen when guests would be at the house, the person or family was likely to come to an agreement much faster. The latter was held to be responsible for the upkeep of these hired protesters so long as they continued their action.[17] Vagharis, a caste of low ritual standing, used similar methods in Kathiawad. They would go in a body and sit before a house holding unused *datun* (tooth-cleaning sticks) to symbolize the fact that they had not yet eaten.[18]

Sometimes Brahmans were employed to perform dharna, as it was considered particularly shaming to cause hardship to members of this caste. In eighteenth-century Maharashtra many Brahmans made a living by hiring themselves out for this purpose.[19] They would sit at the door

[14]P.V. Kane, *History of Dharmashastra*, Vol. III, Pune 1973, pp. 438–9. The five means of recovery advised were persuasion, legal proceeding, trick, sitting before the door, and labour bondage/imprisonment.

[15]Loc. cit.

[16]Bondurant, *Conquest of Violence*, p. 118.

[17]*Report of the Committee on the Riots in Poona and Ahmednagar 1875*, Government Central Press, Bombay 1876, p. 26.

[18]Interview with the folklorist and artist Khodidas Parmar, Bhavnagar, December 1988.

[19]Thomas Broughton, *Letters Written in a Mahratta Camp during the Year 1809*, London 1892, p. 32.

lamenting the wrong, appealing to the gods and abusing and cursing the wrongdoer in a loud voice. They might bring a small *murti* of a deity, to be worshipped at the same time, invoking the blessings of the deity for the protest. They might also fast, or perhaps stand with a stone placed on the head or with their topknot nailed to the wrongdoer's door, so as to increase the moral pressure.[20]

A more extreme form of moral pressure could be exerted by the wronged party threatening to kill himself or herself unless the grievance was redressed. The guilt, and social opprobrium, would be seen to fall on the persons who had caused the injury or death. There is a story of a Brahman in the time of Akbar who had lent a rupee to a shepherd. The Brahman went to the shepherd and said if the rupee was not repaid he would hang himself, making the shepherd responsible for his death.[21] Mahipati likewise recounts an incident in the life of Tukaram when the saint once gave some goods on credit in the Konkan. When one of the people refused to pay him, Krishna is said to have come to Tukaram's aid. He took on the guise of Tukaram's servant and went to the debtor and threatened to hang himself, and thus disgrace the place unless the money was handed over. The neighbours pleaded with the man to relent. When the servant made preparations to hang himself, the neighbours beat the debtor and forced him to pay up.[22]

In Gujarat and Rajasthan, this form of protest was institutionalised in the practice of *traga*, which was carried on by members of the Bhat and Charan communities. They would threaten to inflict severe violence on their own bodies if their grievance was not redressed. If they were so forced to do, it was commonly believed that the person who was responsible would suffer a terrible curse. For example, when the founder of Udaipur, Maharana Udaisingh, confiscated some of the villages of the Bhats and Charans of his state in the sixteenth century, they reacted

[20]Arthur Steele, *The Law and Custom of Hindoo Castes within the Dekhun Provinces*, London 1868, pp. 267–8; *Gazetteers of Bombay Presidency*, Vol. XVIII, *Poona*, Part III, Government Central Press, Bombay 1885, pp. 9 and 12.

[21]The shepherd was contemptuous of the Brahman, and in the story later had his comeuppance. *North Indian Notes and Queries*, 2: 4, July 1892, p. 63.

[22]Justin Abbot, *Tukaram*, Scottish Mission Industries Co., Pune 1930, p. 59.

by performing acts of ritual suicide. Udaisingh was eventually forced to yield and restore their villages.[23] Bhats and Charans were able to earn a living by hiring themselves out to act as protectors of trade-caravans, travelling with them and threatening self-injury if robbers waylaid the caravan or feudal lords tried to levy excessive tolls.[24] Members of the two castes also provided security for tax demands and debts. If the money was not forthcoming they might threaten to injure or kill themselves or a family member.[25] The fear of being stigmatised as a killer of Bhats and Charans was such that few rulers were prepared to defy them openly.

The British had little sympathy for protests involving self-injury. They classified them as acts of 'blackmail' and from the late eighteenth century onwards ruled that the issuing or carrying out of such acts would be treated as a criminal offence.[26] The beliefs surrounding such protests were considered to be a mere 'ignorant superstition'.[27] Those who broke the law were punished despite strong protests by people who believed that they would suffer grave misfortune in consequence. The British claimed that the public subsequently became reconciled to the new situation when they saw that the curses of the Charans and Bhats had had no effect.[28] By 1842 the dread of traga was, according

[23]Kalika Ranjan Qanungo, *Studies in Rajput History*, S. Chand, New Delhi 1960, p. 44.

[24]'Description of the Countries beyond the North Western Frontier of the Bombay Presidency Relating Chiefly to Jodhpur and Jaisalmer by Lieut. A. Burnes; Paper No. 7 on Joodpoor or Marwar', National Archives of India, Foreign Department, 14 October 1830, 3–8 SC.

[25]Thomas Marshall, 'A Statistical Account of the Pergunna of Jumboosur', *Transactions of the Literary Society of Bombay*, Vol. 3, 1823, pp. 372–3.

[26]C.A. Bayly, *Empire and Information: Intelligence Gathering and Social Communication in India, 1780–1870*, Cambridge University Press, Cambridge 1996, p. 152.

[27]Marshall, 'A Statistical Account of the Pergunna of Jumboosur', p. 373.

[28]James Sutherland, March 1834, National Archives of India, Foreign Department Political, 15 May 1834, 34. Sutherland was the first British officer to order the execution of some Charans in Ahmedabad District of Gujarat in 1815. He noted later that the District Collector had been 'assailed by the lamentation of persons at the infringement of their deep-rooted prejudices, which they considered to be the heaviest calamity that could have befallen them. Since then every year

to one official, a thing of the past in Saurashtra: 'I have known several instances of lives being taken and much blood shed without the least effect being produced, whereas, at the beginning of this century a single life offered in traga would have subdued the most stubborn landholder ...'[29] These claims appear to have been over-optimistic, for as late as the 1890s a case was reported in which a Charan protested against a chief of Saurashtra by killing his old mother and daubing her blood on the chief's house. The chief, overwhelmed with guilt, refused to eat and died a few days later, 'virtually a suicide'. The Charan was arrested and later sentenced to transportation for life.[30]

The British also criminalized the practice of dharna, making it an offence under the Indian Penal Code punishable with imprisonment of up to one year and/or a fine.[31] They held that the courts of law constituted by the state should act as the sole authority in such disputes.[32] Despite this, dharna continued to be performed. In 1840 it was reported from Maharashtra that usurers were still hiring people to sit before the houses of their debtors, even though they risked being prosecuted if a complaint was made.[33] However, the colonial civil courts provided such a powerful means for usurers to exert power over their debtors that these various forms of dunning became less common during the course of the nineteenth century.[34]

Acting in these ways and others, the British redefined notions of

---

has tended to divert their persons [e.g. the Charans] as well as Bhats of their sacred character, and to class them within proper places in society as ordinary men.'

[29]George le Grand Jacob, 'Report on Kattywar 1842', in G. le Grand Jacob, *Western India: Before and During the Mutinies*, Henry S. King, London 1872, pp. 33–4.

[30]*North Indian Notes and Queries*, Vol. 4, No. 4, July 1894, p. 60.

[31]Editorial comment in Broughton, *Letters Written in a Mahratta Camp*, p. 32.

[32]For a critical analysis of this process see Upendra Baxi, '"The State's Emissary": The Place of Law in Subaltern Studies', in Partha Chatterjee and Gyanendra Pandey (eds), *Subaltern Studies VII*, Oxford University Press, New Delhi 1992, p. 252.

[33]W. Bartle Frere, Assistant Collector, Pune District, 2 July 1840, Maharashtra State Archives, Bombay, Revenue Department 1844, 107/1664.

[34]David Hardiman, *Feeding the Baniya: Peasants and Usurers in Western India*, Oxford University Press, New Delhi 1998, pp. 187–92.

legitimate protest. Acts involving self-privation and self-injury were deemed criminal. Forms of local disciplinary coercion against tyrannical officials—which in dhandak were considered to be means of serving a ruler by cleansing the realm of rotten elements—were treated under colonial law as criminal assault and made liable to harsh punishment. The colonial state claimed for itself a monopoly of the use of disciplinary violence of all sorts. It was able increasingly to enforce this claim as local warlords and chiefs were subjugated and the populace systematically disarmed, while at the same time it extended the power of the police into even the most remote areas. Any protest that involved violence, even of a relatively petty kind, was considered illegitimate, to be legitimately crushed with what were described as 'salutary' measures, which meant the use of an overwhelming violence, however feeble the resistance might be.

The level of violence used to suppress protest escalated considerably. This was true for both the areas under British rule and for princely states. A good example of this transition comes from Gandhi's home region of Saurashtra, where some Mahiya peasants of Junagadh state carried on a struggle against the nawab's government in the period 1872 to 1882. Previously, the Mahiyas had made a living in part through farming and in part through providing military and police services to the state. As a reward for their service, they did not have to pay land tax. The protest was launched after the state decided that it no longer required their services, so that they became liable to pay land tax. A group of Mahiyas marched on Junagadh town and proclaimed that they were seeking to restore the ancient dynasty of the Chudasma Ras. When the state police disarmed them, they retreated to a hill, where they held a dharna, stating that they would remain there until their demands were redressed. Only after much negotiation did they agree to return to their homes. The state then sought to backtrack on its promises by surveying their land and demanding that they pay the land tax. When they refused to pay, they were not however pressed. The resistance continued for several years, and there were some stray cases of minor violence. In 1882, the British political agent—concerned by such 'lawlessness'—decided that the easy-going attitude of the nawab towards such a protest was no longer acceptable, and he demanded that it be crushed by force. Troops were sent and over eighty Mahiyas massacred.[35]

This brutal escalation of the conflict sent out a clear signal that the older forms of protest had lost their legitimacy under the new dispensation. Redress came in the end through criticism in the Bombay press of the role of the Bombay Political Agency in the affair. Embarrassed by the bad publicity, the Bombay government appointed a commission of enquiry, which led to a reduction of the tax demand by thirty percent. There was a clear lesson here: publicity was crucial to success, and that success would be made much easier if the protest did not incur any taint of 'criminality', as understood under colonial law. In effect, this meant that strict non-violence gave an edge to a protest. Because the Mahiya struggle received a lot of publicity at the time, Gandhi's father—then one of the leading Indian administrators in Saurashtra—would certainly have known about the case in detail. It is probable, therefore, that Gandhi himself would have been aware of this tragic history.[36]

These concerns came to the fore in a powerful manner in the first movement that Gandhi led on his return to India from South Africa. The movement was by the peasants of Champaran district of North Bihar against white indigo planters. Earlier protests against the planters had been accompanied by a considerable degree of low-level petty violence. This had led to police repression, arrests and jail sentences. When Gandhi took over the leadership of the Champaran peasants in 1917, he insisted on strict non-violence, which, in the context of a society in which landlord violence and peasant counter-violence was an everyday fact of rural life, was a very novel idea. He brought in followers of his from Gujarat and recruited like-minded members of

[35]Ian Copland, *The British Raj and the Indian Princes: Paramountcy in Western India 1857–1930*, Orient Longman, New Delhi 1982, pp. 174–81; H.Wilberforce-Bell, *The History of Kathiawad from the Earliest Times*, Ajay Book Service, New Delhi 1980 (reprint), pp. 238–9; Shambhuprasad Desai, *Kanadano Ker*, S. Desai, Junagadh 1984.

[36]There is however no mention of it in Gandhi's autobiography, or in Pyarelal's detailed study of his early years. Pyarelal, *Mahatma Gandhi*, Vol. 1, *The Early Phase*, Navajivan Publishing House, Ahmedabad 1965.

the local middle class to work amongst the people to ensure that there was no violence. As a result, the 1917 protest was characterised by a much lower degree of violence than previous agitations, and it was also far more successful in achieving its aims. The satyagraha was seen throughout India as a triumph for Gandhi's methods and a shining example for others to follow.[37]

We can thus see that Gandhian non-violence provided a potent means for a legitimate and effective form of resistance within the new political order. Under Gandhian leadership the downtrodden were able to advance their cause by adopting a position of superior morality—that of non-violence—in a situation in which the rich and powerful routinely deployed forms of violence that were now, under the law, criminal acts. This allowed for an appeal to higher authority over and against the representatives of the state at the local level, who tended to connive at the extra-legal violence of superordinate groups.[38]

Gandhi similarly sought to reshape the politics of shame and honour that involved, typically, vendettas and blood feuds of a most violent type. Gandhi agreed that the preservation of honour was crucial for self-respect, stating that: 'My honour is the only thing worth preserving.'[39] This, however, was to be achieved through a non-violent refusal to cooperate, rather than through any counter-violence. In fact, it was better to accept death rather than retaliate with force.[40] He also sought to expand the question of honour beyond the realm of the family and local community or caste into a defence of the honour of the people as a whole against the state, through his campaigns of civil disobedience.[41]

He likewise reshaped the politics of dharna and traga, practices that he, like the British, condemned strongly. They were, he believed, ruled

[37]Jacques Pouchepadass, *Champaran and Gandhi: Planters, Peasants and Gandhian Politics*, Oxford University Press, New Delhi 2000, pp. 220–9.

[38]This paragraph owes much to Denis Vidal, *Violence and Truth: A Rajasthani Kingdom Confronts Colonial Authority*, Oxford University Press, New Delhi 1997, pp. 16–17.

[39]'If I were a Czech', *Harijan*, 15 October 1938, *CWMG*, Vol. 74, p. 90.

[40]'The Fiery Ordeal', *Young India*, 4 October 1928, *CWMG*, Vol. 43, p. 59.

[41]Amita Baviskar, *In the Belly of the River: Tribal Conflict over Development in the Narmada Valley*, Oxford University Press, New Delhi 1995, pp. 17–18.

by a spirit of revenge and were violent to both spirit and body.[42] Instead, he advocated self-imposed suffering that was free from any feeling of hatred of the opponent. This might involve the taking of vows to abstain from the use of foreign cloth or liquor and the like, as well as other forms of self-imposed discipline. In his case, this included fasting, though he argued that even a fast could be violent in intent if deployed wrongly.[43] It was best used only in cases in which the two parties knew each other personally and enjoyed a mutual respect.[44] All of this struck a chord with the popular belief that self-suffering in itself legitimised protest.

In these various ways, Gandhi forged a new language of protest for India by both building on older forms of resistance while at the same time accepting the colonial censure of all forms of violent protest. In time his new methods were to become as ritualised as the older forms of resistance. Part of their efficacy lay in the strong theoretical underpinnings that Gandhi gave to this form of protest through his doctrine of satyagraha.

Satyagraha

Satyagraha, as is often pointed out, is an amalgamation of two Gujarati words, *satya* (truth) and *agraha* (taking, seizing, holding), the implication being that one seizes hold of the truth. Gandhi equated satya with God. As he told Lanza del Vasto in 1937:

> I used to say, 'God is truth'. But some men deny God. Some are forced by their passion for truth to say that there is no God, and in their own way they are right. So now I say, 'Truth is God'. No one can say, 'Truth does not exist' without removing all truth from his statement. Therefore I prefer to say 'Truth is God'. It has taken me fifty years of persevering meditation to prefer this way of putting it to the other.[45]

Del Vasto saw this as a fundamental metaphysical breakthrough on Gandhi's part. In fact, the idea flows from the word satya itself, which

[42]Bondurant, *Conquest of Violence*, p. 118.
[43]Statement to the Press, 3 March 1939, *CWMG*, Vol. 75, p. 137.
[44]'Fasting in Satyagraha', *Harijan*, 13 October 1940, *CWMG*, Vol. 79, p. 295.
[45]Lanza del Vasto, *Return to the Source*, p. 122.

in Sanskrit means true, real, actual, genuine, sincere, honest, truthful, faithful, pure, virtuous, good, successful, effectual, valid. Its root is *as*—to be, to live, to exist. It is a quality associated with a range of deities.[46] The meaning of the word was identical in Gujarati, being elaborated on in a number of popular proverbs, such as '*satya tare chhe*'—truth comes to the surface; '*satyamev jayate*'—truth always has firm foundation; '*satyano beli Ishwar*'—God is the protector of truth. The term *satya-svarup* meant 'God, whose form is truth'.[47]

Gandhi understood that truth/satya was reached through a complex dialogue, in which reasoned argument had often to be reinforced with emotional and political pressure. He knew that, in many cases, reason by itself would not win an argument, for people tend to be swayed as much by emotion as by rational argument. This was where self-inflicted suffering, such as fasting, could be important. The large majority of Gandhi's fasts were directed against those over whom he believed he had a strong emotional bond. He never used a fast to gain political concessions from the British. He claimed that he fasted so as to make those who loved him reconsider their actions.[48] Even then, additional political pressure was often needed, entailing mass demonstrations, non-cooperation, tax refusal, *hartals* and the like.[49] During these protests, the satyagrahi had always to be open to the other side, seeking out alternatives that could satisfy both. The aim was to avoid bitterness and resolve conflict by searching for a common truth.[50] This demanded a spirit of give-and-take on both sides, for as Gandhi stated: 'all my life through, the very insistence on truth has taught me to appreciate the beauty of compromise. I saw in later life that this spirit was an essential part of satyagraha.'[51]

Gandhi resisted seeing his adversary as an enemy, insisting that in satyagraha there are no enemies. 'It is a breach of satyagraha to wish

[46] M. Monier-Williams, *A Sanskrit–English Dictionary*, Motilal Banarsidas, New Delhi 1963, p. 1135.

[47] Belsare, *Gujarati-English Dictionary*, p. 1108

[48] Parekh, *Gandhi's Political Philosophy*, pp. 159–60.

[49] Ibid., pp. 149 and 153.

[50] Dalton, *Mahatma Gandhi*, pp. 43–4.

[51] Gandhi, *Autobiography*, *CWMG*, Vol. 44, p. 201.

ill to an opponent or to say a harsh word to him or of him with the intention of harming him.'[52] He stated in 1937:

> I myself have always believed in the honesty of my enemies, and if one believes in it hard enough, one finds it. My enemies took advantage of my trust in them and deceived me. They deceived me eleven times running; and with stupid obstinacy, I went on believing in their honesty. With the result that, the twelfth time, they couldn't help keeping their word. Discovering their own honesty was a happy surprise for them and for me too. That is why my enemies and I have always parted very pleased with each other.[53]

Gandhi contrasted satyagraha with other forms of non-violent resistance, which he believed were based on an appeal to narrow self-interest and which failed to reach out to the opponent. 'It is a bad habit to say that another man's thoughts are bad and ours only are good and that those holding different views from ours are the enemies of the country.'[54] In *Hind Swaraj* he argued that many of the young extremist nationalists in India at that time adopted a needlessly hostile and disrespectful attitude to older nationalists such as Dadabhai Naoroji and Gokhale. They were even more antagonistic towards Englishmen like Hume and Wedderburn who had played a positive role in the early years of the Indian National Congress. Gandhi asserted that it was wrong to condemn them merely because they were English: 'if we shun every Englishman as an enemy, Home Rule will be delayed'.[55]

Some nationalists disliked this strong emphasis on the importance of winning over one's enemies. It was objected that such an approach could at times look suspiciously like collaboration, and it could cause suspicion among followers as to the motives of the leader. Gandhi answered that he let the results speak for themselves. It was also argued that genuine changes of heart by political opponents are rare; civil resistance succeeds mainly by bringing pressures to bear in a way that

[52]'An Impatient Worker', *Harijan*, 15 April 1933, *CWMG*, Vol. 60, p. 381.
[53]Lanza del Vasto, *Return to the Source*, p. 123.
[54]Gandhi, *Hind Swaraj*, in *CWMG*, Vol. 10, p. 250.
[55]Ibid., p. 250.

makes it hard for a regime to operate, thus forcing a stand-down.[56] Gandhi knew that this was often the case, but felt that a victory in such circumstances could only be partial. It was only when the opponent had understood the force of the counter-argument and had acted on that basis that there could be any genuine and durable success. In practice, Gandhi applied a complex mix of moral argument and non-violent coercion (through mass protests or personal fasts), emphasising one or the other as a situation developed and changed. What was crucial in this respect was his political skill in knowing which line to play at each twist and turn.

Individual Conscience

Gandhi always stressed that the decision as to whether or not to embark on satyagraha was a moral choice to be made consciously by each individual. Gandhi took his lead in this respect from European and American traditions in which civil resistance was understood primarily in terms of individual conscientious objection. The Quakers were well known in this respect, and Henry David Thoreau gave their principles a strong theoretical justification in his *Civil Disobedience*. Thoreau stressed that the conscience of an individual came before the will of the majority. He asserted: 'The only obligation which I have the right to assume, is to do at any time what I think is right.' He refused also to accept the legitimacy of a law with which he disagreed, even if it had been passed by a democratically elected legislature: 'Law never made men a whit more just; and, by means of their respect for it, even the well-disposed are daily made the agents of injustice.'[57] Also: 'Under a government which imprisons any unjustly, the true place for a just man is also in prison.' Thoreau believed that the principled resistance of even one person could make a great difference: 'For it matters not how small the beginning may seem to be: what is once well done is done forever.'[58] Leo Tolstoy followed Thoreau in this respect. His *Writings on Civil Disobedience and Nonviolence* (which was read keenly by Gandhi)

[56]Randle, *Civil Resistance*, pp. 105–6 and 111–12.
[57]Thoreau, 'Civil Disobedience', p. 387.
[58]Ibid., pp. 397–8.

also emphasised the imperative for the individual to act according to conscience, regardless of the consequences.[59]

Thoreau and Tolstoy were aggressively individualistic; neither made any attempt to build mass movements of protest. Thoreau's protest against the poll tax in Massachusetts was waged alone, and Tolstoy for his part condemned mass organisation, as it required political work that he saw as inherently corrupting. Gandhi took a very different line; his protests sought to build wide-ranging solidarities. He did, however, at times resort to individual protest, most notably in his fasts and in the so-called 'individual satyagraha' campaign of 1940–1.

In stressing the right of individual dissent, Gandhi followed Thoreau in refusing to accept the liberal principle that in a democracy the citizen had a duty to obey the laws of a democratically constituted legislature. He stated this principle very forcefully in *Hind Swaraj*, arguing that the British parliament danced to the tune of the executive, with members voting according to the party line regardless of their feelings in the matter. Parties were voted into power by people who were swayed by oratory and the biased opinion of the newspapers they read.[60] The parliament then passed laws which people were required to obey, however degrading they might be. 'That we should obey laws whether good or bad is a new-fangled notion.'[61]

> It is a superstition and ungodly thing to believe that an act of a majority binds a minority. Many examples can be given in which acts of majorities will be found to have been wrong and those of minorities to have been right. All reforms owe their origin to the initiatives of minorities in opposition to majorities ... So long as the superstition that men should obey unjust laws exists, so long will their slavery exist. And a passive resister alone can remove such a superstition.[62]

In this, Gandhi did not agree with Tagore's argument that civil resistance was a worse form of authoritarianism, as it involved a vocal minority imposing its will on a passive majority. Neither did he accept

[59]Randle, *Civil Resistance*, pp. 44–6.
[60]Gandhi, *Hind Swaraj*, *CWMG*, Vol. 10, pp. 255–6.
[61]Ibid., p. 293.
[62]Ibid., p. 294.

the contention of the liberal politician Chimanlal Setalvad that 'if you inculcate in the minds of the younger generation the idea of direct action, the ideas of disobeying laws, what will happen to your Swaraj when you get it?'[63] Gandhi countered by arguing that his aim was to build a democracy in which satyagraha could be used against an authoritarian state, as well as 'mobocracy'. Through satyagraha, the people could provide a check on parliament. Respectful obedience to the law should be the norm, but it remained a citizen's duty to discern bad and unjust laws and to disobey them if necessary. Satyagraha was a highly democratic weapon, as women as well as men, those without arms as well as the physically weak could all use it. All that was required was a courageous commitment to a cause.[64]

Gandhi always held that participation in any satyagraha was a matter of individual choice and that it was wrong in principle to use pressure to force people to protest against their will. In this, he distanced himself from the majority of nationalists, who had no qualms about deploying community and caste sanctions to ensure solidarity. This was a marked feature of the swadeshi movement in Bengal between 1905 and 1909.[65] Aurobindo Ghose had made such sanctions a keystone of his programme of nationalist struggle, India being a country 'in which the people are more powerfully swayed by the fear of social excommunication and the general censure of their fellows than by the written law'.[66] Ranajit Guha has argued that such sanctions represented 'the clay that nationalism itself was made of', and that this was true even after Gandhi assumed the leadership of the movement.[67] Despite his frequent strictures, Gandhi found that he could not swim against the tide. All he could do ultimately was to insist that caste sanctions and boycotts be applied non-violently.[68]

The problem in this respect was that individual freedom counted

[63]Dalton, *Mahatma Gandhi*, p. 99.

[64]Gandhi, *Hind Swaraj*, *CWMG*, Vol. 10, pp. 294–5.

[65]Ranajit Guha, 'Discipline and Mobilize', pp. 78–90. Rabindranath Tagore was a prominent critic of such tactics from 1908 onwards (see pp. 77–8).

[66]Sri Aurobindo, *Bande Mataram: Early Political Writings*, Sri Aurobindo Ashram, Pondicherry 1973, p. 87.

[67]Guha, 'Discipline and Mobilize', p. 91.

[68]'Social Boycott', *Young India*, 16 February 1921, *CWMG*, Vol. 22, pp. 351–3.

for little in a society in which the large majority of people were not considered to have a moral presence separate from that of the kinship or community group. If on the one hand this provided a basis for solidarity—as Partha Chatterjee has emphasised in his discussion of the 'communal mode of power'[69]—it also created the conditions for oppression, particularly of women. In standing out against such a mind-set through his stress on the right of individual self-determination, Gandhi was demanding that swaraj be rooted in a very different modality of power, that of individual conscience. As he stressed: 'No society can possibly be built on a denial of individual freedom.'[70] It is clear that India, in common with many other societies, has yet to achieve this ideal, given that powerful social and political leaders habitually apply sanctions and frequent violence against citizens who assert their right to social or ritual equality or freedom of religious belief.

However, as Rammanohar Lohia once argued, what is most important is that Gandhi taught people that, however humble, low and powerless they may appear to be, they had the power in themselves to resist, and that this resistance was entirely legitimate. 'This enabling the individual to resist oppression by himself and without any support is, to my mind, the greatest quality of Mahatma Gandhi's action and life.'[71]

Ahimsa

Gandhi's non-violence *(ahimsa)* represented a creative adaptation of various philosophies of non-violence. As Bondurant has pointed out, ahimsa is valorised strongly in the Hindu tradition. She claims that the aphorism found in the Mahabharata: *ahimsa paramo dharmah* (non-violence is the greatest religion or duty) is 'known in every village in India'.[72] It is particularly important in Jainism, in which it constitutes

[69]Partha Chatterjee, 'Agrarian Relations and Communalism in Bengal, 1926–1935', in Ranajit Guha (ed.), *Subaltern Studies I*, Oxford University Press, New Delhi 1982, pp. 11–18.

[70]'Plain Living and High Thinking', *Harijan*, 1 February 1940, *CWMG*, Vol. 79, p. 267.

[71]Lohia, *Marx, Gandhi and Socialism*, p. 122.

[72]Bondurant, *Conquest of Violence*, p. 111.

the first vow, and it is frequently argued that Gandhi's non-violence was rooted in his experience of Jainism in early life. It is certainly true that Jains sought to practice a most rigorous form of non-violence in their careful avoidance of taking of life, however small and seemingly insignificant. There was however a certain formulaic coldness to the logic of their non-violence which Gandhi found unattractive. Thus, Jain Baniyas could be scrupulous about not harming insects, but treat their fellow human beings with calculating cruelty in matters of business. As a Marwari proverb put it most succinctly:

> Oh Baniya! Nobody knows your doings. Although you do not drink water without straining and sifting it [to ensure that there are no insects in it], you sip the blood of your clients without reserve.[73]

Gandhi's non-violence was, by contrast, rooted in altruism and compassion towards fellow humans. He stated in 1915 that non-violence involved qualities such as *daya*, *akrodh*, and *aman*.[74] In Gujarati, daya meant, according to a dictionary of 1904, pity, compassion, commiseration, mercy, clemency, sympathy, tenderness. This quality was central to Gandhi's understanding of ahimsa. As he said in 1932: 'We can describe compassion as the concrete expression of *ahimsa*.'[75] Akrodh found no place in this dictionary, only akrodhi, an adjective meaning not passionate, habitually abstaining from anger.[76] Aman was from an Arabic word meaning security, and in this context meant essentially 'peace'. The general thrust of Gandhi's injunction was that ahimsa involved qualities of respect and sympathy for the opponent, freedom from anger, and a desire for peace.

Gandhi's non-violence was influenced also by the teachings of Jesus in the Sermon on the Mount and by certain traditions of Christian

[73]The Marwari original reads: '*Baniya thari ban koi ar jane nahin. Pani piye chhan lohi unchhaneo piye.*' *Report on the Census of 1891*, Vol. II, *The Castes of Marwar*, Marwar State, Jodhpur 1894, p. 130.

[74]Gandhi to Maganlal Gandhi, after 14 March 1915, *CWMG*, Vol. 14, p. 383.

[75]Letter to Purushottam Gandhi, 12 May 1932, *CWMG*, Vol. 55, p. 365.

[76]In a later Gujarati–English dictionary of 1974, *akrodh* (noun) appears, meaning absence of anger, patience, peacefulness. P. G. Deshpande, *Gujarati-Angreji Kosh*, University Granth Nirman Board, Ahmedabad 1974, p. 4.

dissent. Mainstream Christian practice had little to contribute on the subject of non-violent resistance, conforming as it generally did to the Pauline doctrine that Christians were obliged to obey civil authority. A number of dissenting sects had refused to accept this principle, notably the Quakers, who believed firmly in the principle of non-violence and non-violent resistance to unjust laws. In America they established a tradition of conscientious objection along principled non-violent lines. They saw this, however, as a matter of individual conscience and there was no involvement in any mass struggles.[77]

These various influences fed into Gandhi's own understanding of ahimsa. He held that as none could know the absolute truth, nobody had a right to commit violence on others lest they be in the wrong. An individual's truth should be asserted 'not by infliction of suffering on the opponent but on one's self.'[78] He believed that one had to be very strong in oneself to be able to practise ahimsa with success. To be non-violent out of weakness was no more than cowardice: 'It is not conceived as a weapon of the weak.'[79] He stated that it was better to resist violently than act in a cowardly manner.[80] He praised the violent resistance of the Polish people to Hitler in 1939, as he recognised that non-violence was not an option for them.[81]

In the context of colonial rule in India, non-violent resistance made strong tactical sense, for it wrong-footed the British, putting them on the defensive. Until then they had been able to counter what was normally the petty violence of protesters with a ruthless use of their superior gunpower. Faced with non-violence they were left in a quandary, as their counter-violence merely served to reveal the moral bankruptcy of their rule. A few British officials even resigned their positions

[77]Randle, *Civil Resistance*, pp. 24–9.

[78]Statement to Disorders Enquiry Committee, 5 January 1920, *CWMG*, Vol. 20, p. 206.

[79]'Notes', *Young India*, 23 March 1921, *CWMG*, Vol. 22, p. 452.

[80]Speech to First Gujarat Political Conference, 3 November 1917, in *CWMG*, Vol. 16, p. 128. In 1925 Gandhi said similarly that it is better to kill than to run away in a cowardly manner. 'Meaning of the *Gita*', *Navjivan*, 11 October 1925, Vol. 33, p. 89.

[81]Randle, *Civil Resistance*, p. 72.

so as to spare themselves from having to sanction violence against unarmed and non-violent crowds.[82] In this respect, Gandhi's insistence on complete non-violence was critical in achieving a moral advantage for nationalists.

In general, the debate on Gandhian non-violence tends to focus on its applicability as an absolute value. It is often argued that non-violence was all very well against opponents with a moral conscience, but useless against an enemy without qualms. Nelson Mandela, for example—who was in other respects a great admirer of Gandhi—felt that non-violence could not succeed in South Africa against a white regime which was not prepared to accept the morality of the struggle for democratic rights, and which was prepared to use the most violent and murderous means to suppress it. As Mandela later wrote: 'Non-violent passive resistance is effective as long as your opponent adheres to the same rules as you do. But if peaceful protest is met with violence, its efficacy is at an end.'[83] Gandhi did not accept this sort of critique—there was, he held, no human without some form of moral conscience, and even the Nazis might be made to yield. As he stated in this context in 1938: 'The hardest metal yields to sufficient heat.'[84] Dennis Dalton, otherwise a strong admirer of Gandhi, feels that Gandhi betrayed a grave ignorance of the situation under such a totalitarian regime. In Nazi Germany, even the slightest dissidence was crushed, with arrests in the dead of night and instant executions or incarceration in concentration camps in such a way that the population as a whole remained in ignorance. He feels that Gandhi discredited himself by advocating civil resistance when it had no chance of the slightest success. Satyagraha can only succeed when the government is ambivalent, as was the case in India and in Western democracies. In situations in which rulers are prepared to eliminate many of their citizens to remain in power, it cannot work.[85]

Dalton argues that Gandhi did not know enough about the situation in Nazi Germany to be able to suggest any effective strategies for those

[82]Dalton, *Mahatma Gandhi*, pp. 132–4.

[83]Nelson Mandela, *Long Walk to Freedom: The Autobiography of Nelson Mandela*, Little, Brown and Co., London, 1994, pp. 146–7.

[84]Quoted in Dalton, *Mahatma Gandhi*, p. 135.

[85]Ibid., pp. 135–8.

who were oppressed by the state. Instead he made absurd suggestions, such as that the Jews should come out *en masse* and be prepared to die in public. This is a valid point—Gandhi would have done better if he had not made specific suggestions in cases in which he had a poor grasp of the complexities of the situation. There is, however, evidence that the Nazi war effort was hampered considerably over the years by civil resistance in the occupied countries. In Norway there was particularly strong opposition of this sort to the Quisling government. The military theorist Basil Liddel Hart interviewed German officers after the war; they said that they had found it much harder to deal with non-violent civilian resistance than guerrilla warfare.[86] Even within Nazi Germany, there are examples of successful resistance. In February 1943 the Gestapo arrested all of the Jews remaining in Berlin, about two thousand of whom had non-Jewish spouses. These spouses, who were mostly women, staged a protest outside the prison where the Jews were held. The police dispersed them, threatening to open fire, but they regrouped time and again over the next week. In the end, fearing the impression that the protest might have on other 'Aryans', the authorities backed down and released the Jews.[87] Elsewhere, many ruthless dictatorships have been undermined as a result of mass protest by unarmed civilians, such as those of the Shah in Iran (1979), Marcos in the Philippines (1986), Pinochet in Chile (1989), Ceausescu in Romania (1989) and Milosevic in Yugoslavia (2000).

In modern India, the issue of non-violence as against violence has been debated in recent years within the Naxalite movement in Bihar. This brings out the strong logic there is for a non-violent strategy within the modern polity. In the early stages, in the late 1960s and 1970s, the chief emphasis in the Naxalite movement was on the violent elimination of notorious landlords. The latter countered by organising their own private armies, which sought to instil terror in the people through massacres of low-caste and Dalit peasants who supported the Naxalites. The Naxalites replied with counter-massacres of high-caste people. There was a tendency for the violence to feed on itself, with one attack being

[86]Randle, *Civil Resistance*, pp. 122–3 and 169.

[87]Nathan Stoltzfus and Walter Lacquer, *Resistance of the Heart*, Norton and Co., New York 1996. I am grateful to Mahesh Rangarajan for this reference.

revenged by another, as in a blood feud. In some cases, Naxalites began to recruit help from bandits and criminals to help them in their work. When some Naxalite groups decided to try to escape this cycle of violence by moving towards open mass campaigns, the groups that condemned this move as 'revisionist' carried out murderous attacks on members and supporters of the rival groups.

The movement thus split into different tendencies, with those who followed the line of open mass struggle soon emerging the stronger. Besides participating in elections, groups such as the CPI (ML) Liberation and Party Unity have organised mass protests to gain land for their supporters, and fought the landlords through demonstrations, protest marches, strikes, blockades and the like. In the process, their low-caste and Dalit supporters have felt empowered in a way that was not the case when the movement had focused on underground guerrilla activity. This does not mean that its aims have been achieved, for the landlords are still very strong and enjoy state support, and problems of poverty and exploitation are still acute in rural Bihar.[88] Also, the Naxalites have ignored many areas of constructive work of a Gandhian sort, such as campaigns to educate the poor and build a culture of economic self-help in the villages. However, the fact that they are now accountable to their supporters means that Naxalite cadres have an interest in addressing such issues as well.[89]

In Andhra Pradesh the Peoples War Group has opened up an internal debate on this matter. In 1998 the leaders called for a process of 'remorseful introspection' on the issue of violence. It was felt that too frequently violence had been deployed in ways that were counter-productive. As a result, a document was circulated to cadres setting out new guidelines in this respect.[90] A new human rights organisation was established in India in February 2000—the People's Union for Human Rights—which called on militants everywhere to adopt a more critical

[88]Prakash Louis, 'Class War Spreads to New Areas', *Economic and Political Weekly*, 24 June 2000, pp. 2206–11.

[89]Bela Bhatia, 'The Naxalite Movement in Central Bihar', unpublished Ph.D. thesis, University of Cambridge 2000, pp. 55–63 and 156–70.

[90]Javed Anand, 'A Clarification, and an Apology', *Communalism Combat*, April 2000, p. 32.

attitude towards their use of violence. As Javed Anand has argued: 'Put bluntly, do groups and organisations whose rights we defend themselves believe in democratic forms of mass mobilisation? Is it ethically right and politically tenable that rights groups focus their entire attention on violations by state personnel but remain mum when "militants" maim, rape or kill fellow citizens.'[91] There was a sharp reaction to this by many in the civil rights movement, who argued that it was wrong to equate the violence of the militants with that of the state, and in fact this was the very argument deployed by the state to absolve itself from blame.[92] The debate continues, but it seems that the critique of the 'excessive violence' of the early Naxalites has been having an impact on even the most hardened armed activists.[93]

Satyagraha Within the Indian Polity

The techniques of civil resistance developed by Gandhi rapidly became a central feature of Indian politics, providing a strong counter to the power of the colonial state. It followed its own rituals, with marches, flag-hoisting, and symbolic violations of selected laws, and fasting. As early as 1921, the Sikh Akalis decided to deploy satyagraha in their demand for popular control over Sikh temples. The leaders of this protest, following Gandhi, insisted that there be complete non-violence, and, as if to refute most strikingly that colonial stereotype of the hot-headed and 'martial' Sikh, this rule was complied with to a remarkable degree.[94] There was a similar upturning of a stereotype when the Pukhtuns of the North West Frontier Province launched a series of non-violent

[91]Javed Anand, 'Birth of a New Rights Body', *Communalism Combat*, March 2000, p. 20.

[92]Shekhar Krishnan and Anthony Samy, 'CC Echoes Reactionary Voices', and Vrijendra, 'No Quid Pro Quo in Democratic Rights', *Communalism Combat*, April 2000, pp. 33–6.

[93]In December 2001–January 2002 there was for example a heated debate in Andhra Pradesh on the violence of the Naxalites. In one critique, it was pointed out that over 77 percent of their civilian victims between 1991 and 2001 were Dalits, Adivasis and members of Other Backward Classes, the very groups the Naxalites were meant to be fighting for. *Times of India* (Bombay), 1 January 2002.

[94]Mohinder Singh, *The Akali Movement*, Macmillan, Delhi 1978, p. 52

satyagrahas under the leadership of Abdul Ghaffar Khan.[95] Satyagraha also became a means for protest by depressed groups against their Indian exploiters, as in the protest at Vaikam in Kerala in 1924–5, when Untouchables demanded the right to use a road running past a temple.

Even groups who were politically opposed to Gandhi and the Indian National Congress adopted the weapon of satyagraha. For example, the radical Tamil leader Periyar E.V. Ramasamy had learnt the techniques of Gandhian resistance at Vaikam, but subsequently broke with Gandhi in 1925 because of his refusal to endorse the principle of separate representation for the depressed classes and because he continued to valorise *varnashrama dharma* and Brahmanism. In 1926, he founded the Self Respect Movement. In 1937 he organised strong protests against the Congress plan to make Hindi compulsory in Tamil schools, and he ended up in jail as a result. Despite its opposition to the Gandhian Congress, the movement existed within the political space that had been opened up by Gandhi.[96]

Satyagraha has continued to be a central element within the Indian polity since independence in 1947, again deployed by all sorts of groups and political parties. We can see this in the ritual of the public fast, a form of protest that is taken very seriously by those in authority. This is in marked contrast to the attitude of politicians elsewhere, such as Margaret Thatcher, who felt no qualms about allowing Bobby Sands and nine other Irish nationalist hunger strikers to die in agony in 1981, stating that she would not be 'blackmailed' by terrorists.[97] This harsh reaction was viewed with horror and disbelief in India, where such moral courage is widely respected. Indian political leaders have had to adopt

[95]M.S. Korejo, *The Frontier Gandhi: His Place in History*, Oxford University Press, Karachi 1993, pp. 47–71.

[96]Pandian, '"Denationalising" the Past', pp. 2282–3. Eugene Irschik, *Politics and Social Conflict in South India: The Non-Brahman Movement and Tamil Separatism, 1916–1929*, University of California Press, Berkeley 1969, pp. 330–1 and 345–6. Conversation with M.S.S. Pandian, Oxford, 22 June 1999.

[97]In fact, the ten hunger strikers gained their chief demand posthumously, as Irish republican prisoners were subsequently granted an effective status as political prisoners. Many consider their deaths to have marked a turning point in the Irish struggle in Northern Ireland. Interview with Margaret McCauley by Rosie Cowan, 'Why I had to Let my Brother Die', *The Guardian*, 2 April 2001.

a very different attitude towards political fasting. To take some examples at random, when Indira Gandhi refused to give a date for fresh elections in Gujarat in 1975—even a year after the state assembly had been dissolved—Morarji Desai launched a fast unto death. Six days into the fast, Indira Gandhi agreed to allow the elections to be held.[98] A year later, Vinoba Bhave demanded a total ban on cow slaughter, and announced that he would go on a fast until the government accepted it. The governments of Andhra, Tamil Nadu, Maharashtra, Kerala, West Bengal and Assam promptly announced that they would ban cow-slaughter. Vinoba Bhave then withdrew his threat and publicly thanked Indira Gandhi.[99] In some cases fasting merges with mass protest. For example in 1991, 250 residents of Ralegan Siddhi (Ahmadnagar District, Maharashtra) led by the social worker Anna Hazare went on fast after the government failed to grant recognition to their village school. Within hours, the authorities backed down and recognised the school.[100]

In all these various ways, Gandhi has provided a strong institutional base for the expression of dissent within the modern Indian polity. Its power has, if anything, grown, for in a time of rapid electronic communication a matter which might appear to be of only local concern may be turned through satyagraha into an issue of national, and even international, importance. Through satyagraha, many have come to believe that they have the strength to exert a counter-power against those in authority. Satyagraha thus provides a means through which—to use the language of the new social movements—the personal is made political.

[98] Ostergaard, *Nonviolent Revolution in India*, p. 192.

[99] Ibid., 247–53.

[100] Vivek Pinto, *Gandhi's Vision and Values: The Moral Quest for Change in Indian Agriculture*, Sage Publications, New Delhi 1998, p. 150.

4

An Alternative Modernity

Gandhi is often seen as taking an extreme—even eccentric—stance in regard to what is defined as 'modernity'. His polemic of 1909, *Hind Swaraj*, is quoted as evidence that he rejected almost all aspects of Western civilisation, as imposed on India and other colonised regions of the world by the imperialist powers. There are however problems with this reading of Gandhi, as it assumes a questionable dichotomy between Western civilisational values and Gandhi's alternative morality. The difficulty flows from the term 'modernity' itself. In English, the word dates back to the eighteenth century, and it is frequently taken to denote the paradigmatic philosophical, scientific and governmental beliefs and practices that originated in Europe during that period and were subsequently spread throughout the globe.[1] Gandhi, however, endorsed many key aspects of this modernity, such as the doctrine of human rights, the fundamental equality of all humans, the right of all to democratic representation, the principle of governance through persuasion rather than coercion, and so on. In these respects, he can hardly be said to have been antagonistic to modernity. Rather, he took the position that in these respects Westerners frequently did not practice what they preached. The liberal regimes of the West were, for example, far less democratic than they claimed, and extremely undemocratic in a colo-

[1]The term is deployed in other ways, for example to denote the experimental art and writing of the period *c.*1890–*c.*1940. See Raymond Williams, *Keywords: A Vocabulary of Culture and Society*, Fontana, London 1976, p. 208. However, in recent years it has been taken as a shorthand term for the values associated with the Enlightenment which 'postmodernist' theorists seek to critique.

nial context. When we open up the issue more carefully, we can see that Gandhi was taking up a strategic position within the debates of his day. His relationship to modernity was a dialogic rather than antagonistic one.

What is taken as Gandhi's 'critique of modernity'[2] generally refers to his critique of the doctrines of materialism and instrumental rationality, the belief in scientific and technological progress, practices such as large-scale methods of production, rapid transportation, allopathic medicine, adversarial parliamentary systems of democracy and so on, and the accompanying conviction that it was the duty of those who subscribed to such values to impose them on the rest of the world. Against this, he counterpoised his own definition of what entailed a genuine 'civilisation' that had, he argued, to be rooted in an alternative morality. His position in this respect is set out most clearly in *Hind Swaraj*.

Hind Swaraj

Hind Swaraj was written by Gandhi in Gujarati in 1909, and translated by him into English in 1910. It took the form of a debate between an 'editor' (Gandhi) and a 'reader'. It is significant that this most seminal of Gandhian texts should have taken the form of a dialogue. Gandhi accepted that this was an unusual way of putting forward an intellectual argument in English (though there are of course highly respectable European precedents, notably Plato's *Republic*), but it came naturally to the Gujarati language. No doubt he had in mind here the interchange between Krishna and Arjun in the *Bhagavad Gita*.[3] Gandhi stated in 1910 that he had engaged in a dialogue along similar lines with 'several friends', so that he was reporting a debate of the day.[4] Although he does not state it as such, it almost certainly reflects discussions he had with the India House group in London in 1909, led by Shyamji Krishnavarma and including the militant Hindu nationalist V.D. Savarkar. The group as a whole advocated the use of terrorism and violence against the British

[2]This is the title of Chapter 3 of Terchek, *Gandhi*, as well as Chapter 5 of Bhikhu Parekh, *Gandhi*, Oxford University Press, Oxford 1997.

[3]Arnold, *Gandhi*, p. 65.

[4]'Preface to *Indian Home Rule*', 20 March 1910, *CWMG*, Vol. 10, p. 457.

in India.[5] Clearly, Gandhi saw it as his task to refute their belief in this strategy.

In *Hind Swaraj* Gandhi attacked the common view that civilizational progress could be judged in terms of the sophistication of machines, technology and weapons, and standards of material comfort enjoyed by a society. Such yardsticks ignored issues of morality and religious ethics. In fact, technology had caused terrible harm to the world. In India, it had allowed the British to establish their rule and control the people with an iron hand. The railways, generally seen as one of the great benefits of British rule, had merely spread disease and caused famines, as foodgrains were moved in freight wagons from areas of dearth, and, worst of all, had made people aware of their religious differences, causing confusion and divisions.

Similarly, the printing press and newspapers served to titillate rather than inform. As Gandhi stated later, in 1929:

> What would villagers gain by reading newspapers? They would come to know of the progress of motion pictures, of the progress made in aviation, stories of murders, facts describing the various revolutions that are going on in the world, dirty descriptions of dirty proceedings of law suits, news regarding horse races, the stock exchange and motor-car accidents. Mostly items of news mean only these things.[6]

Gandhi refused to accept modern systems of transport, printing presses and the like as defining features of 'civilization'. In *Hind Swaraj* he put forward a different understanding of the term: 'Civilisation is that mode of conduct which points out to man the path of duty. Performance of duty and observance of morality are convertible terms. To observe morality is to attain mastery over our mind and our passions. So doing we know ourselves. The Gujarati equivalent for civilisation means "good conduct".'[7] In the original Gujarati in which *Hind Swaraj* was written Gandhi used the word *sudharo*, stating that *su* meant 'good' and *dharo* meant 'way of life'. In doing so, Gandhi appeared to have been providing an 'Indian' understanding of the concept. In fact,

[5]Arnold, *Gandhi*, p. 65.
[6]'About *Navajivan*', *Navajivan*, 14 July 1929, *CWMG*, Vol. 36, p. 272.
[7]Gandhi, *Hind Swaraj*, in *CWMG*, Vol. 10, p. 279.

Gandhi's definition was as novel in Gujarati as in English. Belsare's Gujarati–English dictionary, which preceded *Hind Swaraj* by five years, defined *sudharo* as (1) reformation, (2) civilisation, (3) setting to rights, correcting; making accurate and exact, (4) improvement. *Sudharo dakal karvo* meant to introduce a reform, to introduce an innovation, or to introduce or adopt European manners.[8] There was no tension here between Europeanisation and civilisation—*sudharo* was what the British did through their institutions, such as municipalities.[9]

Gandhi was thus putting forward a novel and radical new way of understanding the concept of 'civilisation'. His 'good way of life' meant placing a curb on our material desires and refusing to fetishise technology. Above all, we should not value competition as the supreme value that drives forward 'progress'. He claimed that in pre-colonial India people followed their occupations in uncompetitive ways, being satisfied to earn enough for an adequate subsistence. This allowed for an elevation of morality. He concluded: 'So understanding and so believing, it behoves every lover of India to cling to the old Indian civilisation even as a child clings to the mother's breast.'[10]

Whether or not this was true of the Indian past—and almost certainly it was not—Gandhi was mounting a radical challenge to values that had been propagated so powerfully under colonialism as to have come to be perceived by the Indian middle classes as virtual forces of nature.

The British authorities in India reacted to *Hind Swaraj* by banning it and seizing all copies. Gandhi initially responded by stating that: 'The British Government in India constitutes a struggle between the Modern Civilisation, which is the kingdom of Satan, and the Ancient Civilisation, which is the Kingdom of God.' In this case, he argued, the former had the upper hand, but he hoped that older, more moral civilisational principles would prevail in the end. He advised his fellow

[8]Belsare, *Gujarati-English Dictionary*, p. 1156.

[9]This continues to be the standard meaning of the term. One of the best of more recent dictionaries defines *sudharo* in terms of 'change for the better', 'new custom or fashion', an 'amendment'. There is nothing about 'good conduct'. One meaning of the related word *sudharai* is that of 'municipality'. Deshpande, *Gujarati-Angreji Kosh*, pp. 905–6.

[10]*Hind Swaraj*, *CWMG*, Vol. 10, p. 281.

Indians to assert the latter, rather than worship at the shrine of Western civilisation. If they did so, the English would either have to change their whole way of being or quit India.[11] In 1914 he adopted a more conciliatory tone by insisting that the British were mistaken in their belief that *Hind Swaraj* was filled with hatred against them. He accepted that some Indians had read the tract in such a spirit. He regretted that a few had even felt that it showed that the British should be expelled as quickly as possible by armed force. This, for Gandhi, represented a grave misunderstanding of his intent. He had no hatred for the British, whom he loved as he would any fellow human. All he condemned was 'the present-day civilisation of Europe.'[12]

In later years, Gandhi accepted that in practical terms it was not possible to rid India of many of the attributes of modern civilisation, such as railways, hospitals, law courts, textile mills. He had to accept them as a 'necessary evil'.[13] In 1926 he stated that in an ideal world these institutions and technologies would not be needed, but it would be wrong to get rid of them all at once, as it would cause too much unnecessary disruption. What was needed was a vision of a future in which we would not be ruled by such elements.[14] Near the end of his life, in 1945, Gandhi said that there was no need to give up using facilities such as railway trains; all that was required was that they should be used in a non-attached way, as a utility, rather than consumed as an object of enjoyment.[15]

Some have read *Hind Swaraj* as an attack on the West, or Europe, from an Eastern perspective. However, although Gandhi often does talk in the tract in terms of an East/West dichotomy, this did not for him go to the heart of the matter. The fundamental problem for him was an uncritical assimilation of the civilisational values that were dominant in the West. This is clear from his preface to the English edition

[11] 'Preface to *Indian Home Rule*', 20 March 1910, *CWMG*, Vol. 10, p. 457.

[12] '*Hind Swaraj*', 29 April 1914, *CWMG*, Vol. 14, p. 157.

[13] '"*Hind Swaraj*" or "the Indian Home Rule"', *Young India*, 26 January 1921, *CWMG*, Vol. 22, p. 260.

[14] Interview to Langeloth and Kelly', *Young India*, 21 January 1926, *CWMG*, Vol. 33, p. 418.

[15] Letter to Krishnachandra, 14 June 1945, *CWMG*, Vol. 87, p. 129.

of 1910, in which he states that what he disliked about British rule and much Indian nationalism was that both endorsed 'the evils of modern civilisation' such as 'modern methods of violence'. If the British could reassert older values, they were welcome to remain in India as equal partners.[16] He never sought to deny that there was much to be learnt from the West. As he stated in 1926: 'there is much we can profitably assimilate from the West. Wisdom is no monopoly of one continent or one race. My resistance to Western civilisation is really a resistance to its indiscriminate and thoughtless imitation based on the assumption that Asiatics are fit only to copy everything that comes from the West.'[17]

Gandhi has been harshly criticised for his supposed attack on modernity, even by his strong admirers in other respects. Dalton regards the argument of *Hind Swaraj* as grossly overstated and sometimes absurd—Tolstoy, Ruskin, Thoreau and other figures whom Gandhi admires in the work were, after all, products of modern civilisation. Dalton explains Gandhi's tone in terms of a certain immaturity of style, with an extreme position being advanced which he would later modify to accord with his more inclusive approach to problems.[18] It is true that Gandhi toned down his statements in this respect in later years, although he never actually disavowed what he had said in *Hind Swaraj*. Otherwise, Dalton misses the point. It was in fact the very excess of *Hind Swaraj* that made it such an exceptional statement. Even if Gandhi later found it hard to defend all that he had said in it, he had succeeded in making many people think about the values that they considered civilised. If anything, the appeal of the tract increased over time, as the barbarities of world wars and fascism revealed a rottenness at the heart of Western civilisation.[19] It was taken up as a manifesto by a wide range of groups and tendencies, ranging from critics of capitalism, to pacifists, ecologists and Christians. Its valorisation of the rural and small

[16]'Preface to *Indian Home Rule*', 20 March 1910, *CWMG*, Vol. 10, p. 458.

[17]'Unity in Variety', *Young India*, 11 August 1927, *CWMG*, Vol. 39, p. 370.

[18]Dalton, *Mahatma Gandhi*, pp. 20–1.

[19]This point was made in 1938 about *Hind Swaraj* by the prominent British socialist G.D.H. Cole. See Raghavan Iyer, *The Moral and Political Writings of Mahatma Gandhi*, Volume I, *Civilization, Politics, and Religion*, Clarendon Press, Oxford 1986, p. 283, n. 1.

scale over and against the urban and large-scale also struck a chord with many members of the lower middle-class intelligentsia of India, who communicated the message to the subordinate classes of the rural areas. They in turn interpreted it in their own way, with at times some very radical consequences.

A Gandhian Civilisation

Gandhi's critique was selective. He focused on what he saw as the fetishising of technology and science, with its assumption that any technological improvement or scientific advance represented 'progress'. He condemned the consumerism that this promoted, with a constant valorisation of whatever innovation was seen to be the latest and most sophisticated. In this way, humans mortgaged their lives to the desire to experience and consume novelty, leading to a frenetic, ever-spiralling cycle of acquisitiveness. He also condemned the economic and political rivalry that lay at the heart of Western civilisation, with its emphasis on the value of competition over and above cooperation. These elements of modernity, in his view, compromised the great achievements of this civilization, such as the doctrine of human rights.[20]

Gandhi wanted instead a civilisation rooted in an ethical science and technology, by which he meant investigation and invention that was applied to human need on a human scale. As he said in 1925: 'I think that we cannot live without science, if we keep it in its right place.'[21] He himself was fascinated by science as a subject, and saw no harm in scientific research if it was undertaken for the sake of knowledge rather than for profit or material gain. It had, however, to conform to ethical principles. He considered, for example, vivisection by medical scientists to be a gross violation of animal life.[22] Another problem with

[20]On this latter point, see Nandy, 'From Outside the Imperium', pp. 173–6.

[21]Speech in Reply to Students' Address, Trivandrum, 13 March 1925, *CWMG*, Vol. 30, p. 410.

[22]Again, however, Gandhi refused to adopt an intolerant attitude in this respect. When his follower Ramachandra Rao—a teacher of biology—insisted on dissecting frogs in the Sevagram Ashram (much to the disgust of several of the inmates), Gandhi listened to both sides of the argument and ended by ruling that Rao could continue with his dissections, as they had a scientific rationale. Hugh Grey, '"Gora", Gandhi's Atheist Follower', p. 145.

scientific research was that it was the preserve of élites, who were detached from manual labour. Without an understanding of practical needs, as experienced through such labour, the research was unlikely to be of great benefit to the mass of humans. It was thus far more important to devise a new, improved spinning wheel which could be used by village artisans, rather than invent some dazzling new labour-saving machine which could be afforded only by the rich.[23]

Gandhi's critique of technologism and a materialistic and instrumentalist practice of science can be fitted into the post-Enlightenment thematic of the divide between what Donald Worster has called an imperialistic science and an arcadian sensibility. Following Theodor Adorno and Max Horkheimer, he has argued that, since the eighteenth century, Western thought has been confronted with a choice between two moral allegiances. On the one side there has been the drive to dominate nature in an aggressive way, involving the desacrilization of the world and its reduction to a quantitative, mechanistic scientific understanding. In such a framework, certain humans have sought scientific knowledge with the prime aim of manipulating nature to enhance their power over others. On the other side there has been the demand for an ethical approach to human affairs, and a search for ultimate purpose, the ends of life, and a harmonious coexistence within nature. This is the critical side to the Enlightenment, in which human reason has been driven by the desire to advance towards greater human equality, liberty and fraternity.[24]

The arcadian sensibility was seen in much eighteenth-century landscape painting, which depicted ordered, harmonious and gentle landscapes, with their quiet meadows, herds of cows and flocks of sheep and shepherds. They recalled a myth of the Golden Age that had haunted the European imagination since antiquity. They were given a new significance by Jean-Jacques Rousseau's pastoral primitivism. Rousseau believed the pastoral and pre-agricultural stage of civilisation to have been the happiest for man.[25] There was a strong arcadian sensibility in

[23]Speech in Reply to Students' Address, Trivandrum, 13 March 1925, *CWMG*, Vol. 30, pp. 409–14.

[24]Donald Worster, *Nature's Economy: A History of Ecological Ideas*, Cambridge University Press, New York 1985, pp. x-xi.

[25]Hugh Honour, *Romanticism*, Allen Lane, London 1979, pp. 59–60. It is

India too, with, for example, the celebration in poetry and painting of Krishna the cowherd dallying with peasant maidens in an idyllic pastoral countryside.

Gandhi's position as an arcadian within this 'dialectic of Enlightenment'[26] was always, however, a dialogic one, involving a mediation of the concept of 'nature' through the idea of *prakruti*. The word 'nature', as Raymond Williams has pointed out, is a highly problematic one, with meanings that are not only variable, but at times also philosophically opposed. The English word derives from the Latin *natura*, meaning the essential character and quality of something. In time however it had also come to entail, among other things, an idea of the physical power of the material world, as well as the inherent force that directs the world and humanity.[27] Whereas the emphasis on materiality allowed a separation to be made between nature and the divine, the emphasis on an undefined 'driving force' allowed for reconciliation between the two. Both the 'imperialist' scientist and the romantic could claim to be working 'in tune with nature', even though their understanding of what they were doing was greatly at variance. Gandhi invoked the concept in a way that might appear to have accorded more with the romantic sensibility, for he defined it as no more than a manifestation of God.[28] He did not however seek this pantheistic deity in the wild, as Thoreau and other Western romantics did—implicitly accepting a divide between 'nature' and 'culture'. Thoreau pursued his ecological vision by going to live in the woods near his home town as a hermit in a simple hut, eating berries and nuts, swimming in rivers and lakes, surrendering his being to the transcendental experience of

---

important to distinguish this arcadian sensibility from the *storm und drang* of the romantic structure of feeling—a product of the post-French revolutionary period—which celebrated the wild and uncontrolled forces of nature and psychology. On this see Honour, *Romanticism*, pp. 14–32. In his work, Worster does not distinguish adequately between these two tendencies. Gandhi had little in common with this romantic sensibility.

[26]The phrase used in the title of Adorno and Horkheimer's important book *Dialectic of Enlightenment*, Verso, London 1989.

[27]Williams, *Keywords*, pp. 219–20.

[28]'Answers to Questions from Moolchand Agrawal', 5 August 1927, *CWMG*, Vol. 39, p. 344.

immersion in a wildness free from human presence. In India, many sadhus and renouncers followed a similar path, seeking enlightenment through living in solitude in forests and mountains. Gandhi was rooted too firmly within human society to be attracted in any way by such a life. Gandhi's understanding of 'nature' was a far more inclusive one, rooted in the Gujarati word *prakruti*, which derived from the Sanskrit *prakriti*, meaning 'the original or natural form or condition of anything, original or primary substance', and 'the personified will of the Supreme in the creation ... also considered as identical with the Supreme being'.[29] In this, no separation could be seen to exist between material force and divine being, or nature and culture.

For Gandhi, the power of prakruti made a mockery of even the most advanced technology of the day. When a flood hit Paris in 1910, he observed that the great buildings that were washed away had not been built in anticipation of such an event. 'Only those who forget God will engage in such ostentation.'[30] Humans had however to do their best to bend the forces of nature to their ends. This was an onerous and never-ending task, to be undertaken with a sense of humility. As he stated: 'The great Nature has intended us to earn our bread in the sweat of our brow.'[31] In other words, what was required was an onerous interaction between human and non-human nature, exemplified by the diligent husbandry of the peasant cultivator. Such labour should be undertaken to earn a subsistence and no more. To try to take any more from nature was no more than thieving: 'If I take anything that I do not need for my own immediate use, and keep it, I thieve it from somebody else. I venture to suggest that it is the fundamental law of Nature, without exception, that Nature produces enough for our wants from day to day, and if only everybody took enough for himself and nothing more, there would be no pauperism in this world, there would be no man dying of starvation in this world.'[32] By equating nature with the divine, Gandhi placed himself within a pantheistic tradition that

[29]Monier Williams, *A Sanskrit-English Dictionary*, p. 654.

[30]'Paris Havoc', *Indian Opinion*, 5 February 1910, *CWMG*, Vol. 10, p. 410.

[31]Speech at Moulmein, 12 March 1929, *CWMG*, Vol. 45, p. 225.

[32]Speech on 'Ashram Vows' at YMCA, Madras, 16 February 1916, *CWMG*, Vol. 15, p. 171.

was central to much Hindu culture. From such a standpoint, nature/God can never be comprehended fully by humans, only experienced with a sense of awe, and treated with deference and humility. Such sensibilities have fed into some Western strands of pantheistic thought. For example, earlier forms of romantic nature-mysticism were reworked during Gandhi's lifetime by Henri Bergson, with his philosophy of vitalism, which asserted that plants and animals act according to an indwelling, mysterious power that cannot be measured by physics or chemistry. John Burroughs saw nature as a single huge organism, pulsing with life.[33] James Lovelock has restated this concept more recently with his notion of Gaia.[34]

Like many arcadians, Gandhi hated the modern city, where modern technology was seen in all of its ugliness,[35] and where godlessness reigned. As he stated in 1916: 'It is not possible to conceive gods inhabiting a land which is made hideous by the smoke and din of mill chimneys and factories and whose roadways are traversed by rushing engines ...'[36] His ideal was that of the small-scale agricultural community, cultivating common land in a sustainable and largely self-sufficient way. Following Ruskin and Tolstoy, he emphasised the dignity of manual labour, either on the farm or in artisan manufacture. He experimented with such a way of life in his ashrams, beginning in 1904 with the Phoenix Settlement near Durban. In such an environment, agriculture and craftwork were accorded a spiritual dimension. Once a week, the inmates gathered for a multi-faith service, with readings from the scriptures of a variety of religions. One observer has described Phoenix as 'an agriculture-based religious community'.[37]

Gandhi was keen to apply the most appropriate techniques in his

[33]Worster, *Nature's Economy*, p. 17.

[34]James Lovelock, *Gaia: A New Look at Life on Earth*, Oxford University Press, Oxford 1979.

[35]For a vicious attack on Bombay, which Gandhi said 'looks as if it were the scum of London', see Letter to Maganlal Gandhi, 11 January 1915, *CWMG*, Vol. 14, p. 337.

[36]Speech at Muir College Economic Society, Allahabad, 22 December 1916, *CWMG*, Vol. 15, p. 277.

[37]Pinto, *Gandhi's Vision and Values*, pp. 43–51, quote on p. 51.

agricultural and artisanal activities. Ashramites were for example sent from Phoenix to learn from Trappist monks how to make sandals, the resulting products providing a valuable source of income for the institution. He advocated a careful study of horticulture and the establishment of model farms that would provide an example for surrounding farmers. He argued that refuges for cows maintained by many religious organisations in India should be turned into centres for cattle-research, so as to improve milk-yields.[38] He encouraged his followers to undertake socio-economic surveys of villages, so as to be able to obtain the facts on which appropriate campaigns for rural improvement could be based.[39] Gandhi did not therefore reject rational and scientific approaches to problems, so long as they accorded with his moral principles.

The Constructive Programme

All this fed into what is known as the Gandhian 'constructive programme'. Of all his work, this was closest to his heart, for as he stated in 1940: 'I was born for the constructive programme. It is part of my soul. Politics is a kind of botheration for me.'[40] The programme incorporated principles such as swadeshi (home-based production), in which a village, locality or nation would be as self-reliant as possible, *sarvodaya* (commitment to public welfare) and *aparigraha* (non-possessiveness).[41] Gandhi inaugurated it during the Non-cooperation Movement of 1920–1.[42] Although such activity is often subsumed within the rubric of 'development', this term had connotations of an evolution towards

[38]Speech on Cow Protection, Bettiah, 9 October 1917, *CWMG*, Vol. 16, p. 56.

[39]Pinto, *Gandhi's Vision and Values*, pp. 60–2.

[40]Speech at Gandhi Seva Sangh Meeting, Malikanda, Bengal, 21 February 1940, *CWMG*, Vol. 77, p. 374.

[41]Pinto, *Gandhi's Vision and Values*, pp. 67–9.

[42]The constructive programme also incorporated educational and cultural work, such as establishing national schools, inculcating communal harmony and eradicating the practice of untouchability. These latter two aspects will be examined in later chapters. For details of the constructive programme in Gujarat during Non-cooperation see David Hardiman, *Peasant Nationalists of Gujarat: Kheda District 1917–1934*, Oxford University Press, New Delhi 1981, pp. 118–26.

a Eurocentric model—an anathema to Gandhi. He therefore never used the word.

The Gandhian form of swadeshi sought to nurture forms of technology that were seen to be appropriate to the needs of the majority of the people. It aimed to provide dignity for manual occupations and allow for a more equitable division of labour, with all forms of work, whether public or domestic, being accorded an equal value. There was a place in this for labour-saving devices and technologies, so long as they reinforced this process rather than undermined it, as factory-based production was seen to do at a range of levels. By valorising labour-intensive work so publicly, Gandhi also emphasised that self-reliance through labour would be required for all citizens of a future India. For Gandhi, the winning and maintenance of freedom was impossible without such work-discipline.[43]

The spinning wheel took pride of place in this campaign, as Gandhi believed that it provided the best means through which the poor could earn a supplementary income or save money by producing their own clothes. For him, it epitomised the spirit of self-reliance. He launched the spinning campaign in 1919, persuading one of his followers to offer a prize of Rs.5000 for the best design for a wheel.[44] A simple and portable wheel was produced in the following year. Gandhian activists raised funds to have these wheels manufactured and distributed to the poor. The thread was then supplied to handloom weavers to make into a cloth called khadi. Khadi *bhandars* (stores) were opened to market the results, along with other Indian-made products and nationalist literature. They provided an important focus in a town or village for this work as well as for wider Gandhian activities. Khadi was not however able to compete with mill-made cloth in terms of price, and hand-spinning did not turn out to be an economically viable occupation.[45] In the long

[43]I.P. Desai and Banwarilal Choudhry, *History of Rural Development in Modern India*, Volume II, Impex India, New Delhi 1977, p. 58

[44]'Notes', *Navajivan*, 5 October 1919, *CWMG*, Vol. 19, p. 31.

[45]A British official in Gujarat calculated that daily earnings from hand-spinning were only about half that from agricultural labour. *Land Revenue Administration Report of the Bombay Presidency, including Sind, for the Year 1920–21*, Bombay 1922, p. 27. Several Gandhians who put their savings into *khadi* work suffered

run khadi production survived through subsidies from the rich obtained through the All India Spinners Association, founded by Gandhi in 1925. Khadi was kept alive because of its great symbolic importance for the cause. In strictly economic terms, this work did not provide a good example of self-sufficiency.

This failure gave an edge to criticisms of Gandhian economic theory in general. He was accused of shunning labour-saving devices in favour of older-style labour-intensive methods of production that have historically condemned the poor to long hours of back-breaking labour. Although there was, arguably, some truth in this so far as khadi and other labour-intensive activities were concerned, there were many other areas in which appropriate technologies have proved to be of obvious value to the poor. For example, working conditions for women have been greatly improved through improvements in *chula* (stove) design, the development of *gobar* gas plants and solar cookers, and improvement of hand-pumps. Relatively small changes in the designs of bullock-carts, ploughs and agricultural implements have greatly enhanced the productivity of farmers at a minimum cost. Locally based seed experiments have determined the varieties that provided the highest yield for organic forms of agriculture in a particular microclimate. Cattle have been improved through breeding programmes in *goshalas*, leading to increases in milk yield. Particular strains of grass have been promoted to provide better fodder for livestock. Techniques such as the building of small check-dams on rivers and streams, the lining of tanks with an artificial membrane to prevent seepage, well-replenishment through channelling monsoon rain, water-pumping from rivers, and drip-irrigation have proved to have huge drought-proofing potential.[46]

Even khadi might be made a success. Much of its problem has probably stemmed from the fact that khadi-spinning and weaving were fetishised, while other elements necessary for a sustainable and eco-

---

bad financial losses. For an example see *Navajivan*, 23 August 1925, in *CWMG*, Vol. 28, p. 102.

[46]Work such as this is carried on in a number of Gandhian institutions today, for example, at Lok Bharati in Sanosra village of Bhavnagar District, Gujarat. Unfortunately, such institutions are few and far between, having only a marginal influence on Indian village life at a wider level.

friendly cotton-growing economy were neglected. Recent work by Uzramma Bilgrimi in Andhra Pradesh has indicated that what is required is an agricultural system which incorporates local indigenous forms of short-staple cotton which are relatively drought-resistant and which are ideal for hand ginning and weaving. Such cotton can be interplanted with food crops in a way that minimizes attacks by pests. It is cheap to grow, harvests are more reliable, and the resulting cotton cloth is typically of very high quality—unlike a lot of the cloth sold today in khadi shops—and able, potentially, to earn the producers a good income.[47]

What this brings out is that alternative economic systems cannot be dreamed up and applied in dogmatic ways. There has to be careful open-minded investigations of problems on the ground, followed by slow and cautious experiments with more people-oriented and eco-friendly forms of production. There will be many mistakes, and much fine-tuning will always be required.

Gandhi understood this very well, and was a firm advocate of the careful and scrupulous social survey that was informed by a scientific spirit and open frame of mind. Following the principles of the great Victorian social investigators of Britain, he sought to identify problems through detailed fieldwork, involving the collection of testimonies and statistics. He claimed to be doing this in a neutral way, with his future action being guided by his findings. It was however almost inevitable that such investigation would reveal abuses of power by local élites and officials. The nationalist agenda of Gandhi and his assistants was also well known, and the radicalising potential of such work was only too obvious. Because of this, the local authorities tended to view the whole process with suspicion, and they could be openly hostile.

Gandhi applied such an approach in Champaran District of Bihar, where he went in 1917 to investigate complaints by the peasants against white indigo planters. The local authorities were not impressed, and promptly arrested him. In a statement before the court he asserted:

> I have entered the country with motives of rendering humanitarian and national service. I have done so in response to a pressing invitation to

[47]Rajni Bakshi, *Bapu Kuti: Journeys in Rediscovery of Gandhi*, Penguin, New Delhi 1998, pp. 233–54.

> come and help the ryots, who urge they are not being fairly treated by the indigo planters. I could not render any help without studying the problem. I have, therefore, come to study it with the assistance, if possible, of the administration and the planters. I have no other motive and I cannot believe that my coming here can in any way disturb the public peace or cause loss of life. I claim to have considerable experience in such matters. The administration, however, have thought differently.[48]

The higher authorities in India did not however want to alienate Gandhi at that juncture—for he was supporting the war effort—and they ordered the local authorities to abandon the prosecution and allow the survey to continue. The same method was applied a year later in Kheda District to investigate the grievances of the peasants against the government. Similar surveys were carried out under the direction of his followers, such as Narhari Parikh in Bardoli Taluka of Surat District in 1927 and J.C. Kumarappa in Matar Taluka of Kheda district in 1928–30. The results were published, with suggestions being put forward for appropriate remedies for the various problems that had been exposed.[49] In all of these cases the surveys preceded major nationalist-led protests, that of the Kheda Satyagraha of 1918, the Bardoli no-tax campaign of 1928 and the Kheda no-tax campaign during the Civil Disobedience movement of 1930–1. It was clear from this that such work tended to have very radical consequences.

Gandhi, Socialism, and the Doctrine of Trusteeship

Gandhi did not believe that socialism provided a path to the form of civilization that he advocated. He had a low opinion of the Bolsheviks in Soviet Russia: 'Bolshevism is the necessary result of modern materialist civilisation. Its insensate worship of matter has given rise to a school which has been brought up to look upon material advancement as the

[48]Statement by Gandhi before the Court, Motihari, Champaran District, 18 April 1917, *CWMG*, Vol. 15, p. 345.

[49]Narhari Parikh, *Bardolina Kheduto*, Chhotubhai Gopalji Desai, Bardoli 1927 (in Gujarati); J.C. Kumarappa, *A Survey of Matar Taluka*, Gujarat Vidyapith, Ahmedabad 1931.

goal and which has lost all touch with the finer things of life.'[50] He went on to argue that through satyagraha the people of India could prevent Bolshevism from becoming rampant in the land.

At the time when Gandhi made this statement, few Indian nationalists—even those considered most radical at that time—were socialists. The large majority endorsed the capitalist path, albeit one in which Indians would be free from British imperial control. Gandhi, with his sharp critique of many elements of capitalist modernity, was the one out on a limb. This changed during the 1920s, as a younger generation began to look to the Soviet Union as a model to be emulated. The economic crash of 1929, followed by the slump of the 1930s, strengthened this tendency. We thus find leaders such as B.R. Ambedkar endorsing the capitalist path in his writings of the 1920s, but moving to the left during the 1930s and adopting a far more socialistic position.[51]

Gandhi was not insensitive to this development, and during the 1930s and 1940s he carried on a continuing dialogue with socialist nationalists. He accepted the worth of the socialist goals of eliminating poverty and gross inequalities and their struggle for the right of all to a livelihood. He considered that he was in fact more in tune with such sentiments than most socialists and communists, whose work was, he claimed, dictated more by politics than a sense of heartfelt compassion.[52] He had a particularly close relationship with the Congress Socialist Party leader Jayprakash Narayan, and he debated these issues at length with him. He stated in 1940 that: 'I know many friends who delight in calling themselves communists. They are as harmless as doves. I call myself a communist in their company. The underlying belief of communism is good and as old as the hills.'[53] In 1946 he even came round to the socialist view that key industries should be nationalised. However, he refused to accept that this should be carried out in a coercive or violent manner, arguing that it should be done with the cooperation of

[50]Message to Madras meeting, 30 March 1919, *CWMG*, Vol. 17, p. 367.

[51]Omvedt, *Dalits and the Democratic Revolution*, pp. 233–4.

[52]Interview to Louis Fischer, 17 July 1946, *CWMG*, Vol. 91, p. 299. For another statement along such lines, see 'Answers to Questions at Constructive Workers' Conference, Madras', 24 January 1946, *CWMG*, Vol. 89, pp. 296–7.

[53]'Travancore', *Harijan*, 21 July 1940, *CWMG*, Vol. 79, p. 13.

the owners.[54] In this latter respect, he was in fundamental disagreement with most socialists.

Where Gandhi differed most radically from the socialists and communists was over their belief in the necessity for class struggle. He saw this as inculcating hatred and creating a distance between opponents that was counter-productive. In particular, it entailed violence. He contrasted class struggle with satyagraha:

> By the non-violent method we seek not to destroy the capitalist, we seek to destroy capitalism. We invite the capitalist to regard himself as a trustee for those on who he depends for the making, the retention and the increase of his capital. Nor need the worker wait for his conversion. If capital is power, so is work. Either power can be used destructively or creatively. Either is dependent on the other. Immediately the worker realises his strength, he is in a position to become a co-sharer with the capitalist instead of remaining his slave. If he aims at becoming the sole owner, he will most likely be killing the hen that lays golden eggs. Inequalities in intelligence and even opportunity will last till the end of time.[55]

Gandhi argued that it was possible to appeal to the good in every person, however grasping and oppressive they might appear to be.[56] He sought to inculcate a spirit of aparigraha, or non-possession. This would require that each would hold whatever assets they possessed in trust for the good of society. Thus, the rich were required to deploy their wealth for the benefit of those who worked for them, while labourers were required to provide their labour to those who needed it, e.g. their employers.[57] Owners of the means of production should not take more than was needed for a comfortable, but not extravagant, life. Workers were to be treated as if they were members of a family, with

[54]'Alternative to Industrialism', *Harijan*, 1 September 1946, *CWMG*, Vol. 92, pp. 63–4.

[55]'Can you Avoid Class War?', *Young India*, 26 March 1931, *CWMG*, 51, p. 296.

[56]Ibid., pp. 296–7.

[57]'Of Princes and Paupers', *Navajivan*, 22 March 1931, *CWMG*, Vol. 51, pp. 286–7.

provision being made for healthy working and living conditions and general welfare.

Employers, landlords and capitalist entrepreneurs could very obviously deploy the concept of trusteeship in a self-serving way. It has been strongly condemned by Marxists, such as R. Palme Dutt, who saw this as 'the familiar bourgeois essence' showing through 'the idealistic cover'.[58]

> Herein lies the practical significance of this preaching from the standpoint of the big bourgeoisie, who tolerate and even encourage its Utopian yearnings and naïve fantasies with a smile, because they know its business values for protecting their class interests and assisting to hold in the masses and maintain class peace.[59]

Marx and Engels themselves, however, had criticised what they defined as utopian socialism—associated with Robert Owen and other early nineteenth-century radicals—not only because it downplayed class antagonisms, but because it also, and more importantly, rejected political struggle in favour of isolated social experiments.[60] Clearly, Gandhi could not be placed in the latter category—he was a political activist who fought tirelessly for the rights of the poor and oppressed on a wide stage.

There is no escaping the fact, however, that the faith that Gandhi placed in capitalist entrepreneurs as a class was largely misplaced. Only a few exceptional businessmen of the day, like Jamnalal Bajaj and J.R.D. Tata, may be said to have approached such an ideal. The large majority continued to do everything they could to drive down wages and keep the working classes in their place by denying them basic welfare provisions. This was the case even in Ahmedabad, where the few millowners who subscribed to Gandhian principles were in continuing conflict with the majority who did not. In 1920, the progressive entrepreneur Ambalal Sarabhai, with his visions of industrial harmony, was challenged by a coterie of mean-minded Baniyas led by Sheth Mangaldas

[58]Palme Dutt, *India Today*, p. 514.

[59]Ibid., p. 516.

[60]Karl Marx and Frederick Engels, 'Manifesto of the Communist Party', in Marx and Engels, *Collected Works*, Volume 6, Lawrence and Wishart, London 1976, pp. 514–17.

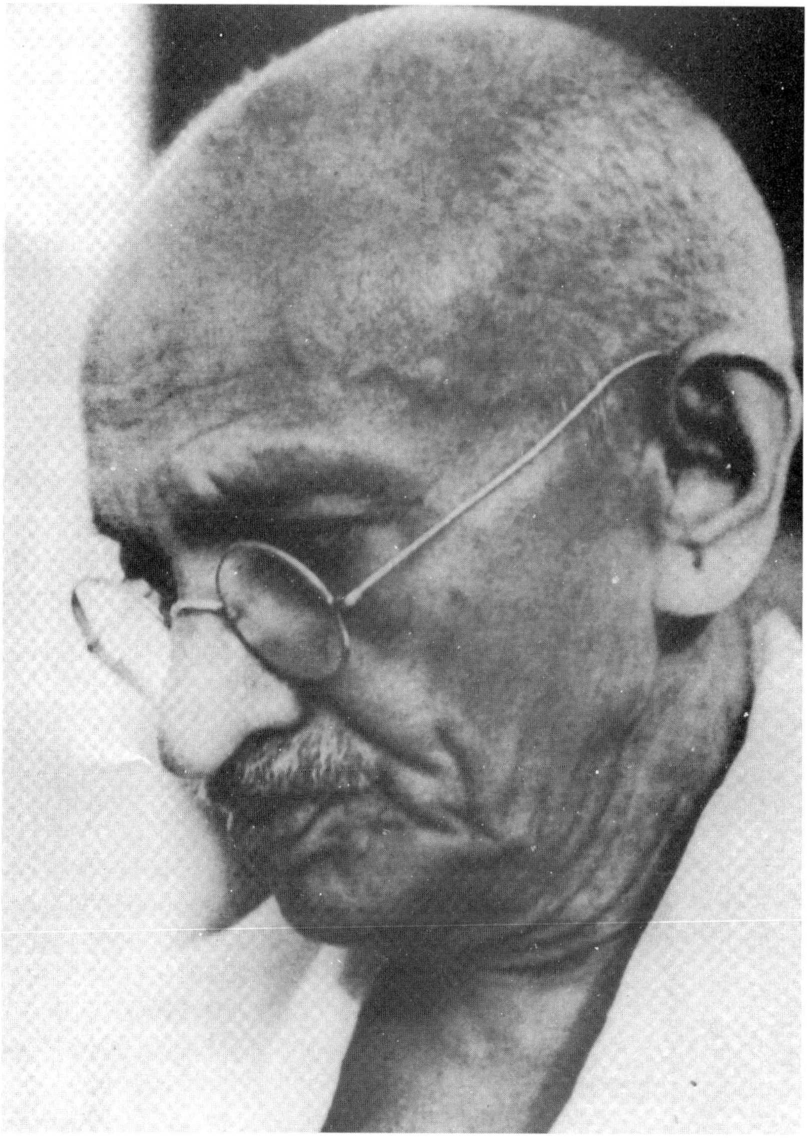

1. M.K. Gandhi

2. Mohandas and Kasturba Gandhi, Johannesburg, July 1914

3. Gandhi on the Salt March, 1930

4. Gandhi in London, 1931

5. B.R. Ambedkar

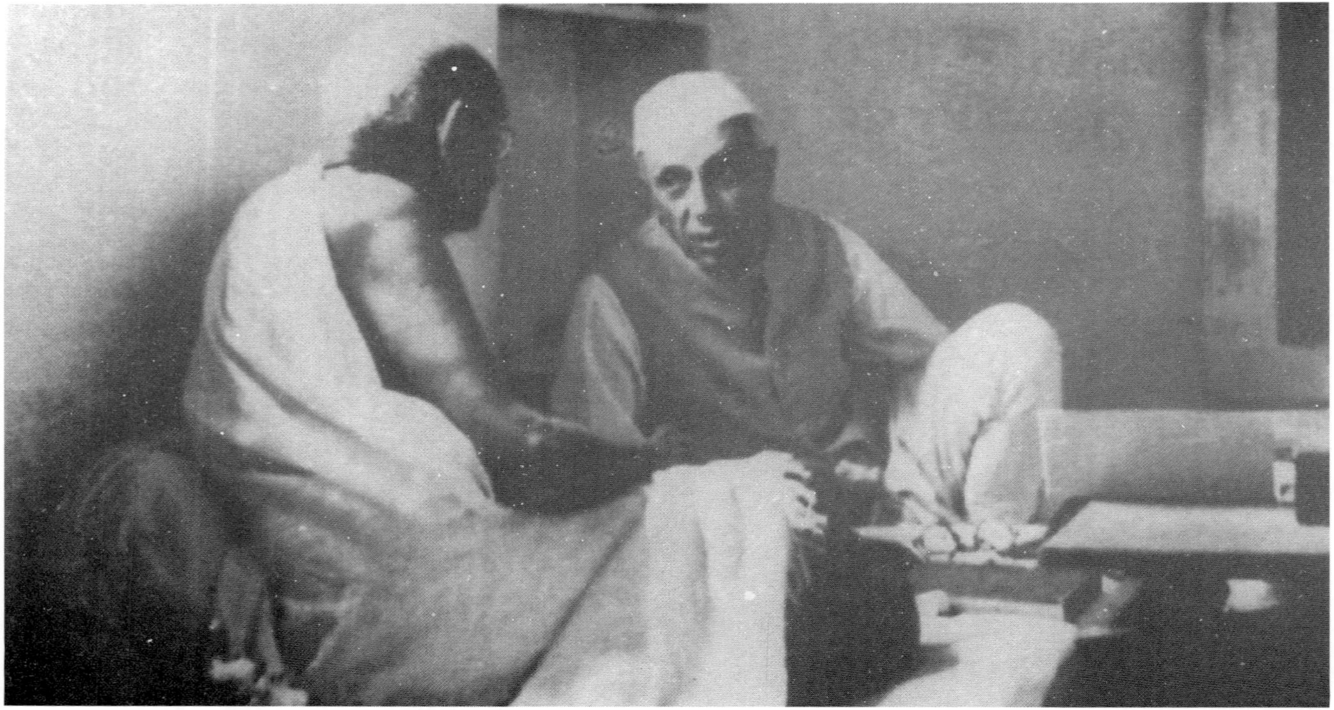

6. Gandhi in dialogue with Jawaharlal Nehru, Delhi, 2 October 1946

7. Jayaprakash Narayan, 1940s

8.Vinoba Bhave on the Bhoodan March 1950s

9. Medha Patkar

10. Protest against the Narmada Dam

11. Martin Luther King leads a march in Selma, Alabama, 30 March 1965 (© Hulton Getty)

12. Petra Kelly

whose main aim was to destroy the Gandhian union that had been established earlier in that year. When Gandhi called a strike and forced the latter to agree to a compromise, the unscrupulous millowner did his best to wreck the agreement. Even in his home city, Gandhi had failed to bring about any genuine or widespread change of heart amongst the majority of capitalists.[61]

Gandhi's position has, however, elements in common with an argument about class struggle put forward by Paul Ricoeur. Ricoeur maintains that many elements of life in a society cut across class boundaries—such as language, culture, sexuality, and nationality. He states that the aim in class conflict should not be the destruction of the enemy through class war, but the forging of a society in which both parties are integrated in an equitable way: 'Some of the European communist parties—particularly in Italy and now in France and Spain—have formulated the idea that the problem is to develop a society better integrated than in the class structure. The point, then, is really to integrate and not to suppress or destroy one's enemy.'[62] This, in many respects, was what Gandhi sought when he became involved in struggles between capital and labour.

The Gandhian Critique Beyond India

In recent years, the Gandhian approach to social and economic problems has been taken up in vigorous new ways, not only in India but in the world as a whole.[63] The person who was probably most responsible for starting this trend was E.F. Schumacher (1911–77). He was a German economist who left Germany in the 1930s and became an economic adviser to the British government in the 1940s and 1950s. After a visit to Burma in 1955 he became convinced that there were serious problems with the economic strategies of the so-called 'developing countries'.

[61] Sujata Patel, *The Making of Industrial Relations: The Ahmedabad Textile Industry 1918–1939*, Oxford University Press, New Delhi 1987, pp. 49–51.

[62] Paul Ricoeur, *Lectures on Ideology and Utopia*, edited by George H. Taylor, Columbia University Press, New York 1986, p. 263.

[63] Bakshi, *Bapu Kuti*, p. 20; Judith Brown, 'Gandhi: Guru for the 1990s?,' in Upendra Baxi and Bhikhu Parekh (eds.), *Crisis and Change in Contemporary India*, Sage Publications, New Delhi 1995, pp. 88 and 95.

The emphasis was on capital-intensive advanced technology that would, it was believed, raise productivity and make those countries competitive in the world economy. They lacked however the human and material infrastructure necessary for these small, highly developed sectors to develop in a dynamic and profitable way. What was needed, he argued, was a form of technology that was appropriate to each particular region. In most cases this would be labour-intensive, small in scale, and not needing huge amounts of investment. He called this 'intermediate technology'.

Schumacher developed the idea through interaction with other economists who had been thinking along similar lines, such as the Gandhian economist J.C. Kumarappa, and the director of the Gokhale Institute in Pune, D.R. Gadgil, who in 1964 put forward a similar concept of 'appropriate technology', arguing that it was imperative that the Indian government give a far higher priority to such a sector.[64] Schumacher, who had been an adviser to the National Coal Board in Britain, also became convinced that the profligate use of energy in industrialised countries was unsustainable, and that the future lay with low-energy production. He was also president of the Soil Association, the foremost body in Britain propagating organic agriculture. His influential book of 1973, *Small is Beautiful*, combined with great power his critique of developmentalism with an ecological awareness.

In this work, Schumacher started with the Gandhian principle that ethics were foremost, contrasting this with the fetishising of economic growth by neo-classical and Keynesian economists, and the 'idolatry of giantism' of twentieth-century governments.[65] Economists, he argued, claimed to be putting forward value-free 'truths', while failing to understand their own metaphysics. What he proposed instead was a 'Buddhist economics', though he noted that the teachings of Christianity, Islam, Judaism or any other great religion would do as well.[66] An ethical economics put humans and their needs first, and evolved economic policies around them.

[64]E.F. Schumacher, *Small is Beautiful: A Study of Economics as if People Mattered*, Abacus, London 1975, pp. 46 & 157–8.

[65]Ibid., pp. 18–19 & 56.

[66]Ibid., pp. 43–4.

He put forward a strongly Gandhian justification for intermediate technology:

> As Gandhi said, the poor of the world cannot be helped by mass production, only by production by the masses. The system of *mass production*, based on sophisticated, highly capital-intensive, high energy-input dependent, and human labour-saving technology, presupposes that you are already rich, for a great deal of capital investment is needed to establish one single workplace. The system of *production by the masses* mobilises the priceless resources which are possessed by all human beings, their clever brains and skilful hands, *and supports them with first-class tools*. The technology of *mass production* is inherently violent, ecologically damaging, self-defeating in terms of non-renewable resources, and stultifying for the human person. The technology of *production by the masses*, making the use of the best of modern knowledge and experience, is conducive to decentralisation, compatible with the laws of ecology, gentle in its use of scarce resources, and designed to serve the human person instead of making him the servant of machines. I have named it *intermediate technology* to signify that it is vastly superior to the primitive technology of bygone ages but at the same time much simpler, cheaper, and freer than the super-technology of the rich.[67]

The élites of the poor countries had reacted to such a suggestion with the retort that they did not want second best. Schumacher commented that this was a reaction of those who were not in desperate need of employment.[68] What he was proposing was not some outdated and anachronistic technology, but an innovative technology that was tailored to the needs of the mass of the people. The greatest ingenuity and skill would be needed to develop such an alternative.[69] In merely seeking to ape the forms of production found in the richer nations, those élites were showing themselves up as unimaginative parasites.[70]

Another powerful plea for an alternative economic order was put

[67]Ibid., p. 128, emphasis in original.

[68]Ibid., p. 151.

[69]Ibid., p. 156.

[70]Schumacher developed his ethical principles further in *A Guide for the Perplexed*, Abacus, London 1978, which was published posthumously.

forward around the same time by Ivan Illich (b.1926). Illich was an Austrian who served as a Catholic priest in a poor parish of New York City in the 1950s. In the 1960s he moved to Puerto Rico and then Mexico, where he wrote four influential books that were published between 1970 and 1975. The second of these books, *Tools for Conviviality* (1973), echoed many of Schumacher's concerns about large-scale industrial society and the marginalisation of the masses. Illich demanded that we develop 'convivial' tools and technologies—the equivalent of Schumacher's intermediate technology—and that we learn to set limits to growth.[71]

Some of Illich's other themes have parallels with the critique being developed at the same time by Michel Foucault of the disciplinary bases to many core modern institutions. In his first book, *Deschooling Society* (1971), Illich focussed on modern education, which he saw as being devised primarily to allow for an authoritarian management of societies, and which inhibited rather than expanded learning opportunities for the mass of the people. He proposed instead decentralised, disestablished and multiple systems of learning, which would develop in pupils a critical and enquiring frame of mind.[72]

In *Medical Nemesis* (1975), he expanded the analysis to the modern health system; which he argued created an unacceptable level of paternalistic control over the patient. In many cases, treatment made people more ill—something he defined as 'structural iatrogenesis'.[73] Although Gandhi is not mentioned at all in this book, his attack on modern medicine echoes that of *Hind Swaraj*. Gandhi had in this work stated that at one time it had been his ambition to serve India by becoming a doctor, but that his observation of the practice of Western medicine had made him change his mind. He had come to see that Western-style doctors used their knowledge to enhance their power over others and fill their pockets with money. They pandered to the rich, treating diseases that were caused by over-indulgence, and did not teach people to control their appetites and discipline their bodies. He had concluded:

[71]Ivan Illich, *Tools for Conviviality*, Fontana, Glasgow 1975.

[72]Ivan Illich, *Deschooling Society*, Penguin, Harmondsworth 1971.

[73]Ivan Illich, *Medical Nemesis: The Expropriation of Health*, Rupa, Calcutta 1975.

'To study European medicine is to deepen our slavery.'[74] The best medicine was a healthy way of life, and this form of medication could only be self-prescribed. Illich came to the same conclusion: 'A world of optimal and widespread health is obviously a world of minimal and only occasional medical intervention. Healthy people are those who live in healthy homes on a healthy diet ...'[75]

Illich's *Energy and Equity* (1974) was a short book that launched a fierce attack on the modern obsession with rapid transport. Huge amounts of energy were consumed, which led to overexploitation of the environment and severe pollution. The costs of building and maintaining these transport systems was also crippling for society. Individuals had to labour long hours to earn sufficient to purchase, maintain and run their cars. It was claimed that rapid transport liberated humans; in fact, he argued, it enslaved them.[76]

Fifty years earlier, Gandhi had also condemned the modern obsession with speed: 'Once we were satisfied with travelling a few miles an hour, today we want to negotiate hundreds of miles in an hour, one day we might desire to fly through space. What will be the result? Chaos—we would be tumbling upon one another, we would be simply smothered.'[77] When he was in London he had observed huge traffic-jams at every corner. This was, he asserted, the inevitable consequence of more and more people having the means to travel long distances *en masse*. When he was asked how he could justify his own use of railway trains, he replied that he wished that he could do his work without the need for such travel. He accepted that modern communication systems allowed certain well-meaning people to carry out valuable social work on a wider stage, but felt that the good they did was far outweighed by the damage caused by the extension of new forms of transport: 'Today two good people come from America with a kind and loving message. But along with the two come two hundred with all sorts of motives. For aught we know a large number may be coming just in search of further avenues

[74] *Hind Swaraj*, *CWMG*, Vol. 10, p. 278.

[75] Illich, *Medical Nemesis*, p. 169.

[76] Ivan Illich, *Energy and Equity*, Rupa, Calcutta 1974.

[77] Interview to Langeloth and Kelly, *Young India*, 21 January 1926, *CWMG*, Vol. 33, p. 417.

of exploitation.'[78] He himself preferred to walk whenever it was practicable to do so. This had in fact been a rule in his South African settlements, and it had not limited his mobility all that much—on one particular day he had even managed to walk fifty-five miles.[79]

Gandhi's critique of rapid transport lacked the ecological element of the later one put forward by Illich. Both shared, however, a belief that the underlying problem was moral—namely that rapid transport benefited the rich at the cost of the poor. Illich proposed an intermediate-level transport system, which was based on bicycles and slow moving and easily maintained motorised vehicles for the masses. 'To expand life beyond the radius of tradition without scattering it to the winds of acceleration is a goal that any poor country could achieve within a few years, but it is a goal that will be reached only by those who reject the offer of unchecked industrial development made in the name of an ideology of indefinite energy consumption.'[80] Twenty years on, these sort of arguments provided a basis for an attack on the modern obsession with road building. Highly effective and well-publicised anti-road protests in Britain and elsewhere forced governments to modify and even abandon some of their more grandiose road-building schemes.

Gandhian economics and constructive work also had a powerful impact on the thinking of workers in non-government organisations that were concerned with the social and economic development of poor countries. We can trace this trajectory in the history of one of the foremost of such agencies, Oxfam. In 1966–7, Oxfam's famine relief work in Bihar brought their representatives into close contact with Gandhian workers. This was the first time that Oxfam had worked in depth with what Maggie Black has classed as 'an agency authentically and inspirationally Indian'.[81] At that time the Oxfam field directors were ideologically committed to the principles of the Green Revolution, with its emphasis on high-yielding plant-hybrids developed by multinational agencies and companies, which needed lavish inputs of irrigation water,

[78]Ibid., p. 418.

[79]Pinto, *Gandhi's Vision and Values*, p. 60.

[80]Illich, *Energy and Equity*, p. 88.

[81]Maggie Black, *A Cause for our Times: Oxfam the First 50 Years*, Oxfam, Oxford 1992, p. 135.

fertilizers, herbicides and pesticides, all of which increased the dependency of farmers on multinational corporations. From a Gandhian perspective, Green Revolution technology was highly divisive, as it increased the gap in wealth between the rich farmers who could afford such inputs and the poor who could not. They were hardly likely to be enthusiastic about such a programme for rural development.

To the credit of the Oxfam fieldworkers, they took the criticisms of the Gandhian workers seriously, and began to ask critical questions of their own. They saw that poor peasants who had obtained land through land reform could only retain control over their new plots if they were able to achieve enough self-sufficiency to break the hold of the rural élites. This was possible if they could gain access to credit that was not controlled by the élites, or given small grants to obtain their own inputs. The partnership with the Gandhians proved to be a turning point for Oxfam in this respect, as it was the first time they had had to grapple with the problem of implementing programmes that would alleviate the problems of the poorest strata of rural society. In the process, they learnt that the 'development' strategies propounded with such bombastic faith by Western governments and transnational organisations were not only failing to help the poor, but were in fact making their situation worse. They began to see very clearly the neo-colonial agendas of such strategies.

During the 1970s Oxfam became known for its critical stance in these respects. It focused on working with local people (which included replacing expatriate field directors with local women and men), and tried to be sensitive to local practice and needs. The emphasis on Green Revolution technology was replaced with the encouragement of appropriate technology and maximum village self-sufficiency. Funds were for example provided for the building of small check dams, which helped raise the water table in a locality. In subsequent years, many other voluntary agencies based in the West were to follow this path also.[82]

Gandhian social and economic theory has also fed into the modern ecology movement. Gandhi is routinely held up as an inspirational figure by ecological thinkers and activists in India and elsewhere. Many of

[82]Ibid., pp. 134–44.

them claim that he foresaw ecological disaster in *Hind Swaraj*. However, as Ramachandra Guha has observed, this work does not in fact have anything to say about ecology as such. For this, we need to look at other writings by Gandhi. In 1928 he stated that if Indians imitated the British in their exploitation of the globe, the world would soon be stripped bare.[83] Otherwise, Guha argues, his programme for an equitable, low technology and largely agrarian human society may be read ecologically, as providing a model for a more sustainable future. In another work, co-authored with Madhav Gadgil, he and Gadgil maintain that many ecologists in India echo Gandhi in seeing this as above all a moral and civilisational problem which is rooted in a materialism and consumerism that alienates people from nature and encourages wasteful ways of life. In this, India is seen to be betraying its civilisational heritage, and such Gandhian ecologists call for a return to a more ecologically harmonious pre-colonial form of social organisation, as invoked by Gandhi in his notion of Ram Rajya. Following this, some Gandhians claim that a reverence for nature is rooted within the Hindu scriptures.[84]

Ramachandra Guha is positive about many aspects of the Gandhian legacy as applied to the ecological movement, but is critical about what he sees as its excessive emphasis on rural life. He argues that Gandhi and his followers have neglected urban environmental problems, which are particularly urgent in India today.[85] This is not altogether fair—in Ahmedabad Gandhi fought for the right of textile millworkers for a dignified life, involving union representation, wages linked to profits,

[83]Ramachandra Guha, 'Mahatma Gandhi and the Environmental Movement in India', in Arne Kalland and Gerard Persoon (eds), *Environmental Movements in Asia*, Curzon, Richmond 1998, pp. 67–9.

[84]Madhav Gadgil and Ramachandra Guha, *Ecology and Equity: The Uses and Abuses of Nature in Contemporary India*, Routledge, London 1995, p. 107. For a critique of the claim that Hinduism endorses an ecological sensibility, see Parita Mukta and David Hardiman, 'The Political Ecology of Nostalgia', *Capitalism, Nature, Socialism: A Journal of Socialist Ecology*, Vol. 11, No. 1, March 2000, pp. 119–21.

[85]Ramachandra Guha, 'Mahatma Gandhi and the Environmental Movement', p. 80.

shorter working hours, better housing and education.[86] What is true, however, is that Gandhi above all valorised a particular type of rural society—that of the smallholding peasant farmer, husbanding fixed fields. He had little to say about forest-dwellers, shifting cultivators or nomadic pastoralists and their various problems.

These considerations have in no way prevented the routine invocation of Gandhi within the ecology movement. For example, when over 1,500 activist groups came together in early 1999 to begin a protest against genetically modified seeds and crops, they chose the sixth of March, the anniversary of the launch of Gandhi's salt march, to inaugurate the 'Bija [seed] Satyagraha'. In addressing the meeting, the noted ecologist Vandana Shiva stated: 'Just as Gandhiji had made salt at Dandi to announce non-cooperation with the unjust British Salt Laws, the Bija Satyagraha is an announcement of people's non-cooperation with the unjust patent laws that make seed saving by farmers a crime ...'[87] She went on to compare the movement against multinational corporations with the earlier struggle for freedom from British rule.

Gandhi's importance for the ecology movement has probably, however, lain most strongly in its use of non-violent forms of resistance. The Chipko and Narmada movements, which will be examined in Chapter 8, have been celebrated by environmentalists in many parts of the world, and the methods of resistance duplicated or used as an inspiration for further innovative forms of protest, such as establishing tree houses in threatened woods.[88]

[86]Patel, *The Making of Industrial Relations.*

[87]'Just say no! to GMO', *Peace News*, May–August 1999, p. 11.

[88]It has however been pointed out that although Indian protests such as Chipko and Narmada have received widespread publicity in Europe and North America, ecological protesters carrying on similar movements in areas such as Latin America are often unaware of these Indian movements. Juan Martínez-Alier and Lori Ann Thrupp, Review of Enrique Leff, *Ecologia y Capital*, in *Capitalism, Nature, Socialism*, No. 3, November 1989, p. 182.

5

Father of the Nation

Although in much of his life and work Gandhi tried to maintain a series of dialogues, there were crucial areas in which his record in this respect was not a good one. This chapter examines one such area, that of his practice of patriarchy. Gandhi always acted the patriarch, and he was expected by many of his followers to do so. They related to him as they would a daughter or son towards a father, addressing him respectfully as 'Bapu' (father). He often signed off his letters to such people with 'Bapu's blessings'. He claimed that he treated all women as he would a 'sister or daughter'.[1] He ran his ashrams as a benevolent but authoritarian patriarch. In his own family life he demanded obedience from his wife, Kasturba, and his four sons and their wives. It was hard for him to accept when a 'daughter' or 'son'—real or adopted—sought to assert their independence; there were acrimonious quarrels, leading in some cases to sharp and bitter breaks. In all these ways he was in a very personal sense the 'father of the nation'.

Patriarchy, by its nature, allows at best only a limited degree of dialogue, whether between husband and wife, father and child, or elder and younger. Patriarchy is characteristically monologic. M.M. Bakhtin has defined the monologic as the voice of an entrenched authority that denies any meaningful dialogue with another person or group. Even when equality is accepted in theory, in practice it perceives the other as 'merely an *object* of consciousness, and not another consciousness', in the process denying that the other has 'equal rights and equal responsi-

[1]'My Life', *Harijan*, 4 November 1939, *CWMG*, Vol. 77, p. 61.

bilities': 'Monologue is finalized and deaf to the other's response, does not expect it and does not acknowledge it in any *decisive* force. Monologue pretends to be the *ultimate word.* It closes down the represented world and represented persons.'[2] In these respects, Gandhi's practice of patriarchy was monologic.

This can be demonstrated to start with through an examination of the history of Gandhi's own family life—an often-distressing and sad affair—to see how his patriarchy was rooted in an everyday familial practice. I shall then go on to look at Gandhi's understanding of sexual desire and female sexuality. From both a feminist and a psychoanalytical perspective, there is much in Gandhi's practice and belief that was problematic in the extreme. I shall also examine how all of this cast a long shadow over his admirable aspiration to better the position of women in India. Although his encouragement of women to take an active part in his campaigns of civil resistance helped to give many women in India a new sense of empowerment, this did not lead, within the nationalist movement, to any ideological challenge to his patriarchal ways.

Gandhi's Family Life

Gandhi was married in 1882, when he was thirteen, to Kasturba, who was the same age. It was an arranged marriage—they had already been betrothed for six years. In his autobiography, he commented that 'I took no time in assuming the authority of the husband.'[3] The marriage was thus consummated, and the couple then lived together while he studied in high school in Rajkot. He doubted her faithfulness to him at that time, and not only kept a close eye on her but tried to restrict her movements. She refused to obey him, going out and about as she wished. As he later stated: 'This sowed the seeds of a bitter quarrel between us.'[4] Within three years, Kasturba was pregnant.

It was at this juncture that his father, Karamchand, became gravely

[2]M.M. Bakhtin, *Problems of Dostoevsky's Poetics*, ed. and trans. C. Emerson, Manchester University Press, Manchester 1984, pp. 292–3. Emphasis in original.

[3]*Autobiography*, *CWMG*, Vol. 44, p. 99.

[4]Ibid., p. 100.

ill. Although Gandhi tended him as a dutiful son, his mind was on his wife and he continued to have sexual intercourse with her. This was to prove for him in retrospect a 'double shame'; first, he was forcing himself on a pregnant woman, and second, he was doing it as his father lay dying.[5] He was in fact having intercourse with Kasturba at the moment of Karamchand's death. His 'lust' at that moment was for him 'a blot I have never been able to efface or forget ...' When Kasturba gave birth soon after, the baby died in a few days. He saw this as a divine judgement on his 'lust', implying that a wife and child should expect to be punished by God for the failings of a husband and father. In future years, he was to implement such a will by continuing to punish Kasturba. As Erik Erikson has pointed out in his psychoanalytical study of Gandhi, the incident provided a 'cover' or reason for a way of behaving that had deeper and more structural roots.[6] Gandhi would also express this logic—of divine retribution on women and children for the sins of men—in a more public sphere, as we shall see later.

Over the following years, Gandhi continued to be harsh in his demands for obedience from Kasturba. Despite claiming in his autobiography that he had regarded her as his equal, he compelled her to do many things that she believed to be wrong. Although he accepted that this was a cause of tension between them, he argued that he acted always for her own good. In his autobiography he recounted one particular instance that occurred in 1898 in South Africa, when he insisted that she empty the chamber pot that had been used by a guest, who was a Dalit Christian. 'Even today I can recall the picture of her chiding me, her eyes red with anger, and pearl drops streaming down her cheeks, as she descended the ladder, pot in hand. But I was a cruelly kind husband. I regard myself as her teacher, and so harassed her out of my blind love for her.'[7] Little respect is shown for his wife in this passage that was written nearly thirty years later.[8]

[5]Ibid., pp. 112–14.

[6]Erik Erikson, *Gandhi's Truth: On the Origins of Militant Nonviolence*, Faber and Faber, London 1970, p. 128.

[7]*Autobiography*, *CWMG*, Vol. 44, p. 296.

[8]Erikson has commented on this passage that it reveals both Gandhi's sadism and an unacknowledged and unconscious hatred towards Kasturba. *Gandhi's Truth*, pp. 234–5.

There was worse to come. He relates how he then objected to her attitude, demanding that she carry the pot cheerfully. She abused him: 'Keep your house to yourself and let me go.' Gandhi lost his temper and, in his words, 'caught her by the hand, dragged the helpless woman to the gate ... and proceeded to open it with the intention of pushing her out.' She shouted back that he was a shameless man: 'Being your wife, you think I must put up with your cuffs and kicks?' Gandhi claimed that he then realised that he was in the wrong and backed down. He commented: 'The wife, with her matchless powers of endurance, has always been the victor.'

We know of this incident because Gandhi was honest enough to describe it in his autobiography, written many years later. He explains his bad behaviour in terms of his continuing sexual 'infatuation', and argues that once he took his vow of celibacy he was able to maintain a strict non-violence in this respect, and that his relationship with Kasturba improved accordingly. In other respects, however, he continued to assert himself against his wife. He refused to give any credence or respect to her opinions or intellect: 'Kasturba herself does not perhaps know whether she has any ideals independently of me.' He then immediately contradicted this by stating: 'It is likely that many of my doings have not her approval even today. We never discuss them, I see no good in discussing them.' He went on to declare that her thoughts were of no matter because 'she was educated neither by her parents nor by me at the time when I ought to have done it.' Kasturba was thus condemned as being ignorant and lacking any worthwhile opinions of her own. All she had were her prejudices that she had learnt to keep to herself.

He wound up this chapter of his autobiography by trying to paper over these glaring contradictions:

> But she is blessed with one great quality to a very considerable degree, a quality which most Hindu wives possess in some measure. And it is this: willingly or unwillingly, consciously or unconsciously, she has considered herself blessed in following in my footsteps, and has never stood in my way of my endeavour to lead a life of restraint. Though, therefore, there is a wide difference between us intellectually, I have always had the feeling that ours is a life of contentment, happiness and progress.[9]

[9]*Autobiography*, *CWMG*, Vol. 44, p. 297.

It seems, however, that Kasturba had little choice but to put up with her family situation without obvious complaint. There could be no real 'contentment' or 'happiness' in such a circumstance. In this, Gandhi showed himself to be very insensitive to his wife's emotional life.

His relationship with his eldest son, Harilal, and Gulab, his wife, was also a troubled one. Harilal was born in 1888, while Gandhi was a college student in Bhavnagar. During the boy's infancy he was away for three years in London. The father whom Harilal first learnt to look up to was the flourishing lawyer of the early years in South Africa, the patriarchal head of a prosperous and westernised family. This all changed radically when Gandhi decided to adopt a simple and austere way of life. He ordered his sons to wash their clothes, cook their own food, chop wood, work in the garden—even in the bitter cold of winter—and forced them to walk long distances rather than use means of transport.[10] Harilal found it extremely hard to adapt to this new regime. He wanted to go to university or study law, but Gandhi would not agree to this as he now held that such institutions were deeply corrupting. At the age of eighteen, Harilal escaped to India, where he hoped to create an independent life for himself. This proved difficult, for Gandhi had not given him a conventional education and he lacked paper qualifications. When Gandhi heard a rumour that he had married Gulab, the daughter of a leading Kathiawadi lawyer who was his friend, Gandhi retorted that he had ceased to think of Harilal as his son 'for the present at any rate'.[11] As Erik Erikson has asked in relation to this episode: how can a son cease to be such on a temporary basis? He sees this as one more example of the 'patriarchal bad manners' that characterised Gandhi's relationship with his eldest son.[12]

A year later, Harilal and Gulab were married. Gandhi told him to return to South Africa alone, but instead Harilal came with his new wife. Gandhi resented the obvious love the couple had for each other, and tried to take her in hand in an authoritarian way, causing her great emotional suffering. He was very annoyed when she became pregnant

[10]Louis Fischer, *The Life of Mahatma Gandhi*, Granada, St. Albans 1982, p. 265.

[11]Ibid., p. 263.

[12]Erikson, *Gandhi's Truth*, p. 243.

and later gave birth to a daughter, as this revealed that the couple were having sexual intercourse despite his injunctions.[13] He punished them by demanding that Harilal be the first to court arrest and go to jail during the satyagraha of 1908. Gandhi acted as his lawyer during his trial, insisting before the judge that the punishment should be as severe as possible.[14] In a public statement made a week later, he said that his twenty-year-old son was 'only a child' and that it was 'a part of Harilal's education to go to gaol for the sake of the country.'[15] Harilal spent nearly a year in prison in all, constantly anxious about Gulab. He had good reason to be, for Gulab developed an alarming cough, excruciating earache and sores all over her body.

Once out of jail, the relationship between father and son deteriorated further. Harilal still wanted to go to university. He objected to Gandhi's treatment of Kasturba, something Gandhi shrugged off by arguing that she did not know her own mind. In 1911, Harilal returned to India, and after some studies in Gujarat tried to establish himself in business in Calcutta. In 1915 the rest of the family followed him back to India, settling in Ahmedabad, a thousand miles away from Calcutta. In 1916 Gandhi's second son Manilal sent some money to relieve his brother's hardships. When Gandhi came to know of this he was furious and expelled him from the ashram. Manilal ended up back in South Africa, where he spent the rest of his days.[16]

Harilal then suffered a deep tragedy when Gulab died suddenly in the influenza epidemic of 1918, leaving him to look after their two daughters and two sons. He took to drink and was often seen to be inebriated in public. His business ran into difficulties in the early 1920s and he embezzled a large sum of money from a friend of his father. When Gandhi heard of this he denounced his son in his journal *Young India*. He stated that the two of them had been at odds for the past fifteen years:

[13]Robert Payne, *The Life and Death of Mahatma Gandhi*, The Bodley Head, London 1969, pp. 185–6.

[14]'Trial of Harilal Gandhi and Others', 28 July 1908, *CWMG*, Vol. 9, pp. 15–16.

[15]Letter to *Indian Opinion*, 8 August 1908, *CWMG*, Vol. 9, p. 42.

[16]Fischer, *The Life of Mahatma Gandhi*, pp. 264–5.

> There is much in Harilal's life that I dislike. He knows that. But I love him in spite of his faults. The bosom of a father will take him in as soon as he seeks entrance. For the present, he has shut the doors against himself. He must wander in the wilderness. The protection of a human father has its decided limitations. That of the Divine Father is ever open to him. Let him seek it and he will find it.[17]

The deity that Harilal eventually embraced was hardly the one that had been in Gandhi's mind, for in 1936 he underwent a conversion to Islam, becoming 'Abdulla Gandhi'. The ceremony of admission to the new faith took place in a Bombay mosque before a large audience, and the news was broadcast all over India.

By now, Gandhi realised that his son was a broken man, and his reaction was one of sadness rather than patriarchal rage, though he still felt compelled to moralise on the subject of conversion. He said that he had no objection to Harilal changing his religion in good faith, but he feared that it was done for selfish reasons.[18] He believed that Harilal had taken loans from some unscrupulous Pathans in Bombay, and they were taking their interest in the form of this 'conversion'. If this was the case:

> Harilal's apostasy is no loss to Hinduism and his admission to Islam a source of weakness to it, if, as I apprehend, he remains the same wreck that he was before. ... conversion is a matter between man and his Maker who alone knows His creatures' hearts. And conversion without a clean heart is, in my opinion, a denial of God and religion. Conversion without cleanness of heart can only be a matter for sorrow, not joy, to a godly person.[19]

Kasturba's reaction to her son's escapades was more direct and emotionally honest. After reading in a newspaper that he had been arrested by the police in Madras for drunk and disorderly behaviour in a public place at midnight, she wrote to him pleading that he change his ways:

[17]'A Domestic Chapter', *Young India*, 18 June 1925, *CWMG*, Vol. 32, pp. 17–18.

[18]Letter to Mirabehn, 30 May 1936, *CWMG*, Vol. 69, p. 59.

[19]Statement to the Press, 2 June 1936, *CWMG*, Vol. 69, p. 78.

> My dear son Harilal, ... I have been feeling very miserable ever since I heard about this incident ... I have been pleading with you all these long years to hold yourself in check. But you are going from bad to worse. Now you are making my very existence impossible. Think of the misery you are causing your aged parents in the evenings of their lives.
>
> Your father says nothing to anyone but I know the shocks you are giving him are breaking his heart. You are committing a great sin in thus repeatedly hurting our feelings. Though born as our son you are indeed behaving like an enemy.
>
> Every morning I rise with a shudder to think what fresh news of disgrace the newspapers will bring. I sometimes wonder where you are, where you sleep, what you eat. Perhaps you take forbidden food ... I often feel like meeting you. But I do not know where to find you.[20]

She told him also that his father loved him very deeply, and was prepared even now to look after him and to nurse him back to health. Kasturba also wrote a distressed letter to Harilal's Muslim friends, saying that they seemed to want 'to make his mother and father a laughing stock of the world ... I am writing this in the hope that the piteous cry of this sorrowing mother will pierce the heart of at least one of you, and you will help my son turn a new leaf.'[21]

Harilal's sad decline seems to have united the ageing father and mother in mutual grief. The anger of the old animosities faded away. But Kasturba's health had suffered, and there is little doubt that her death in jail in Pune in 1944 was hastened by her enduring sadness in this respect. When she lay dying, Harilal came to see her twice. On the first occasion she was overjoyed, but on the second he came drunk and she beat her forehead in anguish. He was removed and she never saw him again. Next day, she begged Devdas to look after Harilal's children. Gandhi was by her bed day and night, nursing her with devoted care and determined to be with her at the end, succeeding here where he had failed with his father. His wish was fulfilled, for she died in his arms on 22 February 1944. She was cremated next day, and Gandhi sat by the pyre from morning to evening. For weeks afterwards he was listless

[20]Fischer, *The Life of Mahatma Gandhi*, pp. 267–8.

[21]Payne, *The Life and Death of Mahatma Gandhi*, p. 474.

and ill.[22] From then until the end of his own life he observed a day of remembrance for her on the 22nd of each month, in which the entire *Bhagavad Gita* was recited at his early morning prayer.[23]

Gandhi continued to try to win back Harilal. In early 1947, he wrote to his son asking him to join him in East Bengal in his work for Hindu–Muslim unity. Harilal never replied.[24] Less than a year later, Harilal was in Delhi when his father was assassinated. His younger brother Ramdas lit the funeral pyre while he remained in the crowd an anonymous watcher. He was suffering from tuberculosis, and in less than six months time was himself dead.[25]

Gandhi and Sexual Desire

Gandhi interpreted his sexual desire for his young wife as a detraction from his duty towards his father. He also believed, following an old tradition in India, that a loss of semen drained a man's vitality. Erikson has pointed out: 'Where such imagery is dominant and some obsessive and phobic miserliness is added, as is universally the case in adolescents convinced that ejaculations are draining them, all sexual life assumes the meaning of depleting a man's essence.'[26] Once in public life, he began to see his sexuality as a hindrance in this sphere also. In this, he regarded his sexuality as a passion to be disciplined, rather than something that provided the basis for a relationship. Love, for him, was defiled by sexual intercourse.[27] In his autobiography he explains many of his early shortcomings and failures, both personal and political, in terms of his continuing sexual profligacy. Only after he had taken his vow of celibacy in 1906 could his full strength be realised. Typically, he took this momentous decision unilaterally, only consulting Kasturba

[22]Ibid., pp. 504–6.

[23]Nirmal Kumar Bose, *My Days with Gandhi*, Orient Longman, Calcutta 1974, p. 55.

[24]Payne, *The Life and Death of Mahatma Gandhi*, p. 526.

[25]Harilal died in a Bombay hospital on 19 June 1948, Fischer, *The Life of Mahatma Gandhi*, p. 490.

[26]Erikson, *Gandhi's Truth*, p. 120.

[27]Bhikhu Parekh, *Colonialism, Tradition and Reform: An Analysis of Gandhi's Political Discourse*, Sage Publications, New Delhi 1989, p. 183.

after he had made up his mind. He stated that she had no objection.[28] Even if she had objected, one doubts that he would have paid her any heed.

Gandhi was not the only Indian nationalist who was striving at that time to be chaste; it was an aspiration shared by many of those who followed the path of violent terrorism during those years. The latter can be seen to have internalised the colonizer's argument that an uncontrolled and lax sexuality had undermined the virility of the Indian people, allowing them to be conquered by a more manly race. Following Swami Vivekananda, they believed that sexual restraint would lead to moral regeneration. Gandhi was not impressed by this desire to build a more 'masculine' Indian persona. His aim was different, that of striving to assert the 'feminine' principles of love, selfless service and non-violence.[29]

For Gandhi, sexuality in men was a powerful, intrinsic force that could be mastered only by hard self-discipline. Sexuality in women, by contrast, lacked such power, for women were, in his eyes, naturally abstemious. He saw women as 'the mother of man' and 'too sacred for sexual love'.[30] Because he expected women to be pure and virtuous, he was harsh and unmerciful with those who failed in this respect. Thus, while on the one hand he placed women on a pedestal as 'sisters of mercy' and 'mothers of entire humanity', on the other he blamed them for luring men into immorality.[31] He refused to sanction the use of contraceptives, as they, in his opinion, encouraged sexual pleasure, profligacy and vice. A woman who used contraceptives was no better than a prostitute.[32]

He reserved a particular loathing for prostitutes, whom he saw as evil temptresses luring men to their ruin. When some prostitutes of

[28]*Autobiography*, *CWMG*, Vol. 44, p. 245.

[29]Parekh, *Colonialism, Tradition and Reform*, pp. 183–4.

[30]'My Life', *Harijan*, 4 November 1939, *CWMG*, Vol. 77, p. 61.

[31]Madhu Kishwar, 'Gandhi on Women, Part 1', *Economic and Political Weekly*, 5 October 1985, pp. 1694 and 1701; Sujata Patel, 'Construction and Reconstruction of Women in Gandhi', *Economic and Political Weekly*, 20 February 1988, p. 378.

[32]Madhu Kishwar, 'Gandhi on Women: Part 2', *Economic and Political Weekly*, 12 October 1985, p. 1755.

Barisal in Bengal asked to be allowed to join the Congress in 1920, he told them that there was no way that he could accept them while they continued in their calling. Madhu Kishwar says in this context: 'It is significant that Gandhi never displayed this kind of self-righteousness *vis-à-vis* better known exploiters of society. The doors of the Congress were not closed to even the most tyrannical of landlords or the most corrupt of businessmen.'[33]

In directing his rebukes at the prostitutes, rather than at their clients, Gandhi revealed a male fear of female sexuality. The idea of women luring men towards doom is of course an inverted understanding of the relationship of power actually experienced by such women. There were other occasions on which Gandhi applied such a logic. When, for example, a young male resident of the Tolstoy Farm in South Africa teased two young women, Gandhi felt that it was not enough to tell off the boy. 'I wished the two girls to have some sign on their person as a warning to every young man that no evil eye might be cast upon them, and as a lesson to every girl that no one dare assault their purity.'[34] After much thought he decided that the only way 'to sterilize the sinner's eye' was by their agreeing to have their hair cut off. They were at first unwilling to accept this, but Gandhi brought them round through pressure, and he himself cut off their hair. He claimed that the two young women gained by this experience and also 'hoped that young men still remember this incident and keep their eyes from sin.'[35] In this case, Gandhi was blaming girls who were being sexually harassed. His assumption was that the young men would not have acted as they did without some laxity on the part of the girls.

Gandhi himself was always in doubt as to his success in achieving full mastery over his passions. He set high standards for himself in this respect, being wracked by a sense of failure whenever he had an involuntary discharge of semen in his sleep. He assumed that he had not entirely conquered his desires.[36] This led to his experiment of 1946–7, when he sought to test his celibacy by sleeping with naked and nubile

[33]Kishwar, 'Gandhi on Women: Part 1', pp. 1693–4.

[34]*Satyagraha in South Africa*, *CWMG*, Vol. 34, p. 202.

[35]Ibid.

[36]Parekh, *Colonialism, Tradition and Reform*, pp. 186–8.

young women without feeling any sexual stirrings.[37] He did this at a time of great difficulty for India, when he felt a need to enhance his spiritual powers so as to be equal to the situation. His success in this respect (his advanced age could have been a factor in this) may have given him the moral strength to act with supreme courage—as he did—in the face of the terrible division and carnage of those years.[38] He does not, however, seem to have been concerned with the psychological effects that this experiment might have on the young women with whom he slept, such as nineteen-year-old Manu, his cousin's granddaughter.[39]

Marriage and Patriarchy

The British had always been highly critical of the way in which women were treated in India, seeing it as one of the chief markers of Indian social and cultural 'backwardness'. Indian social reformers had responded to this by demanding a ban on sati, an end to child-marriage and an acceptance of widow remarriage by high-caste Hindus. They had deplored the illiteracy and ignorance of women in India, and had sought to create a 'new woman' who was literate, cultured and pure. She was to be a well-informed companion and a model wife for her husband, a teacher for her children, and an exemplary manager for the household as a whole. In this way, she would take her place as a worthy yet subordinate citizen of the nation. As Uma Chakravarty puts it: 'the interlocking of an indigenous patriarchy with new forms of patriarchy brought in by the colonial state produced a situation where apparently spaces opened up for women but were simultaneously restricted.'[40]

Gandhi's own thoughts on the women's question were rooted in this patriarchal agenda. The first major statement that he made on the subject after his return to India in 1915 was at an educational conference in Gujarat in October 1917. He focused, appropriately given the venue,

[37]Bose, *My Days with Gandhi*, p. 150.

[38]Parekh, *Colonialism, Tradition and Reform*, p. 202.

[39]Kishwar, 'Gandhi on Women: Part 2', p. 1756.

[40]Uma Chakravarty, *Rewriting History: The Life and Times of Pandita Ramabai*, Kali for Women, New Delhi 1998, pp. 174–5. See also pp. 82–94, 203–9 and 224.

on the need for education for women. It had, however, to be an education with a difference:

> As Nature has made men and women different, it is necessary to maintain a difference between the education of the two. True, they are equals in life, but their functions differ. It is woman's right to rule the home. Man is master outside it. Man is the earner, woman saves and spends. Woman looks after the feeding of the child. She shapes its future. She is responsible for building its character. She is her children's educator, and hence, mother to the Nation ...
>
> If this is the scheme of Nature, and it is just as it should be, woman should not have to earn her living. A state of affairs in which women have to work as telegraph clerks, typists or compositors can be, I think, no good, such a people must be bankrupt and living on their capital.[41]

He went on to deplore the custom of child-marriage that stood in the way of the education of women. The young wife became merely a household drudge and was unable to provide adequate companionship to a husband. He deplored those men who treated their wives as they would an animal and condemned the couplet attributed to Tulsidas: 'The drum, the fool, the Sudra, the animal and the woman—all these need beating,' arguing that it was either a later interpolation or the poet was merely mouthing the prejudices of his time without any reflection. 'We must fight this impression and pluck out from its very root the general habit of regarding women as inferior beings.'[42] Four months later he stated that the maltreatment of women by even the most ignorant and worthless of men impoverished the Indian spirit. Nationalists were to go out and educate women.[43]

Gandhi believed strongly in the institution of marriage, which he saw as a bastion of morality. He refused to consider the relationship between husband and wife as being in any way hierarchical, arguing that it should be considered a partnership between equals. Because of this, men had no right to make sexual claims on their wives without

[41]Speech at Second Gujarat Educational Conference, Bharuch, 20 October 1917, *CWMG*, Vol. 16, p. 93.

[42]Ibid., pp. 94–5.

[43]Speech at Bhagini Samaj, Bombay, 20 February 1918, *CWMG*, Vol. 16, p. 274.

their consent.[44] Until the 1930s, Gandhi preferred that marriages be within broad caste bounds, but in his later years he came round to the view that caste mattered less than compatibility. He was however opposed to marriage customs that he saw as being demeaning towards women. He condemned child marriages, on the grounds that if the child-husband should die, the girl was left a widow for life. He believed that child-widows should be allowed to remarry. In the case of adult widows, he preferred that they should remain unmarried and chaste, but if this proved too hard to maintain, they should remarry. He was opposed also to expensive marriage celebrations and dowries, preferring instead simple weddings, with garlanding of the couple in front of friends and relatives. At the time, this was known as *Gandhi lagan* (Gandhian marriage). Women were also encouraged to stop wearing jewellery, to wear clothes of simple and cheap khadi, and not to overdress. He was opposed to the practice of purdah for women. He also encouraged families to cook simple food so as to save women from drudgery. He also sought to counter the pressure placed on wives to produce children by valorising marriages in which the partners remained chaste. At one wedding, he blessed the couple with the words: 'May you have no children.'[45]

Gandhi was a strong believer in the sanctity of the family, and saw marriage, like religion, as a force for 'restraint'.[46] In this, he failed to take into account the fact that almost the entire burden of restraint rested on women, any failure on their part being punished severely, while the misdemeanours of husbands were generally overlooked. He argued that women could fight oppression within the family through satyagraha against the men, and although he knew that men often enforced their will in a vicious manner, he was confident that the strength of the women would in most cases prevail. He even stated that women who were faced with rape should prefer to give up their lives rather than surrender their virtue and chastity.[47] In this, he once again placed the chief onus for moral behaviour on women rather than men. This

[44] *Harijan*, 5 May 1946. Quoted in Terchek, *Gandhi*, p. 66.

[45] Kishwar, 'Gandhi on Women: Part 1,' pp. 1692–3 and 1696; 'Gandhi on Women: Part 2', pp. 1754–5.

[46] 'Abolish Marriage!', *Young India*, 3 June 1926, *CWMG*, Vol. 35, p. 144.

[47] Kishwar, 'Gandhi on Women: Part 1', pp. 1691 and 1700.

may be taken as a compliment to women, but it seems unreasonable and unfair for Gandhi to have expected women to bear the major burden in such matters.

So committed was Gandhi to the institution of marriage that he even stated in 1917 that children born outside wedlock were like vermin who should not be preserved. For this reason, he had no time for orphanages that brought up such children. In the words of Madhu Kishwar, 'it is hard to comprehend the violence of thought underlying this sentiment considering that he never used similar language or expressed such sentiments against well known exploiters of society, and would not have condoned violence against them as he does against little babies who could not by any stretch of imagination be held responsible for being born of people who refused to take responsibility for them.'[48] Gandhi also revealed his patriarchal sentiments over the matter of defending family or community honour. In disputes over matters of honour, women were frequently made to bear the burden of family or community honour. It was believed to be particularly shaming if a family or community could not defend its female members from sexual violation, rape or murder. Rather than condemn a mentality which made women the prime bearers of such 'honour', Gandhi surrendered to his patriarchal prejudices by arguing that a father would in such circumstances be justified in killing his daughter: 'it would be the purest form of *ahimsa* on my part to put an end to her life and surrender myself to the fury of the incensed ruffian.'[49]

He seems to have modified his opinions on this issue to some extent during the last decade of his life. In 1942 he stated that there was absolutely no justification for holding a woman to blame for being raped and subjecting her to social ostracism as a result: 'Whilst the woman has in point of fact lost her virtue, the loss cannot in any way render her liable to be condemned or treated as an outcast. She is entitled to our sympathy for she has been cruelly injured and we should tend her wounds as we would those of any injured person.'[50] He even said

[48]Kishwar, 'Gandhi on Women: Part 2', p. 1757.

[49]*Young India*, 4 October 1928, in Terchek, *Gandhi*, p. 207.

[50]'Criminal Assaults,' *Harijan*, 1 March 1942, *CWMG*, Vol. 82, p. 41.

that it was acceptable for women to fight back against rapists: 'When a woman is assaulted she may not stop to think in terms of *himsa* or ahimsa. Her primary duty is self-protection. She is at liberty to employ every method or means that come to her mind in order to defend her honour. God has given her nails and teeth. She must use them with all her strength and, if need be, die in the effort.'[51] Men, likewise, were entitled to use violence to prevent a woman being raped.

During the partition period of 1947 there were many cases in which men killed the women of their families rather than have them 'shamed'. In cases in which women were abducted or raped (and rape was assumed whether or not it had occurred), they were commonly rejected by their families as being 'dishonoured'. When confronted with the suffering caused through this logic of 'honour', Gandhi issued repeated appeals to families to accept back with an open heart any women members who had been abducted, stating: 'I hear women have this objection that the Hindus are not willing to accept back the recovered women because they say that they have become impure. I feel that this is a matter of great shame. These women are as pure as the girls who are sitting by my side. And if any one of those recovered women should come to me, then I will give them as much respect and honour as I accord to these young maidens.'[52] No longer, it seems, was he so sure that women deserved to bear the blame for the sexual crimes of men.

Women and Satyagraha

The most significant respect in which Gandhi went beyond the agenda of the nineteenth-century social reformers was in his injunction that women should play an active role in their own emancipation through satyagraha. In a letter of June 1917 he reminded his followers of the bhakti *sant* Mirabai, who, he said, had waged satyagraha against her husband to maintain her chastity, converting him into a devotee through her moral power.[53] He also invoked Sita, who, he claimed, maintained

[51]Ibid., p. 42.

[52]Urvashi Butalia, *The Other Side of Silence: Voices from the Partition of India*, Penguin Books, India 1998, p. 160.

[53]Letter to Esther Faering, 11 June 1917, *CWMG*, Volume 15, p. 436.

her purity by standing up to both Ravana and Ram.[54] He believed very strongly that women who wished to remain chaste should follow the example of Mirabai and refrain from sexual intercourse, even if they were married and had to resist their husband's will in this respect. He praised those women who had made a decision to remain unmarried and chaste throughout life—serving society rather than a family—in the process resisting the huge social pressures there were to get married.

In this respect, Gandhi's emphasis on celibacy, or brahmacharya, had a particular value for women, for it could provide a means for resisting male domination in a way that was legitimised in their culture. For men, it could provide a mark of their commitment to a non-exploitative and equal relationship with women. Critics of Gandhi's brahmacharya tend to ignore this issue and focus on the admittedly problematic matter of his beliefs about male semen and moral power. While Bhikhu Parekh, for example, raises legitimate questions about the efficacy of such beliefs, which he labels as 'largely mystical and almost certainly false', he takes an over-optimistic and gendered view of male sexuality: 'A man who assigns [sexuality] its proper place in life and gratifies it within limits is far more at peace with himself and free of its domination than one locked in a mortal battle with it.'[55] This argument is clearly gendered—a man speaks for his own. It presumes that male sexuality is essentially benign, failing to understand that in a patriarchal society the 'limits' which men define serve their interests rather than women, so that what is 'proper in life' becomes the routine exploitation of women. Gandhi knew that the only effective limit in such a society was strong self-control and moral self-discipline.

Gandhi believed that women had a moral power that was particularly suited to satyagraha. 'To call a woman the weaker sex is a libel; it is man's injustice to woman. If by strength is meant brute strength, then indeed is woman less brute than man. If by strength is meant moral power, then woman is immeasurably man's superior. Has she not greater intuition, is she not more self-sacrificing, has she not greater powers of endurance, has she not greater courage?'[56] Gandhi scorned the extremist

[54]Kishwar, 'Gandhi on Women: Part 1', p. 1691.

[55]Parekh, *Colonialism, Tradition and Reform*, pp. 182–3.

[56]'To the Women of India', *Young India*, 10 April 1930, *CWMG*, Vol. 39, p. 57.

nationalists' attempts to revive a 'male' vigour in India as a counter to the masculinity of British colonialism. In his opinion, this could lead only to violence and hatred.[57] He preferred to stress the 'female' principle of non-violence. Ashis Nandy has argued in this respect that Gandhi 'rediscovered' womanhood as a civilizing force in human society. He holds that Gandhi's role model was above all his mother, who combined a strong religious faith with confidence in her power to have her own way within the family. In valorising such 'female' values, Gandhi was taking on both a patriarchal Sanskritic tradition that devalued woman, and also the colonial valorisation of masculinity. In its place he combined elements of Indian folk culture that celebrated the female principle with a Christian belief that the meek would inherit the earth. Like St. Francis he wanted to be the bride of Christ.[58] Or, we may add, like that of the young cowherd women—the gopis—whose love for Krishna became spiritual rather than physical once they experienced his true being.[59]

Although Gandhi argued that women were best suited for domestic life, he also encouraged them to participate in political activity as the equals of men. At the Gujarat Political Conference at Godhra in 1917 he said that in not including women in their movement they were walking on one leg.[60] During the Kheda Satyagraha of 1918, Gandhi made a point of encouraging women to become involved. He insisted on women sharing the platform with him during meetings—women such as Anandibai, a widow from Pune, who told the audience in Karamsad village that she wished she held land in Kheda so that she could also refuse her taxes and risk having it confiscated.[61] When, on one occasion, Gandhi saw that only men were attending a meeting, he

[57]Dalton, *Mahatma Gandhi*, p. 40.

[58]Ashis Nandy, 'Final Encounter: The Politics of the Assassination of Gandhi', in Ashis Nandy, *At the Edge of Psychology: Essays in Politics and Culture*, Oxford University Press, New Delhi 1993, pp. 73–4.

[59]As Parekh has pointed out, this relationship became inverted at times, with many of Gandhi's female followers relating to him as a *gopi* would to Krishna. Parekh, *Colonialism, Tradition and Reform*, pp. 205–6.

[60]*Secret Bombay Presidency Police Abstract of Intelligence*, Bombay 1917, p. 938.

[61]Shankarlal Parikh, *Khedani Ladat*, Rashtriya Sahitya Karyalay, Ahmedabad 1922, p. 150.

rebuked the audience: 'It was my hope that women also would be present at this meeting. In this work there is as much need of women as men. If women join our struggle and share our sufferings, we can do fine work.'[62] In some cases, special meetings were held for women.[63]

Gandhi's emphasis on hand-spinning from 1920 onwards gave legitimacy to womens' activity and allowed them to participate in the struggle in a new way. He stated that in matters concerning swadeshi, women should put the interest of the nation before even that of their husbands. The nation was thus considered to have precedence over the household.[64] Gandhi also encouraged women to take a leading role in the picketing of liquor shops during the Non-Cooperation movement of 1921–2.[65] This campaign struck a chord with many women, who resented the fact that their husbands squandered their hard-earned incomes on drink rather than provide for their families. Also, their intoxicated husbands often beat them up. Gandhi believed that the presence of women on the picket line helped sustain an atmosphere of non-violence, while at the same time it deterred 'undesirable characters' from joining the protest.[66] Encouraged by the evidence of this new spirit of assertion, he looked forward in July 1921 to the day when 'women begin to affect the political deliberations of the nation', and stated that they should be given the vote and a legal status equal to men.[67]

Women were soon even taking the initiative in protests. During the Bardoli Satyagraha of 1928, for example, Vallabhbhai Patel had advised women not to join the picket lines on one particular occasion as he feared that the police intended to beat up or even fire on the protesters. One woman later recalled: 'Undeterred by the warnings given by Sardar Patel, I led a group of fifty sisters in spite of promulgation of the article under Section 144, broke through the police cordon and joined the picket lines. I was arrested along with twenty-four of my sisters. This

[62] Speech at Uttarsanda, 6 April 1918, *CWMG*, Vol. 16, p. 396.

[63] Parikh, *Khedani Ladat*, p. 221; *Bombay Chronicle*, 30 April 1918, p. 9.

[64] Patel, 'Construction and Reconstruction of Women in Gandhi', p. 380.

[65] 'Women as Pickets', *Young India*, 28 July 1921, *CWMG*, Vol. 24, pp. 15–6.

[66] 'My Notes', *Navajivan*, 31 July 1921, *CWMG*, Vol. 24, p. 33.

[67] 'Position of Women', *Young India*, 21 July 1921, *CWMG*, Vol. 23, p. 469.

was my most unforgettable experience of the satyagraha.'[68] Women's participation in the struggle was taken onto a new plane during the Civil Disobedience movement of 1930–1. Gandhi had initially stated that only men should break the salt laws, but his women followers refused to accept this decree and went ahead and manufactured salt on a large scale. As Usha Mehta says: 'I remember, during the salt *satyagraha*, many women of all ages came out to join the movement. Even our old aunts and great-aunts and grandmothers used to bring pitchers of salt water to their houses and manufacture illegal salt. And then they would shout at the top of their voices: "We have broken the salt Law!"'[69]

Women also took out early morning processions, known as *prabhat pheris*, when they walked through the streets of their towns and villages singing religious and nationalist songs. Because such processions were normally of a purely religious nature, the authorities were reluctant to clamp down on them lest they be accused of religious persecution.

The anti-liquor campaign reached fresh heights in 1930–1. Due to some violence by male picketers during the 1921–2 movement, Gandhi insisted in 1930 that anti-liquor protest should be the preserve of women satyagrahis. Kasturba Gandhi played a prominent role in this campaign, organising the cutting down of around 25,000 toddy trees during the period of the salt satyagraha, and picketing government auctions of liquor shops. In many cases, not a single licence was sold, and in some areas liquor revenues dwindled to almost nothing. The women also attended religious and social functions and urged the people to forsake liquor.[70]

In Ahmedabad city, the Rashtriya Stree Sabha (Nationalist Women's Organisation) launched an intensive swadeshi campaign, which involved almost daily processions of khadi-clad women through the streets singing

[68]Amrut Nakhre, *Social Psychology of Non Violent Action: A Study of Three Satyagrahas*, Chanakya Publications, Delhi 1982, p. 143.

[69]Zareer Masani, *Indian Tales of the Raj*, 1987, quoted in Rozina Visram, *Women in India and Pakistan: The Stuggle for Independence from British Rule*, Cambridge University Press, Cambridge 1992, pp. 27–8.

[70]Frederick Fisher, *That Strange Little Brown Man Gandhi*, Orient Longman, New Delhi 1970, pp. 142 and 148.

patriotic songs, house-to-house collection of foreign cloth which was then burnt in public, the distribution of cyclostyled sheets from door to door, and picketing of shops selling foreign cloth. They also picketed liquor shops—which could be hazardous, as they were subject to abuse by men who wanted to buy liquor. They had however strength in numbers, and many felt exhilarated and empowered in their new public role. Although the police were at first reluctant to arrest women, increasing numbers were sent to prison, becoming celebrated public figures in the process.[71]

As the movement progressed, and more and more of the male participants were arrested and jailed, women came increasingly to the fore. By early 1931, the authorities, frustrated by their inability to break the spirit of resistance, moved onto the offensive against women. The situation became ugly in Gujarat after a seventeen-year-old inmate of Gandhi's ashram in Ahmedabad called Lilavati Asar organised a routine procession of women through the town of Borsad in Kheda District on 15 January. She was arrested, taken to the police station and slapped on the face until she passed out. The police claimed later that she was a hysterical girl, subject to fainting fits.[72] She was then taken to the Sabarmati prison in Ahmedabad. A local woman from Kheda called Benaktiben organised another procession in Borsad on 21 January to protest against the treatment meted out to Lilavati; 1,500 women from 31 different villages participated. They were mostly from the locally dominant caste of Patidar peasants, who were at that time supporting the struggle by refusing to pay their land tax. As soon as they had assembled, the police charged them and beat them with their lathis and rifle butts, at the same time showering them with sexual abuse. Women who fell to the ground were kicked by heavy police boots, or pulled by the hair. The women later stated that the police were reeking of alcohol. Kasturba Gandhi visited the women four days later and saw their cuts and bruises. She stated that: 'This is the first occasion in my life, when I have seen such inhuman treatment meted out to

[71]Aparna Basu, *Mridula Sarabhai: Rebel with a Cause*, Oxford University Press, New Delhi 1996, pp. 34–6.

[72]This particular allegation was reported in *The Times of India*, 10 February 1931, p. 19.

ladies in Gujarat ...', or for that matter, she added, anywhere in India.[73]

The *Borsad Satyagraha Patrika* later published a list of 115 injured women who came from nineteen different villages. The ages of 61 of them were given—the youngest was 15 and the oldest 65. Their overall average age was 25.[74] One of them, sixteen-year-old Kashiben Trikambhai Patel of Bochason, stated that:

> When Madhumati Ben was being beaten I tried to protect the [national] flag when I was given a blow on the left shoulder and was dragged by the hair so forcibly that I fell on the ground. Before falling down, I was given 2 or 3 blows by hand on my cheek, and some blows on the loin. I tried to get up when I got 3 pushes on the chest. They again caught hold of my hair and made me stand. Three blows on the left foot: six to seven on the right thigh and one blow on the back. After receiving two pushes of the butt-end of the rifles, I fainted.[75]

Gangaben Vaidya, an older woman who was on the managing board of Gandhi's ashram, recounted how she had been beaten until blood poured from her head: 'The other sisters bore the blows with exemplary bravery. In some case the assaults were outrageous, many being kicked on their chests with the heels of the policemen's boots. Not one budged an inch, everyone stood unflinching at her post. Whereupon came this sudden access of courage and strength, I wonder. God was with us I am sure. He gave us the strength.'[76] Gandhi praised her fulsomely in his reply: 'How shall I compliment you? You have shown that you are what I had always thought you were. How I would have smiled with pleasure to see your sari made beautiful with stains of blood. I got excited when I knew about this atrocity, but I was not pained in the least. On the contrary, I felt happy.'[77]

[73]*Bombay Chronicle*, 30 January 1931, pp. 13 & 15; *Times of India*, 4 February 1931, p. 11.

[74]Suba, Baroda Division to Manager, Huzur Political Office, Baroda, 9 February 1931, Baroda Records Office, Huzur Political Office file 189 of 1930–1, p. 51.

[75]Servants of India Society Report on the Borsad Incident, published in *The Bombay Chronicle*, 24 February 1931, p. 7.

[76]Letter from Gangaben Vaidya, January 1931, *CWMG*, Vol. 51, p. 442.

[77]Letter to Gangaben Vaidya, 2 February 1931, *CWMG*, Vol. 51, p. 94.

During this period, women from all parts of India proved themselves the equal of the male freedom fighters, and in many cases their superior. In the process, they gained a new sense of empowerment. In the words of Aruna Asaf Ali:

> Gandhiji's appeal was something elemental. At last, a woman was made to feel the equal of man; that feeling dominated us all, educated and non-educated. The majority of women who came into the struggle were not educated or westernised ... The real liberation or emancipation of Indian women can be traced to this period, the 1930s. Earlier, there had been many influences at work, many social reformers had gone ahead, it was all in the air. But no one single act could have done what Gandhiji did when he first called upon women to join and said: 'They are the better symbols of mankind. They have all the virtues of a *satyagrahi*.' All that puffed us up enormously and gave us a great deal of self-confidence.[78]

The Critique of Patriarchy

Fellow nationalists and women activists never subjected Gandhi to any strong criticism for his patriarchal attitudes. In this, we find a contrast to his other major fields of work, in which sharp differences were expressed in a way that forced him to often qualify or modify his position. His close women followers in his ashram and elsewhere revered him as 'father', accepting his patriarchal persona without a murmur. More independent women nationalists never took up this issue. Notable in this respect was Sarojini Naidu, a woman of intellect and power who had fought with success for the women's franchise and who served as President of the Congress in 1925. She described Gandhi as 'my father, my leader, my master'.[79] The strongest dissent came from within his own family, but this was brushed aside as being informed by ignorance in the case of Kasturba and immorality in the case of Harilal. We shall never know how Gandhi might have responded to a strong feminist critique.

[78]Zareer Masani, *Indian Tales of the Raj*, 1987, quoted in Visram, *Women in India and Pakistan*, p. 23.

[79]Sarojini Naidu, *Selected Poetry and Prose*, edited by Makarand Paranjape, Harper Collins, New Delhi 1995, p. 195.

There have, however, been subsequent critiques from a broadly feminist perspective. Madhu Kishwar, as we have seen, points out the 'age-old patriarchal bias' that informed his attitude towards women.[80] Despite her specific criticisms, she holds that Gandhi was far more radical in his actions than in his theory, for he provided an unprecedented role for women in political work. And not only this—he asserted that women were superior to men as satyagrahis.[81] By 1931, she asserts, Gandhi's initiative in this respect was so accepted that the Congress was able to pass a resolution committing itself to the equal rights of women.[82]

Although it is true that many women gained a new self-confidencc and pride through their nationalist work, their participation failed to shake the structure of patriarchy in any very profound way. In an article on women in the nationalist movement in Bengal, Tanika Sarkar, also writing from a feminist perspective, has described the unprecedented degree of public protest by women during the Civil Disobedience Movement there. They took part in processions, picketing and blockading of roads with their own bodies to prevent the passage of police vehicles. When male satyagrahis were arrested, women took their place, and some became the local 'dictators' of the movement. This lead to brutal counter-reprisals, involving insults, molestation, beating and even firing, with one young Mahisya woman, Urmilaben Paria, being shot dead. Sarkar argues that all of this became possible because such militancy was depicted as being almost a religious duty at that time.

> The most crucial element in dovetailing the feminine role with nationalist politics was perhaps the image of Gandhi as a saint or even a religious

[80]Kishwar, 'Gandhi on Women: Part 1', p. 1691.

[81]Ibid.

[82]Ibid., p. 1697. The 1931 resolution of the Congress stated that every citizen of India had a fundamental right to equality before the law 'regardless of caste, creed or sex.' The position of women was one element in a more general statement of principle; this was not a specific pro-woman initiative, as Kishwar makes out. See P. Sitaramayya, *The History of the Indian National Congress (1885–1935)*, Congress Working Committee, Madras 1935, p. 780. Also, the crucial battle in this respect had been for the right for Indian women to have the vote. Women activists fought for this during the 1917–19 period, leading to enfranchisement during the 1920s. This victory had nothing to do with the mobilisation of women in satyagrahas as such. See Visram, *Women in India and Pakistan*, pp. 31–4.

> deity and the perception of the patriotic struggle as an essentially religious duty. According to this perception, joining the Congress agitation would not really be politicisation, a novel and doubtful role for women, but sharing a religious mission—a role deeply embedded in a tradition sanctified by the example of Meera Bai and the 'sanyasinis'. The stress on the personal saintliness of Gandhi, a subtle symbiosis between the religious and the political in the nationalist message under his leadership, enabled nationalism to transcend the realm of politics and elevate itself to a religious domain.[83]

In this, Sarkar argues, Gandhi was in certain respects in tune with a tradition going back to Bankimchandra and the extremist nationalists, in which the country became a part of the Hindu pantheon as the highest deity of all—the Motherland. Women were linked to this, as an embodiment of the Shakti of the Mother Goddess. Through nationalism, this Shakti could be released. In the earlier manifestation, however, this Shakti was seen as a violent power. 'The Gandhian movement resolved the tension beautifully by retaining the religious content of nationalism while turning the movement non-violent and imparting it a gentle, patient, long-suffering, sacrificial ambience particularly appropriate for women. If the movement is non-violent then no dangerous, aggressive note is imparted to the feminine personality through participation.'[84]

The downside to this, from a feminist perspective, was that this militancy failed to mount any challenge to the institution of patriarchy.

> Whether in Gandhian movements or in more militant alternatives to it, nationalists rarely sought a permanent reversal of the customary role of women in and outside political action. Politicisation was internalised as a special form of sacrifice in an essentially religious process. The language, imagery and idiom of the entire nationalist protest remained steeped in tradition and religion as self-conscious alternatives to alien Western norms. And herein lay the paradox: such strong traditionalist moorings alone permitted the sudden political involvement of thousands

[83]Tanika Sarkar, 'Politics of Women in Bengal: The Conditions and Meaning of Participation', *The Indian Economic and Social History Review* 21:1 (1984), p. 98.

[84]Sarkar, 'Politics of Women in Bengal', p. 99.

of women. But that in its turn inhibited the extension of radicalism to other spheres of life.[85]

In Gujarat, too, the vigorous participation of women in the nationalist struggle failed to undermine prevailing patterns of patriarchy in any substantial manner. When I was carrying out interviews of peasant nationalists in the 1970s, I found it hard to gain access to women activists, even though they had played a prominent role in the struggle in 1930–1. The men commonly stated that they could tell me all I needed to know. If pressed, a woman who was known to have participated in the movement was sometimes summoned to the front room of the house. There was no equality in such a space, for while I and the males sat on chairs, the women normally sat on the ground, their heads covered in the presence of the patriarchs, speaking hesitantly and with inhibition. Only in a few exceptional cases, as with the remarkable widow Dahiba Patel, did I manage to obtain any worthwhile testimony through such means.[86] This experience revealed that power relationships in such families had not been altered in any profound way by women's participation in what was in other respects a 'freedom struggle'.

Sujata Patel, in another critique, has argued that there was a strong class and caste bias in Gandhi's prescriptions for women. Most of the women participants in the movement were, she states, from a middle-class, higher-caste background.[87] She criticises Gandhi's claim that women were more biologically suited to life in the home than working

[85]Ibid., p. 101.

[86]Dahiba Patel had persuaded her half-brother to resign his official post as headman, had taken the lead in her village in refusing to pay land-tax, and became the acknowledged leader of the protest there after her half-brother was arrested. She however denied that village women acted as a radical force in general; in most cases, she said, they followed the lead of their husbands. Interview with Dahiba Lallubhai Patel, Boriavi, Anand Taluka, Kheda District, 26 February 1977. In retrospect, I am very aware that I failed to address this issue at all adequately, and it circumscribes the history that was written as a result.

[87]Patel, 'Construction and Reconstruction of Women in Gandhi', p. 377. On this point, I might note that although it is probably true that the majority of women who went to jail were middle class, there is evidence that many peasant women took part in protests such as the salt satyagraha, the no-tax campaigns and forest satyagrahas.

outside it for wages, arguing that his understanding in these respects was that of an upper-caste and middle-class male, whose ideal woman was cloistered in the home. The stricture thus essentialised a sexual division of labour determined by class. It ignored the fact that the majority of Indian women of his day earned their livelihood through field-labour and factory-work and that most were compelled to do so through necessity. The only source of earning he could suggest for women was hand-spinning—something which could earn only very small sums of money in practice. Gandhi thus failed to provide any space within his movement for the economically independent woman.[88] Patel is also highly critical of his opinion that a woman had to make a choice between being either a housewife or a political worker dedicated to an unmarried life of service to the nation. In effect, this meant that women were left with a choice of either looking after the home as a wife, or working outside as an asexual being, in the process denying their biological being. Gandhi does not, in Patel's opinion, provide any grounds for a serious attack on patriarchy. She thus denies that Gandhi can be seen in any way as a messiah of the contemporary women's movement in India.[89]

Besides these critiques by intellectuals, it is important also to examine the way in which modern women activists and political workers have felt either empowered or reduced by Gandhi's legacy. I shall examine women's activism within the Gandhian tradition in the post-independence period in chapter eight, in relationship to the anti-liquor movement after independence and the struggle for peasant women to have the right to gain ownership of land through land reform. In the case of the former, there has been considerable militancy among women, though Gandhi's influence has been patchy. In the case of the latter, women who started within the Gandhian tradition launched a campaign for land for women against the advice of their male colleagues. There was therefore a strong debate, with the women's position being taken up and championed by feminists. In this case, as in others, the Gandhian tradition of resistance has been deployed as a means for

[88]Ibid., p. 379.

[89]Ibid., p. 386.

the empowerment of women, while his patriarchal beliefs are firmly rejected.

To conclude, Gandhi's approach to the question of women's emancipation was one that, on the whole, he shared with many male nationalists and social reformers of his day, namely that women should receive education, should not be married off early and should be allowed to remarry if widowed. He deplored the practice of seclusion and a rigid separation of the sexes. Like the social reformers, he believed that women were biologically more suited to a life in the home. Similarly, he was a strong defender of the institution of marriage, which he saw as inculcating a sense of morality. He believed that women had a duty to defend the honour of their family. He insisted that men should treat their wives with more consideration, advocating, for example, the easing of women's household work through a simple cuisine, and a curb on their sexual demands. The latter was a particularly significant and original intervention in a social milieu in which few women were in a position to resist the unwanted sexual advances of their husbands and other men. By valorizing sexual abstinence and celibacy for men and women, Gandhi provided a means for setting limits on this routine but gross form of exploitation. Gandhi also went further than most of his contemporaries in insisting that women should play an active and positive part in the nationalist movement. In left-led trade union protests of the 1920s and 1930s, for example, women's issues were consistently marginalized by the male leaders. Unlike Gandhi, these leaders did not even attempt to address women's issue in a serious manner.[90] In this way, the Gandhian movement stood out for the way in which it allowed many women in India to gain a new sense of empowerment.

Few feminists can, however, accept his prescriptions for women, arguing that they were rooted in a patriarchal ideology that would always prevent the full self-realisation of women. Gandhian patriarchy has, from this perspective, to be rejected in a wholesale manner. Some feminists would argue that this calls into question Gandhi and his legacy as a whole. Others, like Kishwar, refuse to take such a step, arguing that

[90]Sarkar, 'Politics of Women in Bengal', p. 94.

the negative elements of Gandhi's patriarchy were outweighed by the positive social and political benefits he helped achieve for women.

Patriarchy has survived as an institution in part through its coercive violence, but in part through its inculcation of strong ties of affection. The patriarch is at the same time feared, hated and loved. Such a dialectic has likewise informed the relationship of many Indians towards their own national 'father', and it is one that is likely to continue to resonate so long as patriarchy flourishes.

6

Dalit and Adivasi Assertion

The period of British colonial rule saw the forging of a series of wholly novel all-India collectivities, two of which in time came to be described as the 'Dalits' and the 'Adivasis'.[1] In the past, the groups that were later slotted into these categories occupied a series of positions in hierarchies that were relatively local in form. Those who now regard themselves to be Dalits (or 'the oppressed') were members of particular *jatis*, or sub-castes, who were considered to be at the lowest ends of the social scale. They themselves had their own internal hierarchies. In Gujarat, for example, a Dhed or Wankar regarded a Bhangi as of lower standing and ritually polluting.[2] The colonial state lumped all of these diverse jatis into a single monolithic all-India category. Groups that were seen to lie below a particular threshold of pollutability in caste terms were defined initially as the 'depressed classes' and, from 1909, the

[1]In using these terms to describe these groups in the past I am aware that my usage is anachronistic. However, rather than deploy a series of evolving terms—such as 'Untouchables', 'Depressed Classes', 'early tribes', 'Harijans', 'Scheduled Castes and Tribes' and the like—I have used the terms that these people commonly use to describe themselves in contemporary India. It will be clear from the text that other terms were used at different times. For a fuller justification of my usage as regards the Adivasis, see my book *The Coming of the Devi*, pp. 11–16. It should also be noted that there have been moves in recent years to build a wider 'Dalit' alliance of the oppressed that includes Adivasis. Generally, however, the two groups continue to regard themselves as distinct, and my usage here reflects this.

[2]Shalini Randeria, 'The Politics of Representation and Exchange among Untouchable Castes in Western India (Gujarat)', unpublished Ph.D. thesis, Freien Universität Berlin, 1992, pp. 102–35.

'Untouchables'.[3] The process was often arbitrary at the margins—in Gujarat, for example, the Vagharis, who were considered generally to be a low and polluting caste, were not classed as Untouchables, while the Dheds, Bhangis, Garudias, Khalpas and Sindhvas were.[4] Similar boundaries were established between Adivasis—the so-called 'tribals'—and non-Adivasis, with various communities being lumped together under the category of 'early tribes', in a manner that was again arbitrary at the margins.[5] As a whole, both the 'depressed classes' and 'early tribes' were placed in the category of 'Hindu', as opposed to Muslim, Christian or Parsi. This implied that a Dalit or Adivasi was not a Muslim, Christian, etc. by origin or nature.

From 1909 onwards, the British treated these various imagined collectivities as political constituencies that were expected to represent their particular interests in a unified way, becoming a congeries of lobbies within the liberal polity. This gave rise to a form of politics in which certain politicians sought to build careers by claiming to speak for these collectivities. This process meshed in complex ways with another very different development, that of new forms of self-assertion arising from within these most subaltern of communities. From the late nineteenth century onwards, there were a series of local movements that took the form of self-cleansing. Often they were initiated and led by inspired leaders who claimed to be in touch with God. In many cases, they involved a process of spiritual renewal, in which old beliefs were discarded and new values and deities embraced. The characteristic response of the local élites was to repress such strivings in an often brutal manner. In some cases, however, the subaltern groups sought and gained support from powerful sympathisers. Most notable in this respect were Christian missionaries, who suddenly found themselves—to their astonishment—being asked to provide guidance and leadership in movements of mass conversion to Christianity. From the second decade of the twentieth century onwards, leaders of the Indian nationalist struggle became increasingly called on to play such a role. Eager to build their

[3]Randeria, 'Politics of Representation', pp. 21–3.

[4]*Gazetteer of the Bombay Presidency*, Vol. IX, part I, *Gujarat Population: Hindus*, Government Central Press, Bombay 1901, pp. 331–47 & 510–18.

[5]Ibid., pp. 290–330.

constituencies as 'representatives' of the newly defined subaltern collectivities, these leaders seized the opportunity and claimed to speak for the 'depressed classes' or 'tribals'.

Of all the nationalist leaders, the one who became the foremost embodiment of such popular hopes and desires was Gandhi. Through his life and personal struggles, Gandhi forged a persona that resonated among the Indian masses in a manner that was unprecedented. Often, he himself was taken by surprise by the forms that this popular adulation took. He sought to distance himself, at times through denials of popular beliefs which circulated about his supposed miraculous powers;[6] at times through an irritated scolding of the tumultuous crowds which pressed about him eager for his darshan. Yet, still the people were drawn to him, bearing out V.N. Volosinov's maxim—'if a thought is powerful, convincing, significant, then obviously it has succeeded in contacting *essential* aspects in the life of the social group in question, succeeding in making a connection between itself and the basic position of that group in the *class struggle*, despite the fact that the creator of that thought might himself be wholly unaware of having done so.'[7] Gandhi sought to channel the hopes and dreams that he had aroused in this way into an orderly programme of constructive work that would integrate these communities within the nationalist movement. In doing so, he adopted the language of the all-India collectivity, claiming in particular to be the spokesman for 'Untouchables' throughout India. The history which ensued, and which is the subject of this chapter, involved a dialogue between Gandhi and the Dalits and Adivasis that in part voiced common desires, but which also became grounded at times on the emancipatory limitations of Gandhi's own programme, the élitism of many of his followers, and opposition to his message from within these very communities.

[6]Gandhi stated in 1928 that 'I don't know how the story about miraculous powers possessed by me has got abroad. I can only tell you that I am but an ordinary mortal susceptible to the same weakness, influences and the rest as every other human being and that I possess no extraordinary powers.' Letter to Barbara Bauer, 13 July 1928, *CWMG*, Vol. 42, p. 234.

[7]V.N. Volosinov, *Freudianism: A Marxist Critique*, Academic Press, New York 1976, p. 25.

Dalits

Gandhi had from the earliest years in South Africa strongly opposed the practice of treating certain communities as being ritually polluting. In this, he was in line with several Indian social reformers and religious leaders of the late nineteenth century, such as Dayanand Saraswati, Swami Vivekananda and B.G. Tilak. He saw the practice as a corruption of Hinduism. It also, he believed, revealed the hypocrisy of demands by high-caste Hindus for Indian self-determination, for they were not themselves prepared to offer the same to these lowest of subaltern communities.[8] By taking such a stand, Gandhi involved himself in a long and often acrimonious debate with orthodox Hindus on the one hand and, from the early 1930s onwards, with self-assertive leaders of the Dalits themselves on the other.

Although the institution of untouchability was inseparable from the caste system, Gandhi did not during his early years as a nationalist leader in India push his condemnation of the latter towards a critique of caste in general. Later, he was to be severely criticised for this by many Dalit activists. During the South African years, however, Gandhi had appeared to have little time for the caste system. He had been expelled from his own Baniya sub-caste for travelling overseas—considered a 'polluting' act at that time—and had never sought to gain readmission to the caste. In 1909, he condemned the caste system and 'caste tyranny'.[9] On his return to India he adopted a much softer line on the question. He denied that the caste system had harmed India, arguing that it was no more than a form of labour division, similar to occupational divisions all over the world.[10] It was in fact superior to class divisions, which were based on wealth primarily.[11] He also believed that reform could be brought about through caste organisations.[12]

[8]Parekh, *Colonialism, Tradition and Reform*, p. 215.

[9]Dalton, *Mahatma Gandhi*, p. 49.

[10]'Speech on Caste System, Ahmedabad', 5 June 1916, *CWMG*, Vol. 15, p. 226.

[11]'Caste "Versus" Class', *Young India*, 29 December 1920, *CWMG*, Vol. 22, p. 154.

[12]'The Hindu Caste System', *Bharat Sevak*, October 1916, *CWMG*, Vol. 15, p. 258.

He was influenced in this by his admiration at that time for caste associations such as the Patidar Yuvak Mandal, in which young Arya Samajist social reformers had sought to reform the Patidar caste and promote self-help educational activities.[13] He believed that marriage should be within caste.[14] In 1918 he clarified that by this he meant *varna*, rather than narrow jati.[15] In 1925 he was talking of the need for jatis to merge into varnas based on occupation.[16] In 1931 he condemned the jati system, but praised a fourfold varna system consisting of (1) imparters of knowledge, (2) defenders of the defenceless, (3) farmers or traders, (4) labourers. He believed now that there should be intermarriage.[17] He also endorsed interdining, including with Dalits.[18] In the mid-1930s, Gandhi moved towards a more radical critique of caste. This was largely in response to Ambedkar, as we shall see below. In 1935 he thus argued that *varnashram* no longer existed in practice and that: 'The present caste system is the very antithesis of varnashram. The sooner public opinion abolishes it the better.'[19] In 1936 he stated that the dowry system was an evil propped up by caste, and that if removing it meant breaking the bonds of the caste system, then he would endorse such a move.[20] By 1946 he was urging caste Hindu girls to marry Dalits.[21]

In all of this, Gandhi never compromised over the issue of untouchability, which he always regarded as an out-and-out perversion. He fought hard against the practice after his return to India in 1915. In the ashram that he established in Ahmedabad in 1915 he banned any observation of untouchability. However, he refused to force any inmate

[13]Bhatt, 'Caste and Political Mobilisation in a Gujarat District'.

[14]'The Hindu Caste System,' *Bharat Sevak*, October 1916, *CWMG*, Vol. 15, p. 259.

[15]Letter to "The Indian Social Reformer", 26 February 1919, *CWMG*, Vol. 17, pp. 320–1.

[16]'Invasion in the Name of Religion', *Navajivan*, 7 June 1925, *CWMG*, Vol. 31, pp. 445–6.

[17]'A Caste and Communal Question', *Young India*, 4 June 1931, *CWMG*, Vol. 52, p. 256.

[18]Dalton, *Mahatma Gandhi*, p. 52.

[19]'Caste Must Go', *Harijan*, 16 November 1935, *CWMG*, Vol. 68, p. 152.

[20]'Marriage by Purchase', *Harijan*, 23 May 1936, *CWMG*, Vol. 69, p. 31.

[21]Dalton, *Mahatma Gandhi*, p. 53.

to eat with a Dalit against their will, arguing that he had no reason to believe that eating in company promoted brotherhood in any way whatsoever.[22] In September 1915 Gandhi admitted a member of the Dhed (a Dalit) community to the ashram, causing great hostility within and outside the institution. Kasturba Gandhi was particularly upset.[23] During the Non-Cooperation Movement of 1921–2 he called on Hindus to 'remove the sin of untouchability', otherwise there would be no swaraj, even in a hundred years.[24]

After his release from jail in 1924, with the political struggle in the doldrums, Gandhi took up the issue of untouchability as a central concern. He debated the matter with orthodox Sanatanist Hindus. They provided textual evidence that justified the practice. He argued that what was at stake was morality, and he refused to accept the moral validity of such texts, arguing that they were no longer appropriate for the present times. Such an argument merely riled the orthodox; they accused Gandhi of being corrupted by Christian propaganda. Gandhi countered by arguing that Hinduism was not a text-based religion, but one that was rooted in moral precepts, and texts that conflicted with morality could be discounted. Neither side was prepared to yield any ground on the matter.[25]

During 1924–5 there was a protest by an Untouchable community of Kerala, the Iravas, against a ban on their using a street in front of a temple at Vaikam that was controlled by Nambudiri Brahmans. This was described as a 'satyagraha', and it in fact popularised the use of the term in Kerala, along with 'khadi' and 'ahimsa'.[26] Gandhi took up the issue, travelling to Kerala to negotiate with the Brahmans who controlled the temple. During the debate, one of them stated that the Iravas had been born as Untouchables because of their karma, for example because of their misdeeds in past lives, and that it was therefore God's will that

[22]'Draft Constitution for the Ashram', 20 May 1915, *CWMG*, Vol. 14, pp. 456–7.

[23]Letter to V.S. Srinivasa Sastri, 23 September 1915, *CWMG*, Vol. 15, p. 46.

[24]Parekh, *Colonialism, Tradition and Reform*, pp. 215–16.

[25]Ibid., pp. 217–20.

[26]Robin Jeffrey, 'A Sanctified Label—"Congress" in Travancore Politics, 1938–48', in D.A. Low (ed.), *Congress and the Raj: Facets of the Indian Struggle 1917–47*, Heinemann, London 1977, p. 446.

they be excluded from the precincts of the temple. Gandhi took a soft line on this, accepting that the Iravas were indeed victims of karma, but he added that humans had no right to add to the punishment awarded by God. He thus refrained from condemning the whole baggage of beliefs that justified such discrimination.[27]

In this, Gandhi was adopting a position of seeking to reform Hindu practice from within, rather than attack it from the outside. His aim was to bring about a gradual delegitimisation of the practices of such Brahman priests. In Vaikam, the latter had showed themselves up when their representative had pleaded before him pathetically: 'Mahatmaji, we beseech you to prevent Avarnas [Untouchables] from depriving us of our old privileges.'[28] The heart of the matter thus stood revealed—theology provided no more than a cover for social privilege.

Gandhi was reluctant to involve the state in this process of soul-searching from within, as he felt that this would not bring about any profound change of heart among the orthodox. Persuasion was the best method. Educated leaders of the Dalits saw this approach as too gradualist. They saw that the Vaikam Satyagraha had achieved only limited results—the road past the temple was shifted, so although Iravas could now use it, they did so at a distance from the holy place. They were certainly not allowed entry into the temple. B.R. Ambedkar, who was emerging in the 1920s as a powerful young leader of the Dalits of Maharashtra, praised Gandhi for his work for Untouchables—far surpassing that of any other major Indian nationalist leader—but felt that he needed to take a far more radical stance. He noted that the Brahmans at Vaikam had used the Hindu scriptures to justify their position, and regretted that Gandhi had not subjected these pernicious texts to a rigorous criticism.[29]

Ambedkar then extended the Gandhian approach into a new area, that of highlighting the civil rather than religious discrimination suffered by Untouchables. He launched a satyagraha at Mahad in the Konkan

[27]The interchange between Gandhi and the Brahman is set out in full in Eleanor Zelliot, *From Untouchable to Dalit: Essays on the Ambedkar Movement*, Manohar, New Delhi 1996, p. 161.

[28]Ibid., p. 161.

[29]Ibid., p. 163.

in 1927 in which Dalits asserted their right to use a public tank in the Brahman quarter of the town. The protesters invoked the name of Gandhi, displaying his portrait. Around ten thousand Dalits came from all over Maharashtra to participate, and Ambedkar led a procession to the tank and drank water from it. The Brahmans ceremoniously re-purified the tank after they had gone, and then secured a court injunction that temporarily banned Ambedkar and three of his colleagues from using the tank. Another meeting was held at Mahad at which Ambedkar staged a public burning of the *Manusmrti*—the text *par excellence* of Brahmanical privilege. He did not however defy the injunction by drinking from the tank. He preferred to fight the matter out in court, a long-drawn-out process that went eventually in his favour after three years.[30]

In 1929 Ambedkar took the fight to the heart of Brahmanical power in Maharashtra, launching a satyagraha in Pune city to gain entry to the Parvati temple. Gandhi did not approve of this, believing it to be too confrontational a move. The right-wing Congressmen M.M. Malaviya and Jamnalal Bajaj were sent to investigate; they reported that the affair was causing great resentment in Maharashtra, and they condemned it. Without Congress support, the satyagraha failed, leaving Ambedkar and his followers bitter. The same happened with a further satyagraha which began in 1930 in the pilgrimage town of Nasik. The Dalits of Maharashtra began to doubt Gandhi's commitment to their cause as well as the efficacy of satyagraha.[31]

This distrust was compounded by the way in which Gandhi related to Ambedkar during these years. On their first meeting in Bombay in August 1931, Gandhi treated Ambedkar in a brusque manner, believing that he was a Brahman who was claiming to speak for Untouchables in a questionable manner.[32] They were in contact with each other again across the negotiating table at the Second Round Table Conference in London in late 1931. Although Gandhi now knew that he was an Untouchable, he continued to question his status as a spokesman for

[30]Ibid., pp. 68–9; Omvedt, *Dalits and the Democratic Revolution*, pp. 151–2.

[31]Zelliot, *From Untouchable to Dalit*, pp. 163–5.

[32]Mahadev Desai, *The Diary of Mahadev Desai*, Vol. 1, *Yeravda-Pact Eve, 1932*, Navajivan Publishing House, Ahmedabad 1953, p. 52.

the community. When Ambedkar argued that Untouchables should be granted separate seats in the proposed constitutional reforms—something Muslims had already been granted—Gandhi asserted: 'I say that it is not a proper claim which is registered by Dr Ambedkar when he seeks to speak for the whole of the Untouchables of India ... I myself in my own person claim to represent the vast mass of the Untouchables.'[33] When in 1932 the British announced that they accepted Ambedkar's demand, and that there would be separate electorates for Untouchables, Gandhi launched a fast to death in opposition. He had a strong case—distinct electorates for Muslims had undoubtedly been divisive, creating as they did a class of politicians whose basis was that of a separatist politics. Ambedkar's own position also had a strong justification: the interests of Dalits, who were in a minority everywhere, would be submerged in the politics of the majority. These substantial points of difference were however overlain by much personal rancour. Gandhi appears to have resented Ambedkar as an upstart. In an aside to Vallabhbhai Patel that was overheard by his secretary, Mahadev Desai, he voiced right-wing Hindu prejudices in a most shabby manner, stating that if Untouchables had separate electorates they would make common cause with 'Muslim hooligans and kill caste Hindus'.[34] In the end, it was Ambedkar who bowed to the pressure, agreeing to abandon separate electorates in favour of reserved seats for Untouchables within a general electorate. This system has continued in India to this day.

Gandhi and Ambedkar tried to work together in the All-India Anti Untouchability League, formed immediately after the conclusion of the fast. With Gandhi then propagating a new term for Untouchables—that of Harijans or 'People of God'—the body was soon renamed the Harijan Sevak Sangh.[35] Gandhi launched a major campaign in 1933–4 against the practice of untouchability, touring India in person to put

[33]Zelliot, *From Untouchable to Dalit*, p. 166.

[34]Mahadev Desai, *The Diary of Mahadev Desai*, Vol. 1, p. 301.

[35]Gandhi was unhappy with the Gujarati term for 'Untouchable'—that of Antyaja—and asked the readers of *Navajivan* to suggest a better word. Jagannath Desai of Rajkot pointed out that the great bhakti sant of Saurashtra, Narsinh Mehta, had described his Antyaja devotees as 'Harijans'. Gandhi promptly adopted the term. 'My Notes', *Navajivan*, 2 August 1931, *CWMG*, Vol. 53, p. 166.

pressure on caste Hindus to open up access for Untouchables to public wells, tanks, roads, schools, temples and cremation grounds. In response to Ambedkar, Gandhi had extended his battle for the Untouchables into the civil sphere. Previously, his challenge had been restricted to temple entry. However, Ambedkar soon left the organisation, for the differences between the two were profound. Gandhi insisted that the organisation was to be run primarily by caste Hindus as a means for their self-purification, whereas Ambedkar demanded that the leadership be by the Dalits themselves. He found Gandhi's approach to be tainted with an insufferable paternalism, of a sort that he himself had experienced in a humiliating way throughout his life in his dealings with high-caste people. Ambedkar condemned the caste system in its entirety, whereas Gandhi continued for the moment to cling onto a belief that it was possible to return to an idealised four-caste system of social organisation. Ambedkar rejected Gandhi's belief that there could be any meaningful dialogue with Brahmans and the high castes over the matter of untouchability, and he saw the idea of them undergoing a voluntary 'change of heart' as a chimera. In addition, Ambedkar could see that Gandhi was out on a limb, being opposed in his Harijan work by large numbers of caste Hindus, many of whom were Congress members, as well as by members of the socialist and communist left, who dismissed such work as a culturalist and superstructural distraction from the struggle against imperialism and capitalism.[36]

Once this break from Gandhi had been made, Ambedkar went in yet more radical directions. He stopped fighting for temple-entry, stating that Untouchables should no longer aspire for a place in the Hindu fold. However, he implicitly accepted the emphasis that Gandhi had all along placed on religion by mapping out a radical new religious agenda for Dalits.[37] In 1935 he advised them to convert to other religions, such as Islam, Christianity and Sikhism, even though he had misgivings about Islam and Christianity, as they were 'foreign' religions. He also saw that in practice non-Dalit Sikhs discriminated against their Dalit

[36]Omvedt, *Dalits and the Democratic Revolution*, pp. 176–8; Zelliot, *From Untouchable to Dalit*, p. 69.

[37]This point is made by D.R. Nagaraj, *The Flaming Feet: A Study of the Dalit Movement in India*, South Forum Press, Bangalore 1993, p. 24.

co-religionists. It was at this time that he began his move towards Buddhism.[38]

Gandhi, meanwhile, was extending his own Harijan movement all over India, in what was known as the 'Harijan Yatra', with considerable success in some regions. For example, after he had toured Mysore State in January 1934 the authorities responded by agreeing to fund the improvement of facilities for Untouchables. Branches of the Harijan Sevak Sangh were established all over the state, and its workers were encouraged to open schools for Harijans. In 1936, Untouchables were invited for the first time by the maharaja to participate in the annual Dashera Darbar. The state also supported temple entry in principle, though it proved hard to implement in practice.[39]

The campaign not only put caste Hindus throughout India on the defensive, but enraged many Brahmans. Notable among the latter were some Hindu nationalists of Pune. On 25 June 1934 they even attempted to assassinate Gandhi by throwing a bomb at a car in which he was believed to be travelling. They had in fact mistakenly attacked the car of the chief officer of the municipal corporation, who was severely injured by the blast along with nine other bystanders. Gandhi, in the following car, escaped unharmed. The attackers escaped and no arrests were made.

Despite all these efforts, the majority of Dalits throughout India remained unaware of these campaigns, whether by Gandhi or Ambedkar. Ambedkarite radicalism had the greatest impact amongst the Mahar community of Maharashtra, and with educated Dalits and industrial workers in some of the larger cities. Gandhi and his Harijan Sevak Sangh had a greater sway in the city of Ahmedabad, where members of the Vankar community were his strong supporters, and among the Valmikis of Delhi. In rural areas in general, Gandhian anti-untouchability work had the higher profile. Often, the only voices to be heard speaking up for Dalit rights were those of Congress activists aligned to the Harijan Sevak Sangh. Few Dalits, however, took these injunctions

[38]Zelliot, *From Untouchable to Dalit*, pp. 171–2. For a study of Ambedkar's long-drawn-out move towards Buddhism, see Gauri Viswanathan, *Outside the Fold: Conversion, Modernity, and Belief*, Princeton University Press, Princeton 1998, pp. 211–39.

[39]Omvedt, *Dalits and the Democratic Revolution*, pp. 263–6.

very seriously, for they knew too well from bitter experience the likely reactions of the village élites if they did indeed try to assert their rights.[40]

By the 1940s, seeing the slow progress of his Harijan work, Gandhi became more open to the idea of a direct state-led assault on the practice of untouchability. In this, he became more in tune with Ambedkar. He thus supported the banning of the practice of untouchability by law, and gave his full support to a policy of reservation of seats for Dalits in elections (in 1932 he had conceded this point to Ambedkar with great reluctance, as the lesser of two ills). He also insisted that Nehru appoint Ambedkar as Law Minister in the new government, even though he was not a member of the Congress. Many Congress members resented this move, but it followed on from Gandhi's belief that one should always reach out to and try to incorporate an opponent. Ambedkar was to become the leading figure in the drafting of a new constitution for India.[41] Gandhi had at last accepted that Dalits had to exercise power themselves if they were to better their position in any meaningful way. When the Indian Constituent Assembly formally abolished untouchability on 29 November 1948, the house resounded with cries of 'Mahatma Gandhi ki jai!'[42] The law was seen to be a particularly moving tribute to the memory of Gandhi, who had been assassinated ten months earlier.

D.R. Nagaraj has argued that although Gandhi and Ambedkar were in sharp conflict in the 1930s and their differences of that time continue to provide a reference point for the modern Dalit movement, they had in many respects moved towards each other implicitly, if not explicitly, by the end of that decade. He states that 'having jumped into action they cured each other's excesses; they emerged as transformed persons at the end of a very intense encounter.'[43] He goes on to argue that there was in fact always a lot of common ground between them. For example, they both took up the issue of untouchability as a primarily political

[40]Ibid., p. 267.

[41]Parekh, *Colonialism, Tradition and Reform*, p. 240.

[42]Zelliot, *From Untouchable to Dalit*, p. 150. Zelliot detects some irony in this, as Gandhi, she states, did not believe in such legalistic solutions to social problems. This fails to take into account the fact that Gandhi's position had shifted in the 1940s.

[43]Nagaraj, *The Flaming Feet*, p. 2.

one, in contrast to those—such as the bhakti sants—who had previously fought the battle largely in the religious sphere. Also, both emphasised the centrality of this issue for Indian society as a whole.[44] Nagaraj regrets the hardening of position on both sides of the divide today, arguing that the need now is for a synthesis of the two approaches. He accepts that this cannot be done at a strictly logical level, as there are profound theoretical differences between the two approaches, but feels that it can be done if we seek for a deeper underlying truth.[45]

Is this hope an over-optimistic one? In contemporary India, the reality for most Dalits is a continuing routine discrimination in their daily life, with acts of assertion being met by beatings, rape and murder. Although parliamentary and legislative assembly seats are reserved for Dalits, and they are given scholarships and reserved places in schools and colleges, only a small minority benefit from this, and even those who manage against the odds to obtain high qualifications are often denied employment. The large majority of Dalits continue to live in great poverty. The local police often fail to prevent attacks on Dalits, while covering up for the violence of the dominant classes.[46] Politicians seek to win the Dalit vote by claiming to abhor the practice of untouchability, but move to crush any acts that challenge Hinduism itself. In 2001, for example, some Dalits planned to stage a mass conversion to Buddhism in Delhi. Hindutva activists promptly issued a threat that Dalits who attended would be attacked. Others who were not associated with the Hindu right added their voice to the anti-Dalit clamour, arguing that conversion would 'provoke communal tension'. The Bharatiya Janata Party (BJP) government used its power of office to prevent many Dalits from entering Delhi, so that the event turned out to be a damp squib.[47]

In such a climate, it is understandable that few Dalit activists believe

[44]Ibid., pp. 3–4.

[45]Ibid., pp. 21 and 24–5.

[46]These issues were publicised at a major all-India Dalit conference in Bhopal in January 2002. See V. Venkatesan, 'The Dalit Cause', *Frontline*, Vol. 19, No. 3, 15 February 2002.

[47]B.S. Nagaraj, 'Stop "Provocative" Dalit Conversion Plan: NCM', *The Indian Express*, 1 November 2001; Dom Moraes, 'Shorn off [*sic*] an Oppressed Past', *The Hindu*, Magazine Section, 18 November 2001.

that the system will be reformed by caste Hindus from within. They have good reason to question the efficacy of dialogue and compromise. Dalits have however deployed satyagraha to good effect on many occasions, and there is no reason to believe that it is any less efficacious as a means for struggle today. Not only does it continue to provide a powerful means for applying pressure, but it also serves to remind caste Hindus that their continuing maltreatment of Gandhi's 'children of God' represents an enduring insult to his name. In this respect the legacy of both Gandhi and Ambedkar continues to be of crucial importance for the Dalits of modern India.

Adivasis

The Adivasis, or so-called 'tribals', were a disparate group of jatis that had been defined by the British as 'early tribes'. It was argued that these jatis could be characterised, among other things, by their clan-based systems of kinship and their 'primitive' animistic religiosity. In some cases they were defined in terms of their habitat, as 'jungle tribes'. In the twentieth century they were given the bureaucratic label of 'Scheduled Tribes'. In reaction to all of this, many of them claimed, assertively, to be Adivasis, or 'original inhabitants'. In India, the largest concentrations of the people so described were found in the north-east. Elsewhere, many were found in the central-eastern region, in what is now the state of Jharkhand and areas adjoining to it in Bengal, Orissa and Bastar, and in a belt of western India running over the four modern Indian states of Rajasthan, Gujarat, Madhya Pradesh and Maharashtra.[48]

Although there were many jatis that had been classed by the British as 'early' or 'jungle tribes' in Gandhi's own Gujarat, he does not appear to have been conscious of them in any important respect before 1921. He had been brought up in Saurashtra, and had then based himself in Ahmedabad city, neither of which had any significant population of these jatis, and his work in South Africa had not brought him into contact with them, unlike Dalits, some of whom had migrated there. In this, there was a marked contrast to his concern about the

[48] *A Social and Economic Atlas of India*, Oxford University Press, New Delhi 1987, p. 27.

discriminations faced by the Untouchables and the need to incorporate them within the movement—something which had for many years been a central question both for him and other nationalists. Gandhi's attention was drawn to the matter of the 'tribals' of Gujarat for the first time during the Non-cooperation movement. There were two groups concerned—the Bhils and the so-called 'Kaliparaj'.

The Bhils were the largest of the so-called 'tribal' communities of the western Indian region. In the past they had been organised in warlike clans that prevented outside rulers from extending their control over the mountains. The British had subjugated them—with considerable difficulty—during the first half of the nineteenth century. Even afterwards, there were several Bhil revolts. The 'Kaliparaj' were found only in South Gujarat. The term, which meant 'the black people' was a derogatory one used by non-Adivasis to describe members of a variety of local Adivasi jatis, such as the Chodhris, Dhodiyas and Gamits. These jatis were considered to be less warlike than the Bhils. These communities had lived in the past from shifting cultivation, hunting and gathering, and they were encouraged by the British to practice a more settled and intensive agriculture. In many cases, they were excluded from large tracts of forest that they had previously controlled, so that state foresters could exploit the timber wealth of the woodlands.[49] Landlords, usurers and liquor dealers who were protected by the colonial and princely states ruthlessly exploited those who became settled.[50] This frequently created a crisis of confidence among these people in their own cultures, leading them to look for alternative and more efficacious cultural models. Most notable in this respect was a powerful movement among the Bhils

[49]On this, see in particular David Hardiman, 'Power in the Forest: The Dangs, 1820–1940', in David Arnold and David Hardiman (eds), *Subaltern Studies VIII*, Oxford University Press, New Delhi 1994; and Ajay Skaria, 'Timber Conservancy, Desiccationism and Scientific Forestry: The Dangs 1840s-1920s', in Richard Grove, Vinita Damodaran, and Satpal Sangwan (eds), *Nature and the Orient: The Environmental History of South and Southeast Asia*, Oxford University Press, New Delhi 1998.

[50]On usurers see Hardiman, *Feeding the Baniya*; on liquor dealers see David Hardiman, 'From Custom to Crime: The Politics of Drinking in Colonial South Gujarat', in Ranajit Guha (ed.), *Subaltern Studies IV*, Oxford University Press, New Delhi 1985.

of the Gujarat–Rajasthan border region in 1913 that was led by a charismatic leader called Govind, who was believed to have miraculous powers. The British eventually suppressed this movement by force as it was seen to challenge the hegemony of the local princely rulers.

Nationalists of Gujarat began to reach out to the Adivasis from 1918. During the great influenza epidemic of that year some young activists of the Patidar Yuvak Mandal distributed medicine to the 'Kaliparaj' in an attempt to gain their sympathy.[51] In the Panchmahals, where the Adivasis were all Bhils, some local nationalist workers took up their grievances after the monsoon had failed in the same year. Even though many of the Bhils were starving, government officials were confiscating their meagre possessions—even stripping the tiles from their roofs—to realise land-tax demands. In 1919 Gandhi's prominent lieutenant, Indulal Yagnik, and a leading member of Gokhale's Servants of India Society, Amritlal Thakkar, raised funds from capitalists in Bombay to buy food that was then distributed among the Bhils.[52]

This initial work in the Panchmahals was consolidated during the period of the Non-Cooperation movement of 1920–2, when meetings were organised by nationalists to encourage the Bhils to give up drinking liquor. Some took a vow to abjure spirits while bowing to a portrait of Gandhi.[53] Food was again in short supply among the Bhils in 1921, and Yagnik once more raised funds to purchase food for them. In this, he encountered considerable opposition from other leading nationalists of Gujarat, such as Vallabhbhai Patel and G.V. Mavalankar, who did not feel that such work was a priority at that time. Gandhi, however, supported this work.[54] Yagnik also established a National Bhil Hostel that was modelled on similar hostels run by the government and Christian missionaries.[55] Amritlal Thakkar joined him in this work in early 1922 and put the project on a much firmer footing. Another hostel was opened, called 'the Bhil Ashram'.[56] Soon after, Thakkar

[51]Bhatt, 'Caste Mobilization in a Gujarat District', pp. 320–1.

[52]Indulal Yagnik, *Atmakatha*, Vol. 2, Gujarat Grantharatan Karyalay, Ahmedabad 1970, pp. 158–61.

[53]Ibid., pp. 302–5.

[54]Ibid., pp. 316–18, 325 and 328–30.

[55]Ibid., Vol. 3, pp. 8–11.

[56]Ibid., pp. 58–61.

established the Bhil Seva Mandal, which was in overall control of work amongst the Bhils. This organisation laid the foundations for his life's work amongst the Adivasis of India.[57]

It was at this juncture that Gandhi himself took up the problem of assimilating the Adivasis of the region into the movement. The immediate context was provided by the proposal to launch civil disobedience against the British in one taluka, that of Bardoli in South Gujarat. Although Gandhi had been informed that the people of this area were wholly behind the struggle, he soon discovered that about half the population consisted of 'Kaliparaj' who had not been mobilised at all. He demanded that this be rectified. The Congress activists then started going to the Adivasi villages, but with minimal success initially. Meanwhile, a powerful protest movement had developed among the Bhils in the border region between Gujarat and Rajasthan. They were led by a Baniya of Mewar State called Motilal Tejawat, who had once worked for a Rajput lord, but who had resigned in disgust at the way such people treated the Bhils. Tejawat saw the protest as being a part of the wider movement for independence led by Gandhi, then in a most active phase. In speeches he stated that once 'Gandhi raj' was established they would only have to pay one anna in the rupee to their rulers. Some of his followers took to wearing white caps. He clearly believed that in trying to wean the Bhils away from violence he was following the programme of the Gandhian movement closely. As yet, however, Gandhi knew nothing of him or his movement.[58]

In early 1922, Tejawat and several thousand Bhils armed with bows and arrows went on a progress around the villages of the region. There were some minor clashes, with aggressive policemen and officials being beaten. There is no record of anyone being killed by the Bhils—by their standards they were protesting in a remarkably non-violent manner. When however Gandhi heard of this, he wrote an article in *Young India* disowning the Bhils and their leader: 'none has authority to use my

[57]Ibid., pp. 74–6.

[58]Motilal Tejawat's movement is documented in Premsinh Kankariya, *Bhil Kranti ke Praneta: Motilal Tejavat*, Rajasthan Sahitya Academy, Udaipur 1985 (in Hindi); Prakash Chandra Jain, *Tribal Agrarian Movement: A Case Study of the Bhil Movement of Rajasthan*, Himanshu Publications, Udaipur 1989, chapters 3 and 4; Sen, 'Popular Protest in Mewar, chapter 6; Vidal, *Violence and Truth*, chapter 5.

name save under my own writing... nobody has any authority from me to use any arms, even sticks, against any person.' He warned them that if continued in such an aggressive manner, 'they will find everything and everybody arrayed against them and they will find themselves heavy losers in the end.'[59] Gandhi was not however satisfied that he had heard all he needed to know about this movement, and he sent a leading nationalist worker, Manilal Kothari, to investigate. Motilal and the Bhils were then in Sirohi state, and Kothari managed to meet up with them there and take a promise from Tejawat that he would avoid violence. Kothari was impressed by the power of the movement and sent back favourable reports to Gandhi.

Motilal had been both upset and disheartened when he had learnt of Gandhi's disavowal of his activities in the *Young India* article of 2 February, for he saw himself as a faithful disciple. As he stated, however, in a letter to Gandhi of 11 February, he knew he could not prevent his own followers from carrying arms—with all the possible dangers that that entailed. He argued that despite this, Gandhi should view them favourably as an intrinsically peaceful and religious-minded people who were suffering oppression by autocratic and corrupt rulers.[60] Gandhi gave a rather lukewarm response on 26 February, in which he accepted that Tejawat was doing some excellent work among the Bhils, but pointed out that he had failed to grasp his philosophy in certain important respects.[61] Although his tone was more sympathetic, he was still not very welcoming towards his self-avowed disciple. It was at this juncture that the British moved against the protesters, sending the Mewar Bhil Corps to crush the movement. They surprised a meeting of Motilal and his followers on the morning of 7 March, opening fire on the peaceful crowd from a nearby hill. The commander of the Bhil Corps, Major Sutton, claimed that twenty-two Bhils were killed in what

[59]'Danger of Mass Movement', *Young India*, 2 February 1922, in *CWMG*, Vol 22, p. 315.

[60]Motilal Tejawat to Gandhi, 11 February 1922, *Navajivan*, 26 February 1922, p. 203.

[61]'Motilal Tejavat and the "Bhils"', *Navajivan*, 26 February 1922, *CWMG*, Vol. 26, p. 237.

he described as a skirmish.[62] Against this, an oral tradition of the Bhils claims that between 1,000 and 1,500 were killed.[63]

It is almost certainly the case that Sutton's figure of twenty-two was an understatement, and probably a large one at that. A local missionary who treated the wounded stated that 'there were a hundred casualties; dead and wounded were lying all around, some with fearful wounds. Our little hospital was filled and we were bringing in stretcher cases until 10 p.m.'[64] For Sutton, twenty-two was a politic figure—not representing a denial that a serious incident had occurred, but not an indicator, either, that the carnage had been out of all proportion to the seriousness of the situation. Sutton claimed that the Bhils had started firing and that he had ordered a counter-firing in self-defence. As a British official, G.D. Ogilvie, stated a few days later, little more could be expected in a case involving a 'people little removed from savagery ... childishly ignorant and inflammable ...'.[65]

The nationalist press, when it took any notice at all,[66] satisfied itself by merely regurgitating the government communiqué.[67] There was no suggestion that the shooting was in any way a cause for outrage. Even the most obvious questions were not posed; for example, if the Bhils had, as alleged, made a violent attack on Sutton and his men, why had the latter not suffered a single injury? No attempts were made by the Gujarat Congress to investigate the matter any further, even though it had the potential to be 'Gujarat's Amritsar'. Bhil lives, it seems, were of

[62]Press Communiqué of Government of India, 10 March 1922, National Archives of India, Foreign and Political Department, 428–P (Secret-Printed) of 1922–3.

[63]In December 1997 I interviewed a number of old Bhil men and women of the villages around the site of the firing, who asserted that the casualties were of this order.

[64]Reverend J. Irwin Lea, *Report of the Church Missionary Society Western India Mission 1922*, Diocesan Press, Madras 1923, p. 44.

[65]Quoted in a memo. from F. & P. Dept. to India Office, 15 March 1923, National Archives of India (NAI) file on Motilal Tejawat.

[66]No mention of the massacre was made in either of Gandhi's weeklies *Young India* or *Navajivan*.

[67]See for example *Saurashtra*, 25 March 1922.

minor matter.[68] Motilal himself had managed to escape after the firing started, and the movement continued strongly for two more months. There were further shootings and atrocities, though not of the magnitude of that of 7 March. British officials captured Bhil headmen and forced them to break *Eki* (unity) oath in public.[69] By May 1922 the movement had all but collapsed, leaving Motilal a fugitive.

Gandhi and his followers' response to this Bhil movement left a lot to be desired. The situation was not much better in the Panchmahals, where the single most important leader of the Bhils of that area, Govind, became an implacable opponent of the Gandhians during the Non-Cooperation movement. Govind, who had led the Bhil movement of 1913, had been jailed until 1919, when he was released on condition that he take no part in any 'political' activities. In 1921, the Gandhians had persuaded him to attend their Bhil conference in Dahod, which he had agreed to do, as he did not see it as being 'political'. The British thought otherwise and arrested him before he could reach Dahod. He realised that he had been tricked, and as he was led away he showered abuse on the nationalists.[70] Thereafter, the Gandhians had great difficulty in winning any mass support from the Bhils of the region, though the Bhil Seva Mandal itself continued to operate with impressive efficiency.

In South Gujarat, the Gandhians managed eventually to win much wider support among the Adivasis. In a powerful movement for self-assertion that was launched in 1922, Gandhi was projected by the Adivasis as a divine being who was somehow working to ameliorate their condition. Vows were taken in his name, and miracles expected from him.[71] Gandhians sought to channel these hopes in different directions by organising meetings for the Adivasis from 1923 onwards,

[68]Gandhi can be absolved from this particular charge, as he was arrested and jailed immediately after the massacre, on 10 March.

[69]Political Sec. F. & P. Dept., G. of I. to Private Sec. to Viceroy, 13 April 1922; report by H.R.N. Pritchard, 14 April 1922; press communiqué from F. & P. Dept, G. of I., 7 May 1922; report by H.R.N. Pritchard, 13 May 1922, NAI file on Motilal Tejawat.

[70]*Secret Police Abstracts of Intelligence, Bombay Presidency*, Bombay 1921, p. 217.

[71]I have discussed this all in detail in my study of this movement, *The Coming of the Devi*, pp. 166–76.

at which they were encouraged to abjure liquor and meat, to spin khadi, and live a clean, simple and diligent life. This was characterised in high Hindu terms as *atmashuddhi*, or self-purification. Through such a cleansing the Adivasis would, it was believed, become worthy citizens of the Indian nation. They also campaigned to replace the demeaning term 'Kaliparaj' with that of 'Raniparaj', or 'people of the forest'. The leading figure in this initiative was Dr Sumant Mehta, who recalled how humiliated he had been when he was called a 'blackey' while undergoing medical training in England.[72] At the same time, the Gandhians discouraged Adivasis from continuing the labour boycott that they had been waging against local landlords. They were advised to go back to work.[73] In 1924, an ashram was established in the heart of the Adivasi area at Vedchhi to carry on Gandhian work.

Many high-caste supporters of the Gandhian Congress opposed this activity. In early 1924, for example, the Gandhian Narhari Parikh started a night school for Dubla labourers in an area dominated by Anavil and Patidar peasants. The Dublas were a 'Kaliparaj' community who were mostly bonded agricultural labourers working for the two dominant castes. During the Non-Cooperation Movement the Patidars had given strong support to the Gandhian Congress. However, they felt very threatened by the night school, believing that their hegemony over the Dublas would be jeopardised if they became literate. They informed the Dublas that if they wanted to continue in employment they should stop attending the school. Many Patidars returned their spinning wheels to the local ashram at Sarbhan in protest. When the Dublas defied them, they went to the school and drove them out. Parikh launched a fast in protest, sending a message to Gandhi that he was doing this to bring about a change of heart, not because he bore any grudge against the Patidars. Gandhi gave his blessings, and Vallabhbhai Patel travelled down from Ahmedabad to try to persuade the Patidars to withdraw their opposition to the school. The initial response of the Patidars was aggressive—they stated that they did not care if Parikh died. Eventually, Patel persuaded them to accept the school, and Parikh called off his

[72]Yagnik, *Atmakatha*, Vol. 3, p. 249.

[73]Hardiman, *The Coming of the Devi*, pp. 191–3.

fast. Despite this, individual Patidars made it clear to the Dublas that if they attended the class they would remain unemployed. Intimidated, the Dublas stopped going to the class, and it had to be closed down.[74]

In following Gandhi's injunction to carry out social and political work among the poor and marginalized, people such as Amritlal Thakkar and Narhari Parikh demonstrated considerable moral courage. They often had to fight the local élites who profited by exploiting the Adivasis and who considered them troublemakers. There were however limits to their radicalism. They tended to have a superior attitude towards the Adivasis, seeing them as 'primitives' who required to be 'civilised'. For example, Amritlal Thakkar considered that the Bhils were 'hardly conscious of being human'. He saw his task as being that of winning the community 'back to the country and to humanity'.[75] Within the ashrams, the Gandhians never considered putting Adivasis into positions of responsibility, even though there were educated Adivasis who were capable of carrying out such work on equal terms with the caste Hindus. The Gandhians expended a lot of energy attacking aspects of Adivasi culture that were seen to violate upper-caste notions of decency, such as dances in which men and women held each other around the waist. More pressing concerns were ignored, such as the exploitation of the Adivasis by usurers, landlords and rich peasants.[76]

The situation was worse elsewhere, for many high-caste members of the Gandhian Congress became actively hostile when certain Adivasis claimed to be followers of Gandhi. This was apparent in the revolt of the Gond Adivasis of the Rampa and Gudem hill tracts of the Andhra-Orissa border region led by Alluri Sita Rama Raju in 1922–4. There were certain parallels between Sita Rama Raju and Motilal Tejawat, though there were also important differences. Sita Rama Raju was a high-caste Telugu who became a sanyasi and who was believed by the Gonds to have supernatural powers. He appears to have come into

[74] *Secret Police Abstracts of Intelligence, Bombay Presidency*, Bombay 1924, pp. 147 & 158–9; interview with Chhotubhai Gopalji Desai, Puni, Bardoli Taluka, 28 May 1981.

[75] *The Servant of India*, Vol. 6, No. 26, 26 July 1926, p. 311.

[76] Hardiman, *The Coming of the Devi*, pp. 207–8.

contact with the Gandhian movement while on a pilgrimage to Nasik in 1921. He began to wear khadi, and on his return, preached temperance and the need to resolve disputes locally rather than through the British courts. He launched a rebellion in September 1922 that was sustained for nearly two years. In contrast to Tejawat, Sita Rama Raju encouraged his followers to arm themselves with guns and fight the British using guerrilla tactics. He himself dyed his khadi shirt red, and wore a military-style leather belt with a captured police pistol tucked into it. He tried to gain support for his revolt from Congress nationalists in the plains, but they not only refused to support him, but actively opposed his movement on the grounds that it violated Gandhi's principles of non-violence. A more important reason for their hostility was perhaps that they tended to be of the same class as the traders, usurers, contractors, immigrant cultivators and lawyers whom the Gonds were resisting as their exploiters. Sita Rama Raju was eventually captured and summarily executed by the police in May 1924, bringing the revolt to an end.[77]

Another powerful Adivasi movement that claimed to be inspired by Gandhi was that of the Oraons of the Jharkhand region. This movement had begun during the First World War, when large numbers of Oraons had resolved to reform their lives. They became known as Tana Bhagats. Besides giving up liquor, meat eating and their fear of ghosts and evil spirits, they also stopped paying their rents to high-caste landlords. Seeing this as a threat to law and order, the British authorities tried to suppress this non-violent movement, with little success.[78] During the Non-Cooperation movement, the Tana Bhagats became strong supporters of Gandhi and the Congress. About 20,000 of them refused to pay their taxes to the state, believing that 'Gandhi *raj*' had arrived. Many had their land confiscated as a result. Despite this they remained firm, courting jail and travelling long distances to attend Congress meetings.

[77]David Arnold, 'Rebellious Hillmen: The Gudem-Rampa Risings 1839–1924', in Ranajit Guha, ed., *Subaltern Studies I*, Oxford University Press, New Delhi 1982, pp. 134–40.

[78]Sarat Chandra Roy, *Oraon Religion and Ceremony*, Editions India, Calcutta 1972 (1st edn 1928), pp. 246–50.

They had faith that once swaraj was won they would regain all the land that they had lost over the course of the past century.[79] On a tour of Bihar in 1925, Gandhi met some Tana Bhagats who wore khadi. He was very impressed when they demonstrated their skills in spinning in his presence.[80]

Despite the obvious success of his movement among many Adivasis, Gandhi did not devote any great intellectual or political energy to them and their problems. He knew that work was being done in this respect by his followers in various parts of India, such as Amritlal Thakkar in the Panchmahals and Jugatram Dave in South Gujarat, and he was content to let them carry on. He did, however, try to discourage them from proselytising their own values in a heavy-handed manner. As he stated in 1928: 'As regards taking our message to the aborigines, I do not think I should go and give my message out of my own wisdom. Do it in all humility ... What have I to take to the aborigines and the Assamese hillmen except to go in my nakedness to them? Rather than ask them to join my prayer, I would join their prayer.'[81]

During the Civil Disobedience Movement of 1930–1, many Adivasis participated by disobeying the forest laws—an action which became classed as 'forest satyagraha'. Gandhi himself had refused to sanction such action, on the grounds that he was ignorant of forest regulations.[82] Once he had been jailed, local Congress leaders went ahead and launched the satyagrahas. In central India, Gond and Korku Adivasis were led by khadi-clad Congress nationalists in invasions of government forests, where they cut and removed grass in violation of the law. When the police tried to intervene, there were in some cases violent clashes. By August 1930, the nationalists were no longer in control of the protest in many areas, and the government was becoming seriously alarmed.

[79]K.S. Singh, 'Mahatma Gandhi and the Adivasis', *Man in India*, Vol. 20, No. 1, January-March 1970, pp. 7–8.

[80]Ibid., p. 6.

[81]'Discussion on Fellowship', *Young India*, 19 January 1928, *CWMG*, Vol. 31, p. 462.

[82]David Baker, '"A Serious Time": Forest Satyagraha in Madhya Pradesh, 1930', *The Indian Economic and Social History Review*, Vol. 21, No. 1, January-March 1984, p. 75.

Police reinforcements were sent, and the Adivasis were repressed in a heavy-handed manner. By October the protests had died down in most areas, though not all.[83] At the same time, there were forest satyagrahas in the Sahyadri Mountains in Maharashtra, which were generally non-violent. There was also an upsurge in movements of Adivasi assertion that were linked with Gandhi's name, such as the Haribaba movement in Jharkhand of 1931–2.[84]

Despite this widespread Adivasi support for the Congress, Gandhi himself continued to treat Adivasi issues as marginal to the movement as a whole. For example, he insisted that Amritlal Thakkar expend his chief energies on Harijan work, as Secretary of the Harijan Sevak Sangh, rather than on the Bhils and other Adivasis, which was where Thakkar's heart really lay. He also showed little interest in Verrier Elwin's work among the Gonds. Elwin had come to India as a Christian missionary in 1927 and become close to Gandhi during the period of the Civil Disobedience Movement. He came to see Gandhi as a surrogate father, a role Gandhi accepted.[85] Elwin abandoned his missionary work, and in 1932—inspired by the example of Amritlal Thakkar and the Bhil Seva Mandal—decided to establish a Gandhian-style ashram among the Gonds of Mandla District in the Central Provinces, which he named the Gond Seva Mandal.[86]

In 1932 and 1933 Gandhi sent at least fourteen letters to Elwin. These letters were however of a very personal nature—Gandhi showed almost no interest in the Gonds. When Elwin fell ill, he even advised him to give up his work and return to England.[87] Elwin did not follow this suggestion and continued in Mandla. The work was nevertheless raising difficult questions for him. Initially—as a lapsed missionary—Elwin had appreciated the Gandhian principle that it was wrong to seek to convert people to a faith different to the one in which they had

[83]Baker, '"A Serious Time", pp. 75–82.

[84]K.S. Singh, 'The Haribaba Movement in Chotanagpur 1931–32', *The Journal of the Bihar Research Society*, Vol. 49, Pts.1–4, January-December 1963.

[85]Letter to Verrier Elwin, 23 February 1933, *CWMG*, Vol. 59, p. 346.

[86]Ramachandra Guha, *Savaging the Civilized: Verrier Elwin, His Tribals and India*, University of Chicago Press, Chicago 1999, pp. 54, 59–60 & 65–6.

[87]Letter to Verrier Elwin, 14 January 1933, *CWMG*, Vol. 59, p. 13.

been raised.[88] He came to see, however, that the Gandhians who were working among the Adivasis were involved in a conversion of a more subtle sort, namely that of inculcating their own cultural values. Most of these were, Elwin felt, irrelevant to the Adivasis. Khadi-spinning—a major feature of Gandhian constructive work amongst Adivasis—was for example of no use to the Gonds, for cotton was not grown in their tract. Elwin considered the Gandhian condemnation of liquor to be out of touch with Gond beliefs, for they loved their liquor, made from the mahua flower, and in fact they saw this as central to their identity as a community. Mahua grew freely in the area, and the liquor was, Elwin felt, a far more genuinely swadeshi product for Adivasis than khadi. He also found that the Gonds did not respect him for the strict celibacy that he observed in accordance with Gandhi's advice. They saw it, rather, as a perversion. He was attracted by the way that the Gonds expressed their sexuality in an open and uninhibited way, and began to feel that they acted with greater honesty than the uptight and narrow-minded Gandhians who made a great show of repressing their desires in an often hypocritical manner. He soon abandoned his vow and began to have sexual relationships with Gond women.[89] Towards the end of 1933 he came out with a public critique of the nationalists in the *Modern Review*: 'Indian national workers and reformers—with the exception of the heroic little band associated with the Bhil Seva Mandal—have neglected the tribes shamefully. The Congress has neglected them. The Liberals have neglected them. The Khadi workers have neglected them.'[90] Elwin decided to publicise the plight of the Adivasis in a series of articles, pamphlets and books.[91]

In these writings Elwin celebrated a culture which was as yet uncontaminated by 'civilisation'. At the very time he was writing, however, a movement was sweeping through the Gond community in which the people abandoned liquor-drinking, meat-eating, dancing and singing. This was exactly the sort of movement that Gandhian workers had

[88]Ramachandra Guha, *Savaging the Civilized*, p. 88.

[89]Ibid., pp. 89–90 & 95.

[90]Verrier Elwin, 'Gonds', *Modern Review*, November 1933, pp. 547–8, quoted in Ramachandra Guha, *Savaging the Civilized*, p. 98.

[91]Ibid., pp. 99–100.

both encouraged and sought to build on elsewhere in India, and Elwin suspected that in this case the Adivasis were being manipulated.[92] This is unlikely, for—going by all of the detailed studies we have of such movements—the chief initiative almost certainly came from the Adivasis. Elwin also believed that Adivasis who changed their way of life in this respect went 'flat, like stale beer: there was no more kick in them'.[93] He failed to see that considerable moral courage was required to sustain such a reformed way of life. Not only did reformed Adivasis bring themselves into conflict with members of their own community, but their initiative was often resented very strongly by local landlords, rich peasants, liquor dealers and usurers, who saw it as a case of Adivasis getting ideas above their station. As a rule, they reacted with harsh repression. This was not an act of mere unthinking imitation, but rather a form of proud self-assertion with strong political dimensions.[94] In this respect, the Gandhians were more in tune with the sentiments of the Adivasis who participated in such movements. Elwin's own work among the Gonds was soon jeopardised by the strength of the reformist movement, and in 1938 he even had to move his headquarters to a place where it was less pervasive.[95]

In the new Indian constitution of 1935, many Adivasi areas were designated as 'excluded' or 'partially excluded', which meant in effect that the Adivasis were considered too politically 'immature' to deserve any electoral representation. There was an important issue to be fought over here, but Gandhi and the Congress kept silent on the matter. Some Gandhians even agreed with the policy. Amritlal Thakkar's second-in-command at the Bhil Seva Mandal, Lakshmidas Shrikant, wrote an article in *The Times of India* in 1938 in which he argued that the Bhils had no social cohesion or any sense of social responsibility, and were not suited for democratic forms of local government.[96] Elwin was in broad agreement with the policy as well, as he had by then come to the

[92]Ibid., pp. 107–8.

[93]Ibid., p. 108.

[94]I have argued this in the case of the Devi movement in South Gujarat in my book *The Coming of the Devi*, pp. 157–60.

[95]Ramachandra Guha, *Savaging the Civilized*, p. 109.

[96]*The Times of India*, 24 January 1938.

conclusion that paternalistic Britishers were likely to protect the interests of the Adivasis better than the high-caste Hindu Congressmen who would claim to represent them in the legislative councils. He argued that: 'This company of vegetarians and teetotallers would like to force their own bourgeois and Puritan doctrines on the free and wild people of the forests.'[97]

In 1938 Elwin went to meet Gandhi at Wardha to try to persuade him to take a more active interest in Adivasi issues, but found that for 'all his desire for Home Rule Mahatma Gandhi did not appear to think that the original inhabitants of India deserved any special consideration'.[98] Gandhi was however soon pushed towards a more active engagement with the issue through fear that the Adivasis might develop their own separatist sentiments. In 1938 an Adivasi Mahasabha was formed in Jharkhand to press for constitutional rights for the Adivasis of the region. Many of the Adivasis who were involved in this organisation were Christian converts. It developed links with the Muslim League, which saw the party as a possible ally in its struggle against the Congress.[99] Gandhi was worried that under Christian mission influence, the Adivasis would become 'deIndianized'—as he put it—and that the Congress needed to provide a strongly Indian counter. He encouraged his followers to work amongst the Adivasis: 'They provide a vast field of service for Congressmen.'[100] An Adivasi Seva Mandal was established as a counter to the Adivasi Mahasabha; the president of this body was B.G. Kher, who had been Prime Minister of Bombay in the Congress ministry of 1937–9. Gandhi also added the topic of 'service of Adivasis' to a

[97] Ramachandra Guha, *Savaging the Civilized*, p. 105.

[98] Ibid., p. 108.

[99] K.S. Singh, 'The Freedom Movement and Tribal Sub-Movements, 1920–1947', in B.R. Nanda (ed.), *Essays in Modern Indian History*, Oxford University Press, New Delhi 1980, p. 164. Gyanendra Pandey has pointed out that the Muslim League was at that time projecting itself as the representative of a minority group with interests in common with other minorities in India who were all oppressed by the Congress—the party of the high-caste Hindu and capitalist. Gyanendra Pandey, *Remembering Partition: Violence, Nationalism and History in India*, Cambridge University Press, Cambridge 2001, p. 28.

[100] 'Notes: Adivasis', *Harijan*, 18 January 1942, *CWMG*, Vol. 81, p. 419.

manifesto for the constructive programme—it had previously been absent.[101]

From this time on, Gandhi began to use the term 'Adivasi' consistently when talking about this section of the population. He had always disliked colonial terms such as 'animist' or 'aboriginal', stating: 'We were strangers to this sort of classification—"animists", "aborigines", etc.,—but we have learnt it from English rulers.'[102] In deference to his followers who had coined alternatives such as 'Raniparaj' or 'Girijan', he used these terms in the late 1920s and 1930s. Elwin had in 1938 changed the name of his organisation to the Bhumijan Seva Mandal.[103] 'Bhumijan' meant 'people of the soil', and he seems to have preferred it to the Gandhian terms, which defined Adivasis in terms of their place of residence rather than in terms of their attachment to the earth. Elwin saw these people as the 'original inhabitants', and 'Bhumijan' came closer to this than the Gandhian terms. This did not, however, catch on. The term 'Adivasi' was coined in Jharkhand and popularised by the Adivasi Mahasabha. Amritlal Thakkar seized on it and became a major advocate of its use. Gandhi, who then began to apply the term himself, even believed that Thakkar had coined it.[104] The term was disputed strongly by many Hindu nationalists, who saw its acceptance as a tacit acknowledgement that these supposed 'original inhabitants' had been displaced from their land by Hindu invaders. They preferred to think of these people as 'the imperfectly integrated classes of Hindu society'

[101]'Constructive Programme: Its Meaning and Place', 13 December 1941, *CWMG*, Vol. 81, pp. 369–70.

[102]'Discussion on Fellowship', *Young India*, 19 January 1928, *CWMG*, Vol. 31, p. 462.

[103]Ramachandra Guha, *Savaging the Civilized*, p. 109.

[104]'Constructive Programme: Its Meaning and Place', 13 December 1941, *CWMG*, Vol. 81, p. 369. In the late 1920s, Thakkar had written in Gujarati that the Bhils, Santals, Gonds, etc. were '*asal vatani*' (original inhabitants) of India. A.V. Thakkar, Leaflet on the Bhil Seva Mandal, *c.* 1927, in Rajasthan State Archives, Bikaner, Mahakma Khas, file M/30, basta 19, 1918. His close associate, Laxmidas Shrikant told me in an interview at the Bhil Seva Mandal in Dahod on 30 June 1985 that Thakkar had learnt the term 'Adivasi' from a political leader from southern Bihar who was himself an Adivasi.

or 'backward Hindus' who had to be integrated fully into the Hindu mainstream.[105] Gandhi clearly rejected this argument, for he continued to deploy the term 'Adivasi' up until his death.

He feared, however, that the Adivasis might follow the example of the Muslim League and launch a series of campaigns for separate states. He anticipated that this would happen if the caste Hindus continued to grind the Adivasis under their heels.[106] The only way to prevent this, so far as he was concerned, was for nationalists to work amongst them in a selfless manner. If the government tried to ban them from Adivasi areas, they should court arrest and be prepared to go to jail.[107] In an address to the Congress workers of Midnapore district in Bengal—an area with a large Adivasi population—he stated: 'The 1935 Act had separated them [the Adivasis] from the rest of the inhabitants of India and had placed the "excluded areas" under the Governor's direct administration. It was a shame that they had allowed them to be treated like that. It was up to them to make the Adivasis feel at one with them.'[108] In the final three years of his life, he emphasised the need for such work in a way he had never done before, and he made a point of channelling Congress funds in that direction.[109]

This strategy succeeded in a broad way, for such separatist sentiments never became popular among the Adivasis of India in general, though they did in important parts of the northeast. In Jharkhand, for example, the Adivasi Mahasabha was routed by the Congress in the elections of 1946, putting paid to any further separatist moves at that juncture.[110]

[105]G.S. Ghurye, *The Scheduled Tribes of India*, Transaction Books, New Brunswick 1980, p. 19.

[106]Speech at Prayer Meeting, 12 June 1947, *CWMG*, Vol. 95, p. 266. See also Speech at AICC Meeting, 14 June 1947, *CWMG*, Vol. 95, p. 281.

[107]Speech at Congress Workers' Conference, 5 January 1946, *CWMG*, 89, p. 178.

[108]Discussion with Midnapore Political Workers, 2 January 1946, *CWMG*, Vol. 89, p. 157.

[109]See for example Gandhi to Mrs. S.R. Das, 8 December 1945, *CWMG*, Vol. 89, pp. 13–14, and Gandhi to Chimanlal N. Shah, 21 January 1947, *CWMG*, Vol. 93, p. 305.

[110]Singh, 'The Freedom Movement and Tribal Sub-Movements, 1920–1947', p. 165.

Many Gandhians went to work in Adivasi areas in the late 1940s and early 1950s, in some cases as a reaction to the successful Communist Party mobilisation of particular Adivasi communities.[111] Ashrams were established with hostels and schools for Adivasi children. In this way, a generation of Adivasis was giving a training that allowed them to represent their own communities within the liberal polity. In time, this led, inevitably, to them having to challenge the Gandhian paternalists who had nurtured them in the first place.

The Gandhian approach to Adivasis tended to focus on their education into citizenship. There was much less emphasis on the need to struggle for their rights within the polity through satyagraha. The process of education brought limited gains for a few Adivasis, but it failed to bring the more general emancipation that was hoped for. For most Adivasis, their experience since Indian independence was one of displacement, marginalisation and exploitation. British officials, foresters and policemen were replaced by Indians who treated them just as badly, if not worse. They have had their lands seized from them by high-caste farmers, by bureaucrats who want to build large dams or mine valuable minerals or establish tourist resorts and wildlife reserves in their forests and hills. Their villages have not only been starved of state funding, but their lands have suffered severe ecological damage from rampant cutting of the forests by corrupt contractors and foresters and their political backers. Their agriculture has in consequence deteriorated to the extent that many Adivasis can no longer make a living from the land. They have been often forced to migrate out in search of work, in the process becoming victims of the harshest forms of exploitation.[112] Although nominally citizens of India, the majority continue in practice to be a colonised people. This state of affairs can only be resisted through struggle. This has led some Adivasis towards violent resistance, as for example within the Naxalite movement. Others, however, have resisted

[111]As for example in Thana District of Bombay State in 1946–7. See Godavari Parulekar, *Adivasis Revolt: The Story of Warli Peasants in Struggle*, National Book Agency, Calcutta, 1975.

[112]This process is chronicled by Jan Breman, *Of Peasants, Migrants and Paupers: Rural Labour Circulation and Capitalist Production in West India*, Oxford University Press, New Delhi 1985.

non-violently under a leadership that is inspired, broadly, by the Gandhian tradition, as in the Narmada Bachao Andolan.

Dalits, Adivasis, and the Indian Nation

Though his approach towards the Dalit and Adivasi questions had many limitations, Gandhi situated the fraught issue of the position of these two groups within the emerging nation-state squarely on the political agenda. His approach proved to be in tune with certain strands of self-assertion within these communities that stressed cultural and religious reforms that brought them more in line with high-caste Hindu practice. Not all Dalits and Adivasis were comfortable with this development. B.R. Ambedkar, in particular, felt that such a programme would merely lead to the consolidation of their existing social inferiority. He did not believe that the large majority of high-caste Hindus could be trusted to act with benevolence and compassion towards people whom they had exploited to so much advantage for so long. He thus rejected an approach that stressed the reconciling of differences and the forging of a politics of mutual trust and neighbourliness.

Gandhi was not helped in his task by many of his high-caste followers, who were often hostile towards his efforts in this direction. The reaction by Gandhi's Patidar and Anavil Brahman supporters in Bardoli to Narhari Parikh's attempts to run literacy classes for Adivasis has already been discussed. In Kheda, many peasant nationalists of the Patidar caste were similarly opposed towards attempts to integrate the local Dalits within the struggle. When Gandhi toured the area in 1925 he was deeply upset to see that in a meeting at Bhadran—a leading Patidar village—a bamboo fence had been erected to keep the Dalits apart from the high castes. He insisted that the fence be removed. At nearby Sunav, his foremost Patidar supporters were reluctant to hold a meeting in his honour as they anticipated that some of their caste-fellows would insult their leader to his face by openly condemning his work for the Dalits.[113] These were villages that had supported Gandhi strongly in other respects. The prevalence of such attitudes in what was considered to be the Gandhian heartland shows that Ambedkar's fears were well justified.

[113]Hardiman, *Peasant Nationalists of Gujarat*, p. 173.

Gandhi also made mistakes. His initial dismissive attitude towards Ambedkar created a tension between the two that was to continue even after Gandhi was forced to acknowledge that the Dalit was an outstanding leader of his community. Ambedkar tried hard to reach out to Gandhi during the mid-1930s, but Gandhi did not respond with any great generosity of spirit. Though their mutual debate encouraged both to modify their approaches in significant respects—so that by the 1940s there was less of an ideological gap between them—the bitterness of their encounter in the 1930s continues to inform the Dalit movement in India to this day.

Gandhi devoted an immense amount of his energy to the Dalit issue, for he saw it as a crucial index of the commitment of the Indian people in the building of a nation informed by principles of egalitarianism and democracy. The urgency of his commitment stemmed from his realisation that if he did not provide a viable solution, the Dalits might be alienated from the nationalist project as a whole. This urgency was lacking in the case of the Adivasis up until the end of the 1930s, when some of their leaders began to shift towards the Muslim League. It was only after this that Gandhi moved the Adivasi question up the nationalist agenda. Following this, there was an intense discussion in the early 1940s over the place of these peoples within the emerging nation. On one side there were those who argued that the Adivasis should be given legal protection against non-Adivasis, so that they would have space to work through their own destinies within the nation-state; on the other those who believed that the faster the Adivasis were integrated within the wider society, the sooner they would be able to hold their own. Gandhians were mainly in the latter camp. Once again, the parameters were being drawn up for a debate that would be destined to persist, as the quality of life of the large majority of Adivasis continued to deteriorate in post-independence India.

7

Fighting Religious Hatreds

> ... there are two principles embodied in a democratic system: rule by majority is one; but respect for certain individual and collective rights and freedoms is the other and more fundamental one. Should the two principles collide, it is the second that must at all costs be defended. Thus to resist the encroachment of basic rights by a duly elected government is not to deny democracy but to uphold it.[1]

> I do not believe in the doctrine of the greatest good of the greatest number. It means in its nakedness that in order to achieve the supposed good of 51 per cent, the interests of 49 per cent may be, or rather should be, sacrificed.[2]

Gandhi believed that all people had a right to practise any religion they chose to identify with, and that forms of worship should not be dictated by the state. Although himself a Hindu, he carried on a sympathetic dialogue with those of other faiths, arguing that each represented a different path towards Truth. His views were in part a product of his upbringing in Saurashtra, a region in which there was no obvious history of communal antagonism and in which the local rulers had for centuries pursued a policy of religious tolerance. His father, Karamchand Gandhi, was a follower of the Vallabhacharya Vaishnava sect, which was strong among the mercantile and Baniya élites. He was, it is said, always

[1]Randle, *Civil Resistance*, p. 183.

[2]Letter to Jal A.D. Naoroji, 4 June 1932, *CWMG*, Vol. 55, p. 482.

fascinated by the beliefs of those of other faiths and he used to enjoy discussing them in an open-minded way with Muslims, Parsis, and people of other sects who visited their home from day to day.

His mother, Putaliba, was a follower of the syncretic Pranami sect, which was founded in the early eighteenth century by Prannath, who preached that the Puranas, the Koran and the Bible represented merely alternative paths to the One God. No images were allowed in his temples, merely scriptures of different religions. Putaliba was from a relatively humble Baniya family—considered to be much lower in status to that of her husband—and in following the Pranami sect, her family adhered to the popular syncretism of the people rather than the more orthodox Vaishnavism of her husband's family. It is claimed that Gandhi imbibed much of her attitude in his religious belief as well as practice.[3]

Although there is truth in this so far as Gandhi's own upbringing was concerned, being raised in a high-caste family in Saurashtra was no guarantee of such tolerance. Swami Dayanand Saraswati had also been brought up in a wealthy and prominent family of the small state of Morvi, not so far from Rajkot, where Gandhi spent most of his childhood.[4] His Arya Samaj became the foremost vehicle in early-twentieth-century India for an assault on the religious loyalties of non-Hindus, with its strident orchestration of a so-called 'purification' of Muslims and Christians to bring them 'back' to Hinduism. Gandhi viewed such activities with distaste, and criticised Dayanand for his narrow-mindedness and intolerance in this respect.[5]

Gandhi's religious tolerance was reinforced by secularist doctrines that had emerged in Europe in the years after the religious wars of the post-Reformation period. The latter was formulated most clearly by John Locke, who argued that the state should not seek to adjudicate within the sphere of private belief—this was a matter for the subjective conscience of the individual.[6] Gandhi's commitment to this principle comes out very clearly in two statements made at a time when the

[3]Pyarelal, *Mahatma Gandhi*, Volume 1, *The Early Phase*, pp. 213–15.

[4]J.T.F. Jordens, *Dayanand Sarasvati: His Life and Ideas*, Oxford University Press, New Delhi 1978, p. 4.

[5]'Growing Distrust', *Young India*, 29 May 1924, *CWMG*, Vol. 28, p. 53.

[6]Talal Asad, 'Comments on Conversion', in Peter van der Veer (ed.), *Conversion*

division of India along supposedly 'religious' lines was looming before him. In September 1946 he reassured a Christian missionary who had asked him whether religion would be separate from the state after Indian independence: 'If I were a dictator, religion and state would be separate. I swear by my religion. I will die for it. But it is my personal affair. The State has nothing to do with it. The State would look after your secular welfare, health, communications, foreign relations, currency and so on, but not your or my religion. That is everybody's personal concern!'[7] Five months later he condemned the suggestion that the state should concern itself in religious education:

> I do not believe that the State can concern itself or cope with religious education. I believe that religious education must be the sole concern of religious associations. Do not mix up religion and ethics. I believe that fundamental ethics is common to all religions. Teaching of fundamental ethics is undoubtedly a function of the State. By religion I have not in mind fundamental ethics but what goes by the name of denominationism. We have suffered enough from State-aided religion and State Church. A society or group, which depends partly or wholly on State aid for the existence of its religion, does not deserve or, better still, does not have any religion worth the name.[8]

Gandhi, Muslims, and Hindu Nationalists

One of the most important issues which was debated and fought over in Gandhi's time was the question whether or not Indian nationalism was compromised by the presence of large numbers of Muslims in India. There were many Hindu nationalists who believed that Muslims could not be genuine Indian patriots as their religious 'home' lay outside the subcontinent.[9] Many Muslims, on the other hand, saw that the Indian National Congress was dominated by high-caste Hindus, and felt that

---

to Modernities: The Globalisation of Christianity, Routledge, New York 1996, pp. 268–9.

[7]'Talk with a Christian Missionary', *Harijan*, 22 September 1946, *CWMG*, Vol. 92, p. 190.

[8]Gandhi to E.W. Aryanayakum, 21 February 1947, *CWMG*, Vol. 94, p. 19.

[9]According to Gyanendra Pandey, the term 'Hindu nationalist' does not 'refer simply to nationalists who happen to be Hindus. It is, rather, an indication of their

the 'India' which they projected was one ruled by high-caste, and particularly Brahmanical, values. The British argued that India could never be a viable nation-state as Hindus and Muslims could never live in peace because of their inborn enmity. There was nothing peculiarly Indian, or 'Third World', about such debates as such—defining what constitutes the nation has been and continues to be a controversial matter in all parts of the world. In England, for example, 'Englishness' was often associated with Protestantism, particularly Anglicanism, while non-Protestants, particularly Catholics who supposedly owed their allegiance to the Roman pope, were seen to be inadequate as Englishmen and suspect in their patriotism.[10]

Gandhi took a secular line on this question, stating in *Hind Swaraj* that: 'India cannot cease to be one nation because people belonging to different religions live in it. ... If the Hindus believe that India should be peopled only by Hindus, they are living in dreamland. The Mahomedans also live in dreamland if they believe that there should be only Muslims in India.'[11] They were fellow countrymen who had to live in unity.

Gandhi saw the divide as an aberration, being a poisonous consequence of colonial rule. In the past, he argued, peoples of the two religions had flourished under rulers of both faiths, but 'with the English advent quarrels re-commenced'. He sought to counter these artificial divisions by insisting that: 'Religions are different roads converging to the same point.' There was a lot in the Koran which Hindus could endorse, just as there was much in the Bhagavat Gita which Muslims could agree with. It was important that Hindus gained the trust of Muslims by backing their sectional demands.[12] Because of this, Gandhi supported the establishment of separate electorates for Muslims in 1909—as it was a 'Muslim demand'.

brand of nationalism, a brand in which the "Hindu" moment has considerable weight. It is a nationalism in which Hindu culture, Hindu traditions and the Hindu community are given pride of place.' Pandey, *Remembering Partition*, p. 154.

[10]Gauri Viswanathan, *Ouside the Fold*, pp. 25–6.

[11]Gandhi, *Hind Swaraj*, *CWMG*, Vol. 10, p. 270.

[12]Ibid., pp. 270–4.

In 1919, Gandhi extended his support to another supposedly sectional demand of the Muslims, that of the Khilafat. In the short term this brought great political gains for him, for with the support of the Khilafatists he was able to win the crucial vote for non-cooperation at the Calcutta Congress session of August 1920. The Khilafat cause was however a dubious one. Its proponents did not speak for the majority of Muslims in India, who were in general followers of the Sufi, Barelvi and Shia systems of worship. These traditions were known for their tolerance. Likewise, the Khilafatists opposed the secularist Muslims of the Muslim League, led by Muhammad Ali Jinnah, who had engineered the Lucknow Pact with the Congress in 1916.

The Khilafatists represented mainly the group which has been defined as the Muslim 'salariat'—that is, Muslims with an Anglo-Vernacular education who sought jobs in government service and the modern professions, often with limited success.[13] They were readers of the popular Urdu newspapers that had emerged in the past twenty or so years, and which at that time had—to boost their circulation—taken up the issue of the supposed threat to the Khalifa of Turkey as a result of British hostility during the First World War. Populist mullahs and maulanas took up the issue in similar vein. After the war ended, the British in fact went back to supporting the Turkish Khalifa against internal enemies, notably the republican nationalists associated with Mustafa Kemal. The fact that the Khalifa collapsed in 1924 had nothing to do with the British—it represented, rather, a triumph for the forces of change in Turkey against a vicious autocracy. Logically, Muslim nationalists in India should have supported Mustafa Kemal and his republicans, who were fighting against a British-supported tyrant. But, as Hamza Alavi has demonstrated, the whole Khilafatist position was riven by contradiction.[14]

In 1919, so keen was Gandhi to maintain a dialogue with the Muslims that he allowed himself to be persuaded by the rhetoric of Khilafat leaders such as Mahomed and Shaukat Ali, Abul Kalam Azad, Abdul Bari and Hasrat Mohani. In their speeches they claimed that the institution of the Khalifa as the political head of all Muslims was set out in

[13]Hamza Alavi, 'Ironies of History: Contradictions of the Khilafat Movement', *Comparative Studies of South Asia, Africa and the Middle East*, Vol. 17, No. 1, p. 8.

[14]Ibid., pp. 11–13.

the holy scriptures of Islam. In fact, this assertion was false—there was no such sanction for this idea. Indeed, the claim of the Ottoman Sultans to be the Khalifa went back hardly more than one hundred years.[15] Like many others at that time, Gandhi was taken in by this concoction, backed up as it was by seemingly scholarly quotations in Arabic.[16] As a result, he endorsed the Khilafat position through a misplaced trust—believing that this was a heartfelt plea of the 'Indian Muslim', when in fact it was a highly contentious and sectional demand put forward by populist maulanas.

The politics that Gandhi was now endorsing was not defined by the subjective individual conscience, but that of an alleged collective that was defined in religious terms. He thus both politicised religion and communalised the proto-democracy that was being forged in India at that time. By supporting the Muslim clergy, Gandhi also endorsed the position of a group that was often reactionary and divisive. The lasting legacy of this was, in Alavi's words, 'the legitimisation of the Muslim clergy at the centre of the modern political arena, armed with a political organization in the form of the *Jamiat-e-Ulama-e-Hind* (and its successors after the Partition) which the clergy have used to intervene actively in both the political and ideological spheres. Never before in Indian Muslim history was the clergy ever accorded such a place in political life.'[17] At the same time, Gandhi alienated some Muslim secularists who would have been better allies in the long term, notably Muhammad Ali Jinnah. Jinnah's championship of a secularist and cosmopolitan politics for the Muslim League provided a counter to the grandiose claims of the Khilafatists to represent the Muslims of India. They sought to vilify him in whatever way they could; at the Calcutta Congress of September 1920, Shaukat Ali even assaulted Jinnah physically—he had to be wrenched away by the other delegates.[18] Jinnah and Gandhi fell out decisively in October 1920 when Gandhi demanded that the Home Rule League support the Non-Cooperation movement. Jinnah, who was president of the Bombay branch of the League and a leading figure

[15]Ibid., p. 2.
[16]Ibid., pp. 3 and 6.
[17]Ibid., p. 1.
[18]Ibid., p. 14.

in the organisation since its establishment in 1915, argued that the body had been set up to fight for home rule for India by legal means, and that a two-thirds majority was required to change the League's constitution in this respect. Gandhi, who chaired this meeting, ignored him and pushed through a majority vote in his own favour. Jinnah was furious, and resigned his membership.[19] Some of Gandhi's strongest Muslim supporters were very worried by this turn of events. Abbas Tyabji, for example, warned Gandhi that the Ali brothers were effective as rabble-rousers, but that he would never want to have them in positions of responsibility or authority over him.[20] In this, he implied that people like Jinnah were more deserving of their trust.

At the same time, Gandhi was courting Hindu nationalist organisations, in particular the Arya Samaj and the Hindu Mahasabha. Gandhi admired the educational work of the Arya Samaj, with its gurukuls. Even while in South Africa he had been in touch with Mahatma Munshiram, who had founded the Kangri Gurukul at Hardwar in 1902. Munshiram, who became later known as Swami Shraddhananda, had collected funds for Gandhi's work in South Africa. Immediately after his return to India in 1915, Gandhi had visited this institution and praised it highly.[21] In 1916, Gandhi attended an Arya Samaj conference in Surat and performed the opening ceremony of its new temple there. In his speech he said that although he was not an Arya Samajist, he had 'especial respect for the Samaj', and that he had come under the influence of its founder Dayanand Saraswati.[22]

The Hindu Mahasabha was founded at Hardwar in April 1915. Gandhi attended the inaugural meeting and spoke in favour of the body.[23] Its main support came from high-caste Hindu businessmen and professionals in Uttar Pradesh, most of whom were also active in

[19] *Bombay Chronicle*, 5 October 1920, p. 7, and 7 October 1920, p. 8.

[20] Judith Brown, *Gandhi's Rise to Power: Indian Politics 1915–1922*, Cambridge University Press, Cambridge 1972, p. 276.

[21] J.F.T. Jordens, *Swami Shraddhananda: His Life and Causes*, Oxford University Press, New Delhi 1981, pp. 92–3.

[22] Speech at Arya Samaj Annual Celebrations, Surat, 2 January 1916, *CWMG*, Vol. 15, p. 123.

[23] Richard Gordon, 'The Hindu Mahasabha and the Indian National Congress, 1915 to 1926', *Modern Asian Studies*, Vol. 9, No. 2, 1975, p. 161.

Congress politics. Madan Mohan Malaviya, the founder of the Banaras Hindu University and President of Congress in 1909 and 1918, was the most influential figure within it. Gandhi was in close contact with Malaviya from 1915 onwards. In 1919 he praised him as 'a great leader of India' and 'the patriarch of Hinduism'.[24]

Although Gandhi was seeking a base for himself within these Hindu organisations, he did not give unqualified support to their agendas. In 1916 he told some Arya Samajists that they could do better work if they reformed themselves in some important respects. In particular, he disliked the way that the organisation's spokesmen were 'only too ready to enter into violent controversy to gain their end'.[25] He also felt that the education provided by the gurukuls failed to inculcate a spirit of self-sufficiency, and he recommended that they provide training in agriculture, handicrafts and sanitation.[26]

Gandhi claimed at this time to be a highly orthodox Hindu of the Sanatanist persuasion.[27] He took up the issue of cow protection, calling it the central fact of Hinduism that symbolised the Hindu's reverence for all of God's creation.[28] When he was criticised by Goswami Shri Gokalnathji Maharaj, a leader of the Vallabhacharya Vaishnavites, for his rejection of the institution of untouchability, Gandhi argued that he was as orthodox as any. 'Do not conclude that I am a polluted person, a reformer. A rigidly orthodox Hindu, I believe that the Hindu Shastras have no place for untouchability of the type practised now.'[29] On a visit to a Swaminarayan temple in 1921, he exclaimed: 'At this holy place, I declare, if you want to protect your "*Hindu dharma*", non-cooperation is [the] first as well as the last lesson you must learn up.'[30]

[24]Speech at Hindi Sammelan, Bombay, 19 April 1919, *CWMG*, Vol. 17, p. 445; 'Gujarat's Gift', *Navajivan*, 19 October 1919, *CWMG*, Vol. 19, p. 63.

[25]Speech at Arya Samaj Annual Celebrations, Surat, 2 January 1916, *CWMG*, Vol. 15, p. 124.

[26]Speech at Gurukul Anniversary, 20 March 1916, *CWMG*, Vol. 15, p. 207.

[27]Ibid., p. 203.

[28]'Hinduism', *Young India*, 6 October 1921, *CWMG*, Vol. 24, p. 373.

[29]Speech at Bardoli Taluka Conference, 29 January 1922, *CWMG*, Vol. 26, p. 373.

[30]Speech at Vadtal, 19 January 1921, in Mahadev Desai, *Day-to-Day with Gandhi*, Vol. 3, Sarva Seva Sangh, Banaras 1968, p. 227.

With appeals such as these, Gandhi managed to rally a significant number of Hindu nationalists behind him in the period up until 1922. Mahatma Munshiram, who had taken *sannyas* as Swami Shraddhananda in 1917, threw his support behind Gandhi in 1919. Previously he had distrusted the motives of politicians, but he felt that Gandhi's politics were different, being enthused with the spirit of religion.[31] For a time, he became a leading proponent of Hindu–Muslim unity, and was even invited to preach at the Jama Masjid in Delhi.[32] M.M. Malaviya threw his full support behind the Non-Cooperation Movement, and during those years the Hindu Mahasabha was in a state of hibernation.[33] Gandhi sought to win such people to a more tolerant and inclusive nationalism, insisting, for example, that cow protection should not be made a pretext for any antagonism against Muslims—their support for this cause should be won through love.[34]

As with the Khilafat, Gandhi was playing with fire. Although this strategy forged an unprecedented alliance—symbolised most strikingly by the saffron-clad Shraddhananda preaching from the pulpit of the Jama Masjid—it also brought a new credibility to the Hindu nationalists. Shraddhananda's popularity was much enhanced through his participation in Gandhi's movement. Malaviya had been previously an old-style élite Congressman without widespread support among the masses.

The implosion came after Gandhi called off civil disobedience and was arrested and jailed in early 1922. Already, the revolt by Muslim tenants in Malabar in 1921, which had been accompanied by attacks on Hindu landlords and cases of forcible conversion, had caused uneasy stirrings among the Hindu nationalists. They resented the way in which the Khilafat leaders had refused to condemn these attacks.[35] Swami Shraddhananda took it as a sign of Muslim bad faith: 'it appears that the Muslims only want to make India and the Hindus a mere means of strengthening their own cause. For them Islam comes first and Mother

[31]Jordens, *Swami Shraddhananda*, p. 107.
[32]Ibid., p. 109.
[33]Gordon, 'The Hindu Mahasabha', p. 161.
[34]'Hinduism,' *Young India*, 6 October 1921, *CWMG*, Vol. 24, pp. 373–4.
[35]Gordon, 'The Hindu Mahasabha', pp. 163 & 165.

India second. Should not the Hindus work at their own *sangathan* [consolidation]?'[36] In 1922 he turned on the offensive, demanding that the Congress provide funds for a campaign of reconversion of Muslims to Hinduism, known as *shuddhi*, or 'purification'. When this request was turned down, he renounced his affiliation with the Congress and forged new links with the Hindu Mahasabha. An All-India Shuddhi Sabha was formed at Agra in February 1923.[37]

In the same year, V.D. Savarkar published *Who is a Hindu?*, which defined a Hindu as those who regarded Bharatvarsha as their holy land and fatherland. This formula allowed a wide variety of religions within India, such as Shaivism, Vaishnavism, Jainism, Sikhism to be included within the 'Hindu' umbrella, but not religions such as Islam or Christianity, which were considered 'alien', and by extension, unpatriotic. The Hindu Mahasabha endorsed this definition at its session of August 1923. It also called for a campaign of shuddhi and the organisation of Hindu self-defence squads.[38]

Muslim leaders countered all this with their own *tabligh* (propaganda) and *tanzim* (organisation). There followed what has been described as 'a spate of Hindu-Muslim riots from 1923 onwards'.[39] One British observer calculated that eleven serious communal riots occurred in 1923, eighteen in 1924, sixteen in 1925, thirty-five in 1926 and thirty-one in 1927. The worst of these was in Calcutta in 1926 when 67 died and nearly 400 were injured.[40] The most notable victim of this violence was Swami Shraddhananda, who was assassinated in Delhi by a Muslim in December 1926.

One town in which there were disturbances in 1923 was Nagpur in the Maharashtrian part of the Central Provinces. Members of the

[36]Jordens, *Swami Shraddhananda*, p. 126.

[37]Gordon, 'The Hindu Mahasabha', pp. 163, 170 & 172.

[38]Basu *et al.*, *Khaki Shorts and Saffron Flags*, pp. 8–10.

[39]Gyanendra Pandey, *The Construction of Communalism in Colonial North India*, Oxford University Press, New Delhi 1990, p. 234.

[40]R. Coupland, *The Constitutional Problem In India*, Part 1, *The Indian Problem, 1833–1935*, Oxford University Press, Madras 1944, pp. 75–6. Coupland did not define what he meant by a 'serious' riot, so his seemingly exact figures should be taken as only a rough indicator of the gravity of the problem at that time.

local Hindu Sabha had taken out a procession in which they flaunted weapons and played loud music before the mosques of the town. The Muslims had fought back and many people were injured. The Muslims, who were mostly poor weavers, were forced to agree to allow music to be played in front of their mosques, and there were further armed processions with music in the following years.[41] In 1925, K.B. Hegdewar decided to put these activities on a firmer footing by establishing the Rashtriya Swayamsevak Sangh (RSS). Hegdewar was a Maharashtrian Brahman of Nagpur who had condemned Gandhi's alliance with the Khilafatists, arguing that it was impossible to ally with 'foreign snakes'.[42] The RSS ran daily sessions for boys and young men—known as *shakhas*—which involved physical training and the propagation of right-wing Hindu beliefs. There was training in the use of sticks, swords, javelins and daggers—weapons associated with street fighting. In 1927, the RSS played a leading and aggressive role in another riot in Nagpur in which twenty-two people died. From 1928, the body extended their activities to Uttar Pradesh. M.M. Malaviya supported them fully, providing an office for the organisation at the Banaras Hindu University.[43]

Gandhi was sickened by what he saw as an eruption of hatred that was destroying the achievements of previous years. After his release from prison in February 1924 he received many abusive letters from Hindus who accused him of opening the floodgates by uniting the Muslims of India behind the Khilafat cause. They argued that the 'awakened' Muslims had reverted to their true nature by launching 'a kind of jehad' against the Hindus.[44] Muslims wrote to him complaining

[41]David Baker, *Changing Political Leadership in an Indian Province: The Central Provinces and Berar 1919–1939*, Oxford University Press, New Delhi 1979, p. 101.

[42]He used the word '*yavan*', which is a pejorative term in Hindi which can mean 'foreign', 'Muslim', 'European', or 'barbarian'. McGregor, *The Oxford Hindi-English Dictionary*, p. 842.

[43]Basu *et al.*, *Khaki Shorts and Saffron Flags*, pp. 14–18 & 20–1. It should be noted that the RSS was yet to become a major political force and that many nationalists who supported or praised aspects of their work at that time were probably unaware of the more sinister elements of their beliefs and activities.

[44]Gandhi wrote about this correspondence in 'Hindu-Muslim Tension: Its Cause and Cure', *Young India*, 29 May 1924, *CWMG*, Vol. 28, p. 43.

of the shuddhi and sangathan activities of the Hindus.[45] Many Hindus saw non-violence and satyagraha as discredited forces, claiming that contrary to Gandhi's reading, the Bhagavad Gita enjoined violence in defence of one's faith. Gandhi refused, however, to believe that all was lost—this was a sad regression, but not a defeat. The fighting between Hindus and Muslims was a squalid diversion from the much more important struggle for freedom from British rule, and this battle would not be won through violence. Non-violence would be vindicated in the end because it was the only true way forward.[46]

Gandhi warned the Hindus that if they deployed violence in this way, they were likely to come off as losers. This was because: 'My own experience but confirms that the Mussalman as a rule is a bully, and the Hindu as a rule is a coward. I have noticed this in railway trains, on public roads, and in the quarrels which I have had the privilege of settling.'[47] The answer to this was not, however, gymnastic training and physical exercises which had an aggressive intent. Muslims would play the same game, and the violence would merely escalate. What was needed was training in non-violent resistance and a willingness to arbitrate in communal quarrels. This required far more courage. 'The remedy against cowardice is not physical culture but the braving of dangers.'[48]

Gandhi said that he had also been warned that people like M.M. Malaviya, Lala Lajpat Rai and Swami Shraddhananda had had a hand in stirring up this hatred against Muslims. He refused to accept this. He had worked closely with Malaviya since 1915, and knew that hatred was alien to his being. 'He and I are temperamentally different, but love each other like brothers.' Lajpat Rai had assured him personally that he put unity before division as he believed so strongly in swaraj.[49] Gandhi was less generous towards Swami Shraddhananda. Although he admired his bravery and his educational work, his speeches were

[45]Ibid., p. 44.
[46]Ibid., pp. 44 & 47–8.
[47]Ibid., p. 49.
[48]Ibid., p. 50.
[49]Ibid., p. 52.

'often irritating' and had the unjustifiablc ambition of bringing all Muslims into the Aryan fold. Gandhi went on to criticise the Arya Samaj. He had read Dayanand Saraswati's *Satyarth Prakash*—'the Arya Samaj Bible'—for the first time when he was in jail. In his opinion, Saraswati had severely misrepresented all religions, including Hinduism. 'He has tried to make narrow one of the most tolerant and liberal of the faiths on the face of the earth.'[50]

Gandhi then launched an attack on the shuddhi campaign. He argued that proselytism was alien to the spirit of Hinduism, and he accused the Arya Samaj of imitating Christian missionaries. Like the missionary, 'The Arya Samaj preacher is never so happy as when he is reviling other religions.'[51] This all did far more harm than good. 'My Hindu instinct tells me that all religions are more or less true. All proceed from the same God, but all are imperfect because they have come to us through imperfect human instrumentality. The real shuddhi movement should consist in each one trying to arrive at perfection in his or her own faith.'[52] He also condemned the Muslim campaign of tabligh as being alien to the spirit of Islam. He had read some pamphlets from the Punjab, and found them full of hatred and vile abuse.

He went on to examine some of the so-called 'causes' of the animosity, such as cow-slaughter by Muslims and playing music before mosques by Hindus. Gandhi said that although he believed strongly in protecting cows, this worthy principle could never be served by attacking Muslims; indeed, such aggression was likely to make Muslims kill even more cows. The Hindu demand was full of hypocrisy, as Hindus routinely maltreated their cattle, and when they became old they sold them to Muslim butchers well knowing what their fate would be. It was only by befriending Muslims that they could be persuaded to refrain from cow-slaughter. As for music, Hindus should consult with their Muslim neighbours and come to mutually agreeable arrangements in the matter. In many cases, however, music was being played with the sole intention of irritating Muslims, and this was wholly unacceptable.[53] Gandhi concluded:

[50]Ibid., pp. 52–3.
[51]Ibid., p. 56.
[52]Ibid.
[53]Ibid., pp. 58–9.

For me the only question for immediate solution before the country is the Hindu–Mussalman question. I agree with Mr. Jinnah that Hindu-Muslim unity means swaraj. I see no way of achieving anything in this afflicted country without a lasting heart unity between Hindus and Mussalmans of India. I believe in the immediate possibility of achieving it, because it is so natural, so necessary for both, and because I believe in human nature.[54]

In September of that year, Gandhi sought to bring about such a change of heart by fasting for twenty-one days in the house of a Muslim friend. The rioting, however, continued. By 1927 he was forced to admit: 'I am out of tune with the present temper of both the communities. From their own standpoint they are perhaps entitled to say that my method has failed.'[55]

Some commentators have argued that Gandhi's attempt to forge communal harmony was doomed because he was so obviously a Hindu. His massive popularity with the majority was gained through his religious appeal, but in the process he alienated the religious minorities. W. Norman Brown claims, for example, that: 'He could not in his time have become the political leader of the majority group in India, fortified by mass support, without being religious, he could not be religious without being a Hindu. He could not be a Hindu without being suspect to the Muslim community.'[56] This latter argument is wrong empirically, for even after the communal clashes of the 1923–7 period, many Muslims continued to follow Gandhi with fervour. Most notable in this respect was Abdul Ghaffar Khan and his Khudai Khidmatgars or 'Servants of God'. They were from the Pathan or Pukhtun community of the North West Frontier Province, which had been the first in the subcontinent to convert to Islam in the eighth century when the Prophet Muhammad was still living.[57] They were known, stereotypically, for their supposed propensity for violence, and thus seem the most unlikely of satyagrahis. Yet, they became model Gandhians in this respect.

[54]Ibid., p. 61.

[55]*Young India*, 1 December 1927, *CWMG*, Vol. 40, p. 476.

[56]Cited in Martin Deming Lewis (ed.), *Gandhi, Maker of Modern India?*, D.C. Heath, Boston 1966, p. xiii.

[57]Mukulika Banerjee, *The Pathan Unarmed: Opposition and Memory in the North West Frontier*, Oxford University Press, New Delhi 2001, p. 21.

The movement of the Khudai Khidmatgars began in the 1920s as a revolt by tenants and small peasants of the community against the big landlords and reactionary mullahs who, supported by the British, ruled this society. The mullahs, who received stipends from the colonial state, taught the people that one had to suffer in this world to gain paradise; they also opposed popular education, stating that if the poor were educated they would go to hell. Abdul Ghaffar Khan took the mullahs head on, showing that they were the spokesmen for the rich landlords.[58] Because he was known to have a strong grasp of the scriptures and had a reputation for asceticism and holiness, the vilification of him by the mullahs as a kafir, or unbeliever, found few takers. He was in fact known in the area as a faqir, which means both a religious ascetic and a beggar, and in the North West Frontier region was often used by the élites in a contemptuous manner to refer to peasants without land. By making poverty a virtue, he gave a new and positive meaning to the term as it was applied to the landless poor.[59]

Initially, Khan had approached the Muslim League, hoping to affiliate his movement with it. The leaders of this party did not however believe that their interests would be best served by confronting the colonial state and they showed no interest in an alliance with the Khudai Khidmatgars. Khan then approached Gandhi and the Congress and was welcomed with open arms.[60] All Khudai Khidmatgars had to take an oath in the name of God and with one hand on the Koran that they would observe strict non-violence.[61] Khan was very impressed by the way that women had become active in the Gandhian Congress, and encouraged Pukhtun women to play a vigorous role in protests. He knew that the mullahs would damn him for this, but decided that it was a risk worth taking.[62] The British tried to crush the movement in a brutal manner, with beatings, whipping, torture and confiscation of land.[63] The people stood firm with admirable discipline and non-

[58]Ibid., pp. 48, 52 and 62–8.

[59]Ibid., p. 154.

[60]Ibid., p. 69.

[61]Ibid., p. 73.

[62]Ibid., pp. 97–101.

[63]Ibid., pp. 111–20.

violence. The Khudai Khidmatgars saw themselves as being first and foremost good Muslims, and only secondarily as followers of Gandhi.[64] Through their example, they proved that Gandhian methods of resistance could, when the conditions were right, triumph over narrow religious divides.

This gives the lie to arguments of the sort advanced by W. Norman Brown that the divide between Hindus and Muslims in India was such that it was impossible for a saintly leader of one faith to have any appeal to those of the other. The appeal of many Indian saints has, historically, often cut across religious lines. In many cases it has been hard to categorise particular bhakti sants, faqirs and Sufi pirs as unambiguously 'Hindu' or 'Muslim'. Gandhi's identity in this respect was partially forged and partially projected on him by the people out of a *bricolage* of popular religious belief, of the sants, faqirs, pirs, and even the morality of Christ.[65] In the process, he was able to cut across narrow religious divides and built a rapport with people of various faiths. Many Muslims in India revered him as they would a pir or faqir.

This was seen in the matter of his dress. Some have argued that he alienated Muslims by adopting the garb of a 'Hindu' renouncer. He was aware of this particular criticism, and sought to answer it in 1931 by stating that he had taken the decision to wear only a short *langoti* because he had been told by some poor people in 1921 that they could not afford to dress in a long dhoti and kurta made of khadi. In his opinion, the langoti was a mark of an Indian civilisation which 'spells simplicity', and was not to be seen as having any particular religious connotation.[66] In fact, many faqirs and Sufi pirs—who are classed generally as Muslims—adopted such a garb also. Ironically, Winston Churchill—who otherwise projected Gandhi as a narrowly Hindu politician—acknowledged this fact without meaning to when he accused him of 'posing as a fakir of a type well-known in the East.'[67]

[64]Ibid., p. 149.

[65]Sunil Khilnani, *The Idea of India*, Penguin, Harmondsworth 1998, pp. 164–5.

[66]'The Loin Cloth', *Young India*, 30 April 1931, in *CWMG*, Vol. 52, p. 8.

[67]Churchill quote from Martin Gilbert, *Winston S. Churchill*, Vol. 5, *1922–1939*, Heinemann, London 1976, p. 390. Gandhi later said that he had considered

Gandhi was very careful to avoid sectarianism in his daily practice. For example, in his ashram rules he set out the vows that all inmates were required to take, and although each could have been supported by a quotation from the Shastras, he refused to do this on the ground that 'the principles implicit in the vows are not a monopoly of Hinduism but are common to all faiths.'[68] At his daily prayer meetings hymns from different religious traditions were sung as a matter of routine. He also refused to allow the nationalist workers at his ashram to dress in saffron, insisting that they wear white khadi. The reason he gave for this was that he did not want these 'servants of the people' to be confused with Hindu sannyasis.[69]

Despite this there were, as we have seen, certain problems with the way in which Gandhi handled the issue of the communal divide. In addition to his questionable espousal of the Khilafat issue, he tended to tolerate the communalists who were present in the ranks of the Congress. Thus, although he criticised the Arya Samaj for stirring up animosity, he absolved from blame other Hindu nationalists such as Malaviya and Lajpat Rai. For all their claims to love Muslims, their actual politics were hardly conducive to harmonious communal relations. Muslims who had a less sanguine attitude towards their activities were given one more reason to distrust the motives of the Congress as a whole.

Another problem was that Gandhi gave credibility to stereotypes about each community when he talked about 'bullying' Muslims and 'cowardly' Hindus. In this, he was attributing an essential character to each religious group in a way that depersonalised individuals and made each into a supposedly natural representative of the one or the other. The individual thus became a bearer of the supposed characteristics of a group that was divided from others by its very being. Too much ground

---

it to be an honour to be called a 'fakir'. He even wrote to Churchill saying 'I would love to be a naked fakir but was not one as yet.' Fischer, *The Life of Mahatma Gandhi*, p. 547.

[68]'My Notes', *Navajivan*, 17 June 1928, *CWMG*, Vol. 42, p. 128.

[69]Kaka Kalelkar, *Stray Glimpses of Bapu*, Navajivan Publishing House, Ahmedabad 1960, pp. 32–3.

was being conceded to the characteristic argument of the communalist that a people's traits were rooted in their religion.

Gandhi was however not insensitive to the problem of label-sticking, knowing from his own experience the offence it could give. For example, many Punjabi Sikhs had told him that they did not consider themselves to be Hindu, yet when he described them as 'non-Hindu' in *Young India* in 1924, he was swamped by letters of protest from Sikhs. Similarly with Jains and Arya Samajists—some demanded to be considered Hindu, others repudiated the classification strongly. He stated that he personally felt that these particular faiths were a part of a broad Hindu culture, but he was more concerned not to offend them than to press his own views on the matter.[70]

This latter statement might appear to concede ground to the position that only those who belonged to such a broad Hindu culture could be genuine patriots. His position on this was however very firm—patriotism could not be defined in religious terms. Muslims in India were as much Indians as Muslims in Turkey were Turks: 'Islamic culture is not the same in Arabia, Turkey, Egypt and India but is itself influenced by the conditions of the respective countries. Indian culture is therefore Indian. It is neither Hindu, Islamic nor any other, wholly. It is a fusion of all ...'[71] Gandhi increasingly began to see that the problem of Muslim alienation from the Congress was caused as much by the intolerance of many Hindus as by Islamic fundamentalism. He condemned the 'Hindu patronizing attitude' which was causing disgust to many Congress Muslims, stating in July 1946 that: 'Hindu separatism has played a part in creating the rift between Congress and the League.'[72] When told at the same time that Jinnah was accusing him of wanting only Hindu rule he launched an angry attack on both Jinnah and Hindu nationalism: 'He is utterly wrong. That is absurd. I am a Moslem, a Hindu, a Buddhist,

[70]'Are Sikhs Hindus?' *Young India*, 22 May 1924, *CWMG*, Vol. 28, pp. 10–11.

[71]'The Loin Cloth', *Young India*, 30 April 1931, *CWMG*, Vol. 52, pp. 8–9. Parekh argues that Gandhi was classifying Muslims as 'ex-Hindus' in this passage. This is, in my opinion, the direct opposite of what Gandhi was actually saying. Parekh, *Gandhi's Political Philosophy*, p. 178.

[72]Fischer, *The Life of Mahatma Gandhi*, p. 542.

a Christian, a Jew, a Parsi. He does not know me when he says I want Hindu rule. He is not speaking the truth.'[73]

The 'National Duty' of the Hindu Patriot

During the 1920s, Gandhi still sought to win the more chauvinistic Hindu nationalists over to his way of thought. For example, in 1925 he was involved in the establishment of an All-India Cow Protection Sabha which he hoped would pursue this issue in a less confrontational way.[74] By the early 1930s it was apparent that these initiatives were not working—he continued to be the target of venomous hostility from hardline Hindus. Ashis Nandy has argued that Gandhi antagonised the Hindu nationalists not so much by what he said, as by the fact that he took his message to the people. Many were Brahmans who could tolerate intellectual dissent, but not low-caste assertion. Even more galling, Gandhi criticised the westernisation of many Brahmans and projected himself as the 'real' Hindu.[75] In Maharashtra, in particular, Gandhi's popularity with the non-Brahman masses infuriated many members of the Brahman élite, most notably those clustered around the Hindu Mahasabha, RSS and even more extreme groups, such as Nathuram Godse's Hindu Rashtra Dal. Godse was Gandhi's eventual killer.[76]

Nandy's analysis is only partial, for the more extreme Hindu nationalists were also strongly antagonistic to Gandhi's non-violence. They saw this as going against the national interest of the Hindu people, who needed to arm themselves to fight against 'foreign' enemies, such as the British and the Muslims. They considered Gandhi and his doctrine of ahimsa to be the single greatest obstacle to building a strong and militaristic Indian nation, and felt that it would be a boon if he could be removed from the scene, by violence if necessary. V.D. Savarkar set out the intellectual justification for this mindset in a book that he published after Gandhi's death called *Six Glorious Epochs of Indian History.*

[73]Ibid., pp. 543–4.

[74]'All-India Cow Protection Sabha,' 15 March 1925, *CWMG*, Vol. 30, pp. 428–30.

[75]Nandy, 'Final Encounter', pp. 75–6.

[76]Ibid., pp. 76–8 and 81.

There is no evidence that Savarkar himself actually plotted the assassination of Gandhi at any time, but it is known that the actual assassins were his devoted disciples, and they may well have been encouraged in their task by notions that he had put in their head through his particular interpretation of Indian history.[77] In this book, Savarkar is noticeably silent on the subject of Gandhi's murder, for it was hardly a matter he could seek to justify in a direct way at that time. Instead, he used a historical analogy to make his point. He argued that the emperor Ashoka was a ruler of great moral power, but that his endorsement of Buddhism and non-violence had seriously weakened the Indian national polity. Ashoka, he stated, had carried out 'an excessive propaganda in favour of certain Buddhist principles like Ahimsa *and the rest* which have caused so much harm to the Indian political outlook, her political independence, and her empire ...' He condemned such preaching and practice as 'anti-national'.[78] Because of this, India was soon invaded by a foreign power, 'the aggressive Greeks'.[79] Resistance came at last only after a Brahman warrior called Pushyamitra—a staunch devotee of Shiva and follower of the Vedic religion—assassinated the last of the Maurya emperors. Savarkar argued that: 'Pushyamitra had simply done the unavoidable national duty of killing Ashoka's descendant, Brihadrath Maurya, who had proved himself thoroughly incompetent to defend the independence of the Indian empire.'[80] The assassin became emperor and drove the Greeks—whom Savarkar describes as the 'Yavans'—from India, after which he performed the great horse sacrifice.[81]

The message in all this was clear—staunch patriots had a 'national duty' to eliminate influential apostles of non-violence through assassination. Nathuram Godse—an ardent follower of Savarkar—clearly held

[77]The police tried very hard to implicate Savarkar in Gandhi's assassination, but were unable to find any adequate proof. Although he was tried with the known assassins, he had to be acquitted. Manohar Malgonkar, *The Men who Killed Gandhi*, Macmillan, Madras 1978, pp. 160–79.

[78]Vinayak Damodar Savarkar, *Six Glorious Epochs of Indian History*, translated from Marathi by S.T. Godbole, Rajdhani Granthagar, New Delhi 1971, p. 62, emphasis in the original.

[79]Ibid., p. 68.

[80]Ibid., pp. 77–78.

[81]Ibid., pp. 79–80.

such a belief, deeming that it was his patriotic duty to kill Gandhi. The successful assassination of 30 January 1948 was not the first time that Godse had sought to do this. It is likely that he and his associates made an attempt to kill Gandhi with a bomb as early as 1934. In July 1944, Godse had gone to Panchgani, where Gandhi was recuperating from a bout of malaria, with the intention of stabbing him with a dagger. He was overpowered before he could get in his presence. Gandhi, when told of what had happened, asked Godse to spend eight days with him so that they could discuss their differences. Godse rejected the invitation. Gandhi, magnanimously, said that he was free to go.[82]

The contrast between the approaches of Gandhi and Godse was striking. Gandhi clearly put his faith in dialogue and forgiveness. Godse's motives for rejecting Gandhi's offer at Panchgani were less apparent. He was isolated, in a state of mental turmoil and no doubt keen to escape as soon as the opportunity was presented to him. The balance of power in any debate between the Mahatma surrounded by his acolytes and the bitter, disarmed young man would hardly have been an even-sided one. But also, he must have known that any such dialogue was likely to weaken his resolve.

Two months later, in September 1944, Godse and a colleague called Thatte led a group of men to Gandhi's ashram at Sevagram to protest against his forthcoming talks with Jinnah. They were apprehended at the gates by Gandhi's followers and Godse was found to be carrying a dagger. When questioned, either he or Thatte (the report is unclear as to who) stated that Gandhi would be killed and that one of them would become a 'martyr'. He was asked why he did not leave such things to his leader, V.D. Savarkar. In reply, he boasted: 'If Savarkar talks with Gandhi it will be an honour for Gandhi. The time will not come for Savarkar to talk to Gandhi. Gandhi will be dealt with by our lowly Orderly.' He and the others were then allowed to go on their way.[83] Once again, the idea of dialogue was rejected—it was below the dignity of their Great Leader, Veer Savarkar, to stoop to debate. Gandhi deserved only to be silenced, once and for all. Godse's whole approach, like that of the Hindu and Islamic right in general, was strongly monologic.

[82]Tushar A. Gandhi, http://web.mahatma.org.in/lattempts/attempt2.asp
[83]Ibid.

He hated Gandhi not for any one particular and contingent line of action—such as his attempt to protect Muslim lives in 1947–8—but because he represented a living refutation of the monologic mindset which formed the very core of his, Godse's, being.

Gandhi and Christianity

In nineteenth-century India, Christianity was associated strongly with British colonialism. Missionaries tended to be firm supporters of colonial rule, seeing their work as being a part of the colonial enterprise. In some cases they even acted as propagandists for violent imperial expansionism.[84] When describing their work, they frequently deployed the terminology of military aggression: 'recruiting agencies', 'marching orders', 'the far-flung battle line' and so on.[85] They believed that it was their task to 'civilise' heathens, weaning them from idolatry and inculcating Western values and 'Christian' cultural practices. Even the Anglican clergyman C.F. Andrews, who later became a close colleague of Gandhi, had been inspired by tales of imperial glory as a boy, and later, as a young priest, had run a club for boys in a working-class area of England that was named after the great imperial hero General Gordon. He used to tell the boys stories that glamorised imperialism. Only later did he become a strong critic of British rule in India.[86]

Although Gandhi was brought up in an atmosphere of religious tolerance, he developed an early antipathy to Christianity, which he experienced as a colonial subject. When still a schoolboy in Rajkot, he had paused to hear a missionary who was preaching in the street and was disgusted by the way he poured abuse on Hindus and their gods. He was also sickened by stories he heard that converts were made to eat beef, drink liquor and wear Western dress. This created in him an initial dislike for the Christian religion.[87]

[84]A Wesleyan minister, the Reverend William E. Fitchett, thus wrote a series of books glorifying British imperialism, with titles such as *Deeds that Won the Empire, Fights for the Flag, Tales of the Great Mutiny, How England Saved Wellington's Men,* and *Nelson and His Captains*, Green, *The Origins of Nonviolence*, p. 8.

[85]Fisher, *That Strange Little Brown Man Gandhi*, p. 117.

[86]Green, *The Origins of Nonviolence*, p. 8.

[87]Gandhi, *Autobiography*, *CWMG*, Vol. 44, pp. 116–17.

This changed to a certain degree during his period in London when he was studying law. He was given a Bible to read by a Christian, and although he failed to be impressed by the Old Testament with its vengeful God, he was very taken by the New Testament. He was particularly struck by the Sermon on the Mount, which he believed to be equal in moral authority to the *Bhagavad Gita*.[88] He was struck also by the way that Jesus Christ stood up for his principles, in particular when he drove the moneychangers from the temple. This made him more open to Christians and Christianity, and during his years in South Africa he came into contact with Christians whom he respected, including C.F. Andrews. Later, he even claimed that he had derived his idea of non-violence from the Sermon on the Mount, and that Christianity justified satyagraha: 'Jesus's whole preaching and practice point unmistakably to non-co-operation, which necessarily includes non-payment of taxes.'[89] He drew freely on the New Testament and used Christian hymns and Biblical texts in religious services at his ashrams. He also sought to emulate the Christian missionaries in their educational and welfare work, and favourably compared their dedicated work for the poor with the activities of sadhus and pandits.[90]

Gandhi was however careful to distinguish Christianity as a system of morality from Christianity as an arm of British imperialism. As he stated in 1929:

> Unfortunately, Christianity in India has been inextricably mixed up for the last one hundred and fifty years with the British rule. It appears to us as synonymous with materialistic civilization and imperialist exploitation by the stronger white races of the weaker races of the world. Its contribution to India has been therefore largely of a negative character.
>
> It has done some good in spite of its professors. It has shocked us into setting our own house in order. Christian missionary literature has drawn pointed attention to some of our abuses and set us athinking.[91]

[88]Discussion with Christian Missionaries, Jaffna, 27 November 1927, *CWMG*, Vol. 40, pp. 455–6.

[89]'Render unto Caesar', *Young India*, 27 March 1930, *CWMG*, Vol. 48, p. 483.

[90]Nandy, 'From Outside the Imperium', p. 172.

[91]Interview to Dr John Mott, before 1 March 1929, *CWMG*, Vol. 45, pp. 143–4.

Gandhi did not, however, seek to attack the British by condemning Christianity, for example by claiming it to be an inferior religion to Hinduism. Bankimchandra Chattopadhyay adopted such a stance, as have Hindu nationalists subsequently. This merely reversed the approach of Christian chauvinists, replacing one form of intolerance with another. Gandhi, by contrast, saw Christianity as a religion containing great moral truths, and he argued that modern Western civilisation had turned its back on these values.[92] Such an approach made it impossible to take an aggressive position against the 'Other' on the basis of their religion, whether it was Christianity or Islam.

After Gandhi began his work in India after 1915, a small number of Christian missionaries became his admirers, and in the process they often developed a new and more critical attitude towards the colonial state. The American missionary Frederick Fisher, for example, returned to India in 1917 after a seven-year absence, to find the name 'Gandhi' on everyone's lips. He did not know who Gandhi was, but decided to go and meet him. He immediately fell under his spell: 'The power of his personality, the fire in his great brown eyes, his innate dignity, draw you, irresistibly. You forget yourself; you forget Gandhi as a man. His deep voice carries to you his message only. It is because he has sunk himself so deeply in his ideal, that he has lost all self-consciousness; and therefore is greater than his puny body.'[93] For Christians such as Fisher, Gandhi appeared to exemplify all that a good Christian should be. Two years later he wrote a book called *India's Silent Revolution*, which praised Gandhi and the new spirit of nationalist awakening in India.[94]

Some missionaries began to try to adapt their practice more to Indian culture. Notable in this respect was J.C. Winslow, who founded the Christa Seva Sangh, which drew inspiration from the ashram ideals of Hindus as well as from Gandhi. The missionaries wore khadi, ate vegetarian food, lived in austere simplicity, composed bhajans and kirtans, and worked with the lowest castes. The young Verrier Elwin joined this organisation in 1927, and was soon working closely with Gandhi within the nationalist movement. In time, he even abandoned

[92]Chatterjee, *Nationalist Thought and the Colonial World*, p. 93.
[93]Fisher, *That Strange Little Brown Man Gandhi*, p. 78.
[94]Ibid., p. xv.

his desire to proselytise.[95] In 1931 Gandhi held Elwin up as an example of how Christian missionaries should operate in India, and he encouraged the establishment of 'Christian Ashrams'.[96]

Such missionaries were however in a minority. Those who did show sympathy for Gandhi and the nationalist movement soon found themselves under police surveillance. The C.I.D., for example, suspected Fisher—bizarrely—of being a 'Bolshevik agent' working under the cover of the priesthood.[97] He managed to avoid being expelled from India by appealing to the viceroy. Some other American missionaries with similar political opinions were however deported. In one such case, the local magistrate commented that it was the duty of everyone involved in educational, medical or other public work in India to voice his or her disapproval of the nationalist movement. Missionaries who did not follow this precept were in some cases beaten up by the police and even jailed.[98] It was not therefore surprising that missionaries who might otherwise have been sympathetic chose to keep their thoughts to themselves.

Despite his admiration for many individual Christian missionaries, Gandhi felt that missionaries in general had no right to convert people to a faith other than the one they had been brought up with. 'I disbelieve in the conversion of one person by another. My effort should never be to undermine another's faith but to make him a better follower of his own faith. This implies belief in the truth of all religions and therefore respect for them.'[99] What he rejected in other words was the missionary practice of strident proselytisation with a view towards conversion, an idea he found repulsive for any religion, including Hinduism.[100] He believed that people should strive to work through their destiny within

[95]Ramachandra Guha, *Savaging the Civilized*, pp. 25–9, 42–56 and 90–4.

[96]Speech at Conference of Missionary Societies in Great Britain and Ireland, 8 October 1931, *CWMG*, Vol. 53, p. 472; Ramachandra Guha, *Savaging the Civilized*, p. 59.

[97]Fisher, *That Strange Little Brown Man Gandhi*, p. xvii.

[98]Ibid., pp. 107–8.

[99]Interview to Dr John Mott, before 1 March 1929, *CWMG*, 45, p. 145.

[100]Discussion with C.F. Andrews, on or after 9 November 1936, *CWMG*, Vol. 70, pp. 58–60.

the religious tradition in which they were raised. He wanted people to be better people as Muslims, Hindus or Christians. Thus, when his ardent follower Madeline Slade was attracted to the idea of becoming a Hindu, he advised her strongly to remain a Christian, which she did.[101]

In 1936–7 there was a strong and often acrimonious debate between Gandhi and some leading missionaries who were working in India. Some who had been involved in movements of mass conversion of low-caste and Dalit peoples to Christianity argued that the process fulfilled a deeply felt need for many of the most oppressed, and that the prime initiative had come from the latter rather than from themselves. They held that in responding to this need, they were more in tune with lower-class sentiments than Gandhi, despite his claims to be the true champion of such people. In reply Gandhi said that the missionaries were exaggerating their popular strength. Bishop J.W. Pickett, for example, was claiming that four and a half million members of the 'depressed classes' had become Christians through these mass movements. Gandhi disputed these figures, arguing that he had not seen any evidence of such whole-scale conversion during his tours of India. He also doubted whether the converts had really escaped from the taint of untouchability through conversion and had been accepted by their high-caste neighbours, as asserted by Pickett. Gandhi argued that the real 'miracle' lay not in such claims, but in the fact that over two thousand temples in Travancore State had been opened recently to Harijans as a result of self-reform on the part of caste Hindus.[102]

Gandhi was also in dispute with the Anglican Bishop of Dornakal in eastern Hyderabad State—the Indian Christian V.S. Azariah—who had claimed in a Church Missionary society pamphlet that about 40,000 people of that area were asking to be baptised and about a million in all were 'moving Christward'. Gandhi stated that he had travelled in the area often and had never heard of such numbers seeking to be baptised.[103]

[101]Parekh, *Gandhi's Political Philosophy*, pp. 83–4.

[102]'What is a Miracle?', *Harijan*, 19 December 1936, *CWMG*, Vol. 70, pp. 189–90.

[103]'Church Missionary Society', *Harijan*, 26 December, 1936, *CWMG*, Vol. 70, p. 218.

Azariah, who was an admirer of Gandhi, invited him to come and see for himself, but Gandhi did not take up the offer.[104] Azariah argued that if people expressed a genuine desire to become Christians, then it was his duty as a clergyman to baptise them. In this, he was following the command of Jesus Christ.[105] He also asserted that for him Christianity was the only true religion, and that he personally could not accept that other faiths could be adequate to his needs. He argued that all seekers after truth should be free to choose their own religion: 'Each religion stands for certain truths. When a man genuinely seeks after truth, he will come to a point where Truth must win his obedience. This obedience must mean abandoning one religious system and uniting with another. If a man fears this result, he will either effect a compromise with the Truth as he sees it, or yield to an unreality, professing to see in his old religion the new truth he has found in the new religion.' He called for sympathy from Gandhi for their efforts to help the poor and oppressed. 'Hating conversion, and hating the Christian propaganda are not becoming of a true lover of India's poor.'[106]

This was written in January 1937. In the following month he and J.W. Pickett went to meet Gandhi at Segaon to discuss these issues. The meeting was a failure. Not only was there no significant meeting of minds, but a subsequent report about the content of the meeting in the mission press poisoned the atmosphere yet further. An American missionary called Donald A. McGavran who had met Pickett afterwards put together what he claimed to be a statement made by Gandhi to the two bishops: 'You Christians must stop preaching to and making disciples amongst the Depressed Classes. If you do not, we shall make you. We shall appeal to the educated Indian Christians: we shall appeal to your home constituency; and if those fail we shall prohibit by law any change of religion, and will back up the law by the force of the State.'[107] Gandhi denied that he had ever said any such thing, and

[104]Susan Billington Harper, *In the Shadow of the Mahatma: Bishop Azariah and the Travails of Christianity in British India*, William B. Eerdmans, Grand Rapids, Michegan 2000, p. 315.

[105]Ibid., p. 317.

[106]Ibid., p. 337.

[107]Ibid., p. 326.

demanded an apology. Azariah backed Gandhi in this, saying that it was a 'cruel fabrication'.[108] McGavran backed down, admitting that it was not a direct quotation, and he offered an apology. In private, however, he argued that it was an expression of what he claimed were Gandhi's true feelings in the matter.[109] Many missionaries in fact believed that Gandhi was opposing their work because he was at heart a Hindu chauvinist. They were unable to grasp that his real commitment was not to a narrow form of Hinduism, but to religious plurality and a commitment to truths that cut across sectarian divides.

In recent years, Hindu chauvinists have deployed Gandhi's principled opposition to all forms of conversion to justify their attacks on Christian missionaries. Like McGavran, they have sought to twist Gandhi's arguments and attribute to him statements that they like to think he should have made, rather than anything he said as such. For example, Ravindra Agarwal claimed in a book of 1999 titled *Hindu Manch* that Gandhi had stated on 22 March 1931 that if Christian missionaries continued to proselytise by means of education and health provision he would ask them to leave India.[110] No such statement can in fact be found in the *Collected Works of Mahatma Gandhi* for that date. As Sumit Sarkar has pointed out, the only statement made by Gandhi on this subject around that time was on 23 April 1931, when he told reporters that this particular comment had been attributed to him in one newspaper report, and that it represented a travesty of his views. His real view was that Christian missionaries were welcome in India so long as they concentrated on humanitarian work. Their reward should lie in the knowledge that they had relieved suffering, not in conversion. If they tried to exploit such activities so as to proselytise, then he would prefer that they withdraw. Such an activity was not uplifting, and it gave rise to suspicions. He went on to say that he was not against conversion as such, but only a form of conversion that was like a form of business. He recalled with distaste reading a report by a missionary who had set out how much it cost per head to convert, and who then

[108]Ibid., p. 327.

[109]Ibid., p. 328.

[110]Quoted in Sumit Sarkar, 'Conversion and Politics of Hindu Right', *Economic and Political Weekly*, 26 June 1999, p. 1691.

presented his budget for 'the next harvest'. He closed his message by stating that what he desired above all else was that followers of the great religions of the world should coexist in peace and tolerance and stop trying to win converts from each other.[111] This call for tolerance was hardly one that Hindu chauvinists would wish to endorse.

Partition and Gandhi's 'Finest Hour'[112]

For Gandhi, the idea of Pakistan—which became the official objective of the Muslim League from 1940 onwards—represented the most deathly closure of all, as it meant tearing Indians apart and foreclosing the dialogue of centuries. In September 1946 he stated:

> But what a tragic change we see today. I wish the day may come again when Hindus and Muslims will do nothing without mutual consultation. I am day and night tormented by the question what I can do to hasten the coming of that day. I appeal to the League not to regard any Indian as its enemy. ... Hindus and Muslims are born of the same soil. They have the same blood, eat the same food, drink the same water and speak the same language.[113]

Two weeks later he stated:

> But I am firmly convinced that the Pakistan demand as put forward by the Muslim League is un-Islamic and I have not hesitated to call it sinful. Islam stands for the unity and brotherhood of mankind, not for disrupting the oneness of the human family. Therefore, those who want to divide India into possible warring groups are enemies alike of Islam and India. They may cut me to pieces but they cannot make me subscribe to something which I consider to be wrong.[114]

[111] Ibid., p. 1692; 'Foreign Missionaries', *Young India*, 23 April 1931, *CWMG*, Vol. 51, p. 414.

[112] The phrase is from Sumit Sarkar, *Modern India 1885–1947*, Macmillan, Delhi 1983, p. 437.

[113] Speech at Prayer Meeting, 7 September 1946, *CWMG*, Vol. 92, p. 139.

[114] 'Answers to Questions', on or after 23 September 1946, *Harijan*, 6 October 1946, *CWMG*, Vol. 92, p. 229.

He realised that his was, as he put it, 'a voice in the wilderness'. Despite this he launched what was to become his last and greatest battle—that of the fight against communal violence and hatred at a time when it was spreading like a forest fire. His method was to strive at all costs to keep open a dialogue with and between Hindus and Muslims, even in the face of communal rioting. He saw this as his greatest test. In early August 1946, just before the start of the violence which was to tear Bengal apart, Gandhi stated: 'I have never had the chance to test my non-violence in the face of communal riots. ... the chance will still come to me.'[115] Unlike in the 1920s, however, Gandhi did not try to carry out this work through intermediaries such as the Khilafatists. He no longer had any faith in such people. He now went himself to the areas of communal strife and sought to bring about peace through a courageous personal intervention.

In October 1946, Muslims in East Bengal turned on the Hindu minority. In the ensuing violence several hundred were killed.[116] Gandhi went to the area in November and over the next four months toured the villages on foot, unprotected and with a minimal number of companions. Despite the hostility of many Muslims, he insisted on talking to them and managed to obtain many promises that they would guarantee the safety of the Hindus. He met Hindus and tried to persuade them to remain in the villages. He told both groups that if they wanted peace, they would have to forget the desire for vengeance and build a spirit of mutual trust and confidence.[117] Following this, in March 1947 he went to Bihar, after the Muslim minority was attacked. He toured devastated villages and held prayer meetings. In East Bengal in particular he managed to calm the atmosphere to a remarkable degree.[118]

Once the Congress high command had agreed to partition in June 1947, Gandhi accepted it, with distress, as 'an accomplished fact.'[119]

[115] *Times of India*, 5 August 1946, p. 5, quoted in Dalton, *Mahatma Gandhi*, p. 145.

[116] Pandey, *Remembering Partition*, p. 23.

[117] Nirmal Kumar Bose, *My Days with Gandhi*, p. 58.

[118] Dalton, *Mahatma Gandhi*, p. 161.

[119] He had been asked to lead a protest against the partition, but he turned the

He decided to return to East Bengal to ensure that there was no more violence there. If he had carried out this plan, he would have found himself in Pakistan after the partition of 15 August. However, while on the way there was an outbreak of violence in Calcutta, and he decided to halt there. On 11 August he went to stay in a deserted Muslim house in Beliaghata, one of the worst affected areas of the city. The Muslim chief minister of Bengal, H.S. Suhrawardy, agreed to stay with him there. Suhrawardy was generally considered to be a highly devious and untrustworthy politician, and he was loathed by Hindus throughout the city as the chief instigator of the riots of August 1946. Yet, Gandhi won Suhrawardy over through a strong moral appeal, and together they worked to overcome the distrust and quell the violence. Suhrawardy was so moved by Gandhi's trust in him that he even confessed to his culpability in the rioting of the previous year.[120]

Soon after they arrived at the house in Beliaghata, some Hindus broke into the house and smashed doors and windows and accused Gandhi of pandering to the Muslims. He asked how anyone could accuse him of being an enemy of Hindus. The crowd dispersed. On the day of independence and partition, there was fraternisation between Hindus and Muslims in the city. This continued until 31 August, when a crowd of aggressive Hindus again invaded the house in Beliaghata, claiming that a Muslim had knifed a Hindu. Gandhi, who narrowly escaped being wounded, had to be rescued by the police. Next day, the violence resumed with a vengeance.

Many people in Calcutta laid the blame for the violence on so-called 'goonda elements', who had been instigated by unscrupulous Hindu and Muslim leaders. However, as Gandhi had stated in 1940, the society as a whole provided the climate in which the goondas operated: 'Goondas do not drop from the sky, nor do they spring from the earth like evil spirits. They are a product of social disorganisation, and society is therefore responsible for their existence.'[121] Gandhi decided to fast to

---

offer down as he would not agitate against the Congress. 'A Letter', on or after 2 June 1947, *CWMG*, Vol. 95, p. 194.

[120]Dalton, *Mahatma Gandhi*, p. 162; *CWMG*, Vol. 96, pt. 2, p. 330.

[121]Ibid., p. 164.

bring pressure to bear on the gangs who were responsible for the attacks.

The climate of remorse brought about in Calcutta by Gandhi's fast soon saw several of these goondas coming to Gandhi to beg for forgiveness and promise to stop the violence if he called off the fast. On the evening of 4 September a deputation of leaders from the Muslim League, Hindu Mahasabha, Sikh community and other bodies came to plead with him to end his fast. Gandhi demanded that they promise to lay down their lives to prevent further communal violence. If they broke the promise, he would begin an irrevocable fast until death. They agreed, and he called off the fast. There was no more communal violence in Calcutta during that period.[122] Gandhi's success in preventing any widespread rioting in the city, and indeed in Bengal in general at that time, is considered by many to be his most remarkable achievement.

Gandhi then went to Delhi, arriving on 9 September. From around 3 September, there had been a wave of attacks on Muslim houses and shops throughout the city, with large numbers being killed as a form of 'revenge' for the carnage in the Punjab. The police were noticeably partisan, failing in most cases to provide any protection. A high proportion of the Muslim population of the city fled to places where there was safety in numbers, camping in the Purana Qila, Humayun's Tomb, and elsewhere. The authorities initially treated these places as mere transit camps on the route to Pakistan, and made little effort to provide food, water or sanitation, arguing that this was the responsibility of the Pakistan government. The logic was clear: *all* Muslims were to be henceforth considered as 'Pakistanis'. It was in this atmosphere of hatred and suspicion that Gandhi arrived in the city. Many Muslims believed that having performed one 'miracle' in Calcutta, he would do the same in Delhi. Shahid Ahmad Dehlavi, who had taken shelter in the Purana Qila, compared his coming 'to the arrival of the rains after a particularly long and harsh summer.'[123] On 13 September, Gandhi visited the camp there. 60,000 Muslims were crowded within the walls of the old fort, with only a few tents to protect them from

[122]Ibid., pp. 150–9.

[123]Shahid Ahmad Dehlavi, *Dilli ki bipta*, Naya Daur 1948, p. 156, quoted in Pandey, *Remembering Partition*, p. 142.

the rain and mud. There was one tap, and no latrines or bathrooms. Gandhi's arrival in their midst represented a gesture of compassion that sent out a message that the Muslims were Indian nationals who should be protected by the Indian state. The Delhi authorities were shamed into treating it as their problem, and set about organising rations, sanitary facilities and better security. South Indian troops, who were supposedly more 'neutral' than north Indian soldiers, were deployed to guard the camps. Daily meetings were held to review the situation and neighbourhood meetings were organised and peace committees established.

After this the large-scale attacks on Muslims ceased, though there were still stabbings and Muslim houses and shops continued to be raided and appropriated by Hindus and Sikhs. According to Gyanendra Pandey, Gandhi's presence appears to have given the secular nationalists 'the moral strength they needed to renew the fight for the composite and tolerant India that so many had dreamt of; perhaps his very presence stunned the government and an army of stupefied Congress workers into action.'[124] Pandey goes on to record that: 'In November, again with Gandhi's active intervention and not without some expression of dissent, the All India Congress Committee reiterated its commitment to building a non-sectarian, democratic India in which there would be place for people of all faiths.'[125] He argues that it was Gandhi above all who insisted that Muslims should be declared unequivocally to be entitled to full rights of citizenship in the new nation state. In the month after 15 August this outcome had been by no means certain, given the intolerance and blood lust of many of those in positions of authority in India.

The recurring day-to-day violence against Muslims was now less dramatic but still a cause of anguish for Gandhi, for it revealed a profound hatred in the hearts of large numbers of Sikhs and Hindus. On 13 January 1948 he launched an indefinite fast, declaring that 'It will end when and if I am satisfied that there is a reunion of hearts of all communities brought about without any outside pressure, but from

[124]Ibid., p. 141.
[125]Ibid., p. 142.

an awakened sense of duty.'[126] He also stated that 'Death for me would be a glorious deliverance rather than that I should be a helpless witness of the destruction of India, Hinduism, Sikhism and Islam.'[127] However: 'If I am to live I shall ask every Hindu and every Sikh not to touch a single Muslim.'[128] He would only be satisfied when he could be assured that every Muslim would feel safe walking freely in the streets of Delhi.[129] He also called on Muslims to openly declare themselves for the Indian nation state. He knew that many had in the past supported the Muslim League and Pakistan, but if they were to remain in India as respected citizens they had to show that they had changed their attitude in this respect. He thus called for a change of heart from Muslims too. Only on such a basis could trust between Hindus, Sikhs and Muslims be built.[130]

In the words of Abul Kalam Azad: 'The moment it was known that he had started his fast, not only the city but the whole of India was deeply stirred. In Delhi the effect was electric. Groups which had till recently openly opposed Gandhiji came forward and said that they would be prepared to do anything in order to save Gandhiji's precious life.'[131] Nehru and many others fasted with Gandhi, including Hindu and Sikh refugees from Pakistan. On the fifth day of the fast 100,000 government employees signed a pledge to work for peace. The police signed their own pledge. Representatives of the RSS and Hindu Mahasabha came and promised to maintain peace. M.S. Randhawa, the deputy commissioner of Delhi who had not been active in protecting Muslims, took a group of Hindu and Sikh leaders to repair the shrine of the Sufi saint Khwaja Qutubuddin Bakhtiar Chisti near Mehrauli, which had been desecrated in September. Heartened by this response, Gandhi gave up his fast on 18 January.[132]

[126]Speech at Prayer Meeting, 12 January 1948, *CWMG*, Vol. 98, p. 219.

[127]Ibid., p. 220.

[128]Ibid., p. 226.

[129]Ibid., p. 227.

[130]Ibid., p. 225.

[131]Maulana Abul Kalam Azad, *India Wins Freedom: An Autobiographical Narrative*, Orient Longman, New Delhi 1975, p. 194.

[132]Pandey, *Remembering Partition*, pp. 143–4.

On 27 January Gandhi was invited by Muslims to speak to them at one of their shrines in Delhi. Three days later he was shot and killed by Godse. He was considering the idea of establishing a Shanti Sena (Peace Army) that would work actively to prevent rioting through quick intervention. A conference of leading Gandhians had been convened for February 1948, but Gandhi was assassinated before it could be held, and it was called off.

What had been gained? The verdict of the historian Sumit Sarkar is harsh: 'Intensely moving and heroic, the Gandhian way in 1946–7 was no more than an isolated personal effort with a local and often rather short-lived impact.'[133] Dalton argues against this that Gandhi's final heroic struggle that culminated in his martyrdom had a cathartic effect, revealing the depths to which hatred had dragged the Indian people.[134] Hatred was replaced by grief—voiced in the massive funeral procession in Delhi. Along with it developed a mood of collective guilt, and the hatred was spent. In this respect, Gandhi's death in itself went a long way in achieving what he had been striving for in those final months of his life. Gyanendra Pandey states that the assassination jolted the authorities into taking a far less tolerant line towards communalists. There was a clampdown on extremist groups. The RSS, for example, was banned and many of its leaders were arrested. The Maharajas of Alwar, Bharatpur and other states who had aided and abetted, and even organised, attacks on Muslims, were brought sharply into line. There was also much fuller reporting of violence against Muslims in India; hitherto this had been suppressed in the newspapers. Pandey continues: 'Thus Gandhi achieved through his death even more than he had achieved through his fast. His success at this juncture conveys an unusual message about the meaning of politics and the possibility of a new kind of political community. It is an improbable story of how a certain kind of bodily sacrifice in the public sphere—and a refusal by one outstanding leader to give his consent to the particular conception of the political community that was emerging—changed the nature of sociality at the local level.'[135] No longer were demands heard to make

[133]Sarkar, *Modern India*, p. 438.
[134]Dalton, *Mahatma Gandhi*, p. 167.
[135]Pandey, *Remembering Partition*, pp. 144–5.

Delhi or India an exclusively Hindu and Sikh territory, and no longer was a 'Muslim' seen as being synonymous with a 'refugee' or 'alien'.[136]

Many Muslims felt personally bereaved. According to Ebadat Barelvi: 'The fire of sectarian strife that had raged for months, or rather years, died down as if such strife had never occurred... Overnight, such calm was established, such a peace that one could not have dreamed of even a few days earlier.'[137] At last, the Muslims of Delhi felt secure and able to return to their earlier way of life. As Qazi Jalil Abbasi of Delhi later stated with tears in his eyes: 'Gandhiji made it possible for Muslims to continue to live in India.'[138] Some even sent messages to those who had fled to Pakistan that it was now safe for them to return.

The fact that the communal divide continued, and has been one of the most intractable problems in postcolonial India, does not mean that Gandhi's intervention had failed or that his approach was unsound. In fact, his proved to be the most practical and effective strategy of all. The problem has been otherwise: that in the last two decades of the twentieth century—a time when communal violence once more moved centre-stage in India—there was nobody of a similar calibre who was prepared to lay down her or his life to prevent attacks by the majority community on the minority.

It might be argued that we cannot pin our hopes on exceptional individuals whose like emerges only rarely in history. Perhaps, however, we should feel heartened by the fact that the Gandhi of 1946–8 did exist, and was able to achieve so much. This fact alone means that what he preached was not impractical or utopian, and does provide a way through what might appear to be an impasse of division and hatred.

Gandhian Anti-Communal Work Since Independence

Among leading post-independence Gandhians, it was probably Jayprakash Narayan (JP) who took anti-communal work most seriously. When Hindus launched a pogrom in his home region of Bihar in

[136] Ibid., pp. 142 and 146.

[137] Ebadat Barelvi, *Azadi ke saaye mein* (Lahore 1988) p. 119, quoted in Pandey, *Remembering Partition*, p. 145.

[138] Interview with Gyanendra Pandey, Delhi, 31 January 1995, in *Remembering Partition*, p. 145.

October 1946—killing thousands of Muslims in 'retaliation' for the attacks on Hindus in East Bengal—JP launched an outspoken attack on the Congress government of the state for conniving with the Hindus and deliberately failing to protect Muslims. The events of 1946 and 1947 sickened JP; he became a strong believer in ahimsa as a result.[139] In the following years he worked hard to reconcile Hindus and Muslims in Bihar. Although he received a lot of abuse for this, the hatred abated. In March 1950, when a million refugees fled from East to West Bengal he took a strong stand against those who demanded that all Muslims be driven out of India in revenge. He insisted that Muslims should enjoy full rights of citizenship in India and that the state should adopt a strictly secular policy.[140]

In 1957 Vinoba Bhave established a Shanti Sena to combat communal violence, thus taking up the idea that Gandhi had put forward a few days before his death. Most of those who enrolled as Shanti Sainiks were Gandhian workers already. The secretary of the body from 1962 to 1978 was Narayan Desai, son of Gandhi's secretary, Mahadev Desai. Under his vigorous leadership, the membership increased to about 6,000 in the mid-1960s. When rioting was reported in a particular place, Sainiks went there and tried to meet with leaders of the communities involved in the violence. In the words of Narayan Desai: 'We present ourselves not as saviours but as people eager to assist them in their difficulty. We gather information from them and try to understand their minds. And we try to find the forces of peace on both sides. Often there are people who favour peace but do not know how to work for it.'[141] They encouraged the community leaders to set up peace committees with representatives of both rival groups. They also spoke with local political leaders and police officers, requesting them to use methods that would not inflame the situation any further.

As rioting was almost always stoked—often deliberately—by rumours

[139]Wendy and Allan Scarfe, *J.P. His Biography*, Orient Longman, New Delhi 1998, pp. 114 and 117.

[140]Ibid., pp. 220–1.

[141]Mark Shepard, 'Soldiers of Peace: Narayan Desai and the "Peace Army"', www.markshep.com/non-violence/GT_Sena.html

of supposed atrocities, one important task was for the Sainiks to enquire into the substance of a story and then walk around the disturbed neighbourhoods seeking to counter it. They would talk to people, write messages on community notice boards and make announcements through megaphones. As they were often the only people able to pass freely from one part of a city to another, they were able to counter rumours in an authoritative way in this respect. They also stationed themselves at known tension-spots, hoping by their presence—in their distinctive Sainik uniform of white khadi and saffron scarves—to calm the situation. Female and male Sainiks took part in this work.

One drawback to this approach was that the Sainiks often had to travel some distance to the town or city in which rioting was going on. Many of the Gandhian activists worked in rural areas, which made it hard to act promptly enough. Often, they arrived after the worst of the rioting was over. There were however some notable successes. Narayan Desai told of an occasion when there was violence in Bhivandi, near Bombay:

> ... when we met with the Hindus, they said, 'Why talk to *us* about peace? Why don't you try to go to the Muslim part of the city? The minute you go there, you'll be killed!'
>
> So we said, 'All right, we'll go lodge there.' Then we went and lived with the Muslims.
>
> The Hindus of the city were amazed. They never could have imagined that a mostly Hindu group, including five Hindu women, could stay with the Muslims overnight and be alive the next morning. But we were safe. Not only were *we* safe, but the Muslims thought *they* were safe, because they had Hindu Shanti Sainiks protecting them.[142]

In Calcutta in 1964 they organised a silent procession of three thousand people through the riot-torn streets. The tension was defused and the shopkeepers opened their shops, feeling that they would be secure with the Shanti Sainiks in the area. In Orissa some Christians burnt down the houses of their Muslim neighbours. The local Shanti Sainiks persuaded the Christians to donate funds for the rebuilding of these houses. Some of the actual arsonists even donated money.

[142]Ibid.

JP took an active part in this work in 1963–4, when tensions with Pakistan led to many Hindus being expelled from East Pakistan. This set off a wave of retaliatory attacks on Muslims in eastern India. Muslim houses were attacked, the men and children killed and the women raped. JP visited the riot-torn areas and directed the activities of the Shanti Sainiks. In some cases they took huge personal risks in personally persuading angry crowds to disperse. Many Muslims fled their homes, seeking refuge in camps. JP visited some of these places to try to reassure the Muslims.[143]

Although the Shanti Sainiks were invariably Hindu, and they dressed in a manner that would today be associated with the Hindu right, this does not seem to have compromised their work. As always, the non-violent method depended on the skill and moral courage of its practitioners. In the Bhivandi case, the Sainiks under Narayan Desai managed to turn their Hindu identity to their advantage by showing that the Hindus need not fear Muslims and that Hindus would protect the Muslims. In such situations, it was vital to dispel the fear that each community had of the other. In Desai's words: 'Fear and courage are equally contagious. So Shanti Sainiks often go to areas that are supposed to be dangerous to show that there is nothing to fear.'[144]

JP believed that the root cause of communal friction in India was the continuing hostility between India and Pakistan, and he worked hard to try to bring about reconciliation between the two nations. He was highly critical of Nehru's handling of the Kashmir issue, which involved his reneging on his commitment to hold a plebiscite and then suppressing protest and jailing Sheikh Abdulla in 1953. JP continued to demand Sheikh Abdulla's release over the following two decades, succeeding eventually in 1968. In 1964, JP set up a sixteen-member Indo-Pakistan Conciliation Group in India, and worked to establish a similar body in Pakistan. He argued that there should be a constitutional link between India and Pakistan. He attacked Congress and other politicians for their often narrow-minded, chauvinistic nationalism, with its communal underpinnings. He was as a result subjected to abuse

[143]Scarfe, *J.P. His Biography*, pp. 222–3.
[144]Mark Shepard, 'Soldiers of Peace'.

from the Hindu right, with the RSS-inspired Jana Sangh organising a demonstration against him in Delhi in September 1964 just as he was setting out to visit Pakistan on a mission of peace. The mission did not succeed; less than a year later war broke out between India and Pakistan.[145]

After JP died in 1979, no leading Gandhian came forward to replace him in this respect. The Shanti Sena had been split badly in 1975 when Vinoba Bhave supported the Emergency, with one section going with Bhave, the other with JP. Narayan Desai stepped down as secretary in 1978 and the body soon declined into inactivity. Tragically, this was at a time when the Hindu right was beginning to consolidate its power through a deployment of a populist anti-Muslim demagogy. When things came to a head with the vandalistic destruction of the Babri Masjid in December 1992, there were few Gandhians prepared to risk their necks against the saffron fanatics and their criminal hangers-on as they attacked, raped, killed and looted defenceless Muslim citizens in towns and cities throughout India. One notable exception was Baba Amte, who rushed to Surat, where there had been some of the most despicable acts of violence against Muslims, and worked to restore communal peace. When the attacks began again in Bombay in January 1993, he went there and confronted the Shiv Sena workers. In one case he had to plead with them to allow fire engines to reach houses that were on fire.[146]

As the Hindu right strengthened its hold over Indian politics, some tendencies within it sought to appropriate Gandhi's legacy. Their argument was that Gandhi was a 'great Hindu' who had raised the prestige of Hinduism as a world religion. In a lavish and costly Bharat Mata temple at Hardwar, constructed in the early 1980s by a leading ideologue of the Hindu right, Swami Satyamitranand Giri, Gandhi found a place in the 'Shrine of Heroes' alongside M.M. Malaviya and V.D. Savarkar. Nehru was conspicuous by his absence in this pantheon of freedom fighters, as he was seen to be a socialist and secularist, which according to the dogmas of the Hindu right makes him a dubious patriot. Gandhi was included as a symbol of Hindu spirituality and

[145]Scarfe, *J.P. His Biography*, pp. 222–6.
[146]Bakshi, *Bapu Kuti*, p. 225.

ahimsa.[147] In a school textbook on '*Hindu Dharma*' prepared by the cultural wing of the RSS, the Vishwa Hindu Parishad, Gandhi was cited as a great 'Hindu thinker' who fought racism and propounded ahimsa.[148] Gandhi was thus sought to be assimilated to the Hindu right project of a 'world renaissance of Hinduism'.[149]

This line is however rejected by hardline Hindu nationalists, for it is not possible for those who celebrate violence and aggression to assimilate a figure who stood above all for non-violence. We see this very clearly in the writings of François Gautier, a Frenchman resident in India for thirty years who has become a spokesman for the Hindu right. He describes Gandhi as a 'great soul, an extraordinary human being, a man with a tremendous appeal to the people. But, unfortunately, he was a misfit in India.'[150] Why was this so? Because he was, Gautier argues, at heart a European and a Christian. His non-violence was inspired more by Jesus Christ than by Hindu dharma, which insists that violence is often a matter of religious duty. Gandhi brought great harm to India by his pandering to Muslims and Untouchables. His love of Untouchables was based on a Christian notion of equality, and he failed to appreciate that caste is divinely sanctioned. In acting as he did 'he sowed the seeds of future disorders and of a caste war in India, of which we see the effects only today.'[151] As for Muslims, 'nobody more than Gandhi contributed to the partition of India, by his obsession to always give in to the Muslims, by his obstinate refusal to see that the Muslims always started rioting, Hindus only retaliated; by his indulgence of Jinnah ...'[152]

[147]Lise McKean, *Divine Enterprise: Gurus and the Hindu Nationalist Movement*, University of Chicago Press, Chicago 1996, pp. 157–8.

[148]Nawal K. Prinja, *Explaining Hindu Dharma: A Guide for Teachers*, Religious and Moral Education Press, Norwich 1996, pp. 53 & 177.

[149]This move is made by Romesh Dewan in 'Can We Survive without Gandhian Values?', *Economic and Political Weekly*, Vol. 34, Nos.16 and 17, 17–23 April 1999, p. 962.

[150]François Gautier, *Arise Again, O India!*, Har-Anand Publications, New Delhi 2000, p. 85.

[151]Ibid., p. 88.

[152]Ibid., p. 87.

Gautier goes on to cite his own hero, Sri Aurobindo, who criticised Gandhi for making 'a fetish of Hindu-Muslim unity':

> It is no use ignoring facts; some day the Hindus may have to fight the Muslims and they must prepare for it. Hindu–Muslim unity should not mean the subjection of the Hindus. Every time the mildness of the Hindus has given way. The best solution would be to allow the Hindus to organise themselves and the Hindu–Muslim unity would take care of itself, it would automatically solve the problem. Otherwise we are lulled into a false sense of satisfaction that we have solved a difficult problem, when in fact we have only shelved it.[153]

The 'automatic solution' of this passage appears to be that of instilling such fear in Muslims that they will be forced to flee India.

Another hardline ideologue of the Hindu right is the VHP president, Ashok Singhal, who likewise refuses to countenance the idea that Muslims can be genuine Indians. In a speech in Calcutta in 1998 he accused Gandhi of trying to destroy the identity of India through his insistence that all 'invaders' had a right to be considered Indians, stating that 'India must choose between the theories of Mahatma Gandhi and the Rashtriya Swayamsevak Sangh.'[154] From the perspective of the exclusionary and authoritarian politics of this tendency, Gandhi's politics of plurality, incorporation and dialogism continues to be an anathema. It is indeed hard for the Hindu right to incorporate him into their agenda, for his whole life and being represents a standing indictment of their brand of politics.

[153]Ibid., pp. 87–8.

[154]Speech at Salt Lake, Calcutta, 7 May 1998, quoted in Partha Banerjee, *In the Belly of the Beast: The Hindu Supremacist RSS and BJP of India: An Insider's Story*, Ajanta Books, New Delhi 1998, p. 146.

8

Gandhian Activism in India after Independence

India's political leaders paid much lip service to Gandhi and his ideals in the years after Indian independence. There was a stated desire to forge more equitable social and economic relationships in rural areas, with land reform, the regulation of rural usury and minor irrigation projects. There was considerable state investment in small-scale agriculture and support for the khadi and village industries programme, Gandhian education and ashrams, and for the sarvodaya campaign of Vinoba Bhave. Jawaharlal Nehru sought to build on Gandhi's world reputation by claiming that India's foreign policy was motivated by morality rather than power politics. As Sunil Khilnani has pointed out, Nehru followed Gandhi in this by turning around the language of victimhood in an assertive way.[1]

Time and time again, however, the policies pursued in some of the most crucial areas of concern for modern India ignored all that Gandhi stood for. India had inherited an autocratic system of government from the British, and very little of the repressive apparatus was dismantled. Power was concentrated in the hands of a centralised state that was able to take unilateral action against any form of dissidence that was seen to undermine its control. Far from there being any Gandhian-style devolution of power, the state assumed increasingly authoritarian powers.

Little tolerance was shown towards Gandhian-style civil resistance.

[1]Khilnani, *The Idea of India*, p. 178.

In Delhi, matters came to a head in this respect when the Balmiki Dalit sweepers went on strike for improved working conditions. They had a high regard for Gandhi, who had stayed in their slum-quarter in Delhi in 1946 in an act of solidarity. They deployed Gandhian techniques such as strikes, dharnas and protest-fasts to press their demands with the Delhi Municipal Corporation. The state was caught in a cleft over this, but ultimately resorted to aggressive strike-breaking by the police. In July 1957, demonstrating Balmikis were fired on, with one Balmiki protester, Bhoop Singh being killed. Ministers of Nehru's Congress government expressed regret, but argued that for the sake of public health they could not tolerate strikes by essential workers such as public cleaners. The Home Minister G.B. Pant went so far as to say that the Balmikis had a duty to work 'because they are citizens of the country and they have the privilege to serve the people by rendering essential services.' The Minister for Law, A.K. Sen, asserted that 'the right to strike is not a fundamental right'. On 6 August 1957 the Essential Services Maintenance Ordinance was passed in Parliament, which allowed civil liberties to be suspended in an emergency.[2] Jayprakash Narayan roundly condemned this as an example of a 'growing Indian fascism'.

Many Balmikis regarded the police firing as their 'Jallianwallah Bagh'. In interviews in 1992, some remember the incident as having taken place during the colonial period. This was telling; the Congress rulers of 1957 were seen as indistinguishable from the British. One man stated: 'We were only doing what we had learnt from Gandhi, we were seeking what was just by acting peacefully'. In post-colonial India, it was acceptable for leading politicians to invoke Gandhi in symbolic ways, with *padayatras* and the like, but not for poor people to apply his methods of assertive non-violent protest. Their rewards were beatings and police atrocities. As Rattan Lal Balmiki stated: 'The days of Gandhi are over and true Gandhians are now morose.' Today, the Balmikis maintain the room in which Gandhi stayed in their colony as a shrine, and among the relics is a photograph of Bhoop Singh, the martyr of July 1957.

[2]Vijay Prashad, 'Untouchable Freedom: A Critique of the Bourgeois-Landlord Indian State', in Gautam Bhadra, Gyan Prakash and Susie Tharu, *Subaltern Studies X*, Oxford University Press, New Delhi 1999.

Gandhian principles were also ignored in the economic sphere. With the inauguration of the second five-year plan in 1956, the bulk of state development funding was concentrated on heavy industry. Only 22 percent of the budget was allocated to agriculture, despite the fact that 75 percent of the population was engaged in agriculture and only 11 percent of the population in industry.[3] This expenditure was financed in part by the surplus generated by agriculture.

By the 1960s, shortfalls in agricultural production were being made good by imports of food. The remedy for this was seen to be a Green Revolution-style agriculture, which relied heavily on imported seed, chemical fertilizers, pesticides, herbicides and water from expensive foreign-funded irrigation projects. Two-thirds of all expenditure on irrigation between 1951 and 1985 was on such large- and medium-scale projects, even though the cost of irrigating a hectare of land from them has been calculated as being nearly four times as much as from cheap, small-scale irrigation works.[4] All of this ran counter to the ethos of locally self-sufficient agriculture propagated by Gandhi and his followers.

Since around 1956, therefore, the Indian state has supported Gandhian-style constructive work more in a token form rather than as a central strategy for mass welfare. Western-style 'development' has been the model, in which the emphasis has been on creating a 'modern' industrial and capitalist infrastructure.[5]

Although the Green Revolution allowed India to become more—though by no means entirely—self-sufficient in food,[6] it created increasing differentiations between rich and poor in the rural areas. Those who were able to command the capital required to carry on such agriculture benefited, while those who did not lost out. They even found themselves deprived of the chance to earn a livelihood through agricultural labour, as there has been an increasing tendency to employ

[3]Baviskar, *In the Belly of the River*, p. 23.

[4]Ibid., p. 27.

[5]Pinto, *Gandhi's Vision and Values*, pp. 84–92.

[6]It is also unclear as to what extent Green Revolution-style agriculture can be sustained into the future. Even in the Punjab, agrarian productivity has been in a continuing decline since around 1980. For the causes, see Sukhpal Singh, 'Crisis in Punjab Agriculture', *Economic and Political Weekly*, 3 June 2000.

seasonal migrant labourers from distant regions at very low rates of pay. These migrant labourers live in unsanitary camps, are overworked, and are poisoned by the pesticides they have to apply. Many are maimed in accidents involving agricultural machinery. Because they are dismissed each season and re-employed the next, they cannot be easily organised in labour unions. There is certainly no Gandhian-style ethos of trusteeship in this; they are exploited in a pitiless and dehumanising manner, without a shred of any older-style paternalistic feeling. The consequence is that today about 40 percent of the population eats less than the bare minimum needed to preserve good health. Gandhi's demand that the constitution of India should state that no one should suffer from want of food and clothing continues to be ignored by the ruling class.[7]

The agrarian poor are unable, moreover, to turn in any very important way to cottage industries for an adequate supplementary income. Khadi production is on a very small scale, largely for a niche market, and earnings from it are very low. Artisans are in general under-financed, are denied access to raw materials, and find it hard to market their products in a remunerative way. For example, workers in bamboo goods—an important artisan sector—are denied access to forests to collect bamboo themselves and have to buy from the Forest Department at inflated prices. At the same time, the government sells bamboo at highly subsidised rates to large paper and rayon mills. For example, in 1998 it was common for artisans to pay fifteen rupees for one piece of bamboo, while the mills obtained bamboo at a rate of sixty paise per tonne (the equivalent of about 200 bamboo pieces).[8] Mountains of bamboo can be seen stacked in the factory yards, while poor artisans in neighbouring villages are under-employed through lack of ability to pay for this same wood.[9]

Because Gandhian work has been generally marginal to governmental concerns, Gandhian social workers (as opposed to politicians) have on the whole remained outsiders. Effective local work almost

[7]Pinto, *Gandhi's Vision and Values*, pp. 103–5 and 110–11. See also Breman, *Of Peasants, Migrants and Paupers*.

[8]Bakshi, *Bapu Kuti*, p. 16.

[9]Personal observation, Songadh Taluka, Surat District, Gujarat.

inevitably has placed them in an oppositional role. However, they gain legitimacy by invoking the name of Gandhi—the so-called 'Father of the Nation'—and by projecting a morality which is associated with 'Hindu' values. Because of their commitment to non-violence, they are not seen as a direct threat to the state, and are generally tolerated. Also, many of their demands are congruent with official state policy. It is hard to tar them with the brush of 'traitor to the nation', as is the case with many others who work for the poor, such as communist party activists or Christian priests—who are accused, very hypocritically, of being inspired by 'foreign' ideologies. For good or bad, the Gandhian paradigm invites dialogue, rather than out-and-out repression, and it can wrong-foot opponents in highly effective ways. This at least ensures that there continues to be some sort of space for pro-poor activities in India, even in the most adverse climates. The downside to this is that many of those who claim to be 'Gandhians' take refuge in quietism. In this, they betray their calling, for in 1944 Gandhi had said explicitly that he anticipated that he would have to go on waging satyagraha for social justice, even after Indian independence.[10]

The Bhoodan and Gramdan Movements

Bhoodan and Gramdan were Gandhi-inspired initiatives associated most closely with the two figures of Vinoba Bhave and Jayaprakash Narayan (JP). Their work formed a part of the overall Sarvodaya Movement. Sarvodaya ('compassion through service') entailed dedicated work for public welfare, carried out by cadres—known as *lok sevaks* (servants of the people)—who were trained in Gandhian institutions. The Sarva Seva Sangh, founded in 1923 by Jamnalal Bajaj, took the work in hand initially. Bajaj was a successful capitalist who was able to provide generous funding for this body from his own pocket. He worked tirelessly for the constructive programme up until his sudden and premature death in 1942.[11] He had hoped to provide a lok sevak for every village, but this

[10] Interview with Louis Fisher, 1944, quoted in Parekh, *Gandhi's Political Philosophy*, p. 140.

[11] Shriman Narayan, *Jamnalal Bajaj: Gandhiji's 'Fifth Son'*, Publications Division, New Delhi 1974.

ambition was never fulfilled. Large numbers of idealistic young men did however go to live in villages, seeking through their personal example to win support for Gandhian self-help programmes.

Vinoba Bhave (1895–1982) was a Maharashtrian Brahman brought up in Gujarat, who joined Gandhi in 1916 and was active thereafter in constructive rather than political work. A relatively unknown figure within the movement until 1948, he took the initiative in that year in founding the Sarvodaya Samaj. The day before his assassination on January 30 of that year, Gandhi had proposed that the Congress be disbanded and a Lok Sevak Sangh (Association for the Service of the People) be established in its place. This was rejected by the Congress high command, which believed that given the severe problems of the day, it was essential to maintain a cohesive political party to run the country. In response, Bhave set up the Sarvodaya Samaj in March as an alternative.[12]

This was a time when communists had won strong support in rural areas, with powerful peasant movements in areas such as Telangana, Bengal, and Thana District of Maharashtra. After the movement was crushed in Telangana by the Indian army, with the landlords being in many cases given back the land which had been seized from them by the communists, Bhave—who was strongly anti-communist—toured the region, seeking a Gandhian means for mitigating the problems of the rural poor. In April 1950, a landlord donated one hundred acres of land to him to distribute to landless Dalits. Bhave saw this as a sign from God, and set about trying to persuade other landlords to make gifts of land. Thus was initiated the Bhoodan Movement, based on the concept of *hridaya-parivartan* (change of heart). He had considerable success in Telangana, and then in Uttar Pradesh Nehru gave his blessings to the work, hoping it would provide a better climate for the government's land reform legislation.[13] Bhave received widespread international coverage for this work, his anti-communist credential even helping him to make the cover of *Time* magazine,

[12]'Draft Constitution of the Congress', 29 January 1948, *CWMG*, Vol. 98, pp. 333–5; Ostergaard and Currell, *The Gentle Anarchists*, pp. 5–6.

[13]Geoffrey Ostergaard, *Nonviolent Revolution in India*, Gandhi Peace Foundation, New Delhi 1985, pp. 5–6.

with his portrait over the caption: 'I have come to loot you with love.'[14]

Jayaprakash Narayan (1902–1979), who was from Bihar, soon joined Bhave in this work. Like Bhave, JP had had a long and close relationship with Gandhi, but in JP's case it had been a troubled one, as he had veered from an early Gandhism to Marxism, and then back, slowly and painfully, towards a synthesis between the two. JP had first joined the Gandhian movement during Non-Cooperation in 1921. His wife Prabhavati had gone to live and work with Gandhi in his Swaraj Ashram in Ahmedabad, and remained there during the 1920s when JP went to the USA to study social science. There he came into contact with Marxian writings that persuaded him that Gandhi was a counter-revolutionary who was working in the interests of the bourgeoisie. Back in India in 1929 he went to see Prabhavati at the ashram with mixed feelings, but Gandhi quickly won him over emotionally, if not ideologically, in part by pampering him as a so-called 'son-in-law' (Gandhi had assumed the role of father in relationship to Prabhavati) and in part by talking to him with respect as an equal. He participated in the civil disobedience movements of 1930–1 and 1932–4. Disgusted with the communist refusal to join the struggle at that time, he and other young socialists decided in 1934 to form the Congress Socialist Party to work within the Congress.[15]

JP continued his dialogue with Gandhi during these years. He argued that spinning, and even anti-untouchability work, was irrelevant to the wider struggle, which had to be along class lines. He also held that state power had to be seized before there could be real change; Gandhi replied that people had to be convinced intellectually before legislation could succeed. During these years, JP moved further away from the Communist Party, which he saw as apologising for Stalin's tyranny. He was committed to a strongly democratic socialism. He also followed Gandhi in believing in the need for decentralisation and a moral base to action. However, he refused to accept the principle of ahimsa and in the early 1940s worked actively to prepare for an armed revolt against the British. He was a leading figure in the underground movement

[14]Black, *A Cause for our Times*, p. 132.

[15]Scarfe, *J.P. His Biography*, pp. 21–53.

during the Quit India movement of 1942. At the time, Gandhi publicly praised JP, but after his release from jail in 1944, he condemned the violence of the movement. He said that while he admired JP's courage, Prabhavai was the true hero, as she had remained non-violent throughout. JP, then in jail where he had been tortured, felt very bitter about Gandhi's remarks in this respect. However, the terrible carnage of the Partition period, which JP witnessed at first hand in rural Bihar, made him far more sympathetic to Gandhi's principled abhorrence of violence.[16] JP had immense prestige in India at independence, but preferred to go his own way in politics as a Socialist Party leader rather than work within Nehru's Congress. The Socialist Party did not, however, do well in the elections of 1952, and over the next three years it fell apart. It was against this background that JP decided to concentrate his attention on constructive work.

JP joined Vinoba Bhave in the Bhoodan movement in 1953. He marched through his home state of Bihar encouraging landowners to give land to the poor. Many made promises to do so.[17] Bhave and JP then extended the movement into *gramdan* (village gift), which aimed to bring all land in a village under the control of the village community, with individual landowners agreeing to gift their land to the community. This was a radical departure from the principle of bhoodan, which was rooted in the individual ownership of land. Gramdan also involved activities such as the settlement of disputes by voluntarily established village councils without recourse to the police or courts, and the encouragement of village self-sufficiency. By the end of 1956, 1935 villages had elected for gramdan. By 1958, the movement was flagging. One major problem was that village usurers refused to grant loans to villagers who no longer possessed individual land deeds as a security. Also, there was growing unease amongst Sarvodaya workers about Vinoba Bhave's disinclination to resort to satyagraha against those who had promised to hand over land, but refused in practice to do so. Bhave believed that in a democratic country such as India, satyagraha should only be used in very exceptional circumstances. He rejected the demand

[16]Ibid., pp. 56–8, 68–99, 117.
[17]Ostergaard, *Nonviolent Revolution in India*, pp. 7–10.

made by the socialist leader Rammanohar Lohia for mass civil disobedience to force the pace of change. In 1973 Bhave went so far as to state: 'In Gandhi's days, there was no freedom of thought and expression ... But in India today we enjoy the highest measure of freedom in the world ... Every day the newspaper brings to us the highest indictment of the government ... Satyagraha as practised by Gandhi has therefore become quite irrelevant in India.'[18] Bhave appears to have been blind to the fact that abuses of power by the landed élites, politicians, bureaucrats and the police continued apace in independent India, in most cases being entirely unreported in the press.

The growing unease in regard to Bhave's increasingly quietist approach led to dissent within the ranks of the Sarvodaya Movement. Ramachandra Rao, who had won Gandhi's respect in the 1940s for his activism and strongly-held opinions, went so far as to form a separate Satyagraha Sangh that Bhave refused to support.[19] Rao, who was from Andhra Pradesh, staged a satyagraha in front of the legislative assembly in Hyderabad in 1960 in protest at the corruption of politics through the party system. He demanded that voting blocs and party whips be abolished. He was jailed for a short time in consequence. He then decided to stage a march to Delhi to press his demand with Nehru. He set out on 8 October 1960, covering the 1100 miles in 99 days. Although Bhave refused to give his blessing to this protest, many Sarvodaya workers supported him and joined stages of the march. JP gave his full backing. When Rao reached the capital in January 1961, he staged a satyagraha in front of the prime minister's opulent residence in Teen Murti Marg, stating that Nehru should live more simply. He also demanded that the prime minister should place himself above party by standing as an independent. Nehru agreed to see him and expressed sympathy for his point of view, but felt that there had to be parties. He also argued that such a style of life was expected of a prime minister. Rao received a lot of publicity for this protest, and subsequently toured India and various European countries.[20]

[18]Ibid., p. 63.

[19]Ibid., pp. 15 and 20–2.

[20]Hugh Grey, '"Gora", Gandhi's Atheist Follower,' pp. 152–6.

As the pace of the Bhoodan and Gramdan movements slackened in the early 1960s, Bhave relaxed the definition of what constituted a 'gramdan' village, which allowed far more villages to be so defined.[21] By October 1969 it was claimed that 140,020 villages had declared for gramdan. Bihar, where Jayaprakash Narayan was most active, had the largest number. In the large majority of cases, however, the declaration was not followed-up with any active reorganisation of the village property structure, so that gramdan remained an aspiration rather than reality. Ostergaard and Currell have calculated that only about 500 villages of Bihar had achieved any significant gramdan by 1969. The most solid results were achieved in the poorest Adivasi tracts, where there were few internal caste divides, less differentiation of wealth, and strong traditions of community solidarity.[22] Likewise, bhoodan had failed to fulfil the expectations of the early 1950s, though its achievement was not insignificant. In 1969, of the 4.2 million acres of land donated, 1.85 million acres were uncultivable or legally disputed. Of the rest, about a million acres had been redistributed to over 200,000 families. JP was proud of that achievement at least.[23]

The Naxalite Alternative

By the late 1960s an alternative surge of rural revolution was under way in which Gandhi-inspired methods were firmly rejected in favour of violent appropriation of landed property and the elimination of tyrannical landlords. The Naxalite movement began in north Bengal in 1967, with an uprising by peasants led by communist revolutionaries. Sharecroppers seized the land of the landlords and occupied it. Although the police crushed the rising within a few months, the ideas behind it

[21]Under the new definition, a 'Gramdan village' was one in which 75 percent of landowners owning at least 51 percent of the village land had agreed to give at least one-twentieth of their land to the village community. This meant that a minimum of one-fortieth of the land had to be pledged before a village could gain the title. Ostergaard and Currell, *The Gentle Anarchists*, p. 55.

[22]Ibid., pp. 10–12 and 14.

[23]Ibid., p. 13; Scarfe, *J.P. His Biography*, p. 169.

remained alive, inspiring similar revolts in other parts of India in the following years, notably in Andhra Pradesh and Bihar.[24]

The Naxalites had no time for Gandhi and his theories, for, in the words of the Naxalite theorist Saroj Dutta, 'Gandhi was the leader and representative of the bourgeois group which was the agent of the British imperialists ...'.[25] There was an emphatic rejection of the Gandhian dialogic, which was depicted as a bad-faithed attempt to reconcile irreconcilable class antagonisms.[26] Scorn was poured on Gandhi's desire to create a culture of non-violent struggle. Saroj Dutta called on Naxalites to destroy statues of Gandhi and erect in their place statues of the heroes of the 1857 revolt, such as Mangal Pande and the Rani of Jhansi, thus validating and glorifying a history of violent revolt.[27] The killing of landlords by Naxalites was seen as a wholly progressive and positive step: 'The masses never make mistakes. Revolution is bound to signify excess.'[28]

The chief ideologue and leader of the movement in the early years was Charu Mazumdar, who advocated a campaign of terror against the propertied classes, to be carried out primarily by Naxalite militants operating in underground guerrilla bands in great secrecy. The Gandhian and existing communist emphasis on mass mobilisation and struggle to obtain land was rejected in favour of building a 'red army' which would eventually be able to take on the Indian state. As it was, the Naxalite guerrillas were eliminated in a series of ruthless police operations, in which many villagers were killed alongside the Naxalites. Within the movement, Kanu Sanyal expressed his disquiet at Charu Mazumdar's line, arguing that: 'As a result of denying any importance to politics and rejection of the path of mass struggles and mass organisations, the

[24]Sumanta Banerjee, *In the Wake of Naxalbari: A History of the Naxalite Movement in India*, Subarnarekha, Calcutta 1980.

[25]Saroj Dutta, *On Subhash Bose*, CPI (ML) pamphlet of 1970, quoted in ibid., p. 229.

[26]Ibid., pp. 18–19.

[27]Saroj Dutta, 'In Defence of Iconoclasm', *Deshabrati*, 1970, quoted in ibid., p. 234. Banerjee rightly questions the extent to which the Rani of Jhansi can in fact be considered a champion of the poor.

[28]Saroj Dutta, *Poob Akash Lal* (The Eastern Sky is Red), quoted in ibid., p. 238.

combat groups obsessed with actions only, were soon reduced to roving bands.'[29] He felt that a more dialogic approach in relationship to the government of West Bengal could have gained far more for the people in 1967. Instead, they had been crushed.[30]

The Naxalite outbreak in Bengal proved, however, to be a defining moment in modern Indian history. Arun Sinha has gone so far as to see it as providing 'the ideology of India's alternative'.[31] Whether or not this is so, the Gandhian alternative was certainly eclipsed in the late 1960s by a movement that sought to replace dialogue with terror. There were a series of Naxalite-style revolts in various parts of India at that time. The situation caused great concern to the Government of India, with the Home Minister, Y.B. Chavan, going so far as to state in 1969 that the 'green revolution' might not remain green much longer.[32]

Against this backdrop, Vinoba Bhave abandoned his efforts for peaceful land reform and retired to his ashram near Wardha. He refused to designate any clear successor, which left the movement in a state of drift at a crucial juncture. There were demands from within the Sarvodaya Movement for sustained satyagraha against landlords as a counter to Naxalite violence. This chance was passed up. [33]

In JP's home state of Bihar, Naxalites established strong roots in a number of areas in the early 1970s. On the whole, their approach was more that of Kanu Sanyal than Charu Mazumdar. A firm base was established amongst low-caste and Dalit landless labourers, providing an environment in which the armed militants could find shelter between actions. The emphasis was on building a strong movement through solid work over an extended period, rather than through adventuristic acts of dramatic violence. With such a base, Naxalites were able to resist the counter-attacks of the police and the rural rich, and through their

[29]Article by Kanu Sanyal in *Purba Taranga*, 1 May 1974, quoted in ibid., p. 109.

[30]Ibid., p. 117.

[31]Arun Sinha, *Against the Few: Struggles of India's Rural Poor*, Zed Books, London 1991, p. 156.

[32]*Patriot*, 29 November 1969, quoted in Banerjee, *In the Wake of Naxalbari*, p. 119.

[33]Ostergaard, *Nonviolent Revolution in India*, pp. 29–34.

presence force the latter to improve the conditions of work of their labourers.

When some Naxalites issued death threats against two prominent Sarvodaya workers of Muzaffarpur District of north Bihar in 1970, JP decided to go there and work to counter their influence through bhoodan and gramdan. He found that a lot of land that had been declared bhoodan was still under the control of the original owners, and that they had no genuine intention of ever giving it away. He went from village to village for nearly a year trying to persuade the landlords to honour their promises.[34] He had very little success, and began to have profound doubts about the efficacy of hridaya-parivartan within the Sarvodaya philosophy. He decided to emphasise civil resistance over and above moral appeals. He continued to insist on strict non-violence, as Naxalite-style violence would only provoke fierce state repression.[35] By adopting this approach in his subsequent campaign against the corruption of Indira Gandhi's Congress Party, JP then managed to regain much of the ground that had been lost to the Naxalites. This culminated in a massive upsurge in 1974–5, known often as 'the JP Movement'.

The JP Movement

This movement, which became a particularly notable example of Gandhian-style activism in post-independence India, was inaugurated by JP in 1973 against the corruption of Indira Gandhi's government. Students were mobilised to campaign against corrupt politicians, black-marketeering, profiteering and hoarding by capitalists that led to price rises, the evasion of land reform laws, and unemployment. The movement took off in Gujarat in 1974, with the Nav Nirman (new wave) movement, which brought the venal Congress administration of Chimanlal Patel to its knees. Chimanlal—or Chiman *chor* (thief), as he was popularly known—was forced to resign office.[36] The movement then spread to Bihar. JP led the protest actively there, trying to prevent it degenerating into violence by maintaining the momentum with strikes,

[34]Scarfe, *J.P. His Biography*, pp. 209–13.

[35]Sinha, *Against the Few*, pp. 85 and 89–90.

[36]Ghanshyam Shah, *Protest Movements in Two Indian States: A Study of the Gujarat and Bihar Movements*, Ajanta Publications, Delhi 1977.

demonstrations and marches. He called on the students to leave their studies for a year and work for 'total revolution'. Despite his efforts, there were many incidents of violence. Several Sarvodaya workers condemned the movement in this respect, even though the violence of the police was far greater. For them, state coercion did not rank as 'violence'. Vinoba Bhave merely commented—to JP's great disgust—'I leave it to God for his verdict'.[37]

JP publicly condemned Bhave for this statement—the first time he had ever criticised his fellow-Gandhian in public. This allowed Indira Gandhi to set about exploiting the difference between the two men. She turned on JP, calling him a 'believer in violence' and a traitor to the Gandhian movement. She gave the go-ahead for the formation of a paramilitary group called the Indira Brigade, which went so far as to fire on a demonstration in Patna, injuring twenty-one people. In November, while attacking a rally in Patna, the police launched a murderous assault on JP himself, aimed to maim or kill. He was defended bravely by his followers, some of whom were badly injured. JP passed out after two of his ribs and a toe were broken. Coming round, he addressed the crowd, stating that he had not witnessed such state terror in all of his years of public life, including during British times.[38]

At this juncture, JP made a controversial strategic decision. Seeking for allies in his struggle with the Indira Congress, he linked up with the Jana Sangh and its sinister parent body the RSS, who were eager to use this as a means to attack the 'communists' within the Congress (I). Although JP had severe reservations about the RSS, which he regarded as a clique which refused to open itself to internal debate, he was now linking his Gandhian-inspired movement with a group that despised Gandhi and his legacy and which stood for the most authoritarian, intolerant and non-dialogic forms of politics. In JP's defence, it can be argued that he was hoping to bring about a change of heart in the Jana Sangh and RSS, and that he succeeded to the extent that a more moderate group emerged within this tendency under Atal Bihari Vajpayee. The mass of the Hindu right was not however won over ideologically in any significant way.

[37]Ostergaard, *Nonviolent Revolution in India*, pp. 69–90.
[38]Scarfe, *J.P. His Biography*, pp. 238–9 and 242–5.

In the short term, this move greatly strengthened the protest in northern India, where the RSS had an impressive organisation. With RSS support, a huge demonstration of over half a million protesters was staged in Delhi in March 1975. Indira Gandhi was now able to state in March 1975, with some credibility, that the movement had become a front for 'fascists'.[39] However, rather than try to woo JP away from his dubious new allies, which might have been possible with some concessions, she chose instead to smash all of her opponents together, imposing a state of Emergency on 26 June 1975 and arresting and jailing the leaders of the protest. The RSS was driven underground to continue the fight. This boosted the morale of its cadres on the one hand, and on the other helped it gain legitimacy through its participation in what was widely seen as a righteous struggle.

Vinoba Bhave came out in support of Indira Gandhi at this juncture, praising the Emergency as an *anushasan parva* (an era of discipline) that would be good for the health of the nation.[40] Bhave's stance split the Gandhian movement in two, with many Sarvodaya workers refusing to follow his lead. They organised satyagrahas in nearly three thousand places on over five hundred occasions. The police beat up large numbers, and nearly nine thousand were arrested. Despite great provocation, they remained non-violent. Though these protests were ignored in the heavily censored press, in scale this satyagraha was comparable to many of Gandhi's own anti-British campaigns. Counter-meetings by pro-Vinoba groups attracted very little support.[41]

JP's 'Total Revolution'

JP's protest against the government of Indira Gandhi was one strand of what he called his campaign for 'total revolution' in India. This followed

[39]Ostergaard, *Nonviolent Revolution in India*, pp. 153–60.

[40]Ibid., p. 221; Scarfe, *J.P. His Biography*, p. 249. The leading Sarvodaya worker Narayan Desai told me in an interview that Bhave thought that Indira Gandhi did not intend to continue the Emergency beyond a couple of weeks, or at most a month. He was to be proved wrong in this. Interview in Vedchhi, 10 December 2000.

[41]Ostergaard, *Nonviolent Revolution in India*, pp. 225–6.

the old Gandhian path of deploying political discontent to drive forward a wider movement for all-round social, economic and cultural change. JP's followers in the Sarvodaya movement were to the fore in this initially. The movement was strongest in Bihar, where attempts were made to move towards a Gandhian-style polity, known as Janata Sarkar (People's Government). Gram sabhas were established consisting of all adults of a village. They were to refuse to pay taxes to the state, arrange their own policing, and in some cases take over the distribution of rice, sugar and fertilizer from profiteering merchants and sell them at a fair price. There were also attempts to bring about social reforms, such as stopping dowry payments, limiting expenditure on marriages and death ceremonies and discouraging liquor consumption.[42] JP suggested that Sangharsh Samitis (Struggle Associations) should be established to keep a constant check on the activities of the electoral representatives of the people, who would be forced to resign if they acted wrongly. Members of the Legislative Council would thus be responsible to the samitis rather than to their party.

When the movement began to spread to UP, the government became seriously alarmed, accusing their opponents of being either financed by capitalists or acting as agents of the American C.I.A.[43] By March 1975, the continuing hostility of Vinoba Bhave towards the movement led to 21 of the 24 members of the Sarva Seva Sangh resigning in support of JP, after which Vinoba agreed to wind up the body. At the same time, he told JP that he should stop the movement.[44] When Bhave came out in support of Indira Gandhi's declaration of Emergency in June, the split in the Sarvodaya movement was complete.[45]

After the dramatic elections of March 1977 that brought an end to the Emergency, JP appeared to be vindicated, with the way now being open for more active state support for the Gandhian programme at every level. He demanded that people's committees be established as a step towards a genuine devolution of power at village level. The response

[42]Ibid., pp. 112–13 and 204.

[43]Ibid., pp. 116 and 120–2.

[44]Ibid., pp. 171–6.

[45]Ibid., p. 221.

from the politicians who had now won power was less than enthusiastic and the scheme was soon forgotten.[46] JP himself was in very poor health, and was unable to take much personal initiative in the matter. He died in October 1979.

The Chhatra Yuva Sangharsh Vahini

JP's movement had however sowed the seeds for future agrarian struggles. In early 1975 he started an organisation called the Chhatra Yuva Sangharsh Vahini—a non-violent 'army' (*vahini*) to work for his 'total revolution'. This attracted many of the Sarvodaya workers who were loyal to JP rather than Vinoba Bhave. In 1977, after the Janata government had replaced Indira Gandhi's Congress (I), JP stated that his organisation should now work in the class interest of the poorest of the poor, which in Bihar meant the landless labourers. Many Sarvodaya workers were horrified by his language of class struggle, which they saw as profoundly un-Gandhian. JP denied that he was adopting a Marxian position, which would have entailed a focus on the industrial proletariat. The latter class had, in his opinion, become merely a new petty bourgeoisie in India. Marxian analysis was therefore inappropriate for India. This argument not only revealed a very mechanical understanding of Marx, but also failed to convince the critics, many of whom cut their ties with the Vahini.[47]

In 1978, the Vahini leadership decided to pursue the new line by taking up the issue of the blatant evasion of the land ceiling laws by the *mahant* (superior) of the Shaivite *math* (monastery) of Bodh Gaya. The mahant had divided his huge estate into small units, each of which was recorded in the land records as being held by individual monks or various religious trusts. Although the mahant had earlier donated 11,000 acres of his land in bhoodan, most of it was found to be barren. He exploited the labourers on his estates ruthlessly, paying them less than the minimum wages laid down by law. In April 1978, Vahini workers led five hundred women, tenants and landless labourers in a dharna in front of the great wooden doors of the math. They demanded that the

[46] Ibid., pp. 289–91 and 294.

[47] Sinha, *Against the Few*, pp. 90–1 and 96.

land be distributed to the poor. Ironically, the Communist Party of India, then in alliance with the Indira Gandhi's Congress Party, staged a counter-demonstration on behalf of the mahant.[48]

Vahini workers encouraged the labourers of the mahant to cultivate the land collectively, taking the crops for themselves. Three hundred acres were in addition seized and handed over to them. The police supported the mahant, arresting the protesters and forcibly preventing the activists from harvesting crops. Strongmen were also employed by the math to intimidate the labourers. In one incident in 1979, two labourers were killed by the strongmen, which provoked the labourers into killing a manager of one of the estates of the math. JP sent a committee to investigate this incident and decided to see it as an 'aberration' and not a reason to abandon the struggle, as Gandhi might have done in a similar situation.[49] Several local Sarvodaya workers decided to come out in favour of the mahant however.

The movement continued after JP's death, with Vahini activists encouraging the labourers to collectively cultivate the land they had seized. The labourers were however unwilling to do this, preferring to cultivate as individual family units. Their ambition was in other words to become landowning peasant farmers. This once again revealed the limited appeal of the principle of gramdan outside the Adivasi tracts. The repression continued into the early 1980s, with harvesting of crops by scab workers under police protection and police raids on labourers' huts. In 1982, the government of Bihar agreed to distribute a thousand acres of math land—a very partial victory, as investigations carried out in 108 villages at that time found that the math held about 9,600 acres in them. It was in addition known to hold land in a further 426 villages of Bihar, which were not investigated. The labourers who gained the land lost interest in the struggle thereafter. In this manner, aspirations for a 'total revolution' petered out.[50]

[48]The Congress Party had lost power in Bihar in 1977 to the Janata Party, which was associated with JP. Ostergaard, *Nonviolent Revolution in India*, p. 182; Sinha, *Against the Few*, p. 91.

[49]Sinha, *Against the Few*, pp. 106–8.

[50]Ibid., pp. 117 and 119–20; Ostergaard, *Nonviolent Revolution in India*, pp. 295–7.

Women and Anti-Liquor Movements in India

In recognition of the strong movement against liquor which had been inspired by Gandhi and which brought about an empowering mobilisation of many women within the struggle, prohibition was implemented in certain provinces of India after independence in 1947. Enforcement was however lax, and in most cases the policy was abandoned after a few years. Anti-liquor work was left on the whole to Sarvodaya activists. In Uttar Pradesh, Sohanlal Bhubhisuk, a follower of Vinoba Bhave, launched a dharna outside certain liquor shops in 1962, himself staging a fast on the steps of the Legislative Assembly in Lucknow. This movement never really took off, however.[51] In the following year Vimla and Sunderlal Bahuguna, a couple who were active in the Sarvodaya movement, started a far more powerful movement in the Uttaranchal region of the state. After they launched a satyagraha against the awarding of a contract to sell liquor in a village close to their ashram, the government agreed to cancel the arrangement. The movement spread in 1966, with women picketing liquor shops and forcing them to close. Protests continued in the following years, with many women being jailed. In one demonstration in 1971 over ten thousand women took part; with fifty-six being arrested and jailed for picketing a liquor shop.[52] Eventually, in 1972, the government agreed to impose prohibition in Uttaranchal. In the process, many women were politically empowered, feeding into their remarkable participation in the Chipko movement in the same area in the following years.[53]

There were similar anti-liquor campaigns elsewhere in India at that time. In Dhule district of Maharashtra, for example, activists with Gandhian leanings started one such movement amongst Adivasi women. After a women's camp was held in 1973, many women in the area went in groups to smash up illicit village liquor distilleries.[54]

[51]Shekhar Pathak, 'Intoxication as a Social Evil: Anti-Alcohol Movement in Uttarakhand', *Economic and Political Weekly*, 10 August 1985, p. 1362.

[52]Sunderlal Bahuguna, 'Women's Non-Violent Power in the Chipko Movement', in Madhu Kishwar and Ruth Vanita (eds), *In Search of Answers: Indian Women's Voices from 'Manushi'*, Zed Press, London 1984, p. 129.

[53]Vimla Bahuguna, 'The Chipko movement', in Ilina Sen (ed.), *A Space Within the Struggle*, Kali for Women, New Delhi 1990, pp. 113–14.

[54]Mira Savara and Sujatha Gothoskar, 'An Assertion of Womanpower:

In most cases, initial successes were not consolidated. In Uttaranchal, for instance, the subsequent emphasis on forest protest saw a marginalisation of the liquor issue. Soon, many illicit distilleries sprang up, so that within a few years it became one of Uttaranchal's major cottage industries.[55] In 1980 the government decided that the policy had been a failure, and allowed the sale of liquor once more in three districts of Uttaranchal. This led to a resumption of the anti-liquor movement in the region in the early 1980s by a youth group called the Uttarakhand Sangharsh Vahini. There were strong protests in 1984, with demonstrations at the time of liquor-shop auctions and picketing of liquor stills. Women were to the fore in this activity.[56] The Sarvodaya-led anti-liquor movement continued in Uttaranchal, feeding in recent years into the movement for what is now the separate Uttaranchal state.[57]

In the early 1990s, there was a powerful anti-liquor movement in Andhra Pradesh, launched after the state government had set up a new machinery to market arrack in a more efficient and, for the government, more lucrative way. Village women saw that their husbands and brothers were squandering their meagre family earnings on this high-priced arrack. The last straw proved to be the subsequent withdrawal of the state subsidy on rice for poor families. In Andhra, numerous poor women had become more assertive of their rights as a result of literacy programmes run in part by the Communist Party (Marxist-Leninist) and the Naxalite People's War Group, in part by the state. Women launched a series of raids on arrack-shops on their own initiative. Besides smashing liquor containers, they also attacked excise jeeps bringing the arrack to their villages. They put pressure on the men of their families to renounce liquor, fining some of those who continued to drink. Their main grievance was against the high price of the government arrack, which was causing great poverty in families, rather than against liquor as such. They had no strong objection to the consumption of home-made liquor.

A wide range of politicians and NGO workers of various political

Organising Landless Women in Maharashtra', in Kishwar and Vanita (eds.), *In Search of Answers*, pp. 143–4.

[55]Pathak, 'Intoxication as a Social Evil', p. 1362.

[56]Ibid., p. 1363.

[57]Emma Mawdsley, 'After Chipko: From Environment to Region in Uttaranchal', *The Journal of Peasant Studies*, Volume 25, No. 4, July 1998, p. 47.

persuasions supported the movement, hoping thereby to further their own agendas. This included Gandhians, who introduced a call for temperance as a moral principle. The leader of the Telegu Desam party, N.T. Rama Rao—then in opposition to the Congress government—took up the issue in 1992, invoking the memory of Gandhi's opposition to drunkenness and his encouragement of women to lead the fight against this evil. Under this pressure, the state government announced in October 1993 that there would be a ban on arrack throughout Andhra. When the Telegu Desam Party won power in the following year, Rao—now chief minister—announced that liquor would be prohibited throughout the state from immediate effect. A Gandhian temperance agenda had been imposed, although the women in the movement itself had not put forward any demand for complete prohibition.[58]

Vahini and Women's Rights

In contrast to the Sarvodaya workers in Uttaranchal, JP did not see the need for any separate emphasis on women's issues or mobilisation that focused on women's participation. He assumed that women would benefit from his wider struggle.[59] When he declared that his struggle was for the *antim jan* (last person), this meant for him above all the class of landless agricultural workers. In 1979, some women *saathis* (activists) of his Chhatra Yuva Sangharsh, which was waging a battle to gain land for agricultural workers in central Bihar, raised the issue of the position of the women in the struggle. They had noticed that in meetings of the labourers, the working women tended to be excluded from the deliberations, even though their contribution to the struggle was as great as that of the men. The issue of exploitation by male family members was raised; not only did the women perform fieldwork, but also they had to cook and carry out other domestic work for the men. Their drunken husbands often beat them.

[58]Susie Tharu and Tejaswini Niranjana, 'Problems for a Contemporary Theory of Gender', in Shahid Amin and Dipesh Chakrabarty, *Subaltern Studies IX: Writings on South Asian History and Society*, Oxford University Press, New Delhi 1996, pp. 253–60; personal communication from Susie Tharu, 3 October 2000.

[59]Scarfe, *J.P. His Biography*, p. 258.

Clearly, the ultimate *antim jat* was that of women labourers. The women saathis felt justified in launching a campaign to improve the position of the women labourers within their own communities. When the matter was raised with men involved in the movement, they argued that God had determined the position of women, and that husbands had a right to beat wives. The women saathis then sought to have workers who beat their wives expelled from the movement. As the problem was compounded by liquor drinking, an anti-liquor campaign was launched, with raids by activists on liquor stills, which were dismantled or smashed and the liquor poured away. Special women's camps were held, at which poor women were given the opportunity to discuss the many ways in which they were oppressed and denigrated. There were campaigns also against child-marriages, expensive weddings and prostitution. Many male saathis were not happy about this campaign, as they felt that it was a distraction from what they saw as the larger class struggle. As a result it was confined to a few villages where the women saathis were most active.[60]

Women activists also took up the issue of land rights for women. When the government redistributed land belonging to the Bodhgaya math, males were given the title to the land in their name. The activists argued that they might use the land as a security to obtain loans, which they might then squander in drink, gambling and other pleasures. Also, with women having no right over the land, their position in the family was devalued. Women might spend years labouring on the family land, but if their husband wanted to turn them out of their house for whatever reason, they had no means of obtaining compensation. It was argued that land-deeds in women's names would improve their position in all of these respects. Male labourers objected strongly that if land passed from mother to daughter the land would be lost when the girl followed prevailing custom by marrying outside their natal village. This was countered by the argument that such customs could be changed, and that the husband could come to reside in his wife's village. The men

[60]Manimal, 'Zameen Kenkar? Jote Onkar: Women's Participation in the Bodhgaya Land Struggles', in Madhu Kishwar and Ruth Vanita (eds), *In Search of Answers*, pp. 153–63.

also argued that as they ploughed the land, they were the rightful owners. In Bihar, as in many parts of India, there was a taboo on women ploughing. The answer to this was that women could well carry out this task, and in 1980 the Vahini indeed ran a campaign to encourage women to put their hands to the plough.[61]

In 1981 the women of Pipparghati village announced that they would not allow any land to be distributed if it was in the names of the men. The officials in charge of distribution responded by asserting that they had no power to give land in the name of women. This was not in fact true; women were fully entitled under the law to obtain such land. This led to a stalemate, and the land distribution did not take place. Eventually, in 1983, the men took the land in their sole names. Subsequently, the bureaucracy relented somewhat by accepting the principle of registration of the land in the joint names of husband and wife. This became common in subsequent years. Such joint deeds have not however succeeded in shifting the balance of power in the family towards women in any significant way.[62]

The women's struggle in central Bihar lost its momentum after the mid-1980s. However, it had a lasting significance in that it had raised some critical issues, such as that of the benefits for women in having land and other property in their names. It also provided a model for women-centred activism in India. For example, a Chhatra Yuva Sangharsh Vahini was established in the city of Agra that took up the issue of the corrupt nexus between the police and brothel-owners in the city. When prostitutes tried to escape from the brothels they were frequently captured and returned by the police. The police retaliated in 1982 by arresting and beating up some of the women leaders.[63] This revealed that it was possible to use Gandhian techniques in a struggle that went far beyond Gandhi's own patriarchal limits.

[61]Govind Kelkar and Chetna Gale, 'The Bodhgaya Land Struggle,' in Sen (ed.), *A Space Within the Struggle*, pp. 83–4, 100 and 107–8.

[62]Ibid., pp. 101–5.

[63]Agra Jan Sangarsh Sahyog Samiti, 'Sangarsh Vahini's Struggle in Agra: When People Demand that Government Implement its Promises', in Kishwar and Vanita (eds), *In Search of Answers*, pp. 189–91.

Chipko Andolan

The Chipko Andolan, which was started and led by Gandhian activists, was a protest against the forest policy of the government in the Uttaranchal division of Uttar Pradesh. This was a mountainous region that until the 1960s was thickly forested. There was a long history of protest in Uttaranchal against government forest policy, stretching back to 1906.[64] From 1921, this protest had been linked to that of the Gandhian Congress.[65]

With the extensive construction of roads in the region in the 1960s, trucks were able to enter the hills and remove timber on an unprecedented scale. Politicians took bribes to ensure that timber-felling contracts were awarded to industrialists and timber dealers at concessional rates. Local Sarvodaya workers tried to resist this initially by establishing locally-controlled forest co-operatives, so that the benefits would come to the people of the region rather than outsiders. However, they lacked both political clout and money-power, and could not obtain the contracts for the co-operatives.[66] In late 1972 a series of demonstrations were held, demanding an end to the contract system of forest exploitation and the supply of forest produce to local people at cheap rates.[67]

At the same time, a more critical attitude was developing amongst the local Sarvodaya workers towards forestry in general. They had been active in mobilising women in the strong anti-liquor campaign of the late 1960s and during the course of this struggle had learnt from the women that the destruction of the forest was causing them severe hardship. Fuel-wood for daily cooking needs was becoming hard to obtain, and even springs were drying up as rainwater was running off the hills unchecked, and thus not replenishing underground springs. The fast run-off also caused floods and landslides.

[64]Ramachandra Guha, *The Unquiet Woods*, pp. 71–2.

[65]Ibid., pp. 111–12.

[66]Ibid., pp. 142–3.

[67]Vimla Bahuguna, 'The Chipko Movement', in Sen (ed.), *A Space Within the Struggle*, pp. 115–6.

The movement entered a new phase in 1973, with protest against a case of gross discrimination against local people in favour of a rich industrial concern from the plains. In late 1972, the government awarded a contract to a large sports manufacturer of Allahabad to cut hundreds of trees from a forest in the hills. Earlier, it had refused permission for a small local concern run along Gandhian lines which specialised in processing of forest produce to take a few trees from the same forest. The man in charge of this concern was Chandi Prasad Bhatt, a Sarvodaya worker who had been involved already in work against untouchability and liquor consumption. He decided to launch a campaign of civil disobedience that involved physical prevention of the tree-felling. The local people themselves devised the idea of 'hanging on' (*chipko*) to the trees, thus giving rise to the name of the movement. They managed to get the cutting stopped. When the company tried to move its operations to a neighbouring forest, they organised a similarly successful protest there. Soon, villagers all over the region were preventing forest clearance through this form of protest. Village women were to the fore, though men were also strongly involved.[68]

Although the Chipko Andolan became known as a woman-centred movement in which village women fought to preserve the forest around their villages, this represented only one element of the stuggle. Just as important was the demand for self-determination and self-management for the region. In Uttar Pradesh as a whole, the particular needs of Uttaranchal were often ignored, for even though it was an extensive area, its people made up only four percent of the total population of the state. Politicians, traders and industrialists of the plains exploited Uttaranchal as a resource, but little was invested in return to improve the condition of the people. Hill agriculture was hard and with low returns, forest resources were largely monopolised by the forest department and there was little industrial employment. As a result, most people of the region lived in poverty. Many were being forced to migrate out in search of work. To a large extent, the protest was against this general state of affairs.[69]

The movement continued throughout the 1970s, with Sarvodaya

[68]Ibid., p. 116; Mawdsley, 'After Chipko', p. 39.
[69]Ibid., pp. 40–3.

workers such as Sunderlal Bahuguna and Chandi Prasad Bhatt to the fore in the leadership. They insisted that there be complete non-violence, despite much provocation by the authorities and others. In a few cases, the women found themselves fighting alone, as when Gaura Devi—a fifty-one-year-old widow—led some women of her village in a protest against tree-felling that the men of the village were keen to allow, as they earned money from renting their houses to contractors and their workers, and were also themselves employed by the contractors to cut trees. The village men launched a social boycott against Gaura Devi, making her position very difficult. Her son was beaten up, and she received death threats. It was only with the strong moral support of Chandi Prasad Bhatt that she was able to keep up her struggle. In Dongri Paitoli village also a few courageous village women stood against the men, being subjected as a result to threats and insults.[70]

Bahuguna believed that the movement had the potential to bring a wider transformation in India, stating that 'I am waiting for the day when the non-violent movement of the hill woman will help turn upside down the centres of power in this country.'[71] In 1979 he launched a fast to force the government to stop cutting by contractors. He was arrested on the thirteenth day, but continued his fast in jail. On the twenty-fourth day the authorities agreed to discuss the issue, and he withdrew his fast. In 1980, Indira Gandhi invited the Chipko Andolan leaders to Delhi for talks, and as a result banned commercial forestry at a height above a thousand metres in the Himalayas for the next fifteen years. Food, fodder and fuel-bearing trees were to be planted close to villages, and people were to have the right to take dry twigs and leaves from the government forests. This represented a major victory.[72]

The movement succeeded for a number of reasons. It provided a striking example of a Gandhian-style protest driven by a sense of moral outrage against a corrupt and rapacious regime that was impoverishing the people and their environment. It was led by respected Sarvodaya

[70]Gopa Joshi, 'Slandered by the Community in Return', in Kishwar and Vanita (eds), *In Search of Answers*, pp. 125–8.

[71]Sundarlal Bahuguna, 'Women's Non-Violent Power in the Chipko Movement', p. 133.

[72]Vimla Bahuguna, 'The Chipko Movement,' pp. 118–20.

workers who insisted on a rigid adherence to non-violence and who had good relations with many leading Gandhian politicians as well as top government officials. The state had to tread carefully against a movement so clearly informed by the Gandhian ideals. Because of this, the movement escaped the sort of vicious repression experienced by many other protest movements of the day.[73] In the end, they also won the ear of the prime minister, Indira Gandhi. She had come out in favour of environmental protection at the First International Environmental Conference in Stockholm in 1972, and the appeal was addressed to her on that basis, with considerable success.[74]

Chipko became well known throughout the world as an example of Gandhian environmental action, with the image of women embracing trees becoming an icon of the environmental movement as a whole. Chipko gave rise to a series of protests since that time in which activists have embraced trees or established tree houses, so as to prevent commercial felling operations.

Narmada Bachao Andolan

One of the most powerful campaigns of civil disobedience since 1980 has been against the construction of a huge dam on the Narmada River, just below the point at which it flows into Gujarat state. The resulting lake—called the Sardar Sarovar in honour of Sardar Vallabhbhai Patel—will displace from between 100,000 and 250,000 people—the figures are disputed—in about 450 villages.[75] Of these about two-thirds

[73]Ramachandra Guha, *The Unquiet Woods*, pp. 173–7.

[74]In addition to the works cited above, there are various other studies of the Chipko Andolan. See Anupam Mishra and Satyendra Tripathi, *The Chipko Movement*, People's Action/Gandhi Peace Foundation, New Delhi 1978; S.S. Kunwar (ed.), *Hugging the Himalayas: The Chipko Experience*, Dasholi Gram Swarajya Mandal, Gopeshwar 1982; Thomas Weber, *Hugging the Trees: The Story of the Chipko Movement*, Penguin, New Delhi 1988.

[75]The government has estimated that 40,827 families will be displaced by the dam—which means about 150,000 people. The Narmada Bachao Andolan puts the figure at about 250,000. The number of villages which will be affected is accepted as being about 450. V. Venkatesan, 'Sardar Sarovar Project: Drowned Out', *Frontline*, Vol. 17, No. 22, 10 November 2000.

are in the Nimar plain of Madhya Pradesh. These are mainly relatively prosperous high-caste farmers who have benefited from the Green Revolution. They will lose their fertile lands to submergence. About one-third of those affected are Adivasis living in the hills directly behind the dam. The bulk of the finance for the construction was to come from loans of $450,000,000 from the World Bank and $200,000,000 from the Japanese government.

The organisation that was formed to fight this project—the Narmada Bachao Andolan (Save the Narmada Movement)—is often described as 'environmental'. It has in consequence received support from many environmentalist groups around the world. However, the chief stated goal of the movement itself is that of 'creating an alternative political culture based on Gandhian principles'.[76] It has been driven by a very Gandhian belief that modern developmental projects supported by the state run roughshod over the economic needs as well as civil rights of the mass of the rural poor, and that the only way to counter such tyranny is through non-violent mass resistance. The merits of satyagraha as against participation in electoral politics, or even violent resistance, have been debated at length in the movement, and it is generally accepted that non-violent methods are most appropriate. The two main leaders, Medha Patkar and Baba Amte, have also used fasting as a weapon, often with some success.[77] The Narmada Bachao Andolan is best seen, therefore, as a campaign for economic and civil rights that employs Gandhian-style satyagraha to powerful effect.

Protests against the proposed dam began as early as 1978 in Nimar, but the movement flagged in the early 1980s. It was then taken up by local NGO workers active in the Adivasi areas which were due to be submerged, with a series of rallies and protests in the mid-1980s. Medha Patkar came to the area first in 1985 as a member of a research team that was investigating the resettlement of peasants affected by the project. She was deeply disturbed to find that the people were being evicted from their land and livelihood with no proper compensation. She also felt that the adverse environmental effects of the dam had not been

[76]Baviskar, *In the Belly of the River*, p. 227.
[77]Ibid., pp. 224–5.

fully appreciated, as no proper environmental studies had been carried out. In 1987 she decided to settle in the valley and fight against the dam.[78]

The movement gradually gathered momentum, with an escalating series of rallies, protest marches, demonstrations and fasts. Villagers began to refuse to allow officials access to their villages. Medha Patkar herself went twice to Washington to put the case directly to the World Bank. The Narmada Bachao Andolan (NBA) was formed in 1989 to coordinate this work. In the same year, the Gujarat government notified the whole of the dam site a prohibited area under the Indian Official Secrets Act, and threatened that any protester who entered this area would be arrested.[79] Supporters of the movement were terrorised by the police, being beaten, arrested and tortured. Even women were subjected to such abuse.[80]

Their first success came in 1990, when the NBA managed to persuade the Japanese government to withdraw all further funding for the project on environmental and human rights grounds. In the same year, the much-respected Gandhian social worker Baba Amte (b.1914) became actively involved in the struggle. He was known for his dedicated work amongst lepers in Maharashtra. In 1985 he had led a mass protest against the construction of two dams in Bastar that threatened to displace the Adivasis of the area. The two dams were never built. In 1989, he turned his attention to the Narmada dam, publishing a booklet called *Cry O Beloved Narmada*, in which he argued that the desire for large dams was a form of modern superstition and that the future lay with small-scale watershed projects. In 1990 he decided to take up residence on the banks of the Narmada at Kasravad, where he established an ashram at a spot that was scheduled for submergence. He vowed to stay there and fight the dam to his last breath.[81] In May 1990 he staged a dharna in Delhi before the residence of the prime minister, V.P. Singh, demanding

[78]Bakshi, *Bapu Kuti*, pp. 285–90.

[79]Parita Mukta, 'Wresting Riches, Marginalising the Poor, Criminalising Dissent: The Building of the Narmada Dam in Western India', *South Asia Bulletin*, Volume 15, No. 2, 1995, p. 105.

[80]Baviskar, *In the Belly of the River*, pp. 205 and 209.

[81]Ibid., p. 205; Bakshi, *Bapu Kuti*, pp. 193 & 211–16.

that construction work be stopped. The prime minister, under pressure from the Gujarat government, rejected the demand.[82]

In December 1990 three thousand people who were threatened with displacement started out on a march from Nimar to the site of the dam. After eight days, the state police stopped them at the border of Gujarat. Rather than go back, they sat down in protest. Volunteers tried to break through the cordon, their hands tied in front of them to show their non-violent intentions. They were beaten back by the police and some were arrested. Medha Patkar and five others launched an indefinite fast. The Gujarat government then orchestrated a counter-demonstration at the border by supporters of the dam, which included some noted Gandhian workers such as Harivallabh Parikh.[83] Baba Amte tried to reason with them, but they blocked their ears to his appeals, something he found both sad and disconcerting. The Gujarat government likewise refused to enter into any dialogue; every suggestion from the NBA was turned down flat. The stalemate continued until a group of independent citizens agreed to review the matter, after which the fast was called off having lasted twenty-two days. The NBA leaders decided to abandon their sit-in. Despite the failure, the protest had received huge publicity, and Medha Patkar had become an all-India, and indeed international, figure. The World Bank decided to investigate the matter by setting up a commission of enquiry.[84]

The report that this commission submitted in 1992 thoroughly vindicated the NBA. It was highly critical of the whole project, both in terms of its impact on the environment and for the way in which the displaced peoples were being treated.[85] As a result of this report, the World Bank withdrew its financial support for the project in 1993.

Angered by this setback to their ambitions, the political leaders of

[82]Pravin Sheth, *Narmada Project: Politics of Eco-Development*, Har-Anand Publications, New Delhi 1994, p. 75.

[83]Ibid., pp. 77–8.

[84]Baviskar, *In the Belly of the River*, pp. 206–8; Bakshi, *Bapu Kuti*, pp. 218–19, Patrick McCully, *Silenced Rivers: The Ecology and Politics of Large Dams*, Zed Books, London 1996.

[85]Bradford Morse and Thomas R. Berger, *Sardar Sarovar: Report of the Independent Review*, Resource Futures International, Ottawa 1992.

Gujarat launched a yet more vicious campaign of repression. The police thrashed demonstrators, an Adivasi boy was shot dead, and the NBA office in Baroda was ransacked. They continued to build the dam and dig the canals that it was to feed, financing these works from state resources. Soon, eighty percent of the entire irrigation budget of Gujarat was being poured into the work, starving other irrigation projects of funds.[86]

The NBA had meanwhile challenged the legality of the project in the Supreme Court of India in New Delhi in 1994. It was argued that the way that rehabilitation was being carried through violated the terms under which the project had been passed by the government. The court accepted that there had been various irregularities in the implementation of the project. It ruled that construction work should cease for the time being at a height of 88 metres pending a review. As the projected height of the dam was to be 138 metres, this was considered a major victory for the NBA.

The NBA continued its campaign to prevent the waters of the Narmada being dammed at all. However, many people who were sympathetic towards the protest began to feel that the dam was now a *fait accompli*. The majority of Adivasis affected by the existing submergence had by then been resettled, albeit in very inadequate and often squalid camps, and it was argued that rather than go on opposing it in an outright fashion it would be better to work to obtain a better deal for those who were being displaced.

Medha Patkar refused to accept this, arguing that the whole project continued to violate her deepest feelings. She advanced the Gandhian argument that the struggle was for decentralisation of power, with local people having the right to decide how their resources should be utilised.[87] She now focused the campaign on annual protests in villages that were being submerged by the reservoir each monsoon. Activists stayed with the peasants in their villages as the waters rose, refusing to move, even at the risk of drowning. This was called *jal samarpan*—which

[86]Mukta, 'Wresting Riches, Marginalising the Poor, Criminalising Dissent, p. 101.

[87]Suzanne Goldenberg, 'Villagers in Shadow of Dam Await the End of the World', *The Guardian* (London), 30 July 1999.

means 'give one's life to the water'. The first such protest was in 1993 at Manibelli, a village very close to the site of the dam. In 1994, Baba Amte and his wife refused to move from their house by the river and were only saved from drowning by being forcibly removed by the district collector.[88] There was a highly publicised protest along such lines during the monsoon of 1999, when Medha Patkar went to stay in Domkhedi—one of the villages which was being rapidly submerged by the rising waters. She and sixty other protesters were arrested by the police, dragged away and kept in detention until the water receded after the monsoon.[89]

Patkar was joined in the late 1990s by the celebrity author Arundhati Roy, who threw her weight behind this uncompromising stand with a powerful polemic in favour of the movement which gained a lot of media attention both in India and abroad.[90] In January 2000 Roy was arrested while leading a protest march against the dam. Roy's intervention gave a major fillip to the protest after a period of demoralisation.

In October 2000 there was a grave setback to the movement when the Supreme Court ruled by a 2–1 majority that construction work on the dam could be resumed to bring it up to 90 metres, and thereafter in stages to an eventual height of 138 metres. The Gujarat government, now controlled by the BJP, celebrated this news with fireworks, and then organised a big function at the site of the dam to inaugurate the restart of construction. It was held on 31 October 2000, the 125th anniversary of the birth of Sardar Vallabhbhai Patel, and the man after whom the reservoir is named. The celebrations cut across party lines in Gujarat, with the leader of the Congress opposition in the state, Amarsinh Chaudhary, also attending. However, the chief ministers of the three other states affected by the project, Madhya Pradesh, Maharashtra and Rajasthan, did not come. The function was presided over by L.K. Advani, the home minister of India, who had a conceit of being the true heir to Sardar Patel. In his speech he spoke darkly of the

[88]Bakshi, *Bapu Kuti*, pp. 226–7.

[89]Suzanne Goldenberg, 'Indian Dam Protestors Put Behind Bars', *The Guardian* (London), 13 August 1999.

[90]Arundhati Roy, *The Cost of Living: The Greater Common Good and the End of Imagination*, Flamingo, London 1999.

'anti-national forces' that were opposing both the dam and India's nuclear weapons: 'I sometimes wonder whether these people are working at the behest of our own people or outsiders. I want to be proved wrong, but it surprises me. Why is there so much opposition to developmental projects? This attitude clearly suits those who do not wish to see India becoming strong in security and socio-economic development.'[91] Patkar's response to this was: 'At least they have understood us well when he said that we were against Kargil and Pokhran. They have understood that we are against violence.'[92]

Patkar and Roy refused to compromise at all, launching an immediate campaign to have the Supreme Court verdict reversed. The Gujarat government is now pushing ahead with the building work, hoping that they will eventually be allowed to take the dam to the full height of 138 metres. As the Supreme Court is only allowing the height to be raised in stages, depending on whether or not there has been compliance with the terms of the agreement, permission for each stage is likely to be fought out bitterly. In January 2001, the government of Maharashtra—which is generally more prepared to listen to Medha Patkar than the government of Gujarat—let it be known that it is unlikely to agree to a height greater than 110 metres unless very good reasons are given.[93] The struggle thus continues.

To what extent has this been a *Gandhian* movement? Although Baba Amte is very clearly a Gandhian, Medha Patkar makes no such claim. Yet, in the words of Shripad Dharadikari, who has been with the NBA since 1988: 'Gandhi was never a "*mantra*" within the Andolan. Yet all its activists saw themselves as fighting the battle against Nehru's version of "development" and for something closer to "Gandhi's" version which, fifty years ago, had been pushed aside by the forces of history.'[94] And, as Sanjay Sangvai—another leading figure in the NBA—has pointed

[91]Quoted in Vinay Kumar, 'People Cheer as Work on the Narmada Dam Resumes', *The Hindu*, 1 November 2000.

[92]Gagai Parsai, 'It's a Fight to the Finish, Says Medha Patkar', *The Hindu*, 4 November 2000.

[93]Mahesh Vijapurkar, 'Fact-Finding Panel on SSP to be Set up', *The Hindu*, 5 January 2001.

[94]Bakshi, *Bapu Kuti*, p. 291.

out, the tactics that have been adopted exemplify the Gandhian method of struggle.[95]

As in Gandhi's own campaigns and JP's movement, the protest has depended on the leadership and drive of charismatic figures, most notably Medha Patkar and Baba Amte. Initially, the people of Nimar were suspicious of Patkar, who they suspected was motivated by personal political ambitions. But when they saw that this was not the case—that she was driven by a rage against the injustice of such development projects—they became avid followers, regarding her as almost a goddess-like figure in whom they could repose their faith.[96] She and Baba Amte were widely seen to be above narrow party politics and to be true champions of the people—as were Gandhi and JP. Through their inspired leadership, Patkar and Amte managed to bring together rich farmers and Adivasis within one movement, even though the two groups of this region have very little in common in most respects and in the past have generally viewed each other with considerable distrust.

Just as Gandhi managed to win international attention through his adept use of symbols, so the Narmada Bachao Andolan has proved a master of publicity. Adivasis staged their protests wielding bows and arrows. They held meetings in which—in front of the cameras of the world press—they scooped up water from the Narmada and held it in their hands while vowing never to leave their ancestral lands. When portions of their villages were submerged, they were photographed standing in the rising water declaring that they would let themselves be drowned rather than accept rehabilitation.[97] They learnt to use language that went down well with environmentalists, such as that they were children of the earth who were being torn from their mother's breasts.[98] The image of the movement that was thus projected was that of simple Adivasis who had lived in the area since time immemorial in harmony with their environment being brutally displaced by a callous and unfeeling developmental state. The fact that the majority of the people

[95]Ibid., p. 289.

[96]Baviskar, *In the Belly of the River*, p. 214.

[97]One such photograph by Karen Robinson was published in *The Independent* (London), 25 November 1999.

[98]Baviskar, *In the Belly of the River*, p. 262.

due to be displaced were prosperous farmers of Nimar rather than poor Adivasis tended to be overlooked in all this.

Although the appeal to environmental sensibilities has in many respects been extremely successful, it has also opened up the movement to an attack that seeks to trivialise it. The leaders are thus described as 'youngsters' from urban areas who are driven by romantic concerns about 'trees and tigers'.[99] Also, as Michael Dove has argued, environmentalism is easily turned round by states to justify repressive developmental policies, e.g. by refusing local people access to forests on the grounds that they are destroying the forest ecology.[100]

Similar problems are encountered in the attempt to project this as a religious struggle. The Narmada is considered one of the seven great sacred rivers of India, revered by many as 'Narmada Mai', or the goddess Mother Narmada. There are a string of temples along the banks from its source to its mouth, and it is considered particularly meritorious for Hindus to trek on foot from one to the other along the entire length of the river, travelling east on the north bank and back west on the south. This is known as the *Narmada parikrama* (circumambulation), and it takes many months to complete.[101] The construction of the Sardar Sarovar and other dams along the river will destroy this ancient pilgrimage trail and submerge many old and historic temples. There are no plans to save them in any way. The feeling that religious sensibilities are being trampled underfoot by the state provides an added moral appeal for the movement. This has been reinforced by a free use of religious symbols in demonstrations and protests.[102]

The uncompromising attitude of a succession of Gujarat governments—whether of Congress or the BJP—towards the NBA has made this a particularly difficult test of the Gandhian method of resistance. As I have argued throughout this book, this relies on opening up a

[99]Ibid., p. 235.

[100]Michael R. Dove, 'Local Dimensions of "Global" Environmental Debates', in Arne Kalland and Gerard Persoon (eds), *Environmental Movements in Asia*, Curzon, Richmond 1998.

[101]The religious sites along the Narmada are described in Geoffrey Waring Maw, *Narmada: The Life of a River*, Marjorie Sykes, Selly Oak, no date (c.1992).

[102]Baviskar, *In the Belly of the River*, pp. 214–16.

dialogue. Medha Patkar and Baba Amte have been able to carry on fruitful dialogues with the governments of Madhya Pradesh and Maharashtra. The government of Gujarat, on the other hand, has resisted all dialogue, preferring to react with calumny against the leaders and police action against the protesters. Despite all the provocation, the resistance has remained non-violent.

Realising that they had lost the moral high ground in the affair, the supporters of the dam in Gujarat have deployed a further tactic, namely the mobilisation of their religious spokesmen to advance a claim that the dam is *dharmik*. They argue that it will bring the holy water of 'Narmada Mata' to the homes of people throughout Gujarat. A rally to this effect was held in Bombay in 1990, addressed by high-profile Hindu religious figures, such as Morari Bapu and Pramukh Swami of the Swaminarayan sect. The building of the dam was described as a '*yagna*' (religious rite involving—appropriately—sacrifice).[103]

The strongest grounds for this struggle are neither environmental nor religious (though both are important in their different ways), but those of the rights of citizens to a livelihood, a decent standard of living and freedom from arbitrary acts of state coercion. All of these basic rights are violated most blatantly by the Narmada project. The stuggle began as a local demand for social justice, but in the process it expanded to providing a fulcrum for a critique of a whole system of rule which was prepared to ride roughshod over the basic needs of one section of the population for the sake of development projects which enrich those who are already well off. While the state claims that this furthers national interests, it in fact strengthens class divisions and is thus socially divisive.[104] This can hardly be said to represent a healthy form of national development.

[103]Parita Mukta, 'Worshipping Inequalities: Pro-Narmada Dam Movement', *Economic and Political Weekly*, 13 October 1990, p. 2300. It should be noticed that the Hindu right has, ironically, taken the opposite stance in regard to the Tehri Dam on the Ganga, which it condemns as a sacrilege against that holy river. R. Ramachandran, 'The Tehri Turnabout', *Frontline*, Vol. 18, No. 10, 12–25 May 2001.

[104]The process of class polarisation is analysed by Mukta, 'Wresting Riches, Marginalising the Poor, Criminalising Dissent'.

Gandhian Activism Since 1980

Through struggles such as this and various other satyagrahas elsewhere, many Gandhians maintained a radical image into the 1980s. In 1981, Indira Gandhi's increasingly authoritarian government began to investigate these organisations on grounds that they were 'destabilising the country' and 'tarnishing the image' of the Father of the Nation—e.g. Gandhi. It was alleged that they were receiving funding from foreign governments with this end in mind. This was vigorously denied, and in most cases the Gandhian organisations proved that they had nothing to hide. For example, though the Sarva Seva Sangh was shown to have received Rs.20,000 from foreign sources in the previous decade—a tiny amount in proportion to its total income—it had all been channelled to them through the government.[105]

Although the Gandhian constructive movement was split badly in the 1970s between the followers of Vinoba Bhave and JP, it retained much vitality into the 1980s. In addition, when particular local Gandhian workers became reformist and ineffectual, the work was often taken up and continued by people who did not claim to be Gandhians, but in practice built on Gandhian models of struggle. For example, in Bihar, land which had been designated as bhoodan, but which had never been distributed was in many cases occupied in the 1980s by peasants led by Naxalites. Although known for their violent opposition to the landlords, and campaign of extermination of 'class enemies', in practice, on the ground, they most commonly deployed various forms of non-violent action, such as rallies, processions, *dharnas*, *bandhs*, *hartals*. *Jan adalats* (people's courts) and *jan panchayats* (people's councils) were also established. Even the violence of the ruthless and homicidal caste *senas* (armies), which operated in the interests of the landlords, were countered to a large extent by non-violent mass resistance.[106]

Even gramdan maintains its vitality in some Adivasi areas. In Rajasthan, for example, a Gramdan Act was passed in 1971, allowing for the establishment of village councils (*gram sabhas*) with executive and legal

[105]Ostergaard, *Nonviolent Revolution in India*, pp. 339–40.

[106]Bhatia, 'The Naxalite Movement in Central Bihar', pp. 90 and 96–8.

powers to run the village collectively. A recent study of an Adivasi gramdan village of Udaipur District called Seed has shown how the people took advantage of the act by establishing strict environmental protection measures enforced by the gram sabha, leading to a remarkable regeneration of the forest in a region of severe deforestation.[107]

Gandhian-style constructive work has not been confined only to the rural areas. In Ahmedabad there has been a highly successful struggle by self-employed women. Ela Bhatt inaugurated this work by founding the Self Employed Women's Association (SEWA) in 1972. While working in the Gandhian labour union in the city, the Majur Mahajan, she had seen that conventional trades union organisation did not help self-employed workers, many of whom were women. They were employed in activities such as manufacturing goods at home, selling products on the street, pulling carts, and working in the building industry. They were exploited ruthlessly by middlemen and harassed by the police. She established a co-operative bank, funded by self-employed women, and providing loans at low rates of interest. This was a particularly appropriate strategy, as middlemen typically controlled those whom they exploited by advancing loans at high rates of interest. The initiative was highly successful, greatly empowering the poor, who began to demand higher wages and better piece-rates for their goods. Sufficient capital was soon built up to provide funds for other co-operative banks. By 1993 there were 54,000 members of SEWA, with sixty co-operatives in nine districts of Gujarat. Members are almost all of lower caste, or Dalits or Muslims. The emphasis throughout has been on solidarity through self-reliance and campaigns that are strictly non-violent. In addition, SEWA has striven to build communal harmony in Gujarat—and has achieved much despite the viciously communal atmosphere stoked by the Hindu right in the past decade. In all these respects, it exemplifies the best of Gandhian constructive values.[108]

There are of course many critics of such Gandhian-inspired work. In his day, JP was subjected to a strong critique by the political scientist

[107]Pinto, *Gandhi's Vision and Values*, pp. 151–2.
[108]Ibid., pp. 141–6.

W.H.Morris-Jones for his allegedly impractical and utopian approach to politics.[109] The prominent development economist Gunnar Myrdal dismissed JP's ideas as 'escapist'—being no more than a romanticising of a rural past which in reality had been stagnant and backwards.[110] More recently, Sunil Khilnani has argued that much activity by what he labels as 'public action' groups has lacked any very coherent vision. Activists work within civil society to solve various social and economic problems outside the ambit of the state and bureaucracy. Although NGO groups, environmentalist activists, self-help groups like SEWA, women's groups and so on have a vision of working for a universal good, they are constantly in tension with local group and community interests which assert their power in ruthless and frequently violent ways. The victories of the 'public action' groups are at best contingent, and often overturned. They tend to restrict their vision to local and particular problems, and lack a perspective for an overall economic strategy for India.[111] Khilnani also criticises Gandhian socialists like JP and Ram Manohar Lohia, arguing that their projects were poorly run and opened the way for Hindu nationalists.[112] This appears contradictory: Gandhians are condemned for being localised, yet JP and Lohia and many others were in fact active on a national stage. It is also unfair to blame the rise of the Hindu right on them primarily—the causes are more complex. JP's alliance with the Jan Sangh and its RSS backers in 1975 was certainly a grave mistake in the long term, but it was Indira Gandhi's declaration of Emergency that gave them the crucial boost and which paved the way for the incorporation of the Jan Sangh in government, and thus the legitimisation of the Hindu right. Indira and Rajiv Gandhi's populist accommodation of right-wing Hindu programmes to garner votes compounded this process in the 1980s. Gandhian social activists can hardly be blamed for that.

In fact, the Gandhian agenda has a strong vision for India, but one that is totally at odds with the prevailing dogmas of 'economic growth' and liberalisation. Such is the power of the status quo that attacks often

[109]W.H. Morris-Jones, 'The Unhappy Utopia', *Economic Weekly*, 25 June 1960.
[110]Scarfe, *J.P. His Biography*, pp. 199–200.
[111]Khilnani, *The Idea of India*, pp. 104–5.
[112]Ibid., pp. 187–8.

have to be focused on particular local targets. Successes at such a level may appear fragmented, but they demonstrate that there are alternative paths that can be taken, and they provide an inspiration for others.[113] The task then becomes one of building wider coalitions based on an appeal to these alternative visions. This has been done in the past, and the new 'rainbow coalition' of anti-nuclear activists and environmental campaigners might have a similar impact in the future.

[113]Bakshi, *Bapu Kuti*, is a recent, popular study which describes several Gandhian projects and initiatives of very diverse sorts which have been carried through with great success in many different regions of India in the past two decades.

9

Gandhi's Global Legacy

Some Contemporary Western Reactions

The British governing classes, who believed that they had a divine sanction to 'civilise' the rest of the world, were infuriated to be told by Gandhi that what they called 'British civilisation' was only an idea, betrayed by the reality of imperialism. At their most reactionary they retreated into abusive bluster, as did Winston Churchill, who in 1931 called him 'a malignant subversive fanatic', stating that:

> It was alarming and also nauseating to see Mr Gandhi, a seditious Middle Temple lawyer, now posing as a fakir of a type well-known in the East, striding half-naked up the steps of the Viceregal palace, while he is still organising and conducting a defiant campaign of civil disobedience, to parley on equal terms with the representative of the King-Emperor. Such a spectacle can only increase the unrest in India and the danger to which white people there are exposed.[1]

On other occasions, Churchill called Gandhi 'a thoroughly evil force, hostile to us in every fibre', and 'a traitor'.[2] Lord Wavell, viceroy from 1943 to 1947, described him as 'a malignant old man' and 'a very tough politician and not a saint'.[3]

[1]Gilbert, *Winston S. Churchill*, Vol. 5, p. 390.

[2]Patrick French, *Liberty or Death: India's Journey to Independence and Division*, Flamingo, London 1997, pp. 166 & 188.

[3]Penderel Moon (ed.), *Wavell: The Viceroy's Journal*, Oxford University Press, London 1973, pp. 185 & 236.

A similar lack of empathy towards Gandhi was shown by a group of Oxford dons whom Gandhi was invited to meet when he was in England in 1931. The professors, who were touted as the best 'trained minds' of the day, subjected Gandhi to three hours of dry, scholastic questioning. They refused to concede that there could be any justification in resorting to civil disobedience. Gandhi would not concede any ground to them at all in this respect, resulting in a complete impasse. Edward Thompson, one of the Oxford dons present on that day, concluded: 'He can be exasperating', and went on to say that he now understood why the ancient Athenians had demanded Socrates' death.[4]

Men such as these were too limited by their own class horizons to be able to even begin to understand what Gandhi was about. Not all were so blinkered. Many devout Christians in Europe and the USA understood the moral basis to Gandhi's work, and some even compared him with Christ. For example, Fenner Brockway wrote in 1929 that Gandhi 'in living out his creed personally ... has probably succeeded in doing so more completely than any man since the time of Christ.'[5] Lord Irwin, who served as viceroy from 1926 to 1931, was a staunch Christian who appreciated Gandhi as a man of God, and in 1930 he was reluctant to arrest a saint—which gave Gandhi the leeway to carry out his legendary salt march. In a speech of January 1931, Irwin stated that he recognised the spiritual force that impelled Gandhi, and believed that they shared a common desire for the good of India. He politely requested his cooperation in working to restore 'the seal of friendship once again upon the relations of two peoples, whom unhappy circumstances have lately estranged.'[6] The statement was not received well by most of Irwin's compatriots in India, who were not as yet prepared to concede that Gandhi's 'saintliness' was in any way genuine or that his ethics were at all valid.

There were many Westerners whose feelings for Gandhi were not merely sympathetic, but wildly enthusiastic. In the closing years of the nineteenth and early years of the twentieth centuries there were many

[4]Fischer, *The Life of Mahatma Gandhi*, pp. 356–7.

[5]Dalton, *Mahatma Gandhi*, pp. 125–30 and footnote 156, p. 227.

[6]S. Gopal, *The Viceroyalty of Lord Irwin 1926–1931*, Clarendon Press, Oxford 1957, p. 98.

in Europe and America who believed that the salvation of humanity lay in a forthcoming global spiritual awakening. Some anticipated a new millennium to be inaugurated by a coming World Saviour who, it was suggested, would appear in the East, probably from India. The founder of the Theosophical society, Madame Blavatsky, stated shortly before her death in 1891 that the real purpose of the society was to prepare for the coming of 'the Messiah or the World Teacher'.[7] Her successors soon discovered such a saviour in the person of a young and charismatic South Indian Brahman called Jiddu Krishnamurti. He was groomed to assume his great global role by the Theosophists of Adyar in Madras; by 1927 Annie Besant felt that the time was ripe to declare that: 'The World Teacher is here.'[8] Unfortunately for the Theosophists, Krishnamurti promptly dissociated himself from this plan, declaring that the supposed divinity in him was no more than a chimera imposed on him by his disciples.

Many Europeans and Americans projected their spiritual yearnings in these respects onto the figure of Gandhi. We can see this in one of the most important of the early Western biographies of Gandhi, Romain Rolland's *Mahatma Gandhi: The Man Who Became One with the Universal Being* (1924). As the title suggests, the emphasis was on the saintly qualities of the Mahatma: 'With Gandhi, everything is nature—modest, simple, pure—while all his struggles are hallowed by religious serenity ...'[9] Seven years later the two met in Switzerland. Rolland described Gandhi's blessing to him as they parted: 'It was the kiss of St Dominic and St. Francis.'[10]

Another such spiritual pilgrim from Europe was the Sicilian aristocrat Joseph Jean Lanza Del Vasto (1901–81). A scholarly Christian idealist who thirsted for transcendental awakening, he travelled in 1937 to India to meet Gandhi. In a book written in French in 1943, *Le Pèlerinage aux Sources*, he described his feelings as he arrived at the ashram at Wardha for the first time.

[7]Pupul Jayakar, *J. Krishnamurti: A Biography*, Penguin Books, New Delhi 1986, p. 22.

[8]Ibid., p. 76.

[9]Quoted in Fischer, *The Life of Mahatma Gandhi*, p. 365.

[10]Ibid., p. 369

In the middle of the parched field is a small clay hut, open and so low that it makes no break in the countryside. In the doorway under the slope of the thatched roof, a little, half-naked old man is seated on the ground. It's he! He waves to me—yes, to me!—and makes me sit down beside him and smiles to me. He speaks—and speaks of nothing else but me—asking me who I am, what I do and what I want. And no sooner has he asked than I discover that I am nothing, have never done anything and want nothing except to stay like this in his shadow.

Here he is before my eyes, the only man who has shown us a green shoot in the desert of this century. A man who knows the hard law of love, hard and clear like a diamond. The captain of the unarmed, the father of the pariahs, the king who reigns by the divine right of sainthood. He has come to show us the power over this earth of absolute innocence. He has come to prove that it can stop machines, hold its own against guns and defy an empire. He has come into the world to bring us this news from beyond, where nothing changes, to teach us the truth that we have always known, being Christians. Truth so ill-assorted with us, so strangely contradictory to everything that the world and men had taught us, that we did not know what to do with it. We kept it between the four walls of the church and in the dark of our hearts. He, the Hindu, had to come for us to learn what we had always known. While the old man questions me and smiles, I am silent, trying not to weep.[11]

Like many before him and after, del Vasto had fallen under the spell of Gandhi, drawing from him a vindication of his own particular ethical beliefs and yearnings. The passage brings out well Gandhi's remarkable ability to open himself to all sorts of people and then work his ways on them through his engagement with them as individuals. As del Vasto goes on to say: 'Every statement he makes is illuminated by different approaches to the same point, so that the humblest intelligence has access to it and the keenest is riveted. Not even the most trifling detail is beneath his dignity, just as in his eyes every man has his worth and nothing is without its importance.'[12] He became a follower, and Gandhi conferred on him an Indian name—Shantidas, or 'servant of peace'. There were many such others who came to his ashram at that

[11]Lanza del Vasto, *Return to the Source*, pp. 100–1.
[12]Ibid., p. 102.

time. As one Indian follower later wrote: 'At Sevagram I found myself among young people from all around the world—Americans, Japanese, Africans, Europeans, even Britons—who had come to see Gandhi and to help him in his work. Whether a person's skin was white, brown, or black, whether he or she supported or opposed him, seemed to make no difference to Gandhi: he related to all with ease and respect. Almost immediately, he made us feel we were part of his own family.'[13] Del Vasto's search, which had taken him to India and to Gandhi, had started as a spiritual quest, but his close contact with Gandhi soon conferred a harder social edge to his understanding. He returned to Europe fired by the idea of establishing a 'Gandhian Order in the West'. In the years after the Second World War he set up communes known as 'Communities of the Ark' which sought to be as self-sufficient as possible, with members carrying out physical labour without the help of modern machines as a condition of membership. Initially, most of those drawn to these communes came from an intellectual or aristocratic background, though the membership broadened to include other classes in time. Unlike a monastic order—but as in Gandhi's ashrams—men and women lived together in these collectives.

Del Vasto became active in French politics in 1957, fasting for twenty days in protest against the torture of Algerians by the French. In the following year he started a separate organisation, the Action Civique Non-Violent, dedicated to non-violent political action. This body waged a campaign in 1959–61 against the internment camps set up for Algerians in France who were suspected of supporting the liberation war in Algeria. Volunteers went to the camps and demanded to be arrested for the same 'crime'. Support was also extended to those who objected to serving in the army in Algeria. After some arrests, and the launching of an indefinite fast by Louis Lecoin, a prominent conscientious objector since the time of the First World War who had spent ten years in jail for his beliefs, the French government capitulated and accepted that citizens had a right to refuse military service on grounds of conscience. This was recognised in law in 1963. The organisation also campaigned

[13]Eknath Easwaran, *The Compassionate Universe: The Power of the Individual to Heal the Environment*, Penguin Books India, New Delhi 2001, pp. 21–2.

against nuclear weapons, carrying out the first ever occupation of a nuclear power facility in 1958.[14]

The elevated yearnings of men such as Rolland and del Vasto were those of an élite disenchanted with their own civilization. The reaction to Gandhi by the lower classes of Europe were, as in India, a mixture of the earthy, curious and miraculous, though there was often a friendly irreverence which would have been out of place in the subcontinent. Thus, when Gandhi was walking through the streets of the East End of London on his visit in 1931 an urchin was heard to yell: 'Hey, Gandhi, where's your trousers?' Gandhi laughed heartily, and later quipped: 'You people wear plus-fours, mine are minus-fours.'[15]

Gandhi's trouserless apparel also struck the imagination of the working-class youth of Saltburn in the North-East of England. At the time of their annual carnival, when there was a prize of five shillings offered for the best fancy-dress costume, the unemployed lads wondered how they could win this handsome sum. A community storyteller later recalled their ingenious solution:

> 'Yer'd need a real posh costume.' ...
>
> 'Yer don't!' said Nick. 'Look at this.'
> He produced a crumpled sheet of grease-stained newspaper that must have wrapped last night's chips.
> 'See that!'
>
> He pointed to a large photograph under the headline: 'MAHATMA GANDHI. INDIAN LEADER VISITS LONDON.' We peered at a brown spindly figure wearing wire-framed spectacles and a loin cloth; his pathetic thinness accentuated by the plump, well-fed look of the dignitaries around him.
>
> 'This Gandy—he's a famous fella. Like Tom Mix or Hughie Gallagher. I heard me da talkin' about him,' explained Nick. 'He's in aall the papers and on the wireless as well. One of us'll go as Gandy. It'll cost nowt for a costume!'

[14]Lanza del Vasto, *Return to the Source*, pp. 9–13; Mark Shepard, *The Community of the Ark*, Simple Productions, Arcata, California 1990.

[15]Fischer, *The Life of Mahatma Gandhi*, p. 252.

Geordie Skinner was chosen for the part. They improvised a costume out of a white towel and 'grandad's specs', with an old broom handle for Gandhi's staff on which was nailed a placard made from an old shoebox lid stating: 'GANDY FOR HOME ROOL'. They coloured Geordie's skin with a mixture of gravy browning and cocoa. When the procession began, Geordie strode to the front, still wearing his hobnail boots, but promptly dropped his 'staff' down a manhole. As he wrestled to retrieve it, his spectacles fell in as well. In his distress, he took out his large flat cloth cap—which was of a well-worn and indeterminate mushroom colour—and clapped it on his head. When the judges at last reached him they conferred with great solemnity:

> 'Charming! Quite charming. Delightfully different!' said the Vicar. 'Beautifully marked! Such an ingenious idea!' agreed the Mayoress. She turned to the Carnival Secretary who was hovering pencil poised. 'First prize to the toadstool with the elf underneath!'[16]

Would the local élite—we may wonder—have been so delighted had they known that the youth had meant to represent the 'subversive' figure of Gandhi?

There were many other such curious and wonderstruck reactions to Gandhi in England at that time. When he visited Lloyd George at his farm in Surrey, the servants insisted on coming out to meet the 'holy man'. According to Lloyd George, none other of his many distinguished visitors had ever inspired such a reaction. When Louis Fischer interviewed Lloyd George some seven years later, he was told that an unknown black cat had appeared and sat on Gandhi's lap. It disappeared after he had left, only appearing some years later when Gandhi's devoted follower Madeline Slade came to visit the farm.[17]

The popular responses to Gandhi on the European continent were equally unpredictable, and in some cases bizarre. When Gandhi was due to arrive at Rolland's house in 1931, the elderly author received hundreds of letters relating to the visit:

[16]Alan Stewart, 'Gandhi in a Cloth Cap', in *I Remember ... the North East: Recollections of Yesteryear*, The Pentland Press, Bishop Auckland 1993, pp. 3–8.

[17]Fischer, *The Life of Mahatma Gandhi*, p. 353.

> an Italian wanted to know from Gandhi what numbers would win in the next national lottery; a group of Swiss musicians offered to serenade Gandhi under his window every night; the Syndicate of the Milkmen of Leman volunteered to supply 'the King of India' with dairy products during his stay. Journalists sent questionnaires and camped around Rolland's villa; photographers laid siege to the house; the police reported that the hotels had filled with tourists who hoped to see the Indian visitor.[18]

In all of this, one senses that Gandhi struck a chord with the working class in a way that he generally did not among the ruling class. When, for example, Gandhi visited Lancashire, a region of England that had suffered very materially from the Indian boycott of foreign textiles, the local working class gave him a warm and empathetic welcome. One unemployed worker stated: 'I am one of the unemployed, but if I was in India I would say the same thing that Mr. Gandhi is saying.'[19] At the Greenfield Mill in Darwen, a photograph shows him surrounded by women workers, cheering him heartily, raising their fists in a show of solidarity. Despite their subsequent reputation for racism, a significant portion of the English working class appeared at that time to have a remarkable empathy for the man who above all stood for freedom for India, reaching out with a warm-hearted enthusiasm that was almost entirely alien to their hard-faced superiors.

Gandhi and the Pacifist Movement

Gandhi and his movement were of central importance in the development of modern pacifism, which stands for a principled rejection of the use of violence at all levels of politics. This emerged in the West as a full-fledged doctrine only in the 1930s.[20] It originated in protests against the military-industrial complex during the First World War.

[18]Ibid., p. 366.

[19]Ibid., p. 360.

[20]Previously 'pacifism' meant a preference for peace rather than war, and did not imply a rejection of violence in all instances. James Hinton, *Protests and Visions: Peace Politics in 20th Century Britain*, Hutchinson Radius, London 1989, p. x.

After the war, anti-war protesters came to see Gandhi as a shining example of pacifism in action. Frederick Fisher has noted how in this respect, Gandhi appeared on the world stage at just the right psychological moment. Earlier, his message would have been almost certainly ignored. As it was, he struck a chord with a generation that thirsted for peace and demanded that future international conflicts be resolved non-violently.[21]

A central figure within the newly emerging pacifist movement was the Dutch anarcho-syndicalist Bart de Ligt (1883–1938). A Christian pastor, he was imprisoned by his government during the First World War for making anti-war speeches. His church did not support him in this, and he subsequently became disillusioned with Christianity as it was practised in his day. He studied Greek paganism and Eastern religions, moving towards a belief in more cosmic and universal truths. In the 1920s he became active in the Dutch labour movement, giving it a strong anti-militarist thrust. Moving to Geneva in 1925, he came into contact with the Russian exile Pavel Biryukov, who championed the cause of the Russian pacifist Christian sect of the Dukhobors, which had been persecuted by both the Tsars and the Bolsheviks and had been admired by Tolstoy. He came to see pacifism as something rooted in such long-standing traditions, but providing at the same time a revolutionary means towards a transformation of popular consciousness in an age of mass politics.

During these years de Ligt corresponded with Gandhi and met him in Switzerland in 1931. Later, he persuaded Gandhi to join the Paris-based anti-war organisation, the Reassemblement International Contre la Guerre et le Militarisme (RIGM). In his book *The Conquest of Violence* (1937) he argued that the non-cooperation of syndicalist strikes should be joined with Gandhi's principled non-violence. He was however critical of Gandhi in several important respects. He felt that he was often inconsistent in his non-violence, as during the First World War, when he supported the British war effort. Also, he criticised Gandhi's demand that the Indian people should control their defence forces, when in fact he should have been seeking to disband them. He felt that in these

[21]Fisher, *That Strange Little Brown Man Gandhi*, p. 57.

respects Gandhi's nationalism came into conflict with his non-violence. He also disliked the tendency for Gandhi to be idolised as a new and infallible messiah, for there needed to be a continuing critical scrutiny of his practice.[22]

De Ligt was not altogether fair in his criticism. Although Gandhi had supported the British during the First World War, going so far as to lead a recruiting campaign, he admitted his error soon after the war had ended. An Indian who had visited the battlefield at Ypres just after the slaughter, made a point of seeking him out and telling him that he had been wrong to support a conflict that represented the very antithesis of civilized values. After listening to the description of the carnage, Gandhi commented: 'I am sorry I had anything to do with this war. I believed Woodrow Wilson's dream; that it was a war to end war. But I now see that force can never banish force.'[23]

In America, pacifist theory was developed by a lawyer who was active in the labour movement in the 1920s called Richard Gregg. Impressed by Gandhi's campaigns against the British, he went to India to study the Gandhian movement at first hand, and became converted to the principle of non-violence. He published various books on the subject in the 1920s and 1930s.[24] Gregg helped to popularise Gandhian theory in the USA. Following from this, a Committee for Non-violent Revolution was founded there in 1946, which opposed the armaments industry and encouraged people to refuse to serve in the armed forces or work in arms factories, deploying mass civil disobedience if necessary.[25] This fed into the movement against nuclear weapons that emerged in the 1950s in both America and Europe. Gandhi had been an outspoken critic of nuclear weapons after the American atomic bombing of Japan in 1945. He condemned 'the supreme tragedy of the bomb', stating that it revealed most starkly that: 'War knows no law except that

[22]Peter van den Dungen, 'Introduction to the 1989 edition', Bart de Ligt, *The Conquest of Violence: An Essay on War and Revolution*, Pluto Press, London 1989.

[23]Fisher, *That Strange Little Brown Man Gandhi*, pp. 58–9.

[24]Richard B. Gregg, *The Psychology and Strategy of Gandhi's Non-Violent Resistance*, Madras 1929; *Gandhism and Socialism*, Madras 1931; *The Power of Non-Violence*, Philadelphia 1934.

[25]Ostergaard, *Nonviolent Revolution in India*, p. xiii.

of might.'[26] Also that: 'I regard the employment of the atom bomb for the wholesale destruction of men, women and children as the most diabolical use of science.'[27] He refused to accept the argument that possession of nuclear weapons acts as a deterrent against war, on the grounds that there can be no lasting, durable or moral peace through such means. In Britain, Gandhi's outrage and techniques of struggle were invoked in the Direct Action Committee Against Nuclear War, which was formed in 1957. Within a year, it had given birth to the Campaign for Nuclear Disarmament (CND) and its annual Aldermaston March. During the late 1950s the anti-nuclear movement also adopted civil resistance. For example, in 1957, Harold Steele, a Quaker, sailed into the British nuclear testing ground at Christmas Island in the Pacific.[28]

During the 1960s and 1970s CND abandoned civil resistance and it faded from the public eye. The anti-nuclear movement was reinvigorated in Germany in 1979, when NATO announced its plans to station missiles with nuclear warheads on German territory. In early 1980, a million signatures were collected in Germany in protest against the plan to station nuclear missiles there. Leading intellectuals, such as Heinrich Böll, Günter Grass and E.P. Thompson, joined the campaign. This led to the creation of END (the organisation for European Nuclear Disarmament). There were mass demonstrations throughout Europe, including Eastern Europe, one of which involved establishing a hundred-kilometre-long human chain between two US army bases in Stuttgart and Neu-Ulm. In May 1983, West German activists, some of whom were Green Party members of parliament, crossed over to East Berlin and held a demonstration there. The peace movement in East Germany, known as 'Swords into Ploughshares', had already been banned, and they were promptly arrested and deported back to the West. Their demand did not however go unrecognised. The East German leader Eric Honecker promptly sent a message to the activists that

[26]'Atom Bomb and Ahimsa', 1 July 1946, *Harijan*, 7 July 1946, *CWMG*, Vol. 91, p. 221.

[27]'Talk with an English Journalist', before 24 September 1946, *CWMG*, Vol. 92, p. 234.

[28]Randle, *Civil Resistance*, p. 55.

he, like them, wanted to establish a nuclear-free zone in central Europe, and he invited them to meet him. The Soviet bloc had no interest in entering into a ruinously expensive new arms race with the USA. However, when it came to a vote in the German parliament, the vote in favour of accepting American missiles on German soil was passed with a comfortable majority. After this END lost its momentum and went into decline.[29]

Women played a notable role in this wave of protest, particularly in the peace camps established in Britain in the 1980s on the peripheries of military bases, chemical and biological warfare research centres and arms factories. There were over a dozen such camps, the best known being that at Greenham Common, which was set up in 1983 outside a nuclear weapons base.[30] After camping there for years, the base was eventually abandoned, with the land reverting to being a public common. Other peace camps continue outside nuclear submarine bases at Faslane and the Holy Loch in Scotland.

From the 1970s, the peace and ecology movements worked hand in hand against the military-industrial complex. By its very name, Greenpeace exemplifies the unity between these two tendencies. Eco-warriors have deployed non-violent civil resistance by breaking into places where nuclear weapons are kept, or sailing into nuclear testing sites. In 1972 a French naval patrol ship at the Mururoa Atoll nuclear testing site rammed one such vessel, which served to galvanise opposition to the tests throughout the South Pacific.[31] Despite this, they continued. In 1985, French secret agents planted a bomb on the Greenpeace flagship, the Rainbow Warrior, killing one crew member, Fernando Pereiro. The resulting outcry led to the French government having to admit its culpability, two of its agents being convicted of manslaughter and jailed.

Another important international initiative that has flowed from the

[29]Sara Parkin, *The Life and Death of Petra Kelly*, Pandora, London 1994, pp. 112–13 & 133–7.

[30]Alice Cook and Gwyn Kirk, *Greenham Women Everywhere: Dreams, Ideas and Actions from the Women's Movement*, Pluto Press, London 1983, pp. 5 and 32–3.

[31]Randle, *Civil Resistance*, p. 83.

peace movement has been that of the Peace Brigades International (PBI), which was founded in 1981. It was inspired in part by the work of the Gandhian Shanti Sena in post-independence India.[32] The PBI has three main strands, first, to send unarmed volunteers to protect people who are threatened with repression and provide publicity for violations of human rights, second, to train people in techniques of non-violent resistance and conflict resolution, and third, to document successful non-violent initiatives as an example for others.[33] It has carried out such work in trouble spots in central America, the Caribbean, the Balkans, Palestine, Sri Lanka and South Africa. Volunteers have put their lives on the line in very dangerous areas to protect local peace and human rights activists from death squads, in the process often bringing a feeling of new hope and security in conditions of terrible violence.

In India, JP was the leading spokesperson for peace in the period before 1980. He consistently opposed Indian military action in wars against Pakistan, China, the Nagas, and in the conquest of Goa in 1960. He saw war as a crime against humanity and demanded international disarmament. During the armed occupation of Goa, and during the Indo-China war of 1962, JP had wanted to take an active role in stopping the conflict. He was dissuaded from this by Vinoba Bhave, who supported the use of military force by the Indian state and who insisted that Gandhian workers should engage only in social work within India. Although JP felt that Bhave's position was very un-Gandhian, he agreed to keep quiet in deference to his position as elder statesman of the movement. As it was, some people branded JP as 'unpatriotic'.[34] There was a similar divide between the two leaders over the issue of nuclear weapons. When Indira Gandhi exploded an atomic bomb in May 1974, ostensibly for 'peaceful purposes', Bhave took her at her word and stated that nuclear bombs could help to irrigate land and thus wipe out poverty.[35]

[32]'Peace Brigades International: History and Structure', http://www.igc.org/pbi/history.html

[33]'Peace Brigades International: What We Do', http://www.igc.org/pbi/workoverview.html

[34]Scarfe, *J.P. His Biography*, pp. 215–18.

[35]Ostergaard, *Nonviolent Revolution in India*, p. 383, fn. 72. Presumably, the idea was that huge reservoirs, perhaps underground, could be blasted out by such means. The idea appears bizarre, seeing that such reservoirs would have been highly

JP, on the other hand, condemned the atomic explosion strongly.[36]

JP's close lieutenant, Narayan Desai, developed this strand of Gandhian struggle after JP's death. He led a campaign in the early 1980s against the building of a nuclear power plant at Kakrapad, which was near his ashram at Vedchhi in South Gujarat. The police fired on one of the demonstrations in 1986, with a protester being killed. The building went ahead, and the plant went critical in 1991.

This experience has given rise to a small but vocal movement against nuclear power in India, led by Narayan Desai's daughter, Sanghamitra and her husband Surendra Gadekar. She is a qualified doctor who has carried out investigations of the radiation effects of nuclear power plants, uranium mines and the nuclear explosions at Pokhran in 1998. She has found evidence of congenital deformities and lung problems which have been categorised as tuberculosis, but which could well be lung cancer. Gadekar is a scientist who has dedicated his life to exposing the dangers of nuclear power and nuclear weapons. Together, they run a journal called *Anumukti*, which is, in the words of its sub-heading 'devoted to non-nuclear India'.

There are also a group of activists who have been taking a stand against the development of nuclear weapons in India. Although India only became a nuclear power openly with the explosions of a series of atomic bombs by the incoming BJP government at Pokhran in May 1998, this development had long been on the cards.[37]

Two prominent opponents have been Praful Bidwai and Achin Vanaik, who campaigned long and hard against India's endorsement

radioactive and could never have been used to store water which would be safe for human consumption or crop irrigation. Bhave appears to have been very ignorant as to the nature of nuclear weaponry, as well as the appalling consequences of nuclear radiation.

[36]Ostergaard, *Nonviolent Revolution in India*, p. 97, claims that JP gave his 'full support' to the nuclear test. Narayan Desai, who was very close to JP at that time, says that this is quite incorrect—JP was strongly against it. Interview with Narayan Desai, Vedchhi, 10 December 2000.

[37]As far back as 1946, Nehru had stated that India should 'use the atomic force for constructive purposes'. In the next sentence he went on to say that if India was threatened she should use any means of defence available. M.V. Ramana, 'Nehru and Nuclear Conspiracy', *Anumukti*, Vol. 11, Nos. 5 & 6, April-July 1998, p. 5.

of the nuclear option. Although not Gandhians, in their writings they cite Gandhi's principled stand against nuclear weapons as an inspiration.[38] For years they fought against a massive lack of concern within the public as a whole as to the terrifying logic of nuclear weapons. The majority tacitly accepted the argument of the Hindu right that India's position in world politics would be greatly enhanced once the country went nuclear, and there appears to have been general popular support for the 1998 explosions, even though it was an action that provided perhaps the grossest insult imaginable to Gandhi's memory. As was stated by one observer: 'They [the Hindu right] assassinated Gandhi twice, the first time in January 1948, and for the second time in May 1998.'[39]

Since then, doubts have emerged, as Pakistan quickly went nuclear in response, and then a year later launched an invasion of Indian territory at Kargil in Kashmir. Nuclear weapons were of no avail in what turned out to be a very conventional form of warfare. From then on, the anti-nuclear movement took off, with protest groups springing up all over India. In 1999, coinciding with the first anniversary of the tests, there was a march from Pokhran to Sarnath, the place near Banaras where the Buddha lived and preached. Some 30,000 to 40,000 people participated, including some old Gandhians who had participated in the nationalist movement. In October 2000 the BJP leader L.K. Advani noted what was for him a worrying tendency for environmentalist and anti-nuclear activists to make a common cause. He condemned both for being 'anti-national'. A month later, a large National Convention

[38]Praful Bidwai and Achin Vanaik, *New Nukes: India, Pakistan and Global Nuclear Disarmament*, Signal Books, Oxford 2000, pp. 129 and 140–2. In a personal communication of 11 February 2002, Praful Bidwai has stated that: 'Many of us are also especially moved by Gandhi's description of the Bomb as the most "diabolical" misuse of science. His logic, that you can't use the Bomb to fight the Bomb, is unassailable. It contains the seeds of a profound argument against nuclear deterrence. This I consider an especially valuable part of his legacy. However, I wouldn't quite call myself a Gandhian, either within the (Sarvodaya) organisational perspective, or in sharing his absolute—I know this is over-simple—faith in non-violence, with some of its self-purificatory and spiritual references, etc ... I am a bit agnostic about categorical non-violence, but deeply respectful and empathetic.'

[39]Bidwai and Vanaik, *New Nukes*, p. 142.

for Nuclear Disarmament and Peace was held in Delhi, attended by over 600 delegates, including representatives from Pakistan. Arundhati Roy used this forum to mount a fierce attack on Advani, stating that he was mistaken in believing that 'only people who march in khaki and swear by bombs are patriots.' She argued that she was the real patriot in fighting against weapons and irrigation projects that threatened to destroy the lives of millions of Indian citizens.[40] The convention led to the formation of the Coalition for Nuclear Disarmament and Peace, a network of over 200 groups. Many of these came from groups with a substantial Gandhian influence, like the Narmada Bachao Andolan, although to be inclusive it did not endorse non-violence as an absolute principle.

Gandhian Resistance on a World Stage

For large numbers of people in countries which had been colonised by Europeans, or who were tyrannised by authoritarian or racist rulers, Gandhi became a figure who symbolised and stood for the assertion of the oppressed. His position in this respect was secured by the salt march of 1930, the progress of which was reported by the world media on a daily basis. Coming at the dawn of the age of the rapid transmission of sound, photography and film around the globe, this was one of the first such media event in history. The march was mounted as a visual spectacle that focused on the figure of the thin, scantily clad old man surrounded by his khadi-wearing comrades, together defying the might of the empire with strict non-violence. Gandhi employed the language of what is now known as the sound-bite: e.g. 'I want world sympathy in this battle of Right against Might' or 'We are entering upon a life and death struggle, a holy war; we are performing an all-embracing sacrifice in which we wish to offer ourselves as an oblation.'[41] Americans in particular lapped it up, jubilant at what they saw as a further vindication of their own historic rejection of British imperialism. A few months later, *Time* magazine declared Gandhi its 'Man of the Year'.

India's winning of independence in 1947 was widely believed to

[40]'Anti-Dam, Anti-Bomb Activists Join Hands', *The Hindu*, 12 November 2000.
[41]Dalton, *Mahatma Gandhi*, pp. 101–20.

vindicate Gandhi's method of resistance. In most parts of the world it was recognised that armed struggle against authoritarian states was hardly an option, due to the massive discrepancy between the military might of the rulers and people. Violent revolts could succeed only in a few exceptional circumstances, as in China.[42] It came to be seen that modern governments, with their strong and often secretive and authoritarian bureaucracies, but with a nominal commitment to a rule of law, were particularly susceptible to principled non-violent protest. A resistance which revealed the moral failings of those who exercised power while remaining strictly non-violent had the advantage of appealing to many of those in the ranks of the police, bureaucracy and army who propped up the regime. The government, it was argued, would prefer to compromise rather than find itself crumbling from within. This would appear to have been borne out in the case of Iran in 1979, where an autocratic government found its authority eroded so rapidly through mass protest and demoralisation within the police and military that it was forced to surrender power.[43]

The chief opposition to such a strategy came from those who were encouraged by the armed victories of the people in countries such as China, Cuba, Algeria and Vietnam to embrace a romantic notion of the power of revolutionary violence. This was epitomised in the cult of Che Guevara. It was argued that in the last instance all states would defend themselves with a ruthless display of violence. Therefore, however much the state may be put on the defensive by mass strikes and other forms of civil resistance, the movement would at some stage have to escalate to the stage of armed struggle. Some who followed this line formed underground revolutionary terrorist groups such as the Angry Brigade, the Red Army Faction and, in India, the Naxalites.[44]

Most of these terrorist groups have been wiped out without achieving anything concrete. Those that can claim some success have tended to operate in conjunction with mass civil resistance, as with the Palestinians against the Israeli state or the Irish Republicans against the British. Even in these cases, terrorism has had a severe down side. It has given an

[42] Randle, *Civil Resistance*, pp. 8–9.
[43] Ibid., pp. 5–6 and 17.
[44] Ibid., pp. 57–8.

opening for strong state repression, with a suspension of civil liberties and the punishment of the civilian population as a whole. The terrorists then often turned inwards, targeting 'collaborators' for vengeance and resorting to crime to fund their activities, so that the movement ended up being corrupted beyond redemption. Such violence has often hampered the building of alternative democratic and decentralized forms of power rooted in civil society. Underground terrorist organisations also embraced a very macho style of operation that alienated women activists.[45]

It has been argued, following from this, that Gandhian-style non-violent civil resistance has had a greater global impact since 1945 than armed struggles and violent resistance.[46] Such a formulation begs many questions, such as the role that US armed aggression played in shaping struggles during the second half of the twentieth century. Also, there has been often a complex interaction between civil resistance and more violent forms of struggle. It also leaves out of account the question of leadership, for the Gandhian method depends very strongly on the presence of an inspired and charismatic moral leader. The rest of this chapter looks at two resistance movements which have brought such leaders to the fore—that of the self-assertion of African-Americans in the USA and the South African revolt against apartheid—and also at Petra Kelly and the Green Party in Germany, to see to what extent Gandhi has provided both an inspiration and an effective method for struggle in each case.

The African-American Struggle in the USA

Gandhi was admired among African-Americans in the USA from the 1920s onwards. His work was publicised by Marcus Garvey and W.E.B. Du Bois among others. In 1936, Howard Thurman (1900–1981)—a distinguished Baptist minister, theologian and academic who was from the American South—led a delegation of prominent African-American Christians to India to meet Gandhi. Gandhi quizzed him and the others about racial discrimination in the USA, and then expounded on his

[45]Ibid., pp. 8–9.

[46]This is the judgement of *Time* magazine, 31 December 1999, pp. 24–6.

principles of non-violent resistance to injustice. Mrs. Thurman pleaded with Gandhi to come to the USA: 'We want you not for white America, but for the Negroes; we have many a problem that cries for solution, and we need you badly.' Gandhi said that he still had much to do in India, but when he felt the call, he would not hesitate to travel there. Thurman said that what Gandhi had told them resonated strongly with their Christianity. Mrs Thurman then sang two well-known spirituals, and Gandhi—obviously moved—observed that 'it may be through the Negroes that the unadulterated message of non-violence will be delivered to the world.'[47]

Gandhi also inspired Bayard Rustin (1910–1987), who was from an African-American Quaker family of Pennsylvania. He joined the Communist Party in the 1930s, but refused to accept their dogmatic line that racial discrimination would disappear once socialism was established in the USA. He broke with the party in 1941 when it ordered its members to stop fighting for Negro rights, as the USA and Russia were now allies and such internal dissent would, it claimed, detract from the struggle against Hitler. Rustin linked up with A. Philip Randolph, the African-American leader of the Brotherhood of Sleeping Car Porters, a trade union. Together they established the Congress of Racial Equality (CORE) in Chicago in 1942.

Rustin had already been in contact with Krishnalal Shridharani, who after studying at the Gujarat Vidyapith—Gandhi's university in Ahmedabad—had taken part in the salt march of 1930 and had been subsequently jailed. In 1934 Shridharani emigrated to the USA, where he became a prominent advocate of Gandhian non-violence. In 1939 he published an influential book on Gandhian techniques called *War Without Violence*.[48] This book became 'the semiofficial bible of CORE'.[49]

[47]Interview to American Negro Delegation, 21 February 1936, *CWMG*, Vol. 68, pp. 234–8.

[48]Krishnalal Shridharani, *War Without Violence: A Study of Gandhi's Method and its Accomplishments*, Harcourt, Brace and Company, New York 1939. Shridharani describes his participation in the Gandhian movement in India on pp. xxiii–xxxv.

[49]Taylor Branch, *Parting the Waters: Martin Luther King and the Civil Rights Movement 1954–63*, Simon and Schuster, New York 1988, p. 171.

Shridharani himself was a hard drinker, a cigar-smoker and a womaniser, and his African-American disciples learnt through him that 'Gandhian politics did not require a life of dull asceticism.'[50]

CORE staged non-violent protests that challenged racist employment practices in Chicago. Rustin himself refused to serve in the army during the Second World War, and was jailed for three years as a conscientious objector. After his release, he took up the cause of Indian independence, picketing the British embassy in Washington, and being arrested on a number of occasions. In 1947, he and other CORE activists travelled on buses through the South to test a Supreme Court ruling that Negro passengers could sit wherever they wanted to in buses. Rustin was beaten up and jailed for six months under local segregation laws, a sentence which he accepted in a true Gandhian spirit. After his release, he took up an invitation to visit India as a guest of the Congress party.[51] There were further protests, beatings and imprisonments for Rustin in the early 1950s—an experience he described, humorously, as 'going Gandhi'.[52]

While Rustin was carrying on his protests, Martin Luther King was studying at Morehouse College, Connecticut, Crozer Seminary, Pennsylvania, and the School of Theology of Boston University. King, who was born in 1929 in Atlanta, Georgia, was the son of a Baptist minister who was active in fighting for the rights of the African-Americans of that city. A leading member of the National Association for the Advancement of Coloured People (NAACP), the body founded by W.E.B. Du Bois in 1909, Martin Luther King Sr. had led a voting-rights march on the city hall in 1936.[53] While studying at Crozer Seminary, Martin Luther King Jr. attended a lecture on Gandhi by Mordecai Johnson, who had just returned from a visit to India. Johnson argued that Gandhian non-violent protest could be used in the battle for African-American rights. King stated later that the 'message was so profound

[50]Ibid., p. 171.

[51]Ibid., pp. 171–2.

[52]Ibid., p. 172.

[53]Stephen B. Oates, *Let the Trumpet Sound: A Life of Martin Luther King Jr.*, Payback Press, Edinburgh 1998, pp. 7–8.

and electrifying that I left the meeting and bought a half-dozen books on Gandhi's life and works.'[54] He was encouraged in this research by one of his teachers, George Davis, who was a pacifist and admirer of Gandhi.[55] King was particularly impressed by the way in which Gandhi had channelled his anger at injustice into a constructive and creative non-violent engagement. He realised that such a resistance provided a deeply Christian weapon that could provide a strong base for the mass mobilisation of African-Americans. As he stated: 'He was probably the first person in history to lift the love ethic of Jesus above mere interaction between individuals to a powerful effective social force on a large scale.'[56]

King was also influenced strongly by Howard Thurman, who had led the delegation to meet Gandhi in 1936. Thurman was a professor at the School of Theology of Boston University when King was studying there for his doctorate between 1951 and 1954. In 1949 he had published his most important book *Jesus and the Disinherited*, which—inspired in part by Gandhi—sought for a Christian means for combating oppression. Thurman argued that Jesus, who was from a poor Jewish family, had devoted his life to fight for his people. He stood for the self-pride and assertion of the colonized under the tyranny of Rome. Jesus understood, however, that the Roman Empire could not be fought head-on and that the battle had to be of the spirit. Christianity was thus forged 'as a technique of survival of the oppressed. ... Wherever his spirit appears, the oppressed gather fresh courage; for he has announced the good news that fear, hypocrisy, and hatred, the three hounds of hell that track the trail of the disinherited, need have no dominion over them.'[57] Thurman argued that the anger generated by injustice must be transformed into a constructive force. Later, King used to carry this book with him for inspiration during his campaigns.

In 1954, at the age of twenty-five, King was appointed as pastor of

[54]Ibid., pp. 32–3.

[55]Branch, *Parting the Waters*, p. 74.

[56]Oates, *Let the Trumpet Sound*, p. 32.

[57]Howard Thurman, *Jesus and the Disinherited*, Friends United Press, Richmond, IN. 1981, p. 29, quoted in Greg Moses, *Revolution of Conscience: Martin Luther King, Jr., and the Philosophy of Nonviolence*, The Guilford Press, New York 1997, p. 182.

the Dexter Avenue Baptist Church in Montgomery, the capital of Alabama. He could have stayed and worked in the less-segregated North, but he chose deliberately to fight segregation at its core. His chance came soon enough, when in December 1955 an African-American teacher called Rosa Parks refused to give up her seat on a crowded bus to a white man. She was arrested and charged with breaking the local segregation laws. It is perhaps no coincidence that it was a similar experience of racial discrimination on public transport that had first politicised Gandhi in South Africa. It was an experience that King himself had been through. In the words of Greg Moses, 'At the age of fifteen, King won an oratorial prize by celebrating the ideals of the United States Constitution. Riding in a bus on his way home from the speech King was ordered out of his seat. Reflecting behind the veil that was dropped between him and the white passengers ... King recalled, "It was the angriest I have ever been in my life."'[58] When the court punished Parks with a fine of $14, King and other civil rights workers decided to protest the law by organising a boycott of the city's buses. Bayard Rustin, who had long experience of such Gandhi-inspired protests, came to Montgomery to work as an adviser in the campaign. This was the start of a long and fruitful comradeship between two great proponents of non-violence. Rustin prevailed on King to dispense with armed guards and to embrace non-violence as a key element of the struggle. King asserted that they were putting democracy into practice in a truly Christian way and insisted that they should bear no enmity towards their opponents and that they should observe complete non-violence. Rustin also helped forge strong links with African-American radicals of the northern cities who raised funds to support the Montgomery campaign.

After a year of resistance, the Supreme Court came down on the side of the protesters, with bus segregation being ruled illegal. King declared that 'Christ furnished the spirit and motivation, while Gandhi furnished the method.'[59] In this way, the protesters had occupied the moral high ground in a way that proved irresistible. This struggle, coming

[58]Ibid., p. 10.

[59]Dalton, *Mahatma Gandhi*, pp. 178–82. The quote is from Martin Luther King, *Stride Toward Freedom: The Montgomery Story*, Harper, New York 1958, p. 67.

less than a decade after Gandhi's assassination, provided a remarkable vindication of the Gandhian method.

In the following years, King led a series of courageous protests in cities throughout the South against segregation in schools, on buses and at eating places. He also fought for the right to vote. Due to a systematic refusal by white officials to register African-Americans, often on very flimsy grounds, only about a quarter of those eligible to vote were actually registered to do so at that time in the South.[60] King and Rustin established the Southern Christian Leadership Conference (SCLC) in 1957 to carry on this work. In many cases, the Southern whites responded with violence, even bombing African-American churches. King himself was arrested and jailed on numerous occasions. In 1958, for example, he was arrested and beaten up by the police in Montgomery. When a photograph of King was published in the national press showing two policemen twisting his arm behind his back, the police commissioner stated laconically that there was nothing unusual about the behaviour of his officers in this respect.[61]

Although King was always modest about himself, declaring that he had 'no Messiah complex',[62] he believed strongly in the need for powerful and charismatic leadership. As he stated in 1960: 'people cannot devote themselves to a great cause without finding someone who becomes the personification of the cause.'[63] In this, King was influenced by Hegel, whose work he had studied at Boston University. Hegel had argued that throughout history certain 'world historical individuals' who had the vision and intellect to understand the spirit of their age had been able to provide inspiring moral leadership at critical historical junctures. King understood Plato, Aristotle, Lincoln and Gandhi to be such persons.[64] For all his modesty, he saw himself in such a mould.

Like Gandhi, King was nevertheless all too aware of his fallibilities as a leader. Not all of his Southern campaigns were successful. For example, in 1962, he agreed to take personal charge of the campaign in

[60]Oates, *Let the Trumpet Sound*, p. 145.
[61]Ibid., p. 135.
[62]Ibid., p. 157.
[63]Ibid., p. 161.
[64]Ibid., p. 38.

Albany, Georgia, and was soon arrested. There were however various rival groups amongst the local African-Americans, and one paid King's fine, so that he found himself ejected from jail against his will. The local police chief had studied Gandhian methods and was careful to keep his men in order and to treat the protesters with decorum, so that the newspapers were deprived of the usual photographs of police brutalities. King also made tactical mistakes in Albany, as when he agreed to obey a federal court injunction that ruled against the protest, as he did not want to alienate the federal authorities. This angered the radicals in the movement, who saw it as a sell-out. Soon after, there was a riot, in which two thousand African-Americans attacked the police with bottles and stones. King was, inevitably, accused of stoking this violence. The protest lost its momentum and petered out without any substantial gains.[65]

King's methods were nonetheless redeemed by some remarkable successes, as in the campaign in Birmingham, Alabama, of 1963. The target here was the segregation of eating-places in a city that was notorious for the hardline racism of its white population. Only recently, the local Ku Klux Klan had castrated an African-American and dumped his mutilated body in the road.[66] Unlike in Albany, King and his colleagues planned their campaign meticulously. They decided to focus on some prominent retail outlets, such as Woolworth's, harassing them with sit-ins and boycotts that would hit business where it hurt most—in the pocket. They were also careful to ensure that there were plenty of protesters willing to go to jail, so that the jails would be filled in a way that would embarrass the authorities. King anticipated that the local police would not react in a disciplined manner, as they had in Albany. This was crucial, for he wanted to expose the true nature of Southern racism to the outside world, so that the federal government would be forced to intervene. As King stated, he intended to provoke the 'oppressor to commit his brutality openly—in the light of day—with the rest of the world looking on.'[67]

The police commissioner of Birmingham—Eugene 'Bull' Connor—

[65]Ibid., pp. 188–201.
[66]Ibid., p. 210.
[67]Ibid., p. 212.

declared that he was not going to tolerate any 'nigger troublemakers' in his city.[68] Many of the local African-Americans feared what might happen, and King had to use all of his powers of oratory and persuasion to instil the necessary solidarity and enthusiasm for the stuggle. He ran workshops on non-violent resistance, in which the volunteers were trained to resist police provocation without rancour. The jails were soon filling with protesters. When the Alabama state court served an injunction forbidding the protest, King defied it by leading a march. The day was Good Friday, and he talked of 'the redemptive power of suffering', and said that he was heading for jail as 'a good servant of my Lord and master, who was crucified on Good Friday.'[69] His supporters compared him to Jesus, as he marched at the head of a procession, dressed in the faded denim of the African-American worker, and was arrested and jailed.

In prison, he wrote a manifesto that became famous as the 'Letter from Birmingham City Jail'. This was addressed to some prominent white clergymen of Alabama who in January 1963 had published an open letter condemning King for his confrontational tactics at a time when, they alleged, desegregation was being achieved through court rulings. They feared that King's activities would provoke disturbances. King told them that the whites of Alabama had consistently refused to obey court orders in the past and had ruthlessly enforced their own local segregation laws. They had learnt that an oppressor never handed out freedom willingly—it had to be demanded and fought for by the oppressed. They had therefore decided to bring matters to a head: 'Non-violent direct action seeks to create such a crisis and establish such creative tension that a community that has consistently refused to negotiate is forced to confront the issue.'[70] King had been told by the clergymen to be patient and wait. In response he wrote—in a long sentence of great power—of the experiences that had seared his soul:

[68]Ibid., p. 216.

[69]Ibid., p. 221.

[70]'Letter From Birmingham City Jail', in James Melvin Washington (ed.), *A Testament of Hope: The Essential Writings of Martin Luther King, Jr.*, Harper Collins, New York 1991, p. 291.

I guess it is easy for those who have never felt the stinging darts of segregation to say 'Wait.' But when you have seen vicious mobs lynch your mothers and fathers at will and drown your sisters and brothers at whim; when you have seen hate-filled policemen curse, kick, brutalize and even kill your black brothers and sisters with impunity; when you see the vast majority of your twenty million Negro brothers smothering in an airtight cage of poverty in the midst of an affluent society; when you suddenly find your tongue twisted and your speech stammering as you seek to explain to your six-year-old daughter why she can't go to the public amusement park that has been advertised on television, and see tears welling in her little eyes when she is told that Funtown is closed to coloured children, and see the depressing clouds of inferiority begin to form in her little mental sky, and see her begin to distort her little personality by unconsciously developing a bitterness towards white people; when you have to concoct an answer for a five-year-old son asking in agonizing pathos: 'Daddy, why do white people treat coloured people so mean?'; when you take a cross-country drive and find it necessary to sleep night after night in the uncomfortable corners of your automobile because no motel will accept you; when you are humiliated day in and day out by nagging signs reading 'white' and 'coloured'; when your first name becomes 'nigger' and your middle name becomes 'boy' (however old you are) and your last name becomes 'John,' and when your wife and mother are never given the respected title 'Mrs.'; when you are harried by day and haunted by night by the one fact that you are a Negro, living constantly at tiptoe stance never quite knowing what to expect next, and plagued with inner fears and outer resentments; when you are forever fighting a degenerating sense of 'nobodiness'; then you will understand why we find it difficult to wait.[71]

King went on to justify his breaking of selected laws, and made a very Gandhian distinction between just laws which accorded with morality and the will of God—which were to be obeyed—and unjust laws, which they had an obligation to disobey. He argued that any law that degraded a human being could be considered unjust; and also any law imposed by a majority on a minority that was not binding on the

[71]Ibid., pp. 292–3.

majority. He intended to break such laws in an open manner, and in a spirit of brotherly love. He also stated how disappointed he was with white moderates, who criticised the victims of racism for their actions, rather than the racists who provoked them. He warned them that if they did not give a more whole-hearted support to the civil rights movement, African-American anger was likely to vent itself in the racial hatred of Black Nationalism and violence on the streets.

When he was released from jail after eight days, King found that the campaign was flagging. He then took the risky step of mobilising children to court arrest. He knew that he could be criticised for using children, and that some of them might get hurt. But, he reasoned, they were being hurt everyday by whites. He also saw the photo-opportunity provided by the symbol of young children marching against a pernicious segregation. They proved to be exemplary protesters, courting arrest with youthful and fearless enthusiasm in a manner that caused immense logistical problems for the police. On the second day of the children's marches, 'Bull' Connor ordered his men 'Let 'em have it'. Batons, fire hoses and dogs were unleashed in a scene of mayhem that was filmed and broadcast in harrowing detail on television channels throughout America. President Kennedy declared that the sight made him 'sick', and that 'I can well understand why the Negroes of Birmingham are tired of being asked to be patient.'[72]

The protests continued with ever-increasing vigour, as the campaigners sensed that they had forced the white racists of the city on the defensive. Then, confronted by a massive demonstration on 5 May, 'Bull' Connor's men refused to obey him when he ordered them to disperse the crowd by force. As the protesters marched through their ranks, some of the firemen stood holding their unused hoses and wept. Five days later, it was agreed that eating-places throughout the city would be desegregated. King announced that this was a demonstration of the power of non-violence in its purest form: 'I saw there, I felt there, for the first time, the pride and the *power* of non-violence.'[73]

In his application of non-violent resistance, King was far more con-

[72]Oates, *Let the Trumpet Sound*, p. 235.
[73]Ibid., p. 237.

frontational than Gandhi. He actively sought out situations in which he could deploy his techniques of protest, so that his life consisted of a series of engagements in rapid succession, with some being carried on simultaneously. He was always on the front-line himself, heading marches, giving inspirational speeches, courting jail and negotiating with the authorities. Gandhi himself rarely led mass campaigns, and later in life preferred to fight alone rather than risk mass protest that could go awry. King, by contrast, constantly exposed himself to the huge risks involved in such experiments in mass non-violent action.

King's most significant innovation was the concept of 'creative tension'.[74] He spelt this out very lucidly in his speech from Birmingham City Jail:

> I had hoped that the white moderate would understand that the present tension of the South is merely a necessary phase of the transition from an obnoxious negative peace, where the Negro passively accepted his unjust plight, to a substance-filled positive peace, where all men will respect the dignity and worth of human personality. We merely bring to the surface the hidden tension that is already alive. We bring it out in the open where it can be seen and dealt with. Like a boil that can never be cured as long as it is covered up but must be opened with all its pus-flowing ugliness to the natural medicines of the air and light, injustice must likewise be exposed, with all of the tension its exposing creates, to the light of human conscience and the air of national opinion before it can be cured.[75]

To forge such a state of 'creative tension', King learnt to carry out careful research on a situation before he evolved a strategy suited for that particular place and historic moment. If the conditions were not right, he was wary about launching a struggle. What he required above all was a local African-American community with strong internal solidarity and willingness to fight non-violently, and a white population that would react in a ham-fisted and self-defeating way. Birmingham

[74]Ibid., p. 339.

[75]'Letter From Birmingham City Jail', in Washington (ed.), *A Testament of Hope*, p. 295.

was not the only place that fulfilled these criteria: St Augustine in Florida (1964) and Selma, Alabama (1965) were two other places that provided such an environment. King also valued lieutenants who had the ability to provoke retaliation—men such as Hosea Williams, who was known for his non-violent aggression in street confrontations. King celebrated Williams as his 'crazy man', his 'wild man', adding that: 'When Hosea can't have his way, he creates a lot of tension'.[76]

Like Bayard Rustin, King adhered to Gandhian non-violence without trying to follow the Mahatma's ascetic and disciplined way of life. King enjoyed good food (with a high meat content) and fine wines. He stayed in costly hotels on his tours, relishing the luxury. He dressed impeccably in smart and expensively tailored suits.[77] After visiting India in 1959 to tour places associated with Gandhi, King vowed to set aside a day each week for fasting and meditation. The vow was soon forgotten—King had neither the time nor willpower to carry it out.[78] He was also very bad at keeping time, but shrugged off his frequent late arrivals at meetings as being an inevitable case of what he jokingly called CPT, or 'Coloured People's Time'.[79] He had extra-marital sexual relationships with some of his women-followers and admirers. One such intimacy was recorded on tape by FBI snoopers in 1964, and it was to do him considerable political damage over the next four years, as it allowed the sinister FBI boss, J. Edgar Hoover, to mount a smear campaign that undermined his moral reputation. King was guilt-stricken by his failure in this respect, and he resolved constantly not to allow it to happen again.[80]

The period 1964–5 was a turning point for the civil rights movement. 1963 had been a year of triumph, with the victory in Birmingham, followed by the great march on Washington, where King delivered his powerful 'I have a dream' speech. In 1964, President Johnson backed civil rights legislation that made it illegal to practise segregation in any public place in the USA. But in the same year, Newark, Harlem, Chicago, Philadelphia and Jersey City exploded in race riots. King was jeered at

[76]Oates, *Let the Trumpet Sound*, p. 288.
[77]Ibid., p. 282.
[78]Ibid., p. 144.
[79]Ibid., p. 288.
[80]Ibid., p. 283

when he went to Harlem at the invitation of the mayor of New York to try to cool tensions.[81] Harlem was the stronghold of Malcolm X, who in that year denounced what he characterised as the 'Christian-Gandhian groups':

> Christian? Gandhian? I don't go for anything that's non-violent and turn the other-cheekish. I don't see how any revolution—I've never heard of a non-violent revolution or a revolution that was brought about by turning the other cheek, and so I believe that it is a crime for anyone to teach a person who is being brutalized to continue to accept that brutality without doing something to defend himself. If this is what the Christian-Gandhian philosophy teaches, then it is criminal—a criminal philosophy.[82]

Although Malcolm X revealed here a profound misunderstanding of both Gandhi and King's non-violence, for both believed in confronting an oppressor most actively, his words struck a chord with his own followers.

Malcolm X was what was known at the time as a 'Black Nationalist'. He demanded that African-Americans should fight for a separate nation-state in which they would hold power for themselves.[83] He himself rejected Christianity and had converted to Islam. In a debate with Bayard Rustin in 1960, he had criticised the civil rights position that African-Americans should struggle to assert themselves within the American polity, arguing that in a racist society they could never become full-fledged citizens. 'People come here from Hungary and are integrated into the American way of life overnight, they are not put into any fourth or third class or any other kind of class. The only one who is put in this category is the so-called Negro ...'[84] He condemned what he called 'the passive approach' which he saw as a mere palliative preached by liberals.

Arguments such as these began to exert a growing hold over the imagination of young African-Americans of the northern cities. Their

[81] Ibid., p. 306.

[82] Malcolm X, *By Any Means Necessary*, Pathfinder Press, New York 1992, pp. 8–9.

[83] 'An Interview by A.B. Spellman', in ibid., pp. 5–6.

[84] 'Bayard Rustin Meets Malcolm X', *Freedom Review*, January-February 1993.

problems were different to those of the South, for they already had the vote and there was no segregation by law. The vast majority, however, lived in poverty in squalid ghettoes where they were rack-rented by slum lords. Many were unemployed and they were victimised on a daily basis by policemen who 'treated every Negro as a criminal merely because he was a Negro'.[85] Their anger exploded periodically in so-called 'race riots', in which they lashed out at their oppressors and were shot down in the streets.

King decided that he had to extend his movement to the North. In early 1966 he set up home in a cramped and soul-destroying apartment in a Chicago ghetto and launched a movement for integrated housing in the city. He contacted a number of youth gangs, met their leaders and spent long hours in persuading them to embrace non-violence and act as marshalls in demonstrations. He held workshops in non-violence, persuading them that the southern protests had gained far more than the northern riots. Some two-hundred gang members—enthused by the attention given to them by such a famous and charismatic leader—agreed to give non-violence a chance.[86]

Chicago was however not a southern city ruled by hardline racists. The mayor was Richard Daley, a wily politician and a Democrat who claimed to be doing his best to implement President Johnson's anti-poverty programmes. He even boasted that within two years there would be no slums left in the city. He had strong allies within the African-American community of Chicago, and he mobilised them to counter King's threat.[87] By mid-1966, it seemed that the Chicago campaign was going nowhere.

It was at this juncture that King was faced with a rebellion in his ranks. Several young Northerners had been inspired by the civil rights movement and had gone south to participate in the protests. By 1966, however, some of them were becoming disillusioned with King's methods. Matters came to a head in June 1966, during a protest march in Mississippi. After a white man had shot one of the marchers, King overheard some of his fellow-protesters saying that the days of non-

[85]Oates, *Let the Trumpet Sound*, p. 378.
[86]Ibid., pp. 392–3.
[87]Ibid., pp. 293–4.

violence were passing. Some began to arm themselves with guns so that they could fight back. Others accused white sympathisers of trying to appropriate the movement and told King that they didn't want any whites marching with them: 'This should be an all-black march. We don't need any more white phonies and liberals invading our movement.'[88] This was a direct rejection of King's stress on inclusion.

The leading figure in this group was Stokely Carmichael, then twenty-four years old and a magnetic young leader who had been involved in the civil rights movement since 1961. By 1965 he had come round to the Black Nationalist position. During the Mississippi march he told King that African-Americans should grab power wherever they were in a majority: 'I'm not going to beg the white man for anything I deserve. I'm going to take it.'[89] A few days later he proclaimed before a crowd: 'We been saying freedom for six years now and we ain't got nothin'. What we gonna start saying now is Black Power!' The crowd roared back: 'BLACK POWER!! BLACK POWER!! BLACK POWER!!'[90] To King's disgust, the media quickly took up this slogan, with all of its potential for sensation.

During the next three years, King devoted his energies to countering what he saw as the profound errors of Black Power. He understood the anger which had produced this new militancy, and he was always more sympathetic to it than the white liberals, most of whom felt not only threatened by the slogan, but bitter that a movement with which they had sympathised had spawned—so they believed—such rabid hatred. King felt, however, that the Black Power celebration of violence was completely misguided. They could never hope to defeat white America in a show of force, and their relatively feeble violence would provide an excuse for white racists to unleash a wave of genocidal killings of blacks, no doubt under the slogan of 'White Power'.[91] King went on to argue that in advocating violence, Black Power was not adopting a revolutionary line: 'One of the great paradoxes of the Black Power movement is that it talks unceasingly about not imitating the values of

[88]Ibid., p. 397.
[89]Ibid., p. 398.
[90]Ibid., p. 400.
[91]Moses, *Revolution of Conscience*, p. 191.

white society, but in advocating violence it is imitating the worst, the most brutal and the most uncivilized value of American life.'[92] King also condemned Black Power for its repudiation of all whites as racists: 'I reminded them of the dedicated whites who had suffered, bled and died in the cause of racial justice, and suggested that to reject white participation now would be a shameful repudiation of all for which they had been sacrificed.'[93]

For all the rationality of his arguments, King was well aware that what mattered most were results. He had to prove to the African-Americans of the northern cities that they would gain more through non-violent protest than rioting in the streets. In this respect, Chicago became of crucial importance to his movement. He decided to launch mass civil disobedience in the city. He was heckled by supporters of Black Power at one of the first meetings in July 1966. Although bitterly upset, he took it as a challenge and pressed ahead with protests. He was not, however, able to generate any 'creative tension'. There were street riots that July, and although not connected in any way with the campaign, they underlined the extent to which King's movement was a mere sideshow in the violent life of that city. King rushed from riot-spot to riot-spot, calming the people and persuading the authorities to act in a constructive manner. He met with the gang leaders and took from them renewed promises to remain non-violent. The rioting stopped before it gained any further momentum, and several commentators felt that King had been instrumental in this.[94]

King then pressed ahead, announcing a series of marches to all-white neighbourhoods. They were met with racist taunts by working-class white men and women, who waved American Nazi Party insignias and Confederate flags and taunted them with cries of 'you monkeys' and 'Nigger go home!' The white suburbanites even taunted the police who protected the marchers with being 'nigger-lovers' and 'white trash'. Rocks, bricks and bottles were hurled at the marchers. On one occasion a brick hit King, bringing him to the ground. A knife was also thrown at him,

[92]Martin Luther King, *Where Do We Go From Here: Chaos or Community?* Beacon, Boston 1967, p. 64.

[93]Ibid., p. 28.

[94]Oates, *Let the Trumpet Sound*, pp. 409–10.

but missed its target. King was astonished at the sheer venom of the reaction—he stated that he had seen nothing like it in the South. He rejoiced, however, that the young gang leaders who had marched with them had remained non-violent. Mayor Daley retaliated with an injunction banning such marches, on the grounds that they stirred up trouble. King then decided to lead a march on Cicero, a suburb outside the city limits that was not covered by the injunction. Cicero—previously known as the home of Al Capone—was a notoriously racist place that had in 1951 reacted with violence when an African-American family had tried to settle there. To forestall this march, Daley met with King and worked out a plan to reform the city's housing. King then called off the march. Although many saw this as a victory, black radicals accused King of selling out. In general, there was a feeling that the Chicago campaign of 1966 had flopped. Daley was still in control, promising change but doing very little to eradicate African-American poverty and poor housing in any meaningful way.[95] King continued to be haunted by the hate-filled screams of the whites of Chicago, even stating that southern whites should go to Chicago 'to learn how to hate'.[96] In contrast to previous campaigns, Chicago left him depressed rather than elated.

There were further riots in the northern cities in 1967. As Greg Moses has written: 'In the last years of King's life, non-violence was losing its tenuous hold on the American imagination.'[97] Radicals everywhere were celebrating the cathartic power of revolutionary violence and terror. Black Power was only one example of this tendency. To counter this, King wrote his last book *Where Do We Go From Here: Chaos or Community?*. Published in 1967, it represented a heartfelt plea for the continuing relevance of non-violence. He argued that: 'Returning violence for violence multiplies violence, adding deeper darkness to a night already devoid of stars. Darkness cannot drive out darkness: only light can do that. Hate cannot drive out hate: only love can do that.'[98] He demanded a politics that was driven by love and not hate. 'What is

[95]Ibid., pp. 412–16.
[96]Ibid., p. 418.
[97]Moses, *Revolution of Conscience*, p. 149.
[98]Martin Luther King, *Where Do We Go From Here*, p. 63.

needed is a realization that power without love is reckless and abusive and that love without power is sentimental and anaemic.'[99] Black Power, he asserted, divorced power from love and based itself on hatred. He refused to accept that love was associated with resignation of power. 'Power at its best is love implementing the demands of justice. Justice at its best is love correcting everything that stands against love.'[100] Greg Moses has argued that King's position represented an important theoretical breakthrough:

> From King's point of view, the error of separating power from love has been tragically compounded by Christian thinkers who, in divorcing their ethereal Platonic version of love from their temporal struggles for power, left themselves open to Nietzsche's withering attacks. As Nietzsche rejects the 'Christian' concept of love, Christians reject the 'Nietzschean' will to power. All this mutual rejection is unfortunate in King's view, because the two concepts are not really 'polar opposites' but necessary co-conceptions of ethical development.[101]

King himself claimed that Gandhi had been the first to grasp this great truth: 'What was new about Mahatma Gandhi's movement in India was that he mounted a revolution on hope and love, hope and non-violence.'[102]

King always knew that his life was in danger; death-threats were an almost everyday feature of his life.[103] When he heard the news of John F. Kennedy's assassination in November 1963, his first reaction was 'I don't think I'm going to live to reach forty.'[104] Although he proved to be prescient in this respect (he was thirty-nine years of age when shot and killed in Memphis by a white racist on 4 April 1968), his faith in God gave him the strength to carry on with undiminished militancy despite the threats. What mattered, he said, was the quality and not the quantity of one's life: 'If you are cut down in a movement that is

[99]Ibid., p. 37.
[100]Ibid.
[101]Moses, *Revolution of Conscience*, p. 191.
[102]Martin Luther King, *Where Do We Go From Here*, p. 44.
[103]Oates, *Let the Trumpet Sound*, p. 182.
[104]Ibid., p. 270.

designed to save the soul of the nation, then no other death could be more redemptive.'[105] In a speech during a demonstration in Alabama in 1965 he stated: 'I do not know what lies ahead of us. There may be beatings, jailings, and tear gas. But I would rather die on the highways of Alabama than make a butchery of my conscience. There is nothing more tragic in all this world than to know right and not do it. I cannot stand in the midst of all these glaring evils and not take a stand.'[106]

This faith allowed him to conquer his fears, even in the face of terrifying physical aggression. Hosea Williams—whose non-violent courage King himself had praised—recounted being with King in situations in which 'I had so much fear the flesh trembled on my bones.' He added: 'He was the truest militant I ever met. He not only talked that talk; he walked that walk.'[107]

King's assassination had been preceded by that of Malcolm X three years before. During the last year of his life, Malcolm X had been moving towards King in spirit, and had begun to try to patch up their differences in the weeks before his death. Although in certain respects the antithesis of King, he was also a man of strong moral principles and a brilliant and charismatic leader in his own right. Despite his harsh comments on King's non-violence, his courageous struggle for the moral self-assertion of the poor African-Americans of the northern cities was in practice also waged without the use of violence. He just refused to accept non-violence as a principle. As he stated at a mass meeting in 1965: 'I don't advocate violence, but if a man steps on my toes, I'll step on his. ... Whites better be glad Martin Luther King is rallying the people because other forces are waiting to take over if he fails.'[108] The Nation of Islam, in which Malcolm X was a leading figure until his acrimonious break with the organisation in the final year of his life, sought to inculcate an upright, puritanical, moralistic, disciplined and deeply religious approach to life. Followers were expected to give up liquor, drugs and tobacco. Breaking such lifelong habits helped

[105]Ibid., p. 285.

[106]Ibid., p. 351.

[107]Ibid., p. 285.

[108]Malcolm X, *The Autobiography of Malcolm X*, with the assistance of Alex Haley, Penguin Books, Harmondsworth 1968, pp. 51–2.

inculcate what Malcolm X saw as 'black self-pride'.[109] The founder of the Nation of Islam, Elijah Muhammad, taught that 'idleness and laziness were among the black's greatest sins against himself', and Malcolm X himself was punctilious in keeping to time.[110] In these particular respects he was closer in spirit to Gandhi than Martin Luther King ever was. By breaking with Christianity and asserting that Islam was the true religion for the African-American, the organisation sought to break their inferiority complex—the 'Uncle Tom' attitude which saw salvation as lying in imitation of the whites. However, although Elijah Muhammad had an elaborate theology which depicted the white men as devils, he sought to opt out in an essentially quietist way rather than challenge white power head-on. Malcolm X, who took the Nation of Islam from being a tiny, obscure body in the early 1950s to being a mass organisation in the early 1960s, extended the theoretical denunciation of white Americans into a political confrontation.[111]

The first such clash occurred in Harlem in New York in 1958 when a member of the Nation of Islam who happened to be a bystander during a scuffle between the police and some African-Americans was beaten viciously and arrested by the police. Malcolm X immediately organised a mass protest by the Muslims, who stood in massed ranks, silently, before the building in which he was being held. The police had never experienced anything like this before, and agreed to take the wounded man to the local hospital. A large and swelling crowd marched behind them as they took him there. When a police officer ordered them to disperse, Malcolm X told him that they were not breaking any law. Only later, when he gave the word, did they go home. This stand had an electrifying effect in Harlem—the 'Black Muslims' were now seen as an activist body taking on white racism in an entirely new way.[112]

In 1963, Malcolm X broke with the Nation of Islam after Elijah Muhammad, who had been exposed as having sexual relations with two young secretaries, refused to admit his human frailties and instead turned on his most important follower in a vicious way.[113] To give himself breathing space, Malcolm X went on hajj to Mecca in early

[109]Ibid., p. 365.
[110]Ibid., pp. 289 & 303.
[111]Ibid., pp. 397–8.
[112]Ibid., pp. 335–6.

1964. This experience transformed him. He found in the Islamic countries a world in which people were not judged by their colour, and he came to see that the hatred of whites that he had previously propounded was itself a product of American racism. In Islam, he found a sense of brotherhood which transcended race.[114] From Mecca, he travelled to countries in black Africa that were newly liberated from colonial rule. There, he found black people living with dignity and self-respect. On his return to America in May 1964 he told the waiting press that he would never again make sweeping indictments of all whites: 'The true Islam has shown me that a blanket indictment of all white people is as wrong as when whites make blanket indictments against blacks.'[115]

In the last year of his life, Malcolm X began to make conciliatory moves towards Martin Luther King. King himself had criticised Malcolm X strongly as an extremist who was bringing 'misery upon negroes'.[116] Malcolm X, however, wanted to reach out and build a new alliance between the civil rights movement of the South and his own Black Pride movement of the northern ghettoes. In one of his last statements he said:

> Sometimes, I have dared to dream to myself that one day, history may even say that my voice—which disturbed the white man's smugness, and his arrogance, and his complacency—that my voice helped to save America from a grave, possibly even fatal catastrophe.
>
> The goal has always been the same, with the approaches to it as different as mine and Dr Martin Luther King's non-violent marching, that dramatizes the brutality and the evil of the white man against defenceless blacks. And in the racial climate of this country today, it is anybody's guess which of the 'extremes' in approach to the black man's problems might *personally* meet a fatal catastrophe first—'non-violent' Dr King, or so-called 'violent' me.[117]

On 21 February 1965, Malcolm X was shot dead while addressing a meeting in Harlem. Although the hand of Elijah Muhammad and

[113]Ibid., pp. 403–4, 408, 413, 415, 416 & 419.
[114]Ibid., pp. 447, 449 & 454.
[115]Ibid., p. 479.
[116]Ibid., p. 21.
[117]Ibid., p. 496.

the Nation of Islam was suspected, it is likely that there were elements within the CIA or FBI that had either connived in the assassination or been actively involved.[118]

Although Malcolm X refused to be associated with Gandhian non-violence, there were certain parallels between the two men. Malcolm X may have attacked Gandhian non-violence, but he was a great admirer of the man who had fought British imperialism in India. He regarded Gandhi as a great 'leader of the people' who had been politicised by his experience of white racism in South Africa.[119] Both were fighters against injustice and were charismatic figures who based their message on a strongly moral appeal that was rooted in a firm faith in God. Malcolm X's strong anti-white message was intended to shock people out of their complacency in a way that paralleled Gandhi's sweeping rejection of Western civilisation in *Hind Swaraj*. In the last year of his life, Malcolm was moving towards new forms of dialogue—with white sympathisers, pan-African nationalists, the radical regimes in Algeria, Tanzania, Cuba, and with Martin Luther King and the civil rights movement. It was almost certainly this attempt to build a powerful new alliance of those opposed to American racism and imperialism which proved the last straw for certain forces within the American state system. Like Gandhi, Malcolm X died fighting intolerance and hatred. Martin Luther King was to die three years later while struggling to build a similar solidarity of the oppressed.[120]

Although King's death in 1968 brought an end to the period of the great campaigns for African-American civil rights, the movement had changed the political scene in the USA in a radical new direction. Gandhian techniques of resistance had been shown to work in an American context, in a way that legitimised them for a generation of Americans. It had forged a whole vocabulary of protest, with songs such as 'Freedom Now!' and 'We Shall Overcome' becoming the new anthems

[118]He himself in his final days suspected that there was an organised plot to kill him which came from forces other than the Nation of Islam. Ibid., pp. 55 & 57.

[119]Ibid., pp. 271, 344 & 375.

[120]For King's launching, in his last year, of a new campaign against poverty which cut across racial divides see Moses, *Revolution of Conscience*, pp. 33–4.

of dissent. In his last two years, King himself became a leading figure in one such protest, that against the war in Vietnam. Besides massive marches and street demonstrations, there were public burnings of draft cards. Such protest was then extended into campaigns for womens', gay and lesbian rights, and the environmental movement. As Greg Moses has noted: 'it is commonplace to announce that King's death marked the end of an era, but in the broader life of the mind a logic of non-violence was just beginning to make its way into the world.'[121]

The Revolt Against Apartheid in South Africa

After Gandhi left South Africa in 1915, he placed his third son Manilal in charge of his work there. Manilal ran the Phoenix Ashram, published *Indian Opinion*, and kept up the struggle for the rights of Indians.[122] In 1946 he played a leading role in a major campaign of protest against new legislation that discriminated against those of Indian origin that built directly on the legacy of Gandhi's own resistance to the white regime three to four decades earlier. The satyagraha continued for two years, with mass rallies and the picketing of and squatting on of land reserved for whites-only occupation. Indians of all classes were involved—men and women alike—and around two thousand were jailed, including the two main leaders, Yusuf Dadoo and G.M. Naicker. Although confined to the Indian community, many blacks were deeply impressed by the power of the protest. As Nelson Mandela later wrote:

> It instilled a spirit of defiance and radicalism among the people, broke the fear of prison, and boosted the popularity and influence of the NIC [Natal Indian Congress] and TIC [Transvaal Indian Congress]. They reminded us that the freedom struggle was not merely a question of making speeches, holding meetings, passing resolutions and sending deputations, but of meticulous organisation, militant mass action and, above all, the willingness to suffer and sacrifice. The Indians' campaign harkened back to the 1913 passive resistance in which Mahatma Gandhi

[121]Ibid., p. 202.

[122]For a report of 1925 on Manilal Gandhi's work, see Fisher, *That Strange Little Brown Man Gandhi*, pp. xvii–xviii and 46.

> led a tumultuous procession of Indians crossing illegally from Natal to the Transvaal. That was history; this campaign was taking place before my own eyes.[123]

Blacks felt a novel sense of solidarity with a community hitherto regarded by them as being little better than lackeys of the whites.[124]

The 5th Pan-African Congress, which had met in Manchester in 1945, had already endorsed Gandhian passive resistance as the preferred method for resistance to colonialism in Africa. In 1949 the African National Congress (ANC) in South Africa committed itself to non-violence in its struggle against apartheid. Manilal Gandhi wanted them to state that non-violence was a moral principle to be observed at all costs, but the majority of the ANC leaders saw it as a tactical matter, arguing that in a situation of an overwhelming control of force by the white regime, violent resistance would have been futile. This became the official ANC line, despite Manilal's vigorous objections.[125]

In 1952 the ANC launched a campaign against the pass laws in which blacks violated the law by entering white areas. There was however some violence, which gave the rulers an excuse to crush the movement ruthlessly. Non-violent protest continued in the 1950s and 1960s under the leadership of Albert Luthuli (1899–1967), who was strongly committed to non-violence as a principle. This courageous Zulu chief was awarded the Nobel Prize for Peace in 1960.

Long before this, however, many of the ANC leaders had begun to question the strategy of non-violence. New laws were being passed which criminalized even the mildest displays of dissidence. Protesters could now be detained indefinitely without trial. As Mandela stated:

> I began to suspect that both legal and extra-constitutional protests would soon be impossible. In India, Gandhi had been dealing with a foreign power that ultimately was more realistic and far-sighted. That was not the case with the Afrikaners in South Africa. Non-violent passive resistance is effective as long as your opposition adheres to the same rules as you do. But if peaceful protest is met with violence, its efficacy

[123]Mandela, *Long Walk to Freedom*, p. 98.
[124]Ibid., pp. 97–8 and 119.
[125]Ibid., p. 119.

is at an end. For me, non-violence was not a moral principle but a strategy; there is no moral goodness in using an ineffective weapon.[126]

The matter came to a head after the Sharpeville massacre of 1960, in which sixty-nine non-violent protesters were shot and killed by the police in cold blood. The ANC leaders retaliated by burning their passes in public, which led to a declaration of martial law and their being thrown in jail. Many of these leaders felt that non-violence had had its day. After their release, there was a heated debate within the ANC, with Luthuli standing up for non-violence. He was supported by J.N. Singh, an Indian ANC leader, who advanced the Gandhian argument that: 'Non-violence has not failed us, we have failed non-violence'.[127] Eventually, the Gandhians were forced to bow to the majority line—that there should be underground violent resistance. The military wing of the ANC was however to be separate, and under the leadership of Mandela, Walter Sisulu and Joe Slovo.

Mandela did not however turn his back on Gandhi entirely. He could never forget J.N. Singh's words—they continued to reverberate in his head even thirty years later.[128] He continued to be a passionate admirer of Gandhi, whom he saw as a champion of the rights of the colonised and racially oppressed. He never forgot that Gandhi's fierce anti-colonialism was born in South Africa from bitter experiences of racial discrimination and from seeing the brutal repression of the Bambata rebellion by white British troops.[129] Mandela argued that Gandhi did not in any case rule out violence in extreme circumstances, in particular when non-violence was a cover for cowardice, or when honour was at stake. Mandela believed that what mattered was not so much whether a movement was strictly non-violent so much as the balance maintained between non-violence and violence. 'Violence and non-violence are not mutually exclusive; it is the predominance of the one or the other that labels a struggle.'[130] He therefore advocated a limited form of violence, involving acts of sabotage against government installations and property,

[126]Ibid., pp. 146–7.
[127]Ibid., p. 261.
[128]Ibid.
[129]Nelson Mandela, 'The Sacred Warrior', *Time*, 31 December 1999, p. 96.
[130]Ibid., p. 94.

taking care to avoid injuring people. Mandela felt that it was vital that they did not set off a blood feud between black and white: 'Animosity between Afrikaner and Englishman was still sharp fifty years after the Anglo-Boer war; what would race relations be like between black and white if we provoked a civil war?'[131] Non-violent civil resistance continued, with strikes, demonstrations, boycotts and moral pressure from church leaders such as Desmond Tutu and Alan Boesak. The work of these latter figures greatly enhanced the moral power of the struggle.[132]

Although he had turned his back on strict non-violence, Mandela, like Gandhi, understood that a struggle that created bitterness between opponents made it harder in the long term to reach a lasting solution to a problem. He himself had an almost saintly ability to refuse to think badly of his enemies, believing very strongly that: 'Man's goodness is a flame that can be hidden but never extinguished.'[133] He felt himself vindicated in this when he saw certain whites rise above their prejudices—men such as Justice Rumpff who in a celebrated judgement of 1961 refused on the basis of the evidence before him to convict the ANC leaders for acts of violence or being communists, even though the government demanded it.[134] Even during the long and terrible years in jail, Mandela continued to appeal to the humanity of his jailors, and a small number of these hardest of people responded with sympathy.[135] After his release, he sought to bring these qualities to his negotiations with President W.F. de Klerk: 'To make peace with an enemy, one must work with that enemy, and that enemy becomes your partner.'[136]

By the late 1960s, it was clear that the ANC strategy of violent underground struggle was going nowhere. Many of its best leaders were in jail and silenced, while those in exile found that they could do little to pursue their strategy to any effect, and began to quarrel amongst themselves.[137] It was against this background that a new leader emerged

[131]Mandela, *Long Walk to Freedom*, p. 272.

[132]Randle, *Civil Resistance*, pp. 73–4.

[133]Mandela, *Long Walk to Freedom*, p. 615.

[134]Ibid., pp. 248–9.

[135]Ibid., p. 552.

[136]Ibid., p. 604.

[137]Martin Meredith, *Nelson Mandela: A Biography*, Hamish Hamilton, London 1997, pp. 347–8.

who reasserted the principle of struggle through open and non-violent resistance in a most powerful way. This was Steve Biko, who was born in the eastern Cape Province in 1946. While a medical student in the late 1960s, he had taken the leading role in formulating a new creed of Black Consciousness. There were strong parallels between Biko's position and that of Malcolm X. Like Malcolm X, Biko criticised the blacks for their complicity in their own subjugation: 'The type of black man we have today has lost his manhood. Reduced to an obliging shell, he looks with awe at the white power structure and accepts what he regards as the "inevitable position".'[138] He argued that there could be no genuine liberation until the blacks learnt to be proud of themselves and consider themselves to be the equal of the whites. He rejected the ANC strategy of building a multi-racial political alliance, as this tended to reinforce a mentality of dependency on whites. Biko was the most articulate and charismatic of this new generation of young black activists, and was soon the acknowledged leader of the new Black People's Convention (BPC). Discussion groups were set up, and local community self-help projects inaugurated, involving educational, health, welfare and cultural activities.[139]

Biko's aim was to build the strength of the blacks so that they would be eventually in a position to negotiate with the white regime from a much more powerful base. He never rejected the possibility of dialogue. For this reason, he stressed that, in contrast to the ANC, the BPC did not have any armed wing and that: 'We operate on the assumption that we can bring whites to their senses by confronting them with our overwhelming demands.'[140] He refused to rule out the possibility that violence might be needed at a future date, but felt that they had other better methods of struggle available to them, such as attacking the South African economy from within. He predicted that once investors lost confidence in the apartheid regime, capital would drain away and induce a panic amongst the whites, who would then be forced to negotiate. He thought that this process would begin to work its way through by the late 1970s.[141]

[138]Ibid., p. 327

[139]Ibid., pp. 327–8.

[140]Donald Woods, *Biko*, Paddington Press, London 1978, p. 104.

[141]Ibid., pp. 104–5.

The Black Consciousness movement rejected direct political work with whites, and was very critical of white liberals who, they said, only criticised the regime to salve their conscience, while still enjoying a white lifestyle. Biko was however careful to distinguish between whites as people, whom he refused to hate, and whites as part of 'the System', which he opposed in an uncompromising manner. As he once stated about Black Consciousness:

> it isn't a negative, hating thing. It's a positive black self-confidence thing involving no hatred of anyone, not even the Nats [the hardline white supremacist Nationalist Party]—only of what they represent today. ... Our main concern is the liberation of the blacks—the majority of South Africans—and while we want to establish a country in which all men are free and welcome citizens—white as well as black—we have to concentrate on what means most to us blacks.[142]

These were very Gandhian sentiments, and Biko had other qualities of a leader in this mould. He lived in a simple and austere way. He always reached out to others, striving to meet them as human beings, whatever their political or racial differences. He did this with humour and without a trace of arrogance. If he realised that he had made a mistake, or that an argument of his was faulty, he was prepared to accept his error with grace. He had a firm vision of what he stood for and wanted in politics, and was prepared to die for it if necessary. His close friend Donald Woods said of him: 'He had a rocklike integrity and a degree of courage that sent one's regard for the potentialities of the human spirit soaring skyhigh.'[143] He was in every respect a figure of towering moral stature.

Biko carried on his political work in Durban until 1973, when a banning order was passed on him, restricting him to his own King William's Town. He carried on working there openly, until stopped from doing so in 1975. Thereafter he continued his activities secretly, often breaking the banning order. He was arrested several times and

[142] Ibid., p. 55.

[143] Ibid., p. 61. Woods (1933–2001) was a white journalist who fled South Africa in late 1977 to escape persecution for his anti-apartheid work. Obituary in *The Guardian*, 21 August 2001.

spent periods in jail. Then, after being caught breaking the banning order in 1977, he was interrogated and tortured by the police, being beaten so severely that he suffered brain damage. He died, untreated, five days after this murderous assault. The police claimed that he had been injured in a scuffle.

When the news of this atrocity broke, there was a sense of profound shock, followed by riots in the streets. The government responded by clamping down on the Black Consciousness movement. Many of its leaders were arrested and jailed, and banning orders were issued on white supporters. Internationally, there were renewed demands for economic sanctions against South Africa, and the United Nations passed a vote that there should be no future arms sales to the apartheid regime. The events frightened many foreign investors, who began to withdraw their capital.[144] Biko's murder showed very clearly that the white regime was not prepared to engage in any dialogue with the blacks, even those who believed in non-violent resistance and a gradual and peaceful transition to majority rule.

Over the next decade, the white regime continued in its hardline stance, even though Prime Minister P.W. Botha took steps to 'modernize' the regime, which involved watering down some aspects of what was called 'petty apartheid'. The town of Soweto went into revolt, with a whole generation of young black women and men dedicating their lives to the struggle. The collapse of the Portuguese empire in Africa and then the apartheid state in Rhodesia saw the emergence of new black regimes in neighbouring regions. There was a revival of the guerrilla campaign of the ANC, and raids on South Africa were carried out from bases in Angola and Mozambique. Botha allowed the military a free hand to fight the guerrillas, both in South Africa and in the neighbouring countries—to considerable effect.

During the 1980s the international anti-apartheid movement grew in strength, with demands for Mandela's release and attacks on multinational corporations which continued to have dealings with South Africa. However, it was only in 1989, when F.W. de Klerk replaced Botha as prime minister, that the Nationalist Party changed its policy

[144] Meredith, *Nelson Mandela*, pp. 339–40.

of all-out repression of the black movement. Until then, black resistance—non-violent and violent, national and international—had failed to undermine the regime in any very serious way. De Klerk seems to have realised, nonetheless, that opposition was building an irresistible momentum, and that it would be in the long-term interests of the Afrikaners to negotiate with moderate blacks and reach a settlement rather than risk a revolutionary explosion in which they would lose everything.[145]

The implementation of this policy brought Mandela's release in 1990 and the move towards the transition to black rule, which took place in 1994. Once in power Mandela refused to sanction any recriminations against whites and their erstwhile supporters. This was despite the terrible violence of the final years of apartheid, seen in particular in a wave of murderous attacks on ANC activists and supporters by followers of Chief Buthelezi with the connivance of the white state. For Mandela, the process of healing was of far greater importance than satisfying an understandable desire for revenge. The moral stature that he has as a result achieved throughout the world is one that in modern times has been equalled only by that of Gandhi himself.[146]

Petra Kelly and the German Greens

In Europe, one of the most prominent figures in recent years to be inspired by Gandhi has been Petra Kelly, a leader of the German Green Party (Die Grünen). However, unlike Gandhi she fought elections and represented her party in parliament. This caused tensions that were never resolved in a satisfactory manner before her violent and tragic death in 1992. The manner of her death also raised questions about her possible failure to reconcile her private life with her non-violent beliefs.

Kelly was born in Bavaria in 1947, moving with her family to southern USA in 1960. There, she was inspired by the civil rights and anti-Vietnam war movements. Returning to Europe in 1972, she was actively involved in the anti-nuclear movement, and in 1980 was a co-founder and first leader of the German Green Party, which brought together a

145 Ibid., pp. 396–7.

146 On the dust jacket of his autobiography he is described as 'the world's most significant moral leader since Mahatma Gandhi'. *Long Walk to Freedom.*

wide variety of ecological action groups. In 1983 she and twenty-six other Greens were elected to the Bundestag. She served there until the 1990 elections, when the Greens suffered an electoral reverse. While a member of the Bundestag, she led a series of non-violent protests against nuclear installations and military bases. These included protests in East Berlin and Moscow. She also took part in an occupation of the German embassy in Pretoria in protest at German economic ties with the apartheid regime in South Africa. She was also to the fore in protesting against the violation of human rights in Tibet by the Chinese government (she had adopted an orphaned Tibetan girl in 1973).[147]

Kelly drew her inspiration directly from the Gandhian tradition of non-violent moral activism. One of her earliest political heroes was Martin Luther King. She studied political science at university in Washington, where she was introduced to Thoreau and his theory of civil disobedience. She was impressed by the way that King had acknowledged Gandhi and Thoreau as inspirational examples. According to her biographer, Sara Parkin: 'Petra's gods were Gandhi and Martin Luther King. Her bibles were Thoreau and Gene Sharp ...'[148] She became strongly committed to a thoroughgoing non-violence in pursuit of a politics informed by truth.[149] Her non-violence, like that of Gandhi, was not passive but active, and it entailed 'seeking opportunities for dialogue or taking actions which would liberate people from the violent system (of thinking) which prevented them from seeing the power and rightness of non-violence.'[150]

As with Gandhi, these politics flowed from a deep inner spirituality. Kelly had been brought up in Bavaria in a devout family of Roman Catholics, and in her childhood had wanted to become a nun.[151] She was drawn to Martin Luther King in part by his strong Christian faith.

[147]Petra Kelly, *Nonviolence Speaks to Power*, edited by Glenn D. Paige and Sarah Gilliart, Centre for Global Nonviolence Planning Project, Hawaii, 1992, pp. 161–6.

[148]Gene Sharp was an American who wrote widely on the techniques of Gandhian non-violent action. Parkin, *The Life and Death of Petra Kelly*, p. 106.

[149]Petra Kelly, 'Gandhi and the Green Party', *Gandhi Marg*, July-September 1989, pp. 192–202.

[150]Parkin, *The Life and Death of Petra Kelly*, p. 108.

[151]Ibid., pp. 21 & 26.

Later, she became drawn to Catholic liberation theology.[152] During the 1970s her Catholicism gave way to a more eclectic and humanistic faith, a new 'holy trinity of non-violence, personal responsibility and truth.'[153] These became her guiding spiritual truths. She insisted that 'The spiritual dimensions of non-violence as lived by Gandhi are to me most important,'[154] and that—quoting Martin Luther King—'unarmed truth and unconditional love will have the final word in reality.'[155] She also believed that 'we cannot solve ... political problems without addressing our spiritual ones.'[156]

She even claimed that her ecological values flowed from Gandhi:

> In one particular area of our political work we have been greatly inspired by Mahatma Gandhi. That is in our belief that a lifestyle and method of production which rely on an endless supply of raw materials and which use those raw materials lavishly, also furnish the motive for the violent appropriation of raw materials from other countries. In contrast, a responsible use of raw materials, as part of an ecologically-oriented lifestyle and economy, reduces the risk that policies of violence will be pursued in our name. The pursuit of ecologically responsible policies within a society provides preconditions for a reduction of tensions and increases our ability to achieve peace in the world.[157]

She saw her work as being informed above all by a respect for all life forms and an understanding of their interconnectedness.

Kelly engaged with issues at a global level, whether they related to human rights, women's oppression, the environment, the structured violence of the military and nuclear complex, or the divide between rich and poor. She saw herself as speaking for the poor and oppressed: 'To my mind, the purpose of politics and of political parties is to stand up for the weak, for those who have no lobby or other means of exerting influence.'[158]

[152]Ibid., pp. 48 & 65.
[153]Ibid., p. 105.
[154]Kelly, *Nonviolence Speaks to Power*, p. 33.
[155]Parkin, *The Life and Death of Petra Kelly*, p. 114.
[156]Kelly, *Nonviolence Speaks to Power*, p. 17.
[157]Ibid., p. 33.
[158]Ibid., p. 125.

In marked contrast to most such non-violent activists, she was not only involved in party politics as a founder member of Die Grünen, but was also served as a member of parliament. She claimed that Die Grünen was what she called an 'anti-party party'. Kelly took this concept from the Hungarian philosopher Gyorgy Konrad, who called for what he called an 'anti-politics' which 'strives to put politics in its place and make sure it stays there, never overstepping its proper office of defending and refining the morals of the game in a civil society—where a civil society is the antithesis of a military society.'[159] Kelly believed that party work within the legislatures should be carried on in a close symbiosis with action on the streets. Such a programme required that Die Grünen remain a perpetual opposition, the assumption being that any holding of office would lead to inevitable compromises with power and the violent apparatus of oppression controlled by the state. There was much in this that echoed Gandhi's sharp critique of the corruptions of parliamentary power. She was also trying to create a culture of Gandhian-style civil disobedience that would permeate all levels of the polity: 'All of us in Germany would benefit if we were to learn at last the liberating and constructive art of civil disobedience—not just in the extraparliamentary movement, but also within parliament and political parties. Civil disobedience has to be practiced in parliament or even within our own party if we become too dogmatic, powerful, or arrogant.'[160] There were, however, many within the party who did not envisage this as their prime aim and role. This group, known as the *Realos*, hoped to gain enough strength to become partners in a governing coalition, from which position they would be able to push through green policies. Joschka Fischer was the leading figure in this group—he was elected to the Bundestag along with Kelly in 1983. Those who rejected this line came to be known as the *Fundis*. Although Kelly tried to project herself as being above the two factions, she was in practice more in tune with the *Fundis* than the *Realos*.

Another very serious tension within Die Grünen concerned the role of the leader. Kelly wanted to create a party of people who were com-

[159]Gyorgy Konrad, quoted in Parkin, *The Life and Death of Petra Kelly*, p. 128.

[160]Kelly, *Nonviolence Speaks to Power*, p. 148.

mitted to a thorough non-violence in thought, word and deed. Its members would, ideally, be free from any egoistical desire for power, their motivation being a selfless and genuine desire to further the interests of the socially excluded and oppressed and to forge a society which would nurture rather than exploit its environment.[161] In Kelly's words, their party was 'based on human solidarity and democracy among its members and on the rejection of a performance and hierarchy-oriented approach governed by rivalry hostile to life.'[162] Power within the party was to emerge from the bottom up, rather than from the top down, as in conventional party politics. Activism within civil society would be valued as much as parliamentary work. To further this aim, Greens who were elected to the Bundestag were to relinquish their position after two years, handing it over to another party member.

However, although Kelly supported this idea when it was formulated, she soon turned against it and refused to stand down when her turn was up. One reason was personal. She had given up her job to serve as a member of parliament, and had moved her house and home to the capital, Bonn. The Bundestag gave her a superb platform for her particular form of oppositional politics, and she found that her demands and the many causes she championed were taken with greater seriousness both in Germany and internationally, in a way which brought many solid gains. In several instances, she managed to obtain cross-party support for her proposals as a result of her committed and painstaking advocacy of the issue. She felt that the requirement for her to give up such work in two years would also be counterproductive for the party. Kelly also observed that the process of rotation generated a poisonous sense of rivalry between members of the party. She dismissed the argument that rotation helped prevent the concentration of power in particular hands—the real power coteries survived in spite of it.[163]

Although most of the *Realos* within the party accepted that the two-year rotation principle was in practice not workable and soon accepted that it had to be abandoned, it was clear that Kelly and others within

[161]Glenn D. Paige, 'Introduction' to Kelly, *Nonviolence Speaks to Power*, pp. 7–11.

[162]Parkin, *The Life and Death of Petra Kelly*, p. 131.

[163]Kelly, *Nonviolence Speaks to Power*, p. 154.

the party had not thought through this particular strategy adequately. The way she changed her position in a unilateral manner, forcing the party to accept her turnabout, opened her up to the criticism that she had ditched her principles in pursuit of her political ambitions.[164] There was a strongly anti-hierarchical and democratic culture within the party that stemmed in part from the profound and understandable suspicion there was on the German left of charismatic leadership. The fact that Kelly was popularly regarded in Germany and beyond as 'the leader' of Die Grünen added to their fears in this respect. By 1986 a strong antipathy to such 'celebrities' had developed and she found herself increasingly isolated within the party.[165]

It was widely accepted by political commentators that the attempt to exercise power in a plural and decentralised way had meant that the party lacked any clear structures of power and means for delegating authority. Party members had become wary of taking initiatives. Political work became fragmented and there was a lack of unity in policy pronouncements, which caused widespread confusion in Germany.[166] Its parliamentarians operated in an amateurish and ineffective manner. Kelly's partner and fellow Green, Gert Bastian, stated that there was what he called a 'dictatorship of incompetence' within the party.[167] This all raised the question as to whether or not it was possible in a system of liberal democracy, party politics and media-driven political debate to abandon the figure of the 'strong leader'. The whole system craves such personalities, even trying to create them when no such talent is about. It may also be observed that in all spheres of public life, leaders who can provide a sure, courageous and visionary leadership can give a powerful sense of mission and direction to a movement, a political party or other form of institution. One that fails to value and nurture such leadership is unlikely to flourish. In the USA, Malcolm X was, for

[164]Thomas Poguntke, *Alternative Politics: The German Green Party*, Edinburgh University Press, Edinburgh 1993, p. 145; E. Gene Frankland and Donald Schoonmaker, *Between Protest and Power: The Green Party in Germany*, Westview Press, Boulder, Colorado 1992, p. 113.

[165]Parkin, *The Life and Death of Petra Kelly*, pp. 138, 159–60, 162 & 173–4.

[166]Frankland and Schoonmaker, *Between Protest and Power*, p. 218.

[167]Kelly, *Nonviolence Speaks to Power*, p. 155.

example, subjected to a ruthless campaign of cutting to size within the Nation of Islam, to the severe detriment of that body in the long term.

Kelly herself was a great media star, and this provided further ground for distrust within the party. Many in Die Grünen displayed a contempt for the media which infuriated her. As she stated in an open letter to the party in 1991:

> One of the great weaknesses in both the parliamentary group and in the party has been that of media relations. The party must have the courage to appoint really independent, bright, and audacious media spokespersons who are very experienced and competent in dealing with the national and international media. One thing must change very quickly in the Greens' public presentation. We have to try to brighten up our party's image because until now we have appeared unremittingly gloomy and intolerant. We are no longer able to laugh or show a bit of enthusiasm and zest for life. This is particularly evident at the national party conferences, and it is very depressing.[168]

Like Gandhi, Kelly not only appreciated the importance of a good press, but also knew how much the media loves a leader who can project a feeling of inspiration and conviction. In this way, a moral activist could gain crucial publicity and support for her or his cause.

In 1990, Die Grünen found no place for Kelly on its list of parliamentary candidates for the general election of that year. They insisted on running a 'personality-free' campaign. The internal fighting within the party had however lost it crucial electoral support in West Germany. This was the first post-war election in which both East and West Germany voted together, and Die Grünen failed to forge an alliance with the Greens of the East. The latter gained 6.0 percent of the vote there, while the former gained only 4.8 percent in the west. Under Germany's constitution, a party had to win at least 5 percent of the vote to gain any seats in parliament. If they had been formerly allied, they would have gained 5.1 percent of the vote and around 40 seats in the Bundestag. As it was, Die Grünen got nothing.[169]

[168]Ibid., p. 158.

[169]Frankland and Schoonmaker, *Between Protest and Power*, pp. 220–1.

On 19 October 1992, the police entered a house in a suburb of Bonn and discovered the decomposing bodies of Petra Kelly and Gert Bastian. They had each died of a single bullet wound to the head, inflicted on 1 October. It appeared that Bastian had shot Kelly as she lay sleeping in bed and then committed suicide. Although the police claimed that they found no evidence to contradict this assumption, there were inevitable doubts. There were no suicide notes or any intimations of a suicide pact. Friends insisted that Kelly was not a suicidal type, and—even if she had been—that she would never have participated in a suicide pact without leaving an explanation for her family and for the world. Forensic evidence showed that she had been deeply asleep when she was shot in the head. Some suspected that her fight against the military-industrial complex had led to her murder by the 'nuclear mafia', by shadowy government agents of either the capitalist or communist blocs, or perhaps by neo-Nazis. Others suggested that Bastian had become depressed by his own sense of mortality (he was sixty-nine years old), the down-turn in the fortune of Die Grünen and the rise of neo-Nazis in Germany, and decided that it would be best if both died together.[170]

Glenn D. Paige, who edited a collection of speeches and essays by Petra Kelly that was published just before her death, commented in his introduction: 'conventional problems of political leadership are compounded for non-violent leaders who seek to question, challenge, and change the policies and institutions of violence-prone societies—political, military, economic, social, cultural, and ecological—not only locally but also globally. The lonely paths to martyrdom of Gandhi and King provide prototypical examples.'[171] By a deep irony, before that year was out, Petra Kelly was also dead, killed by a lethal shot. One more person of fearless integrity and champion of non-violence in an ethical politics had died suddenly and in shocking circumstances.

If, as could be possible, skilled and trained assassins carried out a double murder so as to leave no trace, then Petra Kelly was a martyr in the same way as Gandhi, Martin Luther King, Malcolm X and Steve

[170]Parkin, *The Life and Death of Petra Kelly*, pp. xxv, 4–5 & 12; *Who killed Petra Kelly?*, www.motherjones.com/motherjones/JF93/hertsgaard.html

[171]Glenn D. Paige, 'Introduction' to Kelly, *Nonviolence Speaks to Power*, p. 9.

Biko had been—killed by political foes. From the evidence, however, this appears unlikely. Kelly's activist career was in the doldrums at that juncture, and with the easing of the Cold War, it hardly seems likely that any secret service would have seen her as a threat that had to be eliminated. Most probably, Bastian murdered Kelly without any foreknowledge or consent on her part. This conclusion accords best with what we know about both Petra Kelly and Bastian. She was a person of principled non-violence and could hardly have allowed her life-message to have been negated so absolutely by choosing to die in such a way (her bedroom was splattered with her blood from the point-blank shot). Gert Bastian on the other hand was still, in himself, a man of violence.

Born in 1923, he had been a fervent member of the Hitler Youth organisation in his teens, a soldier who was decorated for valour in battle during the Second World War, and a successful army officer afterwards. In 1980, while commanding the 12th Panzer Division, he decided to resign from the army in protest at the stationing of nuclear missiles on German soil. Only then had he become a peace activist.[172] Within a couple of years he was quoting Gandhi and Martin Luther King with facility.[173] Yet, he had kept his guns from his army days, and took them with him into the house he shared with Kelly. She knew about this, but rationalised that they were needed as she had received death threats. His non-violence was in fact a sham, something he parroted without belief.[174] The deeply troubling thought is, therefore, that he had lived for over a decade in intimacy with a woman whose whole being exuded the deepest abhorrence of violence and yet he could still go ahead and violate her deepest convictions so blatantly and for the world to see and judge.

What seems to have driven him to carry out this act was the fact that STASI files relating to him from East Germany were about to be made public. These may well have revealed that he had double-dealings with the former East German secret police. He had a strong sense of honour, inculcated in his upbringing and military career, and realised that

[172]Parkin, *The Life and Death of Petra Kelly*, pp. 93–6.
[173]Ibid., p. 122.
[174]Ibid., pp. 180–1.

such an exposure would have exposed his 'honour' as a sham. Kelly had strongly condemned people who had had dealings with STASI, and he must have feared her censure, and a possible end to their relationship. On the day he carried out the act, he had received a telephone call that his personal file was about to be opened. Once a person was dead, only a family member could demand access to such a file. His sense of military honour was also one that valorised suicide through a shot to the head as an act of redemption when all seemed lost.[175]

In a very Gandhian gesture, Kelly had in the past refused to accept police protection, despite the death threats, on the grounds of her commitment to non-violence.[176] She had however allowed Bastian to maintain his guns. She did so to accommodate a man of violence who was her lover and, ostensibly, her protector. This was to prove to be a fatal compromise. Her life, we must conclude, was brought to an end by an act of assassination, but in her case it was carried out not by a political opponent, but by a person of intimacy who felt he had a moral right to carry out such a crime in order to maintain his own warped and violent sense of honour. Kelly's death represented a profound failure for the principle of non-violence at the most personal of levels.

[175]Ibid., pp. 186–7 & 200.
[176]Ibid., p. 180.

10

The Moral Activists' Lonely Path to Martyrdom

Gandhi sought to forge an alternative modernity. His programme was rooted in part in various Indian traditions, such as that of the bhakti movement, with its critique of caste exclusions and oppressive hierarchies. But also he took from the internal Western critique of the imperialism and autocracy embedded in the dominant strands of post-Enlightenment theory and practice, with his endorsement of an alternative arcadian sensibility. He related to these various traditions in a dialogic manner, questioning them at a whole range of levels, seeking to evolve a new system above all through practice and experience.

He tried to incorporate subaltern politics into his alternative by purging it of its violent aspects, so as to give it a strong moral superiority as against the coercive and violent politics of both the colonial state and the indigenous élites. He carried out this task in a cautious way, being always aware that the state could crush such a politics if it felt overly threatened. There was also much that he found hard to understand or sympathise with in the forces he had unleashed, and he preferred to err on the side of caution. He thus sought to build his alternative system slowly, so that it would—he believed—be on firm foundations.

In all of this, Gandhi rejected an intolerant and hate-filled opposition to the Other, whether it was the white Britisher, the Indian collaborator, the Muslim, or the assertive subordinate. He believed that the Other could almost always be won over through a sympathetic and compassionate process of dialogue. There were times when he did not live up to this principle, as when he shunned Muhammad Ali Jinnah in the period after 1920, treated B.R. Ambedkar with disrespect in their initial meetings, or sought to coerce members of his family or discipline women who failed to conform to his elevated model of female 'purity'. He was at times unjustly opposed to powerful class-based conflicts, as against landlords, usurers or Indian princes. Several people he did reach out to, such as the Hindu extremists in the Savarkar camp, rejected his overtures with contempt. Also, his ideal did not stand for much when the dialogue was conducted from a presumed or actual position of superiority, as was often the case with Dalits and Adivasis. It is wrong, however, to argue that Gandhi's dialogic approach precluded conflict and led to collaboration, as some of his opponents on both the left and right argued. Gandhi's position was that contradictions are best resolved through dialogue, but failing that, a non-violent challenge might be the only strategy of integrity. He himself rarely shied away from such conflict if he judged it to be necessary. However, every effort had to be made to avoid acrimony, so as to make it easier for opponents to live with each other in the future.

After Indian independence, the Gandhian approach was seen most strongly in the Sarvodaya and Bhoodan movements, which were at their height in the 1950s. With their decline in the 1960s, it seemed that the Gandhian model had become outmoded and out of touch with contemporary needs. However, Gandhian-style activism then began to braid with the 'new social movements', such as those demanding lower-class emancipation, women's rights, environmental protection, and a non-belligerent foreign policy for India. The new social movements have provided a strong critique of the path taken by the Indian nation state since independence. They have shown up the hollowness of a democracy that claims to operate in the interests of the mass of the people, yet fails to provide the essential resources that the poor need for a decent livelihood. They have revealed the patriarchy that is entrenched deeply within the polity, its war-mongering and seeking of cheap popularity through attacks on minorities. They have rejected the hegemonic discourse of 'development', with its project of interlinking nation states within the global circulation of capital by fostering a world culture based on modern technology and communications, with each sphere of life becoming a field for capitalist profit.[1] It is argued that, far from helping the poor, such 'development' has at a global level created an ever-widening chasm, for whereas in 1950 the gap in average incomes between the developed and underdeveloped countries was estimated at 35 to 1, in 1992 it was estimated to be 72 to 1. Today, the annual income of 582 million people of all of the underdeveloped countries is said to be equivalent to only thirteen percent of the wealth of the two hundred richest capitalists.[2]

Gandhian ideas and techniques have played an important role in several of these movements. Environmentalism provides a case in point. Gandhi has been seen as an inspiring figure for many in the ecology movement there, which began with the Chipko Andolan in 1973. This involved civil resistance, with protesters hugging trees to save them from the axes of commercial foresters. Chandiprasad Bhatt, who took the lead in this, described himself as a Gandhian, and another prominent leader, Sunderlal Bahuguna, was a Sarvodaya worker. Similarly with the movement against large dams on the Narmada river, which began in the mid-1980s. The prominent leaders Medha Patkar and Baba Amte both acknowledge their debt to Gandhi. Environmentalists have also engaged in a series of Gandhian-style padayatras—long-distance marches—through areas threatened with environmental degradation to draw attention to the problem.[3] As Ramachandra Guha has pointed out, not all ecology activists have claimed to be Gandhians—there are socialists, Marxists, Christians and others—but Gandhi has been probably the most important single influence.[4]

The new social movements operate in a number of discrete spheres. A theoretical justification for this may be found in the writings of Foucault, in his argument that hegemonic power is dispersed through-

[1]Pramod Parajuli, 'Power and Knowledge in Development Discourse: New Social Movements and the State in India', *International and Social Science Journal*, February 1991, No. 127, pp. 174–6.

[2]These estimates are from *United Nations Human Development Report*, June 2000, reported in *The Guardian*, 29 June 2000.

[3]Gadgil and Guha, *Ecology and Equity*, p. 101.

[4]Ramachandra Guha, 'Mahatma Gandhi and the Environmental Movement', pp. 65–7.

out the social formation in various sites, with each site expressing a particular relationship of domination and subordination.[5] The new social movements seek to challenge these relationships of power at each of the levels at which they operate. They do not do this through the direct capture of state power through elections, but through trying to transform the nature of politics itself. This in itself is a very Gandhian approach.

The problem then becomes one of articulation between the different spheres—an ongoing problem, but a dialogic process. In practice, the issues taken up by the new social movements may braid with each other, allowing for solidarity between movements. For example, the movement against big dams—which is ostensibly 'environmental'—is also a struggle for Adivasi rights. It has parallels, furthermore, with the struggle for land waged by groups such as Vahini in Bihar, both being concerned with access to crucial productive resources for the poor.

We can argue that in fact Gandhi was in the long run very successful in building such an alternative politics, as seen in the modern ubiquity of satyagraha in India. In this respect, we may see people such as Baba Amte and Medha Patkar as the truest successors to Gandhi in India today. They continue to uphold an alternative arcadian, anti-imperialist and non-violent vision, the resonance of which appears to be growing today, with an increasing appreciation of the moral superiority of such values. For many, such a politics provides the greatest hope for India in the future.

Outside India, Gandhi has most widely been taken as a symbol of the struggle against European imperialism and white racism. Even those who have condemned his insistence on non-violence as a moral principle—for example Malcolm X—have admired Gandhi's struggle to assert the self-pride of the colonised and oppressed. Gandhi has provided a template for the modern moral activist—that is, a person who assumes moral leadership of the poor and oppressed in an age that

[5]Lawrence D. Kritzman, *Michel Foucault: Politics, Philosophy, Culture: Interviews and Other Writings 1977–1984*, Routledge, New York 1990, p. xvi. It is not of course implied that most of those involved in the new social movements have read Foucault, or even know about him.

aspires to but falls woefully short of the ideal of democracy. Though in the mould of the great saints of the past, they are—in contrast with those saints—people whose work is carried on within civil society. This is a political space which exists in a state of tension with government and which is a creation of post-Enlightenment modernity. Civil society provides a critical instrumental means to check the excesses of governmental power. Within this space, religion finds a place primarily in terms of abstract notions of morality and conscience. The moral activists have operated within this sphere of politics, and their work has been intensely political.

Such people are, ideally, courageous moral leaders—fighters by nature—who engage with the political in the interests of the subaltern without being sullied by power. They have had a powerful sense of destiny and an ability to inspire a fierce loyalty from others within a movement. They are people blessed with a rare quality of leadership, with personalities that may be described as 'electric'[6] and with a sure ability to communicate their beliefs with passion and imagination. They have strong moral standards that they are known to conform to with sincerity in their daily lives, often living in an austere way and rejecting a desire for personal wealth. Although strong in maintaining their own truths, they are open to counter-dialogues, and are big enough as people to change their minds if they see that they are wrong in a particular matter.[7]

Although these moral activists devote themselves to the poor and oppressed, they tend to come from provincial middle-class families. Although of a local élite, such people are relatively marginal, and they have to struggle hard to assert themselves in metropolitan cultures. They have generally received a solid education, which includes professional training. Even Malcolm X, whose father was a small-town church minister, had sufficient education to train to be a lawyer, but was thwarted in his ambition by racial prejudice. Only then did he migrate to New

[6]Alex Hailey thus stated that Malcolm X was 'the most electric personality I have ever met.' Alex Hailey, 'Foreword', *The Autobiography of Malcolm X*, p. 78.

[7]Thus, Malcolm X changed his position very radically in his final year. In his autobiography he described this in very Gandhian terms as his 'intelligent search for truth.' Ibid., p. 454.

York City and become a proletarian hustler and then burglar. He regained his destiny through moral reform and self-education in jail. Their education—often to the very highest levels of academic life—allows them to engage with ideas at a rarefied theoretical level on the one hand, while putting their beliefs into practice in the streets on the other.

Several of these moral activists have followed Gandhi's example by making strict non-violence a principle of their politics. Martin Luther King is the outstanding example in this respect, but another more recent figure of comparable moral stature has been Aung San Suu Kyi in Burma. From 1988 onwards she and her party, the National League for Democracy, have sustained a non-violent protest against the ruthless military junta that has ruled Burma since 1962. The party won over eighty percent of the seats contested in an election held in 1990, but the result was ignored by the junta. Aung San Suu Kyi was placed under house arrest from 1989 to 1995, and has suffered an informal blockade and continuous harassment since then. In 1991 she was awarded the Nobel Prize for Peace—the first person to do so while under detention. Although she has been told that she is free to leave the country, she has refused to do so—even to visit her husband when he was dying of cancer in England—for fear that she would be refused re-entry. Many of her comrades have been jailed and tortured, but her personal and moral prestige is such that the junta has not dared to do the same to her.

Like Gandhi, she adopts non-violent civil disobedience as a matter of principle. For her, it provides a most active form of resistance: 'Some people think that non-violence is passiveness. It's not so. I know it is the slower way, and I understand why our young people feel that it will not work. But I cannot encourage that kind of attitude. Because if I do, we will be perpetuating a cycle of violence that will never come to an end.'[8]

She refuses to hate her opponents, as she feels that she needs to be open always to the possibility that they can be persuaded. Also, she believes that you cannot really be frightened of people whom you do not hate. 'Hate and fear go hand-in-hand.'[9] She is prepared always to

[8]Alan Clements, 'Aung San Suu Kyi: Burma's Gandhi', http://mosaic.echonyc.com/~onissues/f98burma.html, p. 2.

[9]Ibid., p. 4.

hold out the hand of forgiveness and reconciliation. In all of these respects, she is a leader truly in the Gandhian mould.

Although the peace and ecology movements of the richer metropolitan countries have deployed many Gandhian principles to powerful effect, they have been unable to accommodate such charismatic moral leadership. In many respects, this has been a deliberate choice. In part it represents a rejection of the *führer* figure—the leader whose popularity has, in recent European history, degenerated into a dangerous demagogy. It is also a product of the anarchist tradition from which many of these movements have emerged. This antipathy to the leader-figure has been a strength in some respects, allowing as it does for a more democratic practice. For groups involved in campaigns of civil disobedience, it is also harder for the authorities to suppress a movement with multiple leaders. The great drawback has been that potential leaders with great tactical insight and charisma may be silenced. In this way, a movement can undercut its greatest assets, and it might lose direction. The person who more than any other grappled with this dilemma was Petra Kelly.

There are also the great moral activists who do not endorse non-violence as a principle, but whose quality of leadership has parallels with that of Gandhi. Nelson Mandela, Steve Biko and Malcolm X have, in their different ways, been exemplary figures of this sort. They stand for the self-assertion and pride-in-self of the oppressed, being in their own lives outstanding examples of people who have transcended the status imposed on them by white racists and imperialists. They condemn what Steve Biko characterised as 'the system'[10]—that is the structures of racism and imperialism—while recognising that individuals can transcend it from within.[11] They thus seek to open a dialogue with more moderate elements within the structure of power. This striving has often, however, been denied by those within 'the system' whose fear

[10]Steve Biko, *I Write What I Like*, Heinemann, Oxford 1987, p. 37.

[11]While in the Nation of Islam, Malcolm X condemned all whites as 'devils', but after his break with the organisation he moved to a position of distinguishing between sympathetic and unsympathetic whites. Malcolm X, *The Autobiography of Malcolm X*, pp. 26–7 & 447–9.

of any dialogue is such that their only riposte is imprisonment, torture or the assassin's bullet.

The moral activist puts her or his life on the line by challenging the 'system' to do its worst. Too often, the challenge has been taken up, and the activist has been murdered. Each such violent and premature death has been a tragic setback. There is however hope, for people of such ethical power have again and again emerged to pose the questions in new ways and to suggest new answers. They have not been perfect beings—they have had their human weaknesses and sometimes made great mistakes. Their personal family lives have often been sad, even tragic. But still, they are people who in their fierce and uncompromising moral commitment have soared above those around them. They stand for a human spirit that refuses to be crushed by the leviathan of the modern 'system' of violence, oppression and exploitation, and which aspires for a better, more equitable and non-violent future. In this, they inspire huge numbers. In them, Gandhi—their model—still lives.

Bibliography

A Social and Economic Atlas of India, Oxford University Press, New Delhi 1987.

Abbot, Justin, *Tukaram*, Scottish Mission Industries Co., Pune 1930

Adorno, Theodor, and Horkheimer, Max, *Dialectic of Enlightenment*, Verso, London 1989.

Agra Jan Sangarsh Sahyog Samiti, 'Sangarsh Vahini's Struggle in Agra: When People Demand that Government Implement its Promises', in Madhu Kishwar and Ruth Vanita (eds), *In Search of Answers: Indian Women's Voices from Manushi*, Zed Press, London 1984.

Alavi, Hamza, 'Ironies of History: Contradictions of the Khilafat Movement,' *Comparative Studies of South Asia, Africa and the Middle East*, Vol. 17, No. 1.

Alter, Joseph S., *Gandhi's Body: Sex, Diet, and the Politics of Nationalism*, University of Pennsylvania Press, Philadelphia 2000.

Amin, Shahid, 'Gandhi as Mahatma: Gorakhpur District, Eastern UP, 1921–2', in Ranajit Guha (ed.), *Subaltern Studies III*, Oxford University Press, New Delhi 1984.

____, *Event, Metaphor, Memory: Chauri Chaura 1922–1992*, Oxford University Press, New Delhi 1995.

Anand, Javed, 'A Clarification, and an Apology', *Communalism Combat*, April 2000, p. 32.

____, 'Birth of a New Rights Body', *Communalism Combat*, March 2000.

Arnold, David, 'Rebellious Hillmen: The Gudem-Rampa Risings 1839–1924', in Ranajit Guha, *Subaltern Studies I*, Oxford University Press, New Delhi 1982.

____, *Gandhi*, Longman, London 2001.

Asad, Talal, 'Comments on Conversion', in Peter van der Veer (ed.), *Conversion to Modernities: The Globalisation of Christianity*, Routledge, New York 1996.

Aurobindo, Sri, *Bande Mataram: Early Political Writings*, Sri Aurobindo Ashram, Pondicherry 1973.

Azad, Maulana Abul Kalam, *India Wins Freedom: An Autobiographical Narrative*, Orient Longman, New Delhi 1975.

Bahuguna, Sunderlal, 'Women's Non-Violent Power in the Chipko Movement', in Madhu Kishwar and Ruth Vanita, *In Search of Answers: Indian Women's Voices from Manushi*, Zed Press, London 1984.

Bahuguna, Vimla, 'The Chipko Movement', in Ilina Sen (ed.), *A Space Within the Struggle*, Kali for Women, New Delhi 1990.

Baker, David E.U., *Changing Political Leadership in an Indian Province: The Central Provinces and Berar 1919–1939*, Oxford University Press, New Delhi 1979.

——, '"A Serious Time": Forest Satyagraha in Madhya Pradesh, 1930', *The Indian Economic and Social History Review*, Vol. 21, No. 1, January–March 1984.

Bakhtin, Mikhail M., *Problems of Dostoevsky's Poetics*, ed. and trans. C. Emerson, Manchester University Press, Manchester 1984.

——, *Rabelais and his World*, translated by Hélène Iswolsky, Indiana University Press, Bloomington, 1984.

Bakshi, Rajni, *Bapu Kuti: Journeys in Rediscovery Of Gandhi*, Penguin, New Delhi 1998.

Banerjee, Mukulika, *The Pathan Unarmed: Opposition and Memory in the North West Frontier*, Oxford University Press, New Delhi 2001.

Banerjee, Partha, *In the Belly of the Beast: The Hindu Supremacist RSS and BJP of India: An Insider's Story*, Ajanta Books, New Delhi 1998.

Banerjee, Sumanta, *In the Wake of Naxalbari: A History of the Naxalite Movement in India*, Subarnarekha, Calcutta 1980.

Basu, Aparna, *Mridula Sarabhai: Rebel with a Cause*, Oxford University Press, New Delhi 1996.

Basu, Tapan, Pradip Datta, Sumit Sarkar, Tanika Sarkar, Sambuddha Sen, *Khaki Shorts and Saffron Flags: A Critique of the Hindu Right*, Orient Longman, New Delhi 1993.

Baviskar, Amita, *In the Belly of the River: Tribal Conflicts over Development in the Narmada Valley*, Oxford University Press, New Delhi 1995.

Baxi, Upendra, '"The State's Emissary": The Place of Law in Subaltern Studies', in Partha Chatterjee and Gyanendra Pandey (eds), *Subaltern Studies VII*, Oxford University Press, New Delhi 1992.

Bayly, C.A., *Empire and Information: Intelligence Gathering and Social Communication in India, 1780–1870*, Cambridge University Press, Cambridge 1996.

Belsare, M.B., *An Etymological Gujarati-English Dictionary*, H.K. Pathak, Bombay 1904.

Besant, Annie, *The Birth of a New India: A Collection of Writings and Speeches on Indian Affairs*, Theosophical Publishing House, Madras 1917.

Bhatia, Bela, 'The Naxalite Movement in Central Bihar', unpublished Ph.D. thesis, University of Cambridge 2000.

Bhatt, Anil, 'Caste and Political Mobilisation in a Gujarat District', in Rajni Kothari (ed.), *Caste in Indian Politics*, Orient Longman, New Delhi 1970.

Bhattacharya, Neeladri, 'Myth, History and the Politics of Ramjanmabhumi,' in Sarvepalli Gopal (ed.), *Anatomy of a Confrontation: The Babri Masjid-Ram Janmabhumi Issue*, Penguin Books India, New Delhi 1991.

Bidwai, Praful and Achin Vanaik, *New Nukes: India, Pakistan and Global Nuclear Disarmament*, Signal Books, Oxford 2002.

Biko, Steve, *I Write What I Like*, Heinemann, Oxford 1987, p. 37.

Black, Maggie, *A Cause for our Times: Oxfam the First 50 Years*, Oxfam, Oxford 1992.

Bondurant, Joan, *Conquest of Violence: The Gandhian Philosophy of Conflict*, Princeton University Press, Princeton 1958.

Bose, Nirmal Kumar, *My Days with Gandhi*, Orient Longman, Calcutta 1974.

Branch, Taylor, *Parting the Waters: Martin Luther King and the Civil Rights Movement 1954–63*, Simon and Schuster, New York 1988.

Breman, Jan, *Of Peasants, Migrants and Paupers: Rural Labour Circulation and Capitalist Production in West India*, Oxford University Press, New Delhi 1985.

Broughton, Thomas, *Letters Written in a Maratta Camp during the year 1809*, London 1892.

Brown, Judith, *Gandhi's Rise to Power: Indian Politics 1915–1922*, Cambridge University Press, Cambridge 1972.

_____, 'Gandhi: Guru for the 1990s?,' in Upendra Baxi and Bhikhu Parekh (eds), *Crisis and Change in Contemporary India*, Sage Publications, New Delhi 1995.

Butalia, Urvashi, *The Other Side of Silence: Voices from the Partition of India*, Penguin Books, Delhi 1998.

Chakrabarty, Dipesh, *Provincializing Europe: Postcolonial Thought and Historical Difference*, Princeton University Press, Princeton 2000.

Chakravarty, Uma, *Rewriting History: The Life and Times of Pandita Ramabai*, Kali for Women, New Delhi 1998.

Chatterjee, Partha, 'Agrarian Relations and Communalism in Bengal, 1926–1935', in Ranajit Guha (ed.), *Subaltern Studies I*, Oxford University Press, New Delhi 1982.

Chatterjee, Partha, *Nationalist Thought and the Colonial World—A Derivative Discourse?*, Zed Books, London 1986.

____, *The Nation and Its Fragments: Colonial and Postcolonial Histories*, Princeton University Press, Princeton 1993.

Clements, Alan, 'Aung San Suu Kyi: Burma's Gandhi', http://mosaic.echonyc.com/~onissues/f98burma.html, p. 2.

Cook, Alice, and Gwyn Kirk, *Greenham Women Everywhere: Dreams, Ideas and Actions from the Women's Movement*, Pluto Press, London 1983.

Copland, Ian, *The British Raj and the Indian Princes: Paramountcy in Western India 1857–1930*, Orient Longman, New Delhi 1982.

Coupland, R., *The Constitutional Problem In India, Part 1, The Indian Problem, 1833–1935*, Oxford University Press, Madras 1944.

Dalton, Dennis, *Mahatma Gandhi: Nonviolent Power in Action*, Columbia University Press, New York 1993.

de Ligt, Bart, *The Conquest of Violence: An Essay on War and Revolution*, Pluto Press, London 1989.

del Vasto, Lanza, *Le Pèlerinage aux Sources*, translated as *Return to the Source* by Jean Sedgwick, Rider, London 1971.

Desai, I.P. and Choudhry, Banwarilal, *History of Rural Development in Modern India*, Volume II, Impex India, New Delhi 1977.

Desai, Mahadev, *The Diary of Mahadev Desai, Vol. 1, Yeravda-Pact Eve, 1932*, Navajivan Publishing House, Ahmedabad 1953.

____, *Day-to-Day with Gandhi*, Vol. 3, Sarva Seva Sangh, Banaras 1968.

Desai, Morarji, *The Story of My Life*, Vol. 1, Macmillan, Madras 1974.

Desai, Shambhuprasad, *Kanadano Ker*, S.Desai, Junagadh 1984 (Gujarati).

Deshpande, Pandurang Ganesh, *Gujarati-Angreji Kosh*, University Granth Nirman Board, Ahmedabad 1974.

Devji, Faisal Fatehali, 'A Practice of Prejudice', unpublished paper 2001.

Dewan, Romesh, 'Can We Survive without Gandhian Values?', *Economic and Political Weekly*, Vol. 34, Nos 16 and 17, 17–23 April 1999.

Dirks, Nicholas B., 'The Conversion of Caste: Location, Translation, and Appropriation', in *Conversion to Modernities: The Globalization of Christianity*, ed. Peter van der Veer, New York, Routledge, 1996.

Dove, Michael R., 'Local Dimensions of "Global" Environmental Debates', in Arne Kalland and Gerard Persoon (eds), *Environmental Movements in Asia*, Curzon, Richmond 1998.

Easwaran, Eknath, *The Compassionate Universe: The Power of the Individual to Heal the Environment*, Penguin Books, New Delhi 2001.

Erikson, Erik, *Gandhi's Truth: On the Origins of Militant Nonviolence*, Faber and Faber, London 1970.

Fischer, Louis, *The Life of Mahatma Gandhi*, Granada, St. Albans 1982.

Fisher, Frederick, *That Strange Little Brown Man Gandhi*, Orient Longman, New Delhi 1970.

Frankland, E. Gene, and Donald Schoonmaker, *Between Protest and Power: The Green Party in Germany*, Westview Press, Boulder, Colorado 1992.

French, Patrick, *Liberty or Death: India's Journey to Independence and Division*, Flamingo, London 1997.

Gadgil, Madhav, and Ramachandra Guha, *Ecology and Equity: The Uses and Abuses of Nature in Contemporary India*, Routledge, London 1995.

Gandhi, M.K., *Collected Works of Mahatma Gandhi* (*CWMG*), from *Mahatma Gandhi: Electronic Book* (CD Rom version of *CWMG*), Publications Division, New Delhi 1999. Note: the version of the *CWMG* on the CD Rom differs from some of the earlier versions of *CWMG*, so that volume and page numbers will differ.

Gandhi, Tushar A., 'Attempts on Gandhi's Life', http://web.mahatma.org.in/lattempts

Gautier, François, *Arise Again, O India!*, Har-Anand Publications, New Delhi 2000.

Gazetteers of the Bombay Presidency, Vol. IX, Part I, *Gujarat Population: Hindus*, Government Central Press, Bombay 1901.

Gazetteers of Bombay Presidency, Vol. XVIII, Poona, Part III, Government Central Press, Bombay 1885.

Ghurye, G.S., *The Scheduled Tribes of India*, Transaction Books, New Brunswick 1980.

Gilbert, Martin, *Winston S. Churchill*, Volume 5, *1922–1939*, Heinemann, London 1976.

Gopal, S., *The Viceroyalty of Lord Irwin 1926–1931*, Clarendon Press, Oxford 1957.

Gordon, Richard, 'The Hindu Mahasabha and the Indian National Congress, 1915 to 1926', *Modern Asian Studies*, Vol. 9, No. 2, 1975.

Gramsci, Antonio, *Selections from the Prison Notebooks*, Lawrence and Wishart, London 1971.

Green, Martin, *The Origins of Nonviolence: Tolstoy and Gandhi in their Historical Settings*, Harper Collins, New Delhi 1998.

Gregg, Richard B., *Gandhism and Socialism*, Madras 1931.

——, *The Power of Non-Violence*, Philadelphia 1934.

——, *The Psychology and Strategy of Gandhi's Non-Violent Resistance*, Madras 1929.

Grey, Hugh, '"Gora", Gandhi's Atheist Follower', in Peter Robb and David Taylor (eds), *Rule, Protest, Identity: Aspects of Modern South Asia*, Curzon Press, London 1978.

Guha, Ramachandra, *The Unquiet Woods: Ecological Change and Peasant Resistance in the Himalaya*, Oxford University Press, New Delhi 1987.

——, 'Mahatma Gandhi and the Environmental Movement in India', in Arne Kalland and Gerard Persoon (eds), *Environmental Movements in Asia*, Curzon, Richmond 1998.

——, *Savaging the Civilized: Verrier Elwin, His Tribals, and India*, University of Chicago Press, Chicago 1999.

——, *An Anthropologist Among the Marxists and Other Essays*, Permanent Black, New Delhi 2001.

Guha, Ranajit, *Elementary Aspects of Peasant Insurgency in Colonial India*, Oxford University Press, New Delhi 1983.

——, 'Discipline and Mobilize', in Partha Chatterjee and Gyanendra Pandey (eds), *Subaltern Studies VII*, Oxford University Press, New Delhi 1992, p. 107.

——, *Dominance without Hegemony: History and Power in Colonial India*, Harvard University Press, Cambridge, Mass., 1997.

Habib, Irfan, *The Agrarian System of Mughal India 1556–1701*, Asia Publishing House, Bombay 1963.

Hardiman, David, 'The Roots of Rural Agitation in India 1914–47: A Rejoinder to Charlesworth', *The Journal of Peasant Studies*, Vol. 8, No. 3, 1981.

_____, *Peasant Nationalists of Gujarat: Kheda District 1917–1934*, Oxford University Press, New Delhi 1981.

_____, 'From Custom to Crime: The Politics of Drinking in Colonial South Gujarat', in Ranajit Guha (ed.), *Subaltern Studies IV*, Oxford University Press, New Delhi 1985.

_____, *The Coming of the Devi: Adivasi Assertion In South Gujarat*, Oxford University Press, New Delhi 1987.

_____, 'Power in the Forest: the Dangs, 1820–1940', in David Arnold and David Hardiman (eds), *Subaltern Studies VIII*, Oxford University Press, New Delhi 1994.

_____, *Feeding the Baniya: Peasants and Usurers in Western India*, Oxford University Press, New Delhi 1996.

Harper, Susan Billington, *In the Shadow of the Mahatma: Bishop Azariah and the Travails of Christianity in British India*, William B. Eerdmans, Grand Rapids, Michigan 2000.

Hinton, James, *Protests and Visions: Peace Politics in 20th Century Britain*, Hutchinson Radius, London 1989.

Honour, Hugh, *Romanticism*, Allen Lane, London 1979.

Illich, Ivan, *Deschooling Society*, Penguin, Harmondsworth 1971.

_____, *Energy and Equity*, Rupa, Calcutta 1974.

_____, *Medical Nemesis: The Expropriation of Health*, Rupa, Calcutta 1975.

_____, *Tools for Conviviality*, Fontana, Glasgow 1975.

Irschik, Eugene, *Politics and Social Conflict in South India: The Non-Brahman Movement and Tamil Separatism, 1916–1929*, University of California Press, Berkeley 1969.

Iyer, Raghavan, *The Moral and Political Writings of Mahatma Gandhi*, Vols I–III, Clarendon Press, Oxford, 1986.

Jain, P.C., *Tribal Agrarian Movement*, Himanshu Publications, Udaipur, 1989.

Jain, Prakash Chandra, *Tribal Agrarian Movement: A Case Study of the Bhil Movement of Rajasthan*, Himanshu Publications, Udaipur 1989.

Jayakar, Pupul, *J. Krishnamurti: A Biography*, Penguin Books, New Delhi 1986.

Jeffrey, Robin, 'A Sanctified Label—"Congress" in Travancore Politics, 1938–48', in D.A. Low (ed.), *Congress and the Raj: Facets of the Indian Struggle 1917–47*, Heinemann, London 1977.

Jordens, J.T.F., *Dayananda Saraswati: His Life and Ideas*, Oxford University Press, New Delhi 1978.

———, *Swami Shraddhananda: His Life and Causes*, Oxford University Press, New Delhi 1981.

Joshi, Gopa, 'Slandered by the Community in Return', in Madhu Kishwar and Ruth Vanita, *In Search of Answers: Indian Women's Voices from Manushi*, Zed Press, London, 1984.

Kalelkar, Kakasaheb, *Stray Glimpses of Bapu*, Navjivan Publishing House, Ahmedabad 1960

Kane, P.V., *History of Dharmashastra*, Vol. III, Pune 1973.

Kankariya, Premsinh, *Bhil Kranti ke Praneta: Motilal Tejavat*, Rajasthan Sahitya Academy, Udaipur 1985 (in Hindi).

Kelkar, Govind and Gale, Chetna, 'The Bodhgaya Land Struggle', in Ilina Sen (ed.), *A Space Within the Struggle: Women's Participation in People's Movements*, Kali for Women, New Delhi 1990.

Kelly, Petra, 'Gandhi and the Green Party', *Gandhi Marg*, July–September 1989.

———, *Nonviolence Speaks to Power*, edited by Glenn D. Paige and Sarah Gilliart, Centre for Global Nonviolence Planning Project, Hawaii 1992.

Khilnani, Sunil, 'Gandhi and History', in *Seminar*, 461, January 1998.

———, *The Idea of India*, Penguin, Harmondsworth 1998.

King, Martin Luther, *Where Do We Go From Here: Chaos or Community?*, Beacon, Boston 1967, p. 64.

Kishwar, Madhu, 'Gandhi on Women: Part 1', *Economic and Political Weekly*, 5 October 1985; Part 2, *Economic and Political Weekly*, 12 October 1985.

——— and Ruth Vanita, *In Search of Answers: Indian Women's Voices from Manushi*, Zed Press, London 1984.

Kling, Blair B., *The Blue Mutiny: The Indigo Disturbances in Bengal 1859–1862*, University of Pennsylvania Press, Philadelphia 1966.

Korejo, M.S., *The Frontier Gandhi: His Place in History*, Oxford University Press, Karachi 1993.

Krishnan, Shekhar and Samy, Anthony, 'CC Echoes Reactionary Voices', and Vrijendra, 'No Quid Pro Quo in Democratic Rights', *Communalism Combat*, April 2000.

Kritzman, Lawrence D., *Michel Foucault: Politics, Philosophy, Culture: Interviews and Other Writings 1977–1984*, Routledge, New York 1990.

Kumar, Ravinder, *Western India in the Nineteenth Century: A Study in the Social History of Maharashtra*, Routledge and Kegan Paul, London 1968.

____, 'Class, Community or Nation? Gandhi's Quest for a Popular Consensus in India', *Essays in the Social History of Modern India*, Oxford University Press, New Delhi 1983.

Kumarappa, J.C., *A Survey of Matar Taluka*, Gujarat Vidyapith, Ahmedabad 1931.

Kunwar, S.S. (ed.), *Hugging the Himalayas: The Chipko Experience*, Dasholi Gram Swarajya Mandal, Gopeshwar, 1982.

Laclau, Ernesto, and Mouffe, Chantal, *Hegemony and Socialist Strategy: Towards a Radical Democratic Politics*, Verso, London 1994.

le Grand Jacob, George, 'Report on Kattywar 1842', in G. le Grand Jacob, *Western India: Before and During the Mutinies*, Henry S. King, London 1872.

Lewis, Martin Deming (ed.), *Gandhi, Maker of Modern India?*, D.C. Heath, Boston 1966.

Lohia, Rammanohar, *Marx, Gandhi and Socialism*, Rammanohar Lohia Samata Vidyalaya Nyasa, Hyderbad 1963.

Louis, Prakash, 'Class War Spreads to New Areas', *Economic and Political Weekly*, 24 June 2000.

Lovelock, James, *Gaia: A New Look at Life on Earth*, Oxford University Press, Oxford 1979.

Ludden, David, *An Agrarian History of South Asia*, *The New Cambridge History of India*, Volume IV:4, Cambridge University Press, Cambridge 1999.

Luithui, Luingam and Nandita Haksar, *Nagaland File: A Question of Human Rights*, Lancer International, New Delhi 1984.

Malcolm X, *The Autobiography of Malcolm X*, with the assistance of Alex Haley, Penguin Books, Harmondsworth 1968.

____, *By Any Means Necessary*, Pathfinder Press, New York 1992.

Malgonkar, Manohar, *The Men who Killed Gandhi*, Macmillan, Madras 1978.

Mandela, Nelson, *Long Walk to Freedom: The Autobiography of Nelson Mandela*, Little, Brown and Company, London, 1994.

____, 'The Sacred Warrior', *Time: The Weekly Newsmagazine*, 31 December 1999.

Manimal, 'Zameen Kenkar? Jote Onkar: Women's Participation in the Bodhgaya Land Struggles,' in Madhu Kishwar and Ruth Vanita (eds), *In Search of Answers: Indian Women's Voices from Manushi*, Zed Books, London 1984.

Martinez-Alier, Juan and Thrupp, Lori Ann, Review of Enrique Leff, *Ecologia y Capital*, in *Capitalism, Nature, Socialism*, No. 3, November 1989.

Marshall, Thomas, 'A Statistical Account of the Pergunna of Jumboosur', in *Transactions of the Literary Society of Bombay*, Vol. 3, 1823.

Marx, Karl and Engels, Frederick, 'Manifesto of the Communist Party', in Marx and Engels, *Collected Works*, Volume 6, Lawrence and Wishart, London 1976.

Maw, Geoffrey Waring, *Narmada: The Life of a River*, Marjorie Sykes, Selly Oak, no date (*c.*1992).

Mawdsley, Emma, 'After Chipko: From Environment to Region in Uttaranchal', *The Journal of Peasant Studies*, Volume 25, No. 4, July 1998.

McCully, Patrick, *Silenced Rivers: The Ecology and Politics of Large Dams*, Zed Books, London 1996.

McGeary, Johanna, 'Mohandas Gandhi', in *Time*, 31 December 1999.

McGregor, R.S., *The Oxford Hindi-English Dictionary*, Oxford University Press, New Delhi 1993.

McKean, Lise, *Divine Enterprise: Gurus and the Hindu Nationalist Movement*, University of Chicago Press, Chicago 1996.

Mehta, Shirin, *The Peasantry and Nationalism: A Study of the Bardoli Satyagraha*, Manohar, New Delhi 1984.

Meredith, Martin, *Nelson Mandela: A Biography*, Hamish Hamilton, London 1997.

Mishra, Anupam and Tripathi, Satyendra, *The Chipko Movement*, People's Action/Gandhi Peace Foundation, New Delhi 1978.

Monier Williams, M., *A Sanskrit-English Dictionary*, Motilal Banarsidas, New Delhi 1963.

Moon, Penderel (ed.), *Wavell: The Viceroy's Journal*, Oxford University Press, London 1973.

Morris, Pam (ed.), *The Bakhtin Reader: Selected Writings of Bakhtin, Medvedev and Volosinov*, Arnold, London 1994.

Morris-Jones, W.H., 'The Unhappy Utopia', *Economic Weekly*, 25 June 1960.

Morse, Bradford and Berger, Thomas R., *Sardar Sarovar: Report of the Independent Review*, Resource Futures International, Ottawa 1992.

Moses Greg, *Revolution of Conscience: Martin Luther King, Jr., and the Philosophy of Nonviolence*, The Guilford Press, New York 1997.

Mukta, Parita, 'Worshipping Inequalities: Pro-Narmada Dam Movement', *Economic and Political Weekly*, 13 October 1990.

———, *Upholding the Common Life: The Community of Mirabai*, Oxford University Press, New Delhi 1994.

———, 'Wresting Riches, Marginalising the Poor, Criminalising Dissent: The Building of the Narmada Dam in Western India', *South Asia Bulletin*, Volume 15, No. 2, 1995.

———, and David Hardiman, 'The Political Ecology of Nostalgia', *Capitalism, Nature, Socialism: A Journal of Socialist Ecology*, Vol. 11, No. 1, March 2000.

Nagaraj, D.R., *The Flaming Feet: A Study of the Dalit Movement in India*, South Forum Press, Bangalore 1993.

Naidu, Sarojini, *Selected Poetry and Prose*, edited by Makarand Paranjape, Harper Collins, New Delhi 1995.

Nakhre, Amrut, *Social Psychology of Non Violent Action: A Study of Three Satyagrahas*, Chanakya Publications, Delhi 1982.

Nandy, Ashis, 'From Outside the Imperium: Gandhi's Cultural Critique of the "West"'; *Alternatives*, Vol. 7, No. 2, 1981.

———, 'Final Encounter: The Politics of the Assassination of Gandhi', in Ashis Nandy, *At the Edge of Psychology: Essays in Politics and Culture*, Oxford University Press, New Delhi 1993.

———, *The Intimate Enemy: Loss and Recovery of Self under Colonialism*, Oxford University Press, New Delhi 1994.

Narayan, Shriman, *Jamnalal Bajaj: Gandhiji's 'Fifth Son'*, Publications Division, New Delhi 1974.

Nehru, Jawaharlal, *The Discovery Of India*, Signet Press, Calcutta 1946.

Oates, Stephen B., *Let the Trumpet Sound: A Life of Martin Luther King, Jr.*, Payback Press, Edinburgh 1998.

Omvedt, Gail, *Dalits and the Democratic Revolution: Dr. Ambedkar and the Dalit Movement in Colonial India*, Sage Publications, New Delhi 1994.

Ostergaard, Geoffrey and Currell, Melville, *The Gentle Anarchists: A Study of the Leaders of the Sarvodaya Movement for Non-violent Revolution in India*, Clarendon Press, Oxford 1971.

Ostergaard, Geoffrey, *Nonviolent Revolution in India*, Gandhi Peace Foundation, New Delhi 1985.

Palme Dutt, R., *India Today*, Victor Gollancz, London 1940.

Pandey, Gyanendra, 'In Defence of the Fragment: Writing about Hindu-Muslim Riots in India Today,' *Economic and Political Weekly*, Vol. 26, Nos 11 & 12, March 1991.

———, *The Construction of Communalism in Colonial North India*, Oxford University Press, New Delhi 1990.

———, *Remembering Partition: Nationalism and History in India*, Cambridge University Press, Cambridge 2002.

Pandian, M.S.S., '"Denationalising" the Past: "Nation" in E.V. Ramasamy's Political Discourse', *Economic and Political Weekly*, 16 October 1993.

———, 'Stepping Outside History? New Dalit Writing from Tamil Nadu', in Partha Chatterjee (ed.), *Wages of Freedom: Fifty Years of the Indian Nation-State*, Oxford University Press, New Delhi 1998.

Pantham, Thomas, 'Gandhi, Nehru, and Modernity', in Upendra Baxi and Bhikhu Parekh (eds), *Crisis and Change in Contemporary India*, Sage, New Delhi, 1995.

Parajuli, Pramod, 'Power and Knowledge in Development Discourse: New Social Movements and the State in India', *International and Social Science Journal*, February 1991, No. 127.

Parekh, Bhikhu, *Gandhi's Political Philosophy: A Critical Examination*, Macmillan, Basingstoke 1989.

———, *Colonialism, Tradition and Reform: An Analysis of Gandhi's Political Discourse*, Sage Publications, New Delhi 1989.

———, *Gandhi*, Oxford University Press, Oxford 1997.

———, *Bardolina Kheduto*, Chhotubhai Gopalji Desai, Bardoli 1927 (Gujarati).

Parikh, Shankarlal, *Khedani Ladat*, Rashtriya Sahitya Karyalay, Ahmedabad 1922 (Gujarati).

Parkin, Sara, *The Life and Death of Petra Kelly*, Pandora, London 1994.

Parulekar, Godavari, *Adivasis Revolt: The Story of Warli Peasants in Struggle*, National Book Agency, Calcutta 1975.

Patel, Sujata, *The Making of Industrial Relations: The Ahmedabad Textile Industry 1918–1939*, Oxford University Press, New Delhi 1987.

———, 'Construction and Reconstruction of Women in Gandhi', *Economic and Political Weekly*, 20 February 1988.

Pathak, Shekhar, 'Intoxication as a Social Evil: Anti-Alcohol Movement in Uttarakhand', *Economic and Political Weekly*, 10 August 1985.

Payne, Robert, *The Life and Death of Mahatma Gandhi*, The Bodley Head, London 1969.

Pinto, Vivek, *Gandhi's Vision and Values: The Moral Quest for Change in Indian Agriculture*, Sage Publications, New Delhi 1998.

Poguntke, Thomas, *Alternative Politics: The German Green Party*, Edinburgh University Press, Edinburgh 1993.

Pouchepadass, Jacques, *Champaran and Gandhi: Planters, Peasants and Gandhian Politics*, Oxford University Press, New Delhi 2000.

Prashad, Vijay, 'Untouchable Freedom: A Critique of the Bourgeois-Landlord Indian State', in Gautam Bhadra, Gyan Prakash, Susie Tharu, eds, *Subaltern Studies X*, Oxford University Press, New Delhi 1999.

Prinja, Nawal K., *Explaining Hindu Dharma: A Guide for Teachers*, Religious and Moral Education Press, Norwich 1996.

Pyarelal, *Mahatma Gandhi, Vol. 1, The Early Phase*, Navajivan Publishing House, Ahmedabad 1965.

Qanungo, Kalika Ranjan, *Studies in Rajput History*, S. Chand, New Delhi 1960.

Ramachandran, R., 'The Tehri Turnabout', *Frontline*, Vol. 18, No. 10, 12–25 May 2001.

Ramana, M.V., 'Nehru and Nuclear Conspiracy', *Anumukti*, Vol. 11, Nos 5 & 6, April-July 1998.

Randeria, Shalini, 'The Politics of Representation and Exchange among Untouchable Castes in Western India (Gujarat)', unpublished Ph.D. thesis, Freien Universität Berlin, 1992.

Randle, Michael, *Civil Resistance*, Fontana Press, London 1994.

Refai, G.Z., 'Anglo-Mughal Relations in Western India and the Development of Bombay 1662–1690', unpublished Cambridge Ph.D. thesis, 1967.

Report of the Committee on the Riots in Poona and Ahmednagar 1875, Government Central Press, Bombay 1876.

Report on the Census of 1891, Vol. II, The Castes of Marwar, Marwar State, Jodhpur 1894

Ricoeur, Paul, *Lectures on Ideology and Utopia*, edited by George H. Taylor, Columbia University Press, New York 1986.

Roy, Arundhati, *The Cost of Living: The Greater Common Good and the End of Imagination*, Flamingo, London 1999.

Roy, Sarat Chandra, *Oraon Religion and Ceremony*, Editions India, Calcutta 1972 (1st ed. 1928).

Sarkar, Sumit, *The Swadeshi Movement in Bengal 1903–1908*, People's Publishing House, New Delhi 1973.

____, *Modern India 1885–1947*, Macmillan, Delhi 1983.

____, 'Conversion and Politics of Hindu Right', *Economic and Political Weekly*, 26 June 1999.

Sarkar, Tanika, 'The Politics of Women in Bengal: The Conditions and Meaning of Participation', *The Indian Economic and Social History Review* (Delhi), Vol. 21, No. 1, 1984.

Savara, Mira and Gothoskar, Sujatha, 'An Assertion of Womanpower: Organising Landless Women in Maharashtra', in Madhu Kishwar and Ruth Vanita (eds), *In Search of Answers: Indian Women's Voices from Manushi*, Zed Press, London 1984.

Savarkar, Vinayak Damodar, *Hindutva: Who is a Hindu*, Nagpur 1923.

____, *Six Glorious Epochs of Indian History*, translated from Marathi by S.T. Godbole, Rajdhani Granthagar, New Delhi 1971.

Scarfe, Allan and Wendy, *J.P. His Biography*, Orient Longman, New Delhi 1998.

Schumacher, E.F., *Small is Beautiful A Study of Economics as if People Mattered*, Abacus, London 1975.

____, *A Guide for the Perplexed*, Abacus, London 1978.

Sen, Ilina, *A Space Within the Struggle: Women's Participation in People's Movements*, Kali for Women, New Delhi 1990.

Sen Gupta, Kalyan Kumar, *Pabna Disturbances and the Politics of Rent 1873–1885*, People's Publishing House, New Delhi 1974.

Sen, Hari, 'Popular Protest in Mewar in the Late-Nineteenth and Early-Twentieth Centuries', unpublished Ph.D. thesis, University of Delhi 1996.

Shah, Ghanshyam, 'The Experience of Bardoli Satyagraha (1920–28)', *Contributions to Indian Sociology*, new series, 8, 1974.

____, *Protest Movements in Two Indian States: A Study of the Gujarat and Bihar Movements*, Ajanta Publications, Delhi 1977.

Sharma, R.C. (trans. and ed.), 'The Ardha-Kathanak', *Indica*, 7:1, March 1970.

Shepard, Mark, 'Soldiers of Peace: Narayan Desai and the "Peace Army"', www.markshep.com/nonviolence/GT_Sena.html

____, *The Community of the Ark*, Simple Productions, Arcata, California 1990.

Sheth, Pravin, *Narmada Project: Politics of Eco-Development*, Har-Anand Publications, New Delhi 1994.

Shridharani, Krishnalal, *War Without Violence: A Study of Gandhi's Meth and its Accomplishments*, Harcourt, Brace and Company, New York 19

Singh, K.S., 'The Haribaba Movement in Chotanagpur 1931–32', *The Journal of the Bihar Research Society*, Vol. 49, Pts. 1–4, January-December 1963.

____, 'Mahatma Gandhi and the Adivasis', *Man in India*, Vol. 20, No. 1, January-March 1970.

____, 'The Freedom Movement and Tribal Sub-Movements, 1920–1947', in B.R. Nanda (ed.), *Essays in Modern Indian History*, Oxford University Press, New Delhi 1980.

Singh, Mohinder, *The Akali Movement*, Macmillan, Delhi 1978.

Singh, Sukhpal, 'Crisis in Punjab Agriculture', *Economic and Political Weekly*, 3 June 2000.

Sinha, Arun, *Against the Few: Struggles of India's Rural Poor*, Zed Books, London 1991.

Sitaramayya, P., *The History of the Indian National Congress (1885–1935)*, Congress Working Committee, Madras 1935.

Skaria, Ajay, 'Timber Conservancy, Desiccationism and Scientific Forestry: The Dangs 1840s-1920s', in Richard Grove, Vinita Damodaran, Satpal Sangwan (eds), *Nature and the Orient: The Environmental History of South and Southeast Asia*, Oxford University Press, New Delhi 1998.

____, *Hybrid Histories: Forests, Frontiers and Wildness in Western India*, Oxford University Press, New Delhi 1999.

Spivak, Gayatri Chakravorty, *A Critique of Postcolonial Reason: Toward a History of the Vanishing Present*, Harvard University Press, Cambridge, Massachusetts 1999.

Steele, Arthur, *The Law and Custom of Hindoo Castes within the Dekhun Provinces*, London 1868.

Stein, Burton, *Peasant State and Society in Medieval South India*, Oxford University Press, New Delhi 1980.

____, *A History of India*, Blackwell, Oxford 1998.

Stewart, Alan, 'Gandhi in a Cloth Cap', in *I Remember...the North East: Recollections of Yesteryear*, The Pentland Press, Bishop Auckland 1993.

Stoltzfus, Nathan and Lacquer, Walter, *Resistance of the Heart*, Norton and Co., New York 1996.

Tarlo, Emma, *Clothing Matters: Dress and Identity in India*, University of Chicago Press, Chicago 1996.

Terchek, Ronald J., *Gandhi: Struggling for Autonomy*, Rowman and Littlefield, Lanham, Maryland, 1998.

Tharu, Susie, and Niranjana, Tejaswini, 'Problems for a Contemporary Theory of Gender', in Shahid Amin and Dipesh Chakrabarty, eds, *Subaltern Studies IX: Writings on South Asian History and Society*, Oxford University Press, New Delhi 1996.

Thoreau, Henry David, 'Civil Disobedience' in *Walden and Civil Disobedience*, Penguin, Harmondsworth, 1983.

Tolstoy, Lev Nikolaevich, *War and Peace*, J.M. Dent and Sons, London no date, Vol. III.

Touraine, Alain, *What is Democracy?* Westview Press, Boulder 1997.

Vaidya, Babubhai, *Rentima Vahan: Shri Kunvarji V. Mehtana Ajhadni Ladatna Samsmarno*, Sastu Sahitya Vardhak Kalylalaya, Ahmedabad 1977 (Gujarati).

Venkatesan, V., 'Sardar Sarovar Project: Drowned Out', *Frontline*, Vol. 17, No. 22, 10 November 2000.

Vidal, Denis, *Violence and Truth: A Rajasthani Kingdom Confronts Colonial Authority*, Oxford University Press, New Delhi 1997.

Virmani, Arundhati, 'National Symbols under Colonial Domination: The Nationalization of the Indian Flag, March-August 1923', *Past and Present*, 164, August 1999.

Visram, Rozina, *Women in India and Pakistan: The Stuggle for Independence from British Rule*, Cambridge University Press, Cambridge 1992.

Viswanathan, Gauri, *Outside the Fold: Conversion, Modernity, and Belief*, Princeton University Press, Princeton 1998.

Volosinov, V.N., *Freudianism: A Marxist Critique*, Academic Press, New York 1976.

———, *Marxism and the Philosophy of Language*, translated by Ladislav Matejka and I.R. Titunik, Seminar Press, New York 1973.

Washington, James Melvin (ed.), *A Testament of Hope: The Essential Writings of Martin Luther King, Jr.*, Harper Collins, New York 1991.

Weber, Thomas, *Hugging the Trees: The Story of the Chipko Movement*, Penguin, New Delhi 1988.

Wilberforce-Bell, H., *The History of Kathiawad from the Earliest Times*, Ajay Book Service, New Delhi 1980 (reprint).

Williams, Raymond, *Keywords: A Vocabulary of Culture and Society*, Flamingo, London 1983.

Woodcock, George, *Gandhi*, Fontana, London, 1972.

Woods, Donald, *Biko*, Paddington Press, London 1978.

———, *Nature's Economy: A History of Ecological Ideas*, Cambridge University Press, New York 1985.

Yagnik, Indulal, *Atmakatha*, Vol. 2, Gujarat Grantharatan Karyalay, Ahmedabad 1970 (Gujarati).

____, *Atmakatha*, Vol. 3, Vatrak Khedut Vidhalay, Mehmedabad 1956 (Gujarati).

Zelliot, Eleanor, *From Untouchable to Dalit: Essays on the Ambedkar Movement*, Manohar, New Delhi 1996.

Index